NATIONAL GEOGRAPHIC

TRAVELER

Rome

NATIONAL GEOGRAPHIC

TRAVELER

Rome

Sari Gilbert and Michael Brouse

National Geographic
Washington, D.C.

Contents

How to use this guide 6–7 About the authors 8
Areas of Rome 35–222 Excursions 223–234 Travelwise 235–264
Index 265–269 Credits 270–271

**Page 1: Fountain of the
Four Rivers, Piazza Navona
Pages 2–3: The Colosseum
Left: Picturesque
courtyard on one of the
city's quieter backstreets**

How to use this guide

See back flap for keys of text and map symbols

The *National Geographic Traveler* brings you the best of Rome in text, pictures, and maps. Divided into three main sections, the guide begins with an overview of history and culture. Following are 11 area chapters with sites selected by the authors for their particular interest and treated in depth. Each chapter opens with its own contents list for easy reference. A final chapter suggests excursions from Rome.

A map introduces each area of the city, highlighting the featured sites and locating other places of interest. Walks, all plotted on their own maps, suggest routes for dis-

covering the most about an area. Features and boxes offer detail on history, culture, or contemporary life. A More Places to Visit page generally rounds off the chapters.

The final section, Travelwise, lists essential information for the traveler—pre-trip planning, getting around, communications, money matters, and emergencies—plus a selection of hotels and restaurants arranged by chapter area, followed by shops and entertainment possibilities.

To the best of our knowledge, site information is accurate as of the press date. However, it's always advisable to call ahead.

Color coding

58

Each area of the city is color-coded for easy reference. Find the area you want on the map on the front flap, and look for the color flash at the top of the pages of the relevant chapter. Hotel and restaurant listings in **Travelwise** are also color-coded to each area.

Colosseo

- Map p. 57
- Piazza del Colosseo
- 06 3996 7700 or 06 700 5469
- $$ (also valid for Palatino). Audio guide: $. Tours in Eng. daily: $
- Bus: C3, 60, 75, 81, 85, 87, 175, 628. Tram: 3. Metro: Linea B (Colosseo)

Visitor information

Practical information is given in the side column next to each major site (see key to symbols on back flap). The map reference gives the page number where the site is shown on a map. Further details include the site's address, telephone number, days closed, entrance charge in a range from $ (under $4) to $$$$$ (over $25), and nearest public transportation stop. Visitor information for smaller sites is in italics and parentheses in the text.

TRAVELWISE

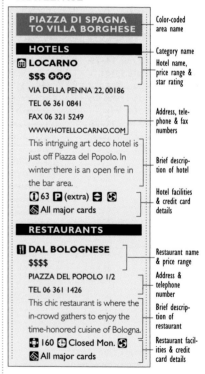

PIAZZA DI SPAGNA TO VILLA BORGHESE — Color-coded area name

HOTELS — Category name

LOCARNO
$$$ ✪✪✪ — Hotel name, price range & star rating

VIA DELLA PENNA 22, 00186
TEL 06 361 0841
FAX 06 321 5249 — Address, telephone & fax numbers
WWW.HOTELLOCARNO.COM

This intriguing art deco hotel is just off Piazza del Popolo. In winter there is an open fire in the bar area. — Brief description of hotel

🛏 63 🅿 (extra) 🔀 🚫 — Hotel facilities & credit card details
💳 All major cards

RESTAURANTS

DAL BOLOGNESE
$$$$ — Restaurant name & price range

PIAZZA DEL POPOLO 1/2
TEL 06 361 1426 — Address & telephone number

This chic restaurant is where the in-crowd gathers to enjoy the time-honored cuisine of Bologna. — Brief description of restaurant

🍴 160 🕐 Closed Mon. 🚫 — Restaurant facilities & credit card details
💳 All major cards

Hotel and restaurant prices

An explanation of the price bands used in entries is given in the Hotels & restaurants section (see pp. 243–55).

CITY MAPS

Rome Metro station

Point of interest

Important featured site

- A locator map accompanies each area map and shows the location of that area in the city.

WALKING TOUR MAPS

Walk route

Direction of route

Red numbered bullet links site on map to description in the text

Point of interest not on walk route

Featured site (in bold) on walk route

Starting point

Building outline

- An information box gives the starting and ending points, time and length of the walk, and places not to be missed along the route.

AREA/EXCURSION MAPS

Point of interest

Important featured town

Road number

- Towns and sites described in the Fuori le Mura (Outside the Walls) and Excursions chapters are highlighted in yellow on the map. Other suggested places to visit are also highlighted and shown with a red diamond symbol.

NATIONAL GEOGRAPHIC

TRAVELER

Rome

About the authors

Sari Gilbert was born and bred in New York City and became interested in things Mediterranean while still attending Hunter High School there. She spent part of her junior year in Italy, at Syracuse University's semester abroad program in Florence. After receiving her B.A. in political science from Syracuse, Sari returned to Italy to attend the Johns Hopkins Bologna Center, and subsequently received an M.A. and a Ph.D. in international relations from the School of Advanced International Studies in Washington, D.C. Her doctoral dissertation was on Italian foreign policy. After concluding her studies, Sari returned again to Rome, where she lives in the heart of the ancient Trastevere district and, for almost 20 years, worked as a correspondent for important U. S. newspapers and magazines. She speaks Italian and French and is currently a full-time reporter for a major Italian daily.

Michael Brouse is a native San Franciscan who spent much of his childhood in Hawaii. After graduating from high school in Marin County, Michael attended the University of Santa Clara, where he received a B.A. in history, but only after spending his junior year abroad, in Rome. Like Sari, Michael returned to Rome in 1972 where, after a stint of teaching English, he worked for many years in men's fashion. His ongoing passion for history and art history found an outlet in popular walking tours he conducts for visitors to the city. Michael is fluent in Italian, French, and German and is an accomplished translator. He returned to his first love (teaching) several years ago and is now a history instructor at St. Stephen's School, an American international high school. Most mornings on his way to work he walks through the Roman Forum.

History & culture

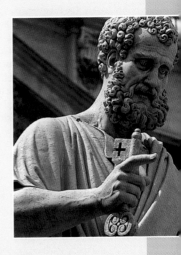

St. Peter with the keys to the Kingdom of Heaven

Rome today

LUCIAN, THE SECOND-CENTURY GREEK RHETORICIAN, DESCRIBED IT AS "a bit of Paradise"; the 15th-century Tuscan scholar, Gian Francesco Poggio Bracciolini, writing centuries later, described the city of Rome as "the most beautiful and magnificent of all those that either have been or shall be"; and in the early 19th century, the English poet, Percy Bysshe Shelley, said the impression of "that majestic city … exceeds anything I have ever experienced in my travels." These are opinions that have survived through time, and today manage to survive even the difficulties of life in modern-day Rome. Labor strikes, pollution, urban disarray, and heavy-handed bureaucracy cannot obscure the beauty and fascination of what is truly the Eternal City.

You can visit this city countless times, or live here for years, and its magnificent light, its colors (soft reds, ochers, and oranges mixed with the off-white and gray of marble and travertine), its harmonies of marble bridges across a curving river, its tree-shaded Renaissance villas and parks, its skyline of domes and *campanili*, will still take your breath away. The Pantheon, the Colosseum, the Campidoglio at sunset, the Roman Forum in the flattening afternoon light—these are timeless wonders that over past centuries (and future ones) make this city a destination for anyone who loves history and admires the artistic capacities of man. While the rampant building speculation that took place after the war has turned the city's outskirts into prosaic concrete canyons, the area within the still resistant Aurelian walls and particularly the *centro storico* (historic center) has—despite uncivilly parked cars, buzzing *motorini*, and ubiquitous dog poop—lost little of its magic.

Rome, of course, has always had its critics. Scan the centuries for the reports of more or less known travelers (or talk to some of today's inhabitants) and words such as decay, dirt, noise, and traffic will literally jump off the pages. Even Poggio Bracciolini, writing in the early 1400s, was moved to dismay, speaking of a city "stripped of beauty, lying prostrate like a giant corpse, decayed and everywhere eaten away." At that time the popes had recently returned from self-imposed exile in Avignon (France), to find a city that plague and factional strife had reduced to severe urban dirtiness and disarray. Other low points were the three-day invasion in 410 by the barbarian Visigoths; the aftermath of the bloody (4,000

dead) Sack of Rome in 1527 by the French and German troops of the Holy Roman Emperor, Charles V; and, centuries later, the brutal German occupation which ended only in 1945 with the Allied liberation.

Italy's capital since 1870, Rome gradually recovered after World War II, thanks largely to the Marshall Plan and to the Italians' natural resilience. The new, democratic party system that was grafted onto the roots of pre-Fascist liberalism, grew quickly, if chaotically. And despite all the problems that have ensued— corruption, government instability, strikes, and terrorism—Rome is now the flourishing capital of a major, and wealthy, European power. Largely a service and administrative center (as well as a tourist destination), its stores and boutiques are elegant (and often expensive). Its restaurants are full. Its parks are lovely and provide bikers, strollers, and mothers and small children with some 21,000 acres (8,400 ha) of green. Its middle-class families are well enough off to give their teenagers motorbikes that often go for as much as $3,000 a throw. Conspicuous consumption is thriving and it's hard to find a Roman who doesn't have—and constantly use—a *telefonino* or *cellulare* (cell phone).

A CITY IN TRANSITION

Rome today is a city of almost three million people, most of whom have come from the

Louis XV of France helped pay for this 18th-century monumental staircase, which ironically has always been called the Spanish Steps. A central feature of the city, it is used for fashion and flower pageants.

surrounding Lazio region or from the Italian south. Drawn to the capital by the possibility of work and the political contacts that, in this Mediterranean country, can be oh-so-useful, they have helped the city to expand far beyond its original perimeters. This was never an industrial capital, and for decades Rome's 20-odd government ministries were swollen repositories of political patronage. The head-quarters of most major banks are located here as are those of airlines, labor unions, and the

unbelievable, and still expanding, plethora of Italian political parties. Many young Italians have poured into Rome to attend its three open-admission public universities and some newer private ones. And, of course, Rome is the capital of Alta Moda (High Fashion or couture) as well as the home of the Vatican and of the pope. It thus attracts hundreds of thousands of tourists and pilgrims. According to City Hall, in 2004 the number of tourists reached almost seven million, two-thirds of

whom were foreigners, with the three biggest groups being the Americans, Japanese, and British, followed by the Germans, French, and Spanish. And in April 2005 alone, more than four million pilgrims came here to honor Pope John Paul II.

Despite this constant influx, for decades Rome was strongly resistant to most foreign influences, boasting a society that was almost stiflingly homogeneous: Almost everyone was white and Catholic (at least nominally). As

Ancient art and artifacts, authentic or not, are part of Italian culture and are everywhere in this city. At the Sunday flea market at Porta Portese, buyers look for images of the past.

recently as the mid-1970s, the number of foreign restaurants could be counted on two hands. Now all this has changed and Rome appears to be on the brink of recapturing the multiracial and polyglot atmosphere

it surely had during the imperial period, when people from all corners of the Roman Empire came here, albeit—in the case of slaves—not always voluntarily.

The arrival of tens of thousands of immigrants from Africa, Asia, and the Middle East, has set in motion an ethnic revolution that in the long run is bound to have profound social and cultural implications—not least because the Italian birthrate is one of the lowest in the world. Many immigrants are illegal, many others have succeeded, thanks to Italy's frequent amnesties, in getting work papers. At present, more than 8 percent of the city's population is foreign-born. The biggest foreign group is from the Philippines. They are followed, in order, by Rumanians, Poles, Peruvians, Bangladeshis, and Egyptians. People from developing countries work as domestic help, construction workers, housepainters, or home aides for the elderly. Many Senegalese are street peddlers. Chinese run

food shops and scores of Chinese restaurants and carry-outs. Egyptians work in restaurant kitchens and may have cooked that luscious *all'amatriciana* that you are eating.

LA DOLCE VITA, ROMAN STYLE

Most of the new arrivals have come to Rome for very clear, work-related reasons. They are part of a huge south–north, east–west migration toward Europe that reflects the sharp differences in living standards that

The Swiss Guard was instituted in the 16th century to protect the pope. The uniform has been unchanged since then.

afflict our world. In contrast, foreigners who have come to Rome from developed countries such as the United States and the United Kingdom are generally motivated by different considerations. First, they know that this city is an open-air museum where the ruins of the near and more distant past can be found at

almost every turn in the road and under nearly every step.

Furthermore, Rome would also appear to have an inside track on sensuality, relaxation, and overall hedonism. And how could it be otherwise in a society that puts beauty and pleasure first and foremost? Although they frequently lose their tempers in traffic, Romans have turned being laid-back into an art form. More than two thousand years of history, with all its vagaries, have left the average Roman with one major conviction: Nothing is more important than the here and now. And Romans do their best to live up to that conviction.

How do you know when it's spring in Rome? Because at the first warming of the sun's rays, everyone is outdoors, chatting on street corners, filling sidewalk cafés, or taking prolonged and possibly undeserved coffee breaks. How do you know when it's summer? Because everyone has left the city for the near-

by beaches to soak up the sun, hopefully becoming even more beautiful in the process. During other seasons, they opt for the *gita in campagna,* a country jaunt, or a short trip to some nearby lovely village, especially if there's a good restaurant in the area. In the evenings, except when it's raining or when a soccer match is being telecast, Romans pour into the streets, particularly in neighborhoods such as Trastevere, Testaccio, and the area around the Pantheon. Many head for the local trattorias,

Conspicuous consumption and a passion for luxury products have always been key elements in the *dolce vita*.

since eating is definitely the number one Roman sport. An after-dinner *caffè* or *gelato,* a bit of people-watching, and some gossip are other favorite pastimes of the average Roman, especially since his *telefonino* allows him to keep in touch with his friends and, if necessary, reschedule. ■

History of Rome

ROME IS ONE OF THE FEW CITIES IN THE WORLD TO HAVE BEEN CONTINU-
ously inhabited for the last 2,700 years, which is why so few traces of early settlement have
been found. Centuries have passed but the influence of its ancient heritage remains para-
mount and holds the key to understanding its later development.

THE FOUNDING OF ROME

From a literary point of view it sounds great:
Aeneas flees Troy by boat, carrying his aged
father Anchises on his back and leading his
small son Ascanius by the hand. He lands in
Italy and founds the city of Lavinium on the
coast. When Ascanius grows up, he founds
Alba Longa in the Alban Hills but because of
family squabbles over the throne in the suc-
ceeding generation, Romulus and Remus are
thrown into the Tiber River and wash up on
the slopes of the Palatine Hill where they are,
in short order, suckled by a she-wolf and res-
cued by a shepherd. The boys grow up, and set
about founding their own city. In the process
they quarrel: Remus is killed and Romulus
becomes the first king of Rome.

Unfortunately, very little of this may be
true. The Romans, in fact, were just one of the
many various peoples to inhabit the central
portion of the peninsula in the late Iron Age,
sharing the land with the Etruscans, the
Latins, and the Samnites. The original population of the area occupied by the future city of
Rome was therefore probably composed of an
aggregation of local tribes. In this context,
the legend of the Sabine women makes sense.
The women were probably kidnapped by
Romulus's men because of a real shortage
of females.

What is instead surely true, according to
the traces that have been found of Rome's
early Iron Age dwellings on the Palatine
Hill, is that whoever settled this area probably
had an instinct for survival and then some.
The Palatine was, after all, the most strategic
location for a primitive settlement: A hill
that was easy to defend, but at the same
time was close to a major river with natural
port facilities. Even more to the point the
hill was not too distant from the most
fordable spot on the river, where the
existence of Tiber Island made crossing
considerably easier.

ROYAL & REPUBLICAN ROME

Romulus, then (or someone like him), was
Rome's first king, and legend tells us that he
was the first of seven, the others being Numa
Pompilius, Tullus Hostilius, Ancus Marcius,
Tarquinius Priscus, Servius Tullius, and
Tarquinius Superbus ("the proud"). The
existence of the first four rulers cannot be
proved. But indications are that the last three,
all with Etruscan names, did exist, and their
Etruscan origin testifies to the likelihood of
some degree of tribal intermingling. Another
clue is that the Etruscans had highly developed
engineering skills and it was precisely then, in
the sixth century B.C., that the marshy area
between the Palatine and Capitoline Hills, the
future Roman Forum, was drained.

Tarquinius Superbus is believed to have
been deposed in 509 B.C. and the monarchy
was then replaced by a republic with two consuls elected annually by the men of the city.
The consuls appointed the members of an
advisory council which eventually became
known as the Senate. Formally at least, this
political system was to last until the advent of
imperial rule under Octavius, or, as he preferred to be called after 27 B.C., Augustus. But
over the centuries it evolved and changed. At
first, the government was dominated by a
patrician elite whose influence derived largely
from the wealth that allowed them to lead the
republic's armies and, later, when qualifica-
tions including wealth and land owning were
set, to dominate the Senate. The result was
years of conflict with the unlanded and the
unwealthy plebeians. During the fourth
century B.C., after skillful manipulation of
public opinion in the Forum's open-air assem-
blies, the dispossessed finally won the right to
equal representation. In fact, say historians,

**The pontiff performs ceremonial rites at
his altar under Bernini's bronze canopy in
St. Peter's Basilica.**

Rome's first expansionist forays into surrounding areas may have been designed to acquire territory needed to distribute among the newly enfranchised.

THE ROMAN EMPIRE, ITS RISE & ITS DECLINE

Rome had an empire long before it had an emperor. In fact, despite the on-going conflict between plebeians and patricians (or perhaps because of it!), the Roman Republic gradually gained control of the city's hinterland. The twin deities, Castor and Pollux, are said to have lent a hand during the Battle of Lake Regillus in 496 B.C., where the Romans defeated the Latin League. Be that as it may, this proved to be the start of an almost unbroken series of military successes, ending with the conquest of all the other peoples of Latium (the area surrounding Rome), be they Latins, Etruscans, Volsci, or Aequi to name but a few. And if the invasion of central Italy by the Gauls in 390 B.C. looked like it was about to become a major setback, it didn't: The young republic was saved when the Veneti attacked the Gauls on their northern flank, forcing them to head back home.

By the middle of the third century B.C., Rome's armies had conquered most of southern Italy. It was in this period that the major consular roads, beginning with the Via Appia to the south and the Via Aurelia and Via Flaminia to the north, were built to facilitate both troop movements and trade. Expansion almost to the shores of Sicily, until then considered to be a part of Carthage's sphere of influence, brought Rome into open conflict with that North African stronghold. The three Punic wars, lasting on and off for 118 years (264 B.C. to 146 B.C.), ended with the destruction of what was then Rome's only major rival for power in the western Mediterranean, and, at the same time, witnessed the first Roman expansion outside the confines of the Italian peninsula: Sardinia, Corsica, and Illyria (today's Dalmation coast) fell under Roman sway, soon followed by Macedonia, Greece, and parts of Asia Minor.

When Julius Caesar appeared on the scene in the first century B.C., Rome's attention had for almost a century been focused on political and social problems at home rather than on

further expansion. During his reign, however, Caesar did manage to defeat and annex Gaul. The social unrest of the era allowed Caesar increasingly to concentrate power in his hands, a trend that was to continue and be further reinforced by Augustus. Under Augustus, who defeated Mark Antony and Cleopatra, Egypt became a Roman province, Spain was completely subjugated, and the empire's borders were extended as far as the Rhine and the Danube. The next hundred years saw more of the same. Britain was conquered, Palestine was annexed, and under Trajan (A.D. 98–117) the empire reached its maximum limits of expansion, stretching from the British Isles to Asia Minor.

By the second half of the second century A.D., however, barbarian tribes had begun

to pose a real threat. Hadrian's decision to build his famous defensive wall in England, completed in A.D. 136, was significant. As Roman competence on the battlefield declined (the empire's overextension was one reason for this), barbarian encroachments increased. In A.D. 330, Constantine inaugurated Constantinople, which soon became the administrative capital of the empire. Not many years after Constantine's death in A.D. 337, the empire was divided in half.

The Eastern Empire, governed from Constantinople, was strong enough to survive for another thousand years. Disaster loomed in the west, however, where repeated barbarian invasions took place. In 410, the Visigoths, led by Alaric, descended on Rome, pillaging for three days and putting an end to the city's

Eight massive columns are all that remain of the Temple of Saturn, located at the western end of the Roman Forum.

reputation of invincibility. In 476, the Germanic warrior, Odovacar, deposed the last emperor, Romulus Augustulus, then but a teenager. Despite its unhappy end, the achievements of the Roman Empire cannot be minimized. Military prowess, combined with an ability to incorporate conquered peoples into its social and political system brought unparalleled success. The proof? Five Latin-based Romance languages (Italian, French, Spanish, Portuguese, and Romanian), the 26-letter Western alphabet, the continued use of Roman numerals, and a calendar of 12 months and 365 days.

CHRISTIANITY & THE PAPACY

It was under Roman rule that Jesus was cruci-fied. It was in Rome that both Peter and Paul suffered martyrdom and where the shrines so dear to future pilgrims were built over their graves. Rome is the center of Catholicism because the popes, in a direct line of Apostolic succession, are considered heirs of St. Peter. The history of Christianity is thus inextricably intertwined with that of the Roman Empire. Indeed, in the Middle Ages many believed that the Roman Empire had been part of a divine plan to provide a stable geographical area and a fertile terrain for the spread of Christianity. Having achieved its purpose, the pagan Roman Empire could decline and disappear, to be replaced by the new universal, but Christian, empire. Unfortunately, things were not quite so cut and dried.

Peter and Paul both died in Rome, proba-bly during the early Neronian persecutions between A.D. 64 and 67. For centuries, how-ever, Christianity remained only one of many cults exported to Rome from the East. And even after it had become the favored sect of the imperial family under Constantine, there were problems. Much of the Roman elite remained fiercely pagan. It was only in the fifth century that Christianity became strong enough to step, definitively, out of the closet. It was in this period that the first grandiose churches, such as Santa Sabina (see pp. 208–209), were built.

As the papacy began to reign supreme in spiritual matters, it also gradually assumed responsibility for the temporal welfare of Rome's population, filling in increasingly for the absentee rulers in Constantinople. In the aftermath of the disastrous sixth-century Gothic wars, Pope St. Gregory the Great (590–604) was forced to provide food and shelter for a population swollen with impover-ished refugees. *Diaconates* were created for the distribution of food, and in the ninth century defensive structures were built around the Vatican by Leo IV to protect it from the marauding Saracens. Greater power meant a larger bureaucratic apparatus and, particularly after the reign (1073–1085) of Gregory VII, an increased determination to remain indepen-dent of any temporal authority, be it king or emperor. This led to the famous conflict over

who had the authority to appoint (or invest) bishops, the so-called Investiture Controversy, between the Holy Roman Emperor Henry IV and Pope Gregory VII, which continued to rankle even after the compromise solution of the Concordat of Worms (1122).

If the 12th and 13th centuries witnessed the papacy's transformation into a first-rate European political power, a gradual decline in status and effective political clout was inevitable. By the beginning of the 1300s, other European nations, as well as the increas-ingly prosperous Italian city-states, were emerging as independent power brokers. In Rome, rampant factionalism and bitter rivalries among the city's noble families led the popes to move the Holy See to Avignon in France (the so-called Babylonian Captivity), where they were to remain for much of the 14th century. During this period a vast reorganization of Church agencies and admin-istration was begun, as were reform measures for the clergy. The close connection to the French court, and the consequent tensions with England and Germany, ended by damag-ing the papacy's prestige.

RENAISSANCE

Historians have been discussing the true significance of the Renaissance (literally "rebirth") almost since its inception. What is not questioned, however, is its outcome (the birth of modern Europe) and its place of ori-gin (Italy). The upsurge of renewed interest in the learning and values of classicism was probably inevitable in Italy with its abundance of classical ruins. The result was humanism, a philosophy propounded by secular men of let-ters as well as Church scholars whose primary emphasis was on the intellectual and artistic capacities of man. This period of heightened artistic expression was to really take off when the prosperous and ambitious princes of the burgeoning Italian city-states, such as the Medici in Florence, summoned to their courts some of the era's most prestigious painters, sculptors, architects, and draftsmen.

The papacy, always resilient, was to reach new heights in the rarefied atmosphere of the Renaissance (and again in the 1500s) in response to the birth of Protestantism, becom-ing an incomparable patron of the arts. By the

Andrea del Pozzo, a 17th-century Jesuit, painted "The Entry of St. Ignatius into Paradise" on the ceiling of St. Ignatius Church.

middle of the 15th century, the pontiffs had reasserted their authority over the Eternal City and, applying their vast resources to the city's embellishment, had shifted the center of the Renaissance from Florence to Rome. Starting about 1450, a series of ambitious, wily, and even (occasionally) erudite popes dedicated much of their attention to beautifying their city. Tuscan and Umbrian artists such as Fra Angelico, Pinturicchio, and Michelangelo were brought to Rome to decorate Vatican interiors such as Nicholas V's chapel, the Borgia apartments, and, of course, the Sistine Chapel, which for close to 60 years kept many famous artists occupied. In architecture, too, the Renaissance was to leave its mark on Rome and here, as well, the Church was to prove a major patron. An eloquent example was Donato Bramante, considered the creator of High Renaissance architecture, who designed the classically inspired Tempietto at San Pietro in Montorio (see p. 189) and then, appointed Papal Architect by Julius II (1503–1513), produced the first designs for the new, gigantic St. Peter's.

COUNTER-REFORMATION & THE BAROQUE

The religious movement identified as the Counter-Reformation was to have a profound effect on its capital, Rome, as well as on the psychology of its governing elite. At its inception, it was a reaction to the Protestant Reformation begun by Martin Luther in the early part of the 16th century. The reforms set off by the challenge of that breakaway movement were to stimulate an era of intense religious fervor, bringing to the fore zealot saints such as St. Philip Neri, St. Theresa of Avila, and, of course, St. Ignatius of Loyola. The latter's soldier mentality (he was once quoted as declaring that he had "never left the army") left its mark on the quasi-military structure of his newly created order, the Society of Jesus (the Jesuits), who were often referred to as the "pope's legions."

The Counter-Reformation also represented a period of serious self-analysis on the part of the Roman Catholic Church. If the three-part Council of Trent (1545–1563) was to establish the doctrinal foundations and the institutional structures that would help the Church

Streets, piazzas, monuments, and high schools throughout Italy are named after Giuseppe Garibaldi.

to survive the Protestant challenge, it also outlined the basic tenets that would govern the life of ordinary Catholics until the Second Vatican Council (1962–65). Primarily conservative in nature, the Trent Council confirmed that the Church alone could interpret Scripture, reformed monastic and religious orders, created a new catechism, and adopted the Tridentine Latin Mass. The renewed vigor brought to the papacy by the Counter-Reformation and the Council of Trent also gave it a new lease on political life and two more centuries as a truly important player on the European stage. The emergence of a new world of young nation-states changed things, however, gradually pushing a reluctant Holy See to the political sidelines.

IL RISORGIMENTO & NATIONAL UNIFICATION

Il Risorgimento (from the Italian verb, *risorgere*, to rise again) was the prime force in 19th-century Italy. The ideological and bureaucratic groundwork laid by the French Revolution and the Napoleonic Wars had set in motion a desire for national unification. Three great men were on hand to make it happen: Giuseppe Mazzini, a democratic nationalist; Giuseppe Garibaldi, a firebrand general whose father was a fisherman; and Count Camillo Cavour, a Piedmontese aristocrat and skilled politician-diplomat. Their combined efforts resulted in the proclamation of the Kingdom of Italy in March 1861. Only two pieces were missing: Venice (to be conquered from Austria in 1866) and Rome, which, thanks to French acquiescence, was to be taken from the pope by Italian armies on September 20, 1870.

Papal rule and the overweening influence of the fractious Roman nobility had not done much for the city. At the end of the 18th century, Rome, with a population of under 200,000, was still a backwater provincial capital. But intellectual currents were running swift. Occupation by Napoleon's armies had infected many Romans with the virus of liberalism and republicanism, and in 1848 Pope Pius IX was forced to grant a constitution. This didn't satisfy Mazzini and his supporters, who, in 1849, proclaimed the short-lived Roman Republic. Despite a valiant defense by the "Garibaldini" and others, the French, acting for the pope, retook the city. But time was running out for the papacy.

Before 1859, as Austria's Metternich had put it, Italy was only "a geographical expression." Divided into eight separate states, it was subject to the domination of foreign powers, mainly France, Spain, and Austria, while the popes still controlled a broad swathe of central Italy. The desire for unification was to snowball, however, particularly after Cavour became prime minister of Piedmont in 1852. Allied with the French, in 1859 the Piedmontese took Lombardy from the Austrians and the next year annexed Umbria and the Marches. In the south, Garibaldi and his Thousand defeated the Bourbon armies, conquering Sicily and then Naples. The remaining Italian states chose union with Piedmont. Rome remained in papal hands, but not for long, although attempts by Garibaldi to capture the city in 1862 and 1867 were unsuccessful. In 1870, with France weakened by its war with Prussia, Italy had its chance. On September 20, Italian troops opened a breach in the city walls (at Porta Pia) and entered Rome. After a plebiscite, Rome became Italy's capital.

FASCISM, WAR, & DEMOCRACY

Rome's population grew rapidly after 1870. By the onset of World War I it had hit 500,000 and by 1930 there were over one million inhabitants. The city had now also expanded well beyond the old Roman walls built by Aurelian. Given the imperial ambitions of the Fascist dictator, Benito Mussolini, it is not surprising that the Fascist regime undertook important archaeological excavations that brought to light or restored many of the monuments of ancient Rome. It was at that time, too, that a major impetus was given to the transformation of the city into a modern capital: The then avant-garde EUR section (for a projected 1942 international fair) was built, as were the new, grandiose avenues such as Fori Imperiali and Conciliazione, although the latter two cost the city the loss of two important medieval neighborhoods.

As the capital of Italy, Rome in the 20th century saw an enhancement of the administrative character that it had already acquired under its popes. But the social stresses and strains of building a nation (and of "making Italians" as the 19th-century statesman, Metternich, had put it) were to have disastrous consequences. Neutral when the Great War began, Italy joined up in hopes of territorial gains, but the war was unpopular and the loss of 600,000 men made it particularly hard to swallow the Triple Entente's refusal to give Italy Dalmatia and Fiume, now part of Croatia, leading nationalists to bemoan a "mutilated victory." Serious postwar economic problems—including galloping inflation and soaring unemployment—increased the social unrest that led both to the growing popularity of the Left and to the rise of the Right. Mussolini's October 1922 march on Rome won him the government, but within two years he had already eliminated democracy,

disbanding most of Italy's constitutional system, banning free speech and association, bridling the press, and, in the late 1930s, introducing anti-Semitic laws. Nevertheless, many aspects of the regime were genuinely popular.

Following Italy's censure by the League of Nations (for invading Ethiopia), Mussolini moved closer to Hitler. The military alliance

This was a favorite pose of Benito Mussolini, the fascist dictator. His urban renovations destroyed medieval areas.

with Germany was to have disastrous economic and military consequences. In July 1943, following the Allied invasion of Sicily, Mussolini was dismissed and arrested and an armistice signed. The Germans immediately occupied Rome and the Italian army disintegrated. Despite the valiant efforts of the Resistance, more active farther north, it was only in June 1944 that the city was liberated by the Allies. After World War II, which had left the country devastated and Rome demoralized, the foundations were laid for a democratic system. In 1946 Italians voted to end the monarchy and found a republic. The new 1948 constitution established a multiparty, parliamentary system which, although chaotic and confusing, has allowed Italy to regain a place of respect within the family of nations. ∎

The arts

THE BEAUTY OF THE ETERNAL CITY IS NOT OF THE CONTEMPORARY KIND.
The two major influences on Rome's artistic heritage were, without a doubt, the Roman
Empire and the papacy and these have left their indelible mark on the city.

ARCHITECTURE & ART

The Emperor Augustus reportedly claimed
that he had found a city made of brick and
left one made of marble. In a sense this is
true. Like his adoptive father, Julius Caesar,
Augustus learned early on that public works
constituted an effective way, not just to
embellish an imperial city and heighten its
prestige, but to gain the good will, or at least
the tolerance, of public opinion. Architectural
extravaganzas were not undertaken simply
because there was an empty space to fill. From
the Colosseum to the Arch of Titus, from the
refurbished Temple of Vesta to the Baths of

Caracalla, the political significance was
fundamental. The concept that "art is the
handmaiden of politics" has been around for
a long time. Perhaps no other country, and
its capital, has so benefited from the
ambitions and, yes, megalomania of its rulers,
be they emperors, popes, or princes. The
final result is layer upon layer of artistic and
architectural glory. Look around you at the
ruins of so many past regimes. The stratification is such that if you observe carefully,
you can usually identify the successive layers
of Rome's past majesty, often in the very
same structure.

Architecture had its first real boom with the advent of the Imperial Roman era. Some emperors built for their own enjoyment alone: Nero and his Golden House come to mind. But in most instances, their major building projects were destined for public use. And the largely unknown architects of ancient Rome did wonders: Some of their constructions—the Pantheon, the Colosseum, Trajan's Markets, the Arches of Titus, Septimius Severus, and Constantine—still stand, mute witnesses of past glories, silent embellishments even today of man's all too brief existence.

Just how different from the emperors of Rome were the popes of the Eternal City? Was not the construction of Santa Sabina in the early fifth century in the midst of an elegant,

The restoration of the Sistine Chapel was completed in 1989. Here, a craftsman works on Michelangelo's "Last Judgment."

and until then largely pagan, aristocratic quarter, a political affirmation of Christianity's march toward primacy? In fact, Catholicism's decision to convert many ancient Roman structures into churches (thereby ensuring their survival), was hardly made on practical grounds alone: The symbolic and psychological content of certain gestures, for example moving the doors of Julius Caesar's Senate to the Basilica of San Giovanni in Laterano, appears obvious. But once again, we are the beneficiaries. Whether we are Catholic, Protestant, Jew, Muslim, or Buddhist, our lives have been enriched by the political decisions of Rome's past secular and religious rulers.

Naturally, some of Christianity's constructions were largely idealistic in inspiration. In some of the earliest churches, built near or over the shrines of early martyrs, or like Santa Maria in Cosmedin, on the site of an early diaconate, you can almost physically sense the aura of Christian faith. Later on, vigorous building campaigns by the papacy, especially in the 9th and 13th centuries, served a dual purpose: New structures were needed to welcome the faithful, but glorification of the mother institution was also part of the process. The building of St. Peter's in the 16th and 17th centuries may have been the most blatant example of architectural self-glorification. The papacy also used interior decoration to effectively reaffirm its precepts; the examples of decorative work with an explicit political undertone are numerous. One of the most eloquent examples from the Middle Ages is the series of 13th-century frescoes in the St. Sylvester chapel in the church of the Quattro Coronati near the Colosseum. The decision to depict events in the life of the Emperor Constantine in such a way as to make him appear subservient to Pope Sylvester is propaganda at its best. How else to explain the final scene in which Constantine, on foot, humbly holds the reins of the pope's donkey!

Starting in the Renaissance, mosaic work—for centuries the most widely used decorative medium in the classical world—was replaced gradually by sculpture and painting, perfect tools for the expression of political concepts and conceits. For centuries, statuary as a medium had been reserved for the representation of gods and secular rulers. One thinks, for example, of the equestrian statue of Marcus Aurelius (long believed to be Constantine) or the statue of Augustus from Livia's villa at Prima Porta. In the 13th century, the popes, too, began to commission statues of themselves—as rulers rather than religious leaders—to be displayed in public. So only a few feet away from Arnolfo di Cambio's statue of Charles of Anjou (dressed as a Roman senator) in the Capitoline Museum are Bernini's statue of Pope Urban VIII, a Barberini, and Algardi's statue of Innocent X, a Pamphili. And you can't miss the political overtones of Raphael's paintings in the so-called Rooms of Raphael in the Vatican Museums. The "Expulsion of Heliodorus from the Temple," for example, was a clear allusion to Pope Julius II's military campaign to expel usurpers from Church lands.

Gian Lorenzo Bernini, "sovereign of the arts, to whom popes, princes and peoples reverently bowed" (see the plaque on his house on Via della Mercede, near the corner with Propaganda Fide), was undoubtedly a genius. The baroque style, of which he is indisputably one of the major creative protagonists, is perhaps the maximum example of art used to convey concepts—primarily faith in the Church and in its doctrines—that transcend the purely ornamental. Designed to combat the rapidly spreading Protestant Reformation and, at the same time, to emphasize the importance of the Catholic religion, the baroque was blatantly propagandistic: All the plastic arts (architecture, painting, sculpture) were used to make an appeal to the faithful that was both sensory and emotional. The magnificence of Rome's baroque churches such as Il Gesù (the mother Jesuit church) or Santa Maria della Vittoria was successfully intended to underscore the splendor and importance of the papacy, to impress the viewer, and convince him that the Roman Catholic Church was the oldest, the best, and the only institution qualified to decipher Divine Will (and scripture) for the faithful. A sharp contrast with the sense of Martin Luther's reforms which stressed the necessity for individual interpretation of scripture.

It was also a lucky break for the Vatican (and for Rome) that three of the great baroque

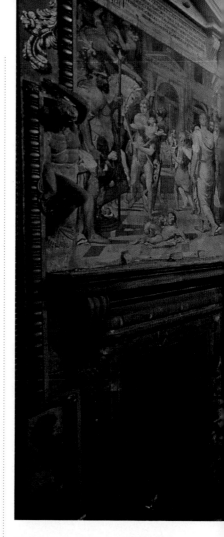

The gloriously decorated Sala Regia was the room in the Apostolic Palace where rulers came to pay homage to the pope.

geniuses (Bernini, Francesco Borromini, and Pietro da Cortona) were contemporaries and spent most of their creative lives in the Eternal City. The extravagant characteristics of their styles (rich colors, gold decoration, unlimited movement, endless depth, diagonal lines, whether concave or convex, dramatic lighting, and theatricality) were utilized in complex compositions to overwhelm the senses, to impress, to underline the importance of the clergy and the Church as an institution, and, through an appeal to the senses, to

stimulate piety and devotion. The overall effect—dynamism and movement in sharp contrast to the stability and unambiguous definition of Renaissance painting and sculpture—is often overwhelming.

The Church also encouraged and utilized musicians. Palestrina, from the nearby town of the same name, was a major innovator of contrapuntal composition. He composed at least 105 Masses while in Rome, many of which he dedicated to Pope Julius III, for a while his patron.

Subsequently, in the 17th century, the Italian baroque was exported abroad and was adopted by secular rulers elsewhere— Versailles in France and the Tsars' Winter Palace in St. Petersburg are good examples— for their own purposes. The situation was different, the message was the same: I am powerful, I am to be admired, feared, and— above all—respected.

In the 20th century, the Fascist government continued (albeit less successfully) with the traditional use of art and architecture by an autocratic government as a means of reinforcing power and prestige. In the 1920s and '30s, Mussolini's regime fostered a style which, although presented in a modern guise, adopted many ancient Roman motifs. The idea was to reinforce its legitimacy as the true heir to the ancient grandeur of Rome. The present-day Via dei Fori Imperiali was, at its inauguration, called the Via dell'Impero (Avenue of the Empire). Some might have thought the reference was to the empire that the Italians were then seeking to create through the annexation of territory in North Africa, but just as likely was the desire to be seen as successors to the "Impero" that, with far greater success, had existed two thousand years before.

The sprawling Foro Italico sports complex was begun by Mussolini's fascist regime. In 1960 it was the site of the Olympic Games.

LITERATURE

In the early days of ancient Rome, educated people used Greek for learning and for literary expression. By the first century B.C., Latin had asserted itself as the medium of artistic expression. Plautus, a comic poet, used colloquial Latin for his plays as did Ennius with his epics and tragedies. By the second half of the first century B.C., there were many writers of distinction, including Julius Caesar. But Cicero—philosopher, orator, and poet—stands out for his use of Latin in the expression of complex, abstract thought. Virgil was not a Roman, but in the capital he became part of an elite circle of poets close to the

Emperor Augustus, and his works—particularly the *Aeneid*—became an inspiration. The poet Horace was lauded for the perfection of form of his *Odes* and *Epistles*. Ovid wrote witty and elegiac poetry. Poems were recited in literary circles and in public, and great importance was given to structure and euphony. Whereas Livy and Tacitus excelled in history, Seneca chose tragedy, and Juvenal, satire. The post-Augustan period, while more subject to political repression, still produced writers as skillful as Petronius, Statius, Martial, and Suetonius. Later, Romans began to write in Greek again; the greatest work by a Roman in the first centuries A.D., Marcus Aurelius's *Meditations*, was composed in Greek.

In the intervening centuries, most writing in Latin was done by prelates or people trained in church schools. The 13th century, however, brought the first examples of literature in the vernacular and the emergence of major Italian writers such as Dante, Petrarch, and Boccaccio, none of whom were Roman, although Petrarch was crowned with laurel at the Campidoglio in 1341. Torquato Tasso, who was born in Sorrento and lived in Urbino, Venice, Padua, Ferrara, and Paris, was also supposed to be made Poet Laureate of Rome, but died shortly after arriving (1595) and is buried in the Church of Sant'Onofrio. It is probable that papal rule was not particularly conducive to the development of secular literature and poetry. It was not until the 19th century, in fact, that a major Roman poet appeared, Giovanni Gioacchino Belli, whose 2,000 sonnets in Roman dialect, for the most part composed around 1830, present a vivid and satirical picture of life in contemporary Rome.

By the late Renaissance, however, Rome had become a magnet for many foreign writers. Well-known early visitors include the French essayist Montaigne and the English poet John Milton. In the 18th and 19th centuries, inspired visitors included the German poet Goethe, the French writer Stendhal, the American writers Nathaniel Hawthorne, Mark Twain, and later Theodore Dreiser, and the English poets Percy Bysshe Shelley, George Gordon Byron, and John Keats as well as Robert and Elizabeth Browning. George Eliot sent her *Middlemarch* protagonist, Dorothea

Brooke, on an eye-opening trip to Rome with her parson husband, and much of Henry James's *Daisy Miller* is set here.

In the 20th century, several major writers emerged in Rome. Alberto Moravia, who died in 1990, started out as a journalist and wrote of alienation in modern society. His first novel, *Gli Indifferenti* (*Time of Indifference*), was published when he was only 21. Other major works, most of which have been translated into English, include *Agostino* (*Two Adolescents*, 1944), *La Romana* (*The Woman of Rome*, 1947), *Il Conformista* (*The Conformist*, 1951), and *La Ciociara* (*Two Women*, 1957), which became a prize-winning movie with Sophia Loren. Moravia was married for a while to the writer Elsa Morante, who died in 1985. Her best-known work, remarkable for its epic quality, is the 1974 *La Storia*, published in English as *History: A Novel*.

Another well-known writer, poet, and movie director was Pier Paolo Pasolini, a northern Italian born in 1922 who came to Rome after the war and used the material from his contacts among the city's down-and-outs for two novels: *Ragazzi di Vita* (*The Ragazzi*, 1955) and *Una Vita Violenta* (*A Violent Life*, 1959). Like his first film, *Accattone*, they deal with the lives of thieves, prostitutes, and other denizens of the Roman underworld. In 1975 Pasolini was murdered by a young man who could have been one of his characters. Other major postwar writers include Italo Calvino, Primo Levi, and Umberto Eco (*The Name of the Rose, Foucault's Pendulum*). More recently, Susana Tamaro, Alessandro Baricco, and Sicilian detective writer Andrea Camilleri have been translated and published abroad.

THE MUSEUM REVOLUTION

In classic terms, Rome is not a cultural center. It is not a city you would visit specifically for a chance to see opera or ballet. The theater, such that it is, is limited to Italian speakers. With a few exceptions, such as the recent opening of the modern Auditorium complex (designed by world-renowned Italian architect Renzo Piano) and the many small, chamber music concerts or recitals held in picturesque churches and palaces, classical music programs leave much to be desired.

Nor are the city's art galleries generally on the international circuit. However, the city has incomparable riches to offer an art lover. Itself an open-air museum where city squares contain Roman temples, Renaissance palaces, and fountains designed by master sculptors, Rome also has a large number of well-endowed museums. The Vatican Museums are known the world over. Many of Rome's museums have been renovated, reorganized, and reopened to become far more user-friendly. A case in point is the Borghese Gallery. Now on everyone's A list (and justly so), it was closed for over a decade while its poorly displayed masterpieces stood alone and ignored. Now, after a glorious restoration (although the internal organization is still far from perfect), it has a modern museum structure to show off its incomparable collections.

The Museo Nazionale Romano (National Museum of Rome), originally housed in the Baths of Diocletian near the station, has also been drastically reorganized; its works, long hidden from view in storerooms and cellars, have been brilliantly distributed among four separate sites. The baths now house the excellently reorganized Epigraphy Museum, while other sections are devoted to pre-Roman history; Palazzo Massimo alle Terme, a former high school right across Esedra Square, harbors magnificent Greek and Roman statuary, mosaics, and frescoes; treasures such as the Ludovisi throne are on display at a former Renaissance cardinal's palace, Palazzo Altemps, near Piazza Navona; and the Crypta Balbi, just a short walk from Largo Argentina, presents relics of the city's history from the end of the ancient Roman period through the later Middle Ages.

Another interesting museum is the Montemartini. Located in a former power plant in the Ostiense neighborhood and originally established to host many artworks from the Capitoline Museums (then under restoration), it has become a permanent structure where alternating parts of the Capitoline's overflow collection can be displayed. The Villa Giulia (the Etruscan Museum) has been refurbished, although too many labels are still in Latin. The National Gallery in the Barberini Palace, though still inefficiently organized, has a new entranceway and will expand now that the Army Officer's Club is giving up part of its space.

And it doesn't end there. In 1827, Stendhal complained in his *Promenades dans Rome* that "the small-minded brains which currently hold power permit us to visit these museums [the Capitoline and the Pio Clementino at the Vatican] only once a week." That was, of course, a long time ago, but until only a few years back the visiting hours at Rome's museums were frustratingly short (most closed at 1 or 2 p.m.) and differed notably one from the other. Now all this has changed. Except for Mondays, when most public museums are still closed (the Vatican Museums and the Roman Houses under the church of Sts. John and Paul on the Celio Hill are exceptions), museums are open all day long and, in summer and during other holiday periods, until late in the evening. Services have become far more efficient, better qualified personnel have been hired, and centralized reservation systems and information offices have been put in place, representing the creativity, flare, and style at which the Italians are so good—when they wish to be.

Rome also has a series of smaller, lesser-known museums that are worth a visit if time permits. The small Museo di Roma, which has artifacts and art related to Rome's later history from the Middle Ages on, has reopened after extensive renovation. The Baracco Museum with its collection of ancient sculpture should reopen in 2006. A new, expanded museum in the Rome synagogue opened in Fall 2005. A Museum of the Imperial Forums is scheduled to open in 2007. And itinerant exhibitions are housed in spaces such as the Palazzo Ruspoli and the Museo del Corso on different ends of Via del Corso, the newly popular Complesso del Vittoriano round the back of the Victor Emanuel Monument, Trajan's Markets on Via IV Novembre, and, the magnificently restored Scuderie, or stables, across the piazza from the Quirinal Palace.

"HOLLYWOOD ON THE TIBER" & AFTER

In the beginning there was Cinecittà, the giant film studio founded in 1937 by Italian dictator Benito Mussolini, who had decided to take on Hollywood and to make Italian film production into a source of national prestige. Ironically, Mussolini's project was to bear its best fruit only once the Fascist regime had been roundly defeated in World War II and superseded by a young democratic republic. As early as the 1950s, neorealism and post-neorealism had put the Italian film industry on the map, and the names of the best directors, actors, and actresses were known throughout the intellectual world. The success of Cinecittà was brought home to all in 1963 on the set of *Cleopatra*, which became the stage setting for a love story between the film's two principal stars, Elizabeth Taylor and Richard Burton. By the end of that decade, "Hollywood on the Tiber" was churning out between 200 and 250 films a year, some of which, over 40 years later, are still considered masterpieces.

Today, all this has changed. Most of the major directors who made their names in that period—Roberto Rossellini *(Roma Citta' Aperta)*, Lucchino Visconti *(Obsession, Senso, The Earth Trembles)*, Vittorio De Sica *(The Bicycle Thief* and *Sciuscià)*, Pietro Germi *(Divorce Italian Style, Seduced and Abandoned)*, Federico Fellini *(La Strada, La Dolce Vita, Roma, Amarcord,* etc.)—have died or, like Michelangelo Antonioni *(Blow Up, L'Avventura)* and Gillo Pontecorvo *(The Battle of Algiers)*, are over 80. Pier Paolo Pasolini *(The Gospel According to St. Matthew, The Decameron)* was murdered in 1975. Major actors such as Marcello Mastroianni and Ugo Tognazzi have passed away or, like Sophia Loren, make few films. Producer Dino De Laurentiis has been in Hollywood since the 1970s, and the only major recent films made in Cinecittà are *Oceans 12* and Martin Scorsese's 2002 hit, *Gangs of New York*.

Today, in fact, Cinecittà Holding rents out the once bustling studios primarily to RAI (Italian state television) and Mediaset (Silvio Berlusconi's film production company). Well-known directors like the Taviani brothers work largely for television, while others, such as Bernardo Bertolucci *(Last Tango in Paris)*, have been working abroad. Nowadays, only 80 to 100 films are produced annually in Italy, and no more than 25 get first-run distribution.

Decidedly, American films are among the most popular in Italy, although European and

**Marcello Mastroianni stars as a frustrated journalist in Federico Fellini's 1960 masterpiece,
La Dolce Vita.**

Asian films have a following among Roman intellectuals. There are, however, a few native bright stars on the horizon. Giuseppe Tornatore *(Nuovo Cinema Paradiso)* and iconoclast Nanni Moretti are popular with many. In March 1999, the Tuscan comedian Roberto Benigni won three Oscars for the touching *Life is Beautiful* about an Italian Jew in a German concentration camp, who convinces his young son to believe it is all a game. And in 2002, new director Gabriele Muccino's l'Ultimo Bacio *(The Last Kiss)* won a prize at the Sundance Film Festival.

L'ESTATE ROMANO (THE ROMAN SUMMER)

The concept of *L'Estate Romano* was first set in motion in the mid-1970s, when city culture commissioner Renato Nicolini turned the city into an outdoor festival with a something-for-everyone flavor. Parks become ballet stages, piazzas are turned into concert halls, basilicas

into auditoriums, riverbanks into bookstalls. Film showings are held at intriguing venues such as the Basilica di Massenzio, the Circus Maximus, and Tiber Island, as well as the area facing the Arch of Constatine where, in September 1981, thousands turned up for the historic screening of Abel Gance's *Napoleon*.

Parks are co-opted, too, with ballet in Villa Ada, concerts in Villa Pamphili, jazz at Villa Celimontana and in the Testaccio neighborhood, and prose near what remains of Tasso's Oak. Concerts, classical to rock, are also held in different downtown sites, while mimes, poets, Sicilian puppet troupes, majorettes, and so forth fan out through less central neighborhoods. In recent summers, events have attracted as many as five million spectators. Critics contend the quality is not what it once was. But there is no doubt that the Roman "Kulturmarket" is alive and well, making sure that tourists and non-vacationers alike have no excuse to be bored (see pp. 260–263). ∎

Food

DORMOUSE GLAZED WITH HONEY, ROLLED IN POPPY SEEDS, AND BAKED (a favorite of Trimalchio, Petronius' intemperate gourmet in *Satyricon*) or, alternatively, stuffed with minced meat, pepper, and nuts, and then roasted or boiled. Sow udders stuffed with oysters, gourds with popular fish sauce made from salted and fermented fish intestines, crushed boiled brains with pepper, milk, and eggs, and then to finish off (after a minimum of seven courses) a roast pig stuffed with live quail (Trimalchio again). But not to worry. Although food, and the eating of it, is as important today as it was in ancient times, some things have changed, and happily dormice and fish sauce are off the menu.

Other things, too, have changed for the better. In fact, if you look through Apicius's *De Re Coquinaria*, the first thing you'll realize is that many of the staple products that we associate with Italian cuisine today were unknown in ancient Rome. Tomatoes, eggplant, and zucchini to name just a few, arrived later from the New World. Instead of durum wheat—not used to make pasta in Naples until the 17th century—the Romans imported a type of grain

A viable alternative to a pasta meal can be a plate of starters or *antipasti* followed by a second meat or fish course.

called *faro adoreum*, and this was used to make *puls*, a boiled cereal that may have been similar to polenta. The unleavened bread of those days was sometimes cut into strips but it was far different from ours. What the two eras have in common, however, is gastronomic enthusiasm. Although the crowded sandwich bars and the

proliferation of fast-food outlets confirm that the three-hour lunch has more or less disappeared (and multicourse dinners are, also, increasingly infrequent), food is still a top priority. In fact, if there is anything a Roman likes to do more than eat, it is to regale his dinner companions with tales of what he ate yesterday, or on some more remote occasion.

Rome has never been cited for the delicacy or the refinement of its cuisine, which is instead hearty and robust, a collection of dishes, often washed down with a bottle of Castelli white, that represent real comfort food but which the wise will ingest only infrequently. The pasta dishes most basic to the Roman cuisine are *rigatoni all'amatriciana* (with smoked pancetta, tomato, and onion), *spaghetti alla carbonara* (pancetta, beaten egg, and onion), *spaghetti alla gricia* (the same but without the egg), or the rudimentary *aglio, olio, peperoncino* (oil, garlic, and chili pepper). Best vegetables include artichokes, Roman style *(carciofi alla romana)* or fried, Jewish style *(carciofi alla giudea)*. Also typical are *puntarelle in salsa d'alici* (raw chicory with anchovy sauce), *peperoni alla Romana* (red and green peppers sautéed with onion), lima beans with pancetta, or wild chicory with oil and lemon.

Another favorite is fried zucchini flowers, often part of a *misto fritto* (mixed fry) of mozzarella, artichokes, olives, and sometimes brains. As far as meat goes, the most characteristic dishes are roast pork *(maialino arrosto)*, baby lamb *(abbacchio)*, and tripe. In fact, innards are an important part of the city's traditional *cucina povera*. In the old days *rigatoni alla pajata* (lamb's intestine) was popular, and some people still swear by lamb heart *(coratella)*, served with artichokes, and *coda alla vaccinara* (oxtail stew). ■

Ave *Caesar* (Hail Caesar). Once the Roman Forum's temples echoed with these words. Today, the heart of ancient Rome is largely silent. But its splendid ruins testify loudly to the magnificent past when Roma was *caput mondi*.

Ancient Rome

Emperor Marcus Aurelius astride his mount at the Campidoglio

Ancient Rome

FROM THE BACK OF THE CAPITOLINE HILL—PROBABLY THE BEST PLACE TO
take your first look at the Roman Forum—you are, in the true sense of the term, a witness
to centuries of history. In front of you, stretching for almost half a mile, is the Roman
Forum and alongside it, flanking the Via dei Fori Imperiali, the excavated portions of the
later imperial *fora* that were built by Julius Caesar, and a series of first-century emperors,
to enlarge and beautify what had become an increasingly cramped downtown area. This
small valley, tucked among several hills (the Palatine, the Capitoline, the Quirinal, and the
Esquiline) is the heart of ancient Rome, in effect its birthplace.

The first Iron Age settlements, dating back to
the ninth and eighth centuries B.C., were on
the hilltops, specifically on the Palatine, which
later became a prized site for imperial
residences. Down below, where a somewhat
marshy enclave was crisscrossed by a road or
two, the foundations were laid for the development of an embryonic forum, an open space
that could and would be used for everything
from town meetings to commerce. In 753 B.C.,
or so they say, Romulus became the first king
of Rome, performing the sacred ceremony
(with a plow drawn by a snow white ox) of
tracing the *pomerium* (perimeter) of the city,
and (but this was not part of the ceremony)
slaying his twin, Remus, for his irreverence. As
the city grew, the forum was gradually transformed into a bona fide civic and religious
center, a site for everything from protests and
funerals to gladiatorial fights and theatrical
presentations. The first monuments made
their appearance during the monarchy. The
Comitium, the circular open space in front of
the Senate building, quickly became institu-
tionalized as a place for discussion and debate.
As Rome's wealth and power grew, and as conquering rulers returned from their first
encounters with the more advanced
Hellenistic world, the forum was to be further
transformed, and increasingly embellished, to
more adequately represent the grandeur of
what was becoming a far-flung empire. From
the fifth century A.D. on, however, it began
declining in importance. Until the excavations
of the 1800s, for most Romans it was of little
interest: They called it Campo Vaccino, the
cow pasture.

From your vantage point on the Capitoline
Hill, you can easily identify the major sites. In
the foreground is the Arch of Septimius

Severus, to its left Diocletian's massive brick
Curia, or Senate building, where Cicero
declaimed against the would-be traitor,
Cataline. The large open space in front of the
arch is the original Roman Forum, for centuries kept cleared of anything but Rome's
three traditional food staples: the olive, the
fig, and the grape. Farther to the right, the
eight large columns belonged to the portico of
the Temple of Saturn. The long rectangle
beyond is all that's left of the Basilica Julia
courthouse. Winding its way toward the Arch
of Titus is the famous Via Sacra, believe it or
not then considered a major thoroughfare,
because there was room for two carts to drive
abreast. Opposite you, toward the right, is the
Palatine Hill, where Romulus and Remus may
have lived, and farther away, to the left, you
can just make out the top of the Colosseum.

Here on the hill, just to your right, you can
see the grey blocks of peperino marble, now
the foundation of the Palazzo Senatorio (see p.
39), that were once part of the Tabularium, the
archives of ancient Rome. Nearby, atop a column, is a copy of the Capitoline wolf suckling
Romulus and Remus. The original wolf, in the
Capitoline Museum, is Etruscan: The infants
were added later. In front of the Palazzo
Senatorio is the Campidoglio, the magnificent
Renaissance complex designed by
Michelangelo to bring renewed glory to a site
that for kings, tribunes, tyrants, and emperors
was the heart of political and religious Rome.
The smallest of the city's seven fabled hills,this
is the most famous, giving us our word "capitol." The Capitoline Museums (see pp. 40–41)
are here, with famed statues such as that of
Marcus Aurelius, the "Dying Gaul" and the
"Boy with a Thorn" as well as the sculpted
faces of the elite of ancient Rome. ■

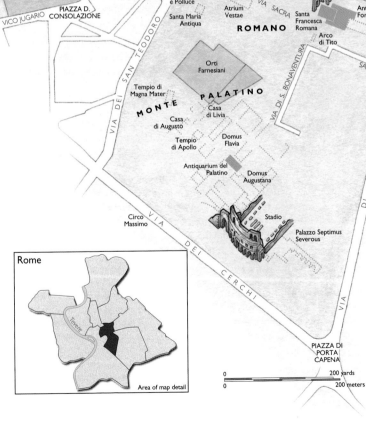

PIAZZA
VENEZIA

VIA IV.
NOVEMBRE

Colonna
Traiana

Mercati
Traianei

FORO

TRAIANO

FORO DI

Tempio di
Venere
Genitrice

FORI

AUGUSTO

Tempio di
Marte Ultore

Scalinata
d'Aracoeli

Santa Maria
in Aracoeli

Palazzo
Nuovo

FORO
DI
CESARE

Cordonata

**Musei
Capitolini**

PIAZZA
DEL
CAMPIDOGLIO

Palazzo
Senatorio

Arco di
Settimio
Severo

FORO DI NERVA

VIA SALARA VECCHIA

IMPERIALI

VIA
DEI
FORI

VIA
CAVOUR

Curia

Comitium

Basilica
Aemilia

FORO DI
VESPASIANO

Entrance to
Roman Forum

Rostra

Colonna
di Foca

Tempio di
Antonino e
Faustina

Santi
Cosma e
Damiano

Basilica di
Massenzio

Palazzo dei
Conservatori

Tempio di
Saturno

FORO

VIA SACRA

Basilica
Giulia

FORO

Tempio di
Cesare

Regia

Tempio del
Divo Romolo

IMPERIALI

MONTE CAPITOLINO

CLIVUS
CAPITOLINUS

Tempio
di Castore
e Polluce

Tempio
di Vesta

Colosseo
M

VICO JUGARIO

PIAZZA D.
CONSOLAZIONE

Santa Maria
Antiqua

Atrium
Vestae

VIA SACRA

Santa
Francesca
Romana

Antiquarium
Forense

Tempio di
Venere e Roma

ROMANO

Arco
di Tito

PIAZZA
DEL
COLOSSEO

VIA DEI SAN TEODORO

Orti
Farnesiani

VIA DI S. BONAVENTURA

VIA
SACRA

Tempio di
Magna Mater

MONTE

PALATINO

Casa
di Livia

Casa
di Augusto

Domus
Flavia

Tempio
di Apollo

DI SAN GREGORIO

Antiquarium del
Palatino

Domus
Augustana

Circo
Massimo

Stadio

VIA DEI CERCHI

Palazzo Septimus
Severous

VIA

PIAZZA DI
PORTA
CAPENA

Rome

Tevere

Area of map detail

0   200 yards
0   200 meters

Campidoglio

THE COMBINATION OF ARCHITECTURE AND HISTORY associated with the Campidoglio, or Capitol (Capitoline Hill), makes it an absolute must for any and every visitor. You should make it your business to come here at least twice: Once during the day, preferably in the late afternoon, for the astonishing view of the sun-kissed Roman Forum below, and again at night, when marvelous lighting (for which the Italians have a real genius) turns the piazza, designed by Michelangelo, and the Roman ruins below into pure magic.

Campidoglio

Map p. 37

Bus: H, C3, 40, 46, 60, 62, 63, 64, 70, 81, 84, 85, 87, 95, 119, 170, 175, 628, 715, 716, 780

The best way to reach the piazza is from the gradually ascending flight of stairs, called the **Cordonata,** designed by Michelangelo in 1536 to provide easy access to the square and flanked at the bottom by two black, basalt Egyptian lions. At the top of the staircase are the giant marble statues of Castor and Pollux, which date back to ancient

times. Before you, in all its splendor (Pope Paul III commissioned it for a planned visit to Rome by the Holy Roman Emperor, Charles V), is **Piazza del Campidoglio,** set in what in ancient times could clearly be seen to be a hollow between two hill crests. You might also want to note the statues of the Emperor Constantine and his son,

Every April 21 a candlelit night-time concert is performed in this piazza to celebrate the founding of Rome in 754 or 753 B.C.

Capitolinus, built in the sixth century B.C. and reputed to be the largest of its kind ever constructed. A circular, glass-enclosed structure, recently inaugurated, was built over the gardens of the palazzo specifically to showcase the excavated portions (the podium and *cella,* or cell) of the temple to Jupiter and to dramatically display the ancient bronze equestrian statue of Marcus Aurelius. Today, the two buildings house different sections of the Musei Capitolini (see pp. 40–41).

Facing you from the bottom of the Cordonata is the **Palazzo Senatorio,** built in various stages in the 13th and 14th centuries on the remains of the Roman Tabularium, and today the seat of Rome's municipal government.

Michelangelo designed the double ramp of stairs at the front, which is embellished by a fountain sporting two enormous reclining river gods, the Tiber on the right and the Nile on the left. In the niche in between is the "Dea Roma," a red-and-white stone composite of two earlier statues of Minerva, the goddess of wisdom and war. The bell tower, designed by Martin Longhi the Elder, was built between 1578 and 1582. The rest of the facade was added a bit later by architects Giacomo della Porta and Girolamo Rainaldi.

At this point, however, you'll probably only have eyes for the equestrian statue of the emperor **Marcus Aurelius** that stands in the center of the square. Actually, what you are looking at is a copy (the original, removed in 1981 for restoration, is now in the Palazzo dei Conservatori). But the copy manages to convey the same sense of history and drama. Keep in mind when you're viewing the original that this is one of the rare surviving equestrian statues from classical Rome, possibly because for

Constantius, as well as two Roman milestones from the Appian Way. The modern statue halfway up the hill, to the left of the Cordonata, marks the spot where Cola di Rienzo, the 14th-century tribune who dreamed of restoring the Roman Republic, was executed.

The two identical buildings on your left and right are, respectively, the **Palazzo Nuovo** (built from scratch in 1655 to Michelangelo's design), and the older **Palazzo dei Conservatori,** the facade of which was redesigned by the Florentine sculptor and further modified by later Renaissance and baroque architects. You should know that the back portion of the Palazzo dei Conservatori (originally called Palazzo Caffarelli) stands on the site of what in ancient times was the temple of Jupiter Maximus

centuries it was believed to be a statue of Constantine, the emperor who converted to Christianity. It was brought to the Campidoglio in 1538 on the recommendation of Michelangelo, who created the pedestal. The bearded emperor has his right hand raised in a gesture of clemency. But don't be fooled! Historians tell us that the horse's raised hoof originally rested on the head of a vanquished barbarian. The bronze statue was originally covered in gold, and Romans used to say that if the gilt coating were to reappear it would be a sign that the day of judgment had arrived.

Walking up the Cordonata, you will have noticed a second, much steeper flight of stairs on the left leading to **Santa Maria d'Aracoeli** (pronounced A-ra-CHEY-li; see p. 139), which translates into "St. Mary of the Altar of Heaven." Don't miss the only partly concealed remains of a multistory, second-century *insula,* on the far side of the steeper staircase. The

122 steps up to the church (not to worry, you can also get in from Piazza del Campidoglio), are said to have been built in 1348 in gratitude for God's deliverance from the plague, and provide a telling contrast to the Cordonata. The Aracoeli staircase reflects the medieval view that to achieve salvation life must be painful and arduous. Michelangelo's design, conceived 200 years later, embodied the concepts of Renaissance humanism; life's final destination is the same—death and salvation—but why not make the intervening voyage more enjoyable?

As you now know, the Palazzo Senatorio rests on the ancient Tabularium and, if you take the road to the left of the building (which leads to a lovely lookout point over the Roman Forum), you will see the blocks of peperino marble from the Tabularium that have been incorporated into the sides of the newer building (as well as the medieval corner towers added later). ■

Musei Capitolini

THE TWO BUILDINGS ON THE RIGHT AND LEFT OF THE Piazza del Campidoglio are identical, even though the one on the right is older and larger. Together they constitute the Capitoline Museums—the city's sculpture and painting gallery and one of the world's oldest public museums. An underground passageway linking the two buildings runs under the Palazzo Senatorio, and thus through the ancient Tabularium, affording a splendid view of the Forum.

Start in the delightful courtyard of the **Palazzo dei Conservatori,** the building on the right; on view here are marble body parts from the colossal statue of Constantine which originally stood in the huge basilica of Constantine (or Maxentius) in the Forum. The marble fragments embedded on the upper portion of the opposite wall are also interesting. Look for the

word "brit" on one of the larger pieces, a relic of the triumphal arch celebrating the Emperor Claudius' military campaigns in Britain. The large marble reliefs below probably come from Hadrian's temple in the Piazza di Pietra (see p. 134).

The first floor of the Palazzo dei Conservatori contains magnificent statuary, including several celebrated pieces such as the "Boy with a

Musei Capitolini

🅐 Map p. 37

✉ Piazza del Campidoglio 1

☎ 06 8205 9127

🕐 Closed Mon.

💲 $$.

Audio guide: $

🚌 Bus: H, C3, 40, 46, 60, 62, 63, 64, 70, 81, 84, 85, 87, 95, 119, 170, 175, 628, 715, 716, 780

Thorn," the Capitoline wolf, and Bernini's statue of Pope Urban VIII. The latter is in the Horatii and Curatii room, which contains frescoes depicting episodes from the days of the earliest Roman kings. This floor also displays the equestrian statue of Marcus Aurelius and a few other giant bronzes next to the extant remains of Jupiter's temple. The **Pinacoteca** (painting gallery) on the second floor includes works by Velázquez, Dosso Dossi, Titian, Antonio Van Dyck, Reni, Annibale Caracci, and Caravaggio. There is also a porcelain collection. On the staircase landings you will find rectangular reliefs showing Marcus Aurelius making sacrifices to the gods. And you should keep in mind that these may be part of the same series that Constantine "borrowed" to decorate the upper portion of the Arch of Constantine.

The **Palazzo Nuovo** (on the left) was built in 1655, primarily to give balance to the piazza and to hide the towering flank of the Aracoeli. It was opened to the public in 1734. The collection includes much of the city's best-known statuary. "Marforio," one of Rome's famous talking statues (see p. 145), reclines in the courtyard. The original bronze statue of Marcus Aurelius is on display here behind a protective glass wall. The **Sala dei Filosofi** (Philosophers' Room) and the **Sala degli Imperatori** (Emperors' Room) contain innumerable Roman busts and heads. Upstairs is the poignant "Dying Gaul," the "Capitoline Venus," and the "Marble Faun" of Nathaniel Hawthorne's last novel. ∎

The torso of this giant statue of Constantine was made of wood and bronze and has been lost. The remaining marble pieces are in the courtyard of the Palazzo dei Conservatori.

Foro Romano

THE ROMAN FORUM CAN BE DIVIDED INTO TWO SECTIONS: the most ancient sector, to the west, and the relatively newer section, the middle and upper realms of the Via Sacra, to the east. There are several entrances, notably the oldest portal accessed from Via dei Fori Imperiali; and the portal accessed via Clivus Capitolinus, which winds down from behind the Palazzo Senatorio on the Capitoline Hill, affording a magnificent overview.

If you choose to take the latter, you pass eight towering Ionic columns on your descent, all that remains of the *pronaos* or porch of the **Tempio di Saturno** (Temple of Saturn). Saturnus was originally the god of seed or sowing and the Saturnalia festival was the Romans' favorite holiday. It lasted seven days and can be compared to a mix of Christmas and Mardi Gras. The temple also served as the state treasury. Note the top line of the inscription on the architrave, "*Senatus Popolusque Romanus*" ("the Senate and People of Rome"). The initials SPQR, a once famous acronym, is nowadays seen mainly on manhole covers and buses.

You enter the Forum from just behind the high Rostra, or speakers platform. The rectangular open space on the far side of the Rostra, currently surrounded by a low iron railing, is the Forum proper. Each of its long sides is flanked by the remains of a basilica and, on its far, short side, you will see the Temple of Julius Caesar.

Measuring approximately 394 by 164 feet (120 by 50 m), the Forum proper was originally paved in travertine by Augustus and deliberately left clear and unencumbered to symbolize the openness of democracy. For centuries its only occupants were the three Mediterranean plants par excellence: the fig, the olive, and the grape. Only later, under the emperors, did other constructions make their appearance around and on it. In later centuries, to the chagrin of traditionalists, the Forum's open space began to get really crowded, with commemorative columns and triumphal arches springing up everywhere. The Emperor Domitian went so far as to erect an equestrian statue of himself here (you can still see the pedestal) and so infuriated everyone that after his death it was torn down and he was erased, in "*dannatio memoriae*," from official history. The lone **Colonna di Foca** (Column of Phocas) in the center, put up in 608 to honor the Byzantine emperor of the same name, was the last monument erected in the Forum.

Next to the Rostra stands the triple apertured **Arco di Settimio Severo** (Arch of Septimius Severus), erected in A.D. 203 to commemorate the tenth anniversary of Septimius's reign and dedicated to his (and his sons') victories over the Arabs and the Parthians. It is considered to be a superb example of the genre because of the harmony of its proportions. Note the barbarians on the column pedestals, who appear (as was intended) to support the weight of the entire arch. Walk through the arch and down the short descent. Immediately to your left is a small area protected by metal railings and paved with bluish gray limestone, below which lies the **Lapis Niger** (literally, the

Foro Romano

🅰 Map p. 37

✉ Main entrances: Piazza Santa Maria Nova 53 (at Colosseum end); Largo Romolo e Remo 5 (off Via dei Fori Imperiali); & Via Clivus Capitolinus (at Campidoglio end)

☎ 06 3996 7700 or 06 699 0110

💲 Audio guide: $. Tours in English daily: $

🚌 Bus: C3, 60, 75, 84, 85, 87, 175. Metro: Linea B (Colosseo)

FORO ROMANO RECONSTRUCTION

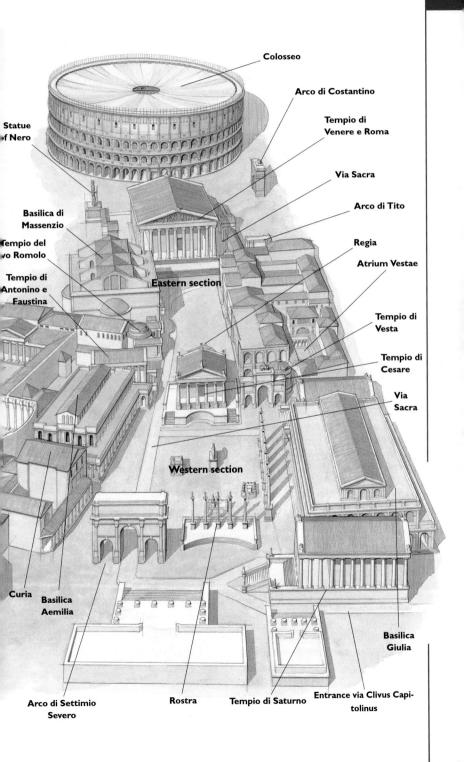

Colosseo

Arco di Costantino

Tempio di
Venere e Roma

Statue
of Nero

Via Sacra

Arco di Tito

Basilica di
Massenzio

Regia

Tempio del
vo Romolo

Atrium Vestae

Eastern section

Tempio di
Antonino e
Faustina

Tempio di
Vesta

Tempio di
Cesare

Via
Sacra

Western section

Curia   Basilica
Aemilia

Basilica
Giulia

Arco di Settimio
Severo

Rostra   Tempio di Saturno

Entrance via Clivus Capi-
tolinus

Julius Caesar's funeral was held in the Roman Forum, and a temple (the low building in the central foreground) was built over the spot where his body was cremated.

black stone). It marks the location of an important archaic grave, possibly that of Romulus himself.

The brick building just beyond is the **Curia,** or Senate, re-oriented on this site by Julius Caesar to make room for his Forum. It was later reconstructed by Diocletian after a fire in A.D. 283. If you are surprised by its fine state of preservation, thank the Christians for converting it into a church in the seventh century. Amazingly enough, the original doors have survived, although they are now at San Giovanni in Laterano. The Curia's marble pavement is a stunning example of what is called *opus sectile*, a repetitive geometric pattern of different colors. The wide steps on the right and left sides of the Senate chamber are the platforms where the senators sat in their portable curile chairs (Julius Caesar's

was reportedly made of gold), moving to the "aye" or "nay" side as necessity dictated. The two marble reliefs or *plutei* (note the Roman buildings in the background) probably decorated the front of the Rostra outside. If you're wondering about the holes on the latter's base, remember it was the custom to insert here the iron "beaks," or "rostra," of captured warships.

Now continue along the Via Sacra. The **Basilica Aemilia,** to your left, was built originally in 179 B.C. and, like all basilicas (which were primarily tribunals or meeting halls rather than churches), had one wide central nave and two narrower side aisles. On the other side of the Forum was the **Basilica Giulia,** another tribunal or courthouse. On its steps you can still see some carved-in-stone game boards that

may have provided diversion to those waiting patiently for the wheels of justice to turn. One game resembles Chinese checkers, another is a circle divided into wedge-shaped sections.

On the Basilica Giulia's east side, the three lovely Corinthian columns you see were part of the temple to the twin semigods **Castore** and **Polluce** (Castor and Pollux), and the focal point of another ancient Roman cult. Legend has it that in the early fifth century B.C. the brothers helped the Romans defeat the Latins in the battle of Lake Regillus and were then seen later the same day at the nearby Fountain of Juturna, touting their victory and watering their mighty, white steeds.

The **Tempio di Cesare** (Temple of Julius Caesar) was built (but not immediately) on the spot where Julius Caesar was cremated after being assassinated in 44 B.C. His body had lain in state on the Rostra in a gilded shrine. Mark Antony's funeral oration so moved the crowd that it was decided to forgo the traditional funeral on the Campus Martius and to cremate him in front of the **Regia.** Today the latter is little more than a pile of rubble, but in Caesar's day it was the headquarters of the chief priest or Pontifex Maximus (a title, by the way, that the Roman Catholic Church still uses for the pope). Although controversial, Caesar's deification soon followed, initiating a practice that would be followed by many of the later emperors, some of whom actually became divine even before death! The remains of his temple, built in 29 B.C., are rather insignificant, but standing in front of it you'll get a nice view of the western Forum with the imposing Tabularium in the background.

EASTERN SECTION

To visit the second part of the Forum, the eastern section, you must walk past the Tempio di Cesare toward the Arch of Titus, and then follow the middle and upper portions of the Via Sacra under cypress trees and through laurel groves. Walk to the left of the temple and stop in front of the steps (on your left) of the **Tempio di Antonio e Faustina,** erected by the Emperor Antoninus in A.D. 141 when his beloved wife, Faustina, died. At his own death 20 years later, the temple was dedicated to him as well. Above the columns, you can see where a second architrave bearing the inscription *"Divo Antonino"* ("Divine Antoninus") was inserted above the original, which had only mentioned Faustina. This temple, too, was later turned into a church.

On your right, on the other side of the jumble of ruins—all that remains of the Regia—you'll find the intriguing Vestal Virgin complex, composed of a circular **Tempio di Vesta,** to the goddess of the sacred fire, and the **Atrium Vestae.** This was where the Vestal Virgins—six priestesses, guardians of the sacred fire—lived in splendid isolation. This cult was of major importance in ancient Rome, surviving until the end of the fourth century, even after Christianity had practically become the state religion. The Vestal Virgins, chosen when they were between six and ten years of age and required to serve for 30 years, may well have been the most important women in Roman society with the exception of the females of the imperial family. The size of their second-century residence gives you an idea of how cosseted and pampered they were. The enormous atrium, with three pools, was surrounded by a colonnade and a multistoried building. The priestesses enjoyed all sorts of privileges, but there was a downside: If it was discovered they were no longer virgins, they were walled up alive.

Back on the Via Sacra, the small **Tempio del Divo Romolo** a little farther up is also round and may have served as a vestibule to Vespasian's Temple of Peace, today occupied in part by the church of **Santi Cosma e Damiano** *(tel 06 699 1540, closed 1–3 p.m.).* The temple's original bronze doors, which still open and shut perfectly, date back to Roman times. The church, the entrance to which is outside the Forum in Via dei Fori Imperiali 1, has a magnificent sixth-century mosaic in its apse; it is one of the few mosaic works in

The Arch of Titus, built in A.D. 81 by Emperor Domitian to commemorate his brother and his father, Vespasian, spans the Via Sacra, which leads from the Roman Forum to the Colosseum.

the late classical Roman style to have survived. It depicts Jesus descending a staircase of multicolored clouds, flanked by saints, while below, between the two holy cities Bethlehem and Jerusalem, 12 sheep represent the Apostles. Its stylized layout was used as a model for later mosaics in many Roman churches.

Next is the **Basilica di Massenzio** (or di Costantino). The building was begun by Maxentius (A.D. 306–312), but before it was finished he was killed by his brother-in-law, Constantine in a battle for the throne at the Milvian Bridge. The giant statue of Constantine you

saw (in pieces) in the courtyard of the Palazzo dei Conservatori originally stood here.

As the Via Sacra continues uphill, you come to a wide flight of steps leading to what appears to be a large open space. The steps are all that remain of the western entrance of the double temple complex erected by the Emperor Hadrian in the second century A.D. and rebuilt later, after a fire, by Maxentius. The **Tempio di Roma** faced the Forum and the **Tempio di Venere** faced the Colosseum, and the two were joined at their apses. **Santa Francesca Romana** *(tel 06 679 5528, closed 12–3:30 p.m.),* also called Santa Maria Nova, was built on the site of the Tempio di Roma. Its lovely cloister has been turned into the **Antiquarium Forense** *(open sporadically; call ahead),* which contains a jumble of marble fragments found in various excavations. The rooms inside exhibit funeral urns, glass, and ceramic pieces, as well as several Roman skeletons. This church, too, is accessible from Via dei Fori Imperiali.

Farther up the Via Sacra, you'll find yourself at the **Arco di Tito** (Arch of Titus), completed in A.D. 81 after Titus's early death. This triumphal arch was built to commemorate his victory over the Jews and the destruction of the Jerusalem Temple in A.D. 70. The reliefs inside the archway are particularly interesting. The one on the south side, that closest to the Palatine, depicts the triumphal procession on its return from the campaign in Palestine. Jewish slaves, money, and the trumpets and menorah from the temple are depicted as campaign booty—one reason why, until the foundation of Israel in 1948, no Roman Jew would walk under it. ■

Palatino

IF YOU'RE NOT TOO TIRED, THIS IS THE TIME TO GO UP TO THE Palatino (or Palatine Hill), the site of both Rome's original paleolithic settlements and, later, of many of its ancient imperial palaces. This is one of the loveliest spots in Rome and definitely not to be missed, although you'd be wise to save this visit for a sunny day, preferably in the afternoon. Lush and green, often breezy, and endowed with a couple of drinking fountains and a reasonable number of park benches, this hill, one of Rome's seven, is a place tailor-made for dreaming and contemplation, rather than for scholarly nit-picking.

In fact, none of the structures are intact and most of the ruins are hard for the average visitor to identify, but because of their extent and intricacy (there are massive substructures beneath these buildings, many of which housed workshops, warehouses, and underground passages), they are imposing. So arm yourself with imagination, and keep in mind that this is where it all started!

This area has always been associated with Rome's founder, Romulus, and his twin, Remus. Supposedly, the two brothers were brought up somewhere on this hill by Faustulus, the shepherd, who had found them after they washed up onto the river bank.

Paradoxically, then, this area was the site of both humble, early Iron Age settlements and—as time went by—a residential neighborhood reserved for the elite. During the late Republican period (the second and first centuries B.C.), notables such as Cicero, the politicians Crassus and Catulus, and the orator Hortensius lived here. Once Octavius (later Augustus) chose to forsake his residence near the Forum for the Palatine house he had bought (from Hortensius), it became the "in" place to live, especially if you were a Roman emperor. It remained the site of the imperial residences until Constantine moved to his new capital in the fourth century in what is today

A desirable address in ancient Rome, Palatine Hill was turned into a Cardinal's private park in the Renaissance.

Palatino

◭ Map p. 37

✉ There are two entrances, one from within the Forum (near Titus's Arch), the other outside, at Via di San Gregorio 30 (near Constantine's Arch)

☎ 06 3996 7700

🕐 Closed Mon.

💲 $$ (also valid for Colosseo). Audio guide: $. Tours in English daily: $

🚌 Bus: C3, 60, 75, 81, 85, 87, 175, 673. Tram: 3. Metro: Linea B (Colosseo or Circo Massimo)

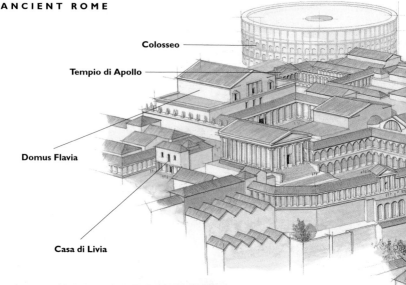

Colosseo

Tempio di Apollo

Domus Flavia

Casa di Livia

In the shadow of the Palatine Hill are the scanty remains of the Circus Maximus, probably the largest racecourse ever.

Turkey. But if Octavius's lifestyle was fairly austere, he found few imitators among his successors (in particular Nero, Domitian, and Septimius Severus), whose unchecked taste for opulence made the Palatine synonymous with luxury. No wonder it is the root of our word "palace."

As we see it today, the Palatine can be divided into three sections. The first includes the ruins from the imperial residences, particularly that of the Flavian emperor Domitian (A.D. 81–96), which is divided into two sections: a private area (Domus Augustana) and the public, or ceremonial part (Domus Flavia). Coming from the Arch of Titus, and once through the turnstyle, walk straight up the path (Via di San Bonaventura) and follow it as it turns left, all the time keeping in mind that much of the Palatine has yet to be excavated.

When you turn left, you will be skirting ruins of the Domus Flavia, including a basilica and an audience hall. This part of Domitian's palace was dedicated to official business and includes the audience hall, or *aula regia*, a basilica for court cases that required the emperor's personal attention, and the enormous *triclinium* for state dining. This must have been impressive. It was decorated in different colored marbles and flanked by courtyards, each containing a fountain. Domitian and his architect, Rabirius, built over earlier buildings constructed by Tiberius and Nero, among others. Despite all the greenery, the ground level has been artificially pumped up (some scholars say by as much as 50 feet/15 m) by layers and layers of used and discarded building materials.

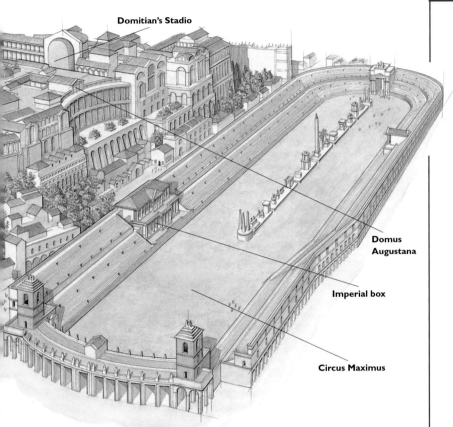

Domitian's Stadio

Domus Augustana

Imperial box

Circus Maximus

Keep on and you will come to **Domitian's Stadio** (or hippodrome), an impressive, large sunken area generally assumed to have been a racecourse or stadium. The ruins directly to the right of the stadium are part of the **Domus Augustana,** a sprawling structure of which lots of bits and pieces—archways, sunken rooms, some of which may have been pools or fountains, and courtyards—are there to explore even if they are not easily identifiable. Gradually work your way toward the terrace from where there is a fantastic view of the **Circus Maximus** below and the Aventine.

Antiquarium del Palatino, located in an ex-convent, is small but displays archaeological finds from the area. Immediately in front

of and to the left of the museum are the remains of the Domus Flavia.

At the southwestern end of the hill are the sites of those Iron Age settlements from the time of Romulus and Remus. There is a temple to Apollo and another to a goddess, Magna Mater. There are also two houses from the late Republican period, the so-called **Casa di Livia** and **Casa di Augusto,** both of which are usually closed to the general public.

The **Orti Farnesiani,** a Renaissance garden once full of rare botanical species, was created in the 16th century. Two pavilions afford a fine view of the Forum below. Steps to the right and the left lead down to another landing with a stupendous, fern-draped nymphaeum. ■

Above: Palatino reconstruction

The emperors: the good ... the bad, & the ugly

The Roman emperors personified the best and the worst of Roman culture. One of the best was Octavius (27 B.C.–A.D. 14), who assumed the title of Augustus in 27 B.C. and is generally considered to be the first true emperor in the Julian-Claudian dynasty started by Julius Caesar. Born in 63 B.C. to a niece of Caesar's and later adopted by his great-uncle, Octavius (Octavian in English) was only 19 in 44 B.C. when his uncle was assassinated. He allied with Mark Antony to punish Caesar's assassins and divided up the empire with him. That alliance ended when Octavian trounced Antony and Cleopatra at the naval Battle of Actium (Greece) in 31 B.C.

Although he always made sure to maintain a facade of republicanism, the rest of Octavian life was dedicated to the process, begun by his uncle, of concentrating power in the hands of one person: himself. But his accomplishments were such that his imperial proclivities can be forgiven. Shrewd, astute, and an able administrator, he reformed the Roman bureaucracy, overhauled the fiscal system, and reorganized the military. Above all, he extended and secured the empire's borders giving rise to what was known as the Pax Romana, a 200-year period of stability and security. It was of course under this same stable and secure regime that the new Christian religion was born. As we know, the solidity of the Augustean Empire proved to be conducive to the new cult's rapid expansion.

Several other "good" emperors have also left important legacies: Vespasian (A.D. 69–79) restored stability after the Neronian chaos, and Trajan (98–117) extended the empire to its furthest limits of expansion. Even more important was his successor, Hadrian (117–138), who is often referred to as the philosopher-emperor because of his devotion to the arts, literature, and architecture. Hadrian enormously embellished the city of Rome: He built a magnificent mausoleum which today we call Castel Sant'Angelo (see pp. 177–78), the sprawling villa in Tivoli that bears his name (see pp. 232–33), and rebuilt

the Pantheon (see pp. 126–29). He put into effect a policy of containment that had a far-reaching impact throughout the empire. Military contingents became fixed rather than mobile. Civilian settlements near military installations thus grew in size, and commerce exploded. Fortification became increasingly important, with defensive architecture reaching new heights in the construction of Hadrian's Wall (in Britain). Hadrian traveled widely during his reign, both for his own pleasure and because of his unusual concept of the Roman Empire: a single, political entity rather than a series of subject states to exploit.

There is no dearth of bad guys in the annals of the empire, and you've probably heard of many of them: Caligula, tall, pale, ungainly, with a wide but sinister forehead and clearly mentally unstable, or Caracalla, who had his younger brother, Geta, killed. But it is Nero who most frequently is seen to personify the worst in Roman imperial rule (among other things he murdered his mother). Nero was born into the imperial family in A.D. 37. Adopted by Claudius after the emperor had married his mother, Agrippina the Younger (Caligula's sister), he became emperor in A.D. 54. During the first ten years of his reign, Nero had a good record. He promoted legal and bureaucratic reform and demonstrated interest for the well-being of his population. All of this changed with the raging, nine-day fire of A.D. 64 during which the Emperor did not actually fiddle, but simply took his own sweet time in leaving his villa in Anzio to come to Rome. Later, he put the blame on the new Christian religious sect, setting off a series of persecutions during which both Peter and Paul were probably martyred. Although after the fire he rebuilt much of the city, Nero gave precedence to his own personal interests, expropriating large tracts of terrain to build the vast and sumptuous Domus Aurea (see pp. 64–65). The populace seethed and rebellion threatened. In A.D. 68, Nero committed suicide thus bringing the Julian-Claudian dynasty to a premature and inglorious end. ∎

This French painting shows the "good" emperor, Augustus, and the Sibyl interpreting his vision of the Virgin and Child.

Above: Like most emperors, Nero minted his own coins. This one is gold and carries his name.

Right: A bust of Julius Caesar on display in the Vatican Museum. Founder of the first imperial dynasty, he never accepted the title of Emperor. After his assassination, the term Caesar was given to all emperors.

Fori Imperiali

IT IS NOT EASY TO COMPREHEND THE LAYOUT OF THE FIVE
Fori Imperiali, or Imperial Forums, because the modern Via dei Fori
Imperiali (built for military parades by the Fascist regime in the early
1930s) cuts directly through them, covering over much of the area.
Ceremonial areas built between the first century B.C. and the start of
the second century A.D., the Imperial Forums were attempts by
Rome's highest leaders both to glorify themselves and to create additional space for the political, religious, and institutional needs of the
expanding Roman Empire. Today they are still only partially excavated although work is now under way. The long-term plan is to
significantly narrow the avenue, but presently the wide Via dei Fori
Imperiali makes the forums of Augustus, Nerva, Vespasian, and
Trajan appear to be totally separate from the Roman Forum
(of which, instead, they formed an integral part).

EARLIER IMPERIAL FORUMS

Julius Caesar was the first to construct his own forum (Foro di
Cesare) which, begun in 54 B.C.,
stands between the Curia or Senate
building and Via dei Fori Imperiali.
He even rebuilt the Senate to bring
it into proper alignment. Measuring
147 by 406 feet (45 by 124 m), the
forum was surrounded by a double
portico of which a small portion is
still visible, as is the base of the
Tempio di Venere Genitrix, the goddess from whom the Julian-
Claudian dynasty traced its descent.

Augustus, Caesar's political heir,
followed suit. The **Foro di
Augusto,** near that of his adopted
father, ends at the high fire wall he
erected to protect the civic center
from the frequent fires in the
densely populated residential
Suburra area on the other side. The
forum took 20 years to complete
and was mostly taken up by the
Tempio di Marte Ultore, which the
young emperor built after killing
Caesar's assassins at the battle of
Philippi in 42 B.C. Three of its 24
tall Corinthian marble columns are
more or less all that remain, but try
to imagine it as it was: The porticoes were dotted with statuary;

floors and walls were done in colored marbles—pure white,
Phrygian purple, Numidian yellow,
Lucullan red or black; there was
even a separate room for a colossus
in precious metal, possibly Caesar
or Augustus himself, and presum-
ably some 33 feet (10 m) tall.

Most of the **Foro di
Vespasiano** (built between A.D. 71
and 75 to mark the defeat of the
Jews) is hidden underneath the Via
dei Fori Imperiali–Via Cavour
intersection. What remains of the
Temple of Peace, as it was called, is
incorporated into the monastery
and church of **Santi Cosma e
Damiano.** In between Augustus's
and Vespasian's forums is Nerva's
Forum **(Foro di Nerva),** which
actually was built by Domitian,
Nerva's predecessor. Long and
narrow, flanked by colonnades, it
was often called the Forum
Transitorium. It transformed the
Argiletum, the route from the
Suburra to the Roman Forum, into
a decorated passageway. All that
remains are two massive Corinthian
columns (the Italians call them the
colonnacce, the ugly columns) in
the corner near Via dei Fori
Imperiali and the podium of a

Fori Imperiali

🅰 Map p. 37

✉ Information Centre
Via dei Fori
Imperiali

☎ 06 679 7786

🕓 At present only
accessible with
guided tour. Tours in
English Wed., Sat., &
Sun. at 3 p.m. (min.
8 people)

💲 $$

🚌 Bus: C3, 60, 75, 84,
85, 87, 175, 673.
Tram: 3.
Metro: Linea B
(Colosseo)

**Opposite: A fluted
column in Trajan's
Forum, where
excavations are
in progress**

Mercati Traianei

🗺 Map p. 37

✉ Via IV Novembre 94. The upper market is closed for restoration until 2007. Entrance to the lower market is on Piazza Madonna di Loreto.

☎ 06 679 0048

🕐 Closed Mon.

$ $$

🚌 Bus: H, 40, 60, 64, 70, 170

temple dedicated to Minerva. The entablature between the columns has a lovely frieze depicting scenes from domestic activity like spinning and weaving, while a statue until recently identified as Minerva keeps watch. Recently a second, sister statue was found, leading archaeologists to wonder if they might instead have represented two imperial provinces.

FORO TRAIANO

The major attraction of the Imperial Forums is the magnificent complex —forum and markets—built by the Emperor Trajan and dedicated in A.D. 112. This was the last of the forums to be built and undoubtedly the grandest and the most splendid; at the time it was considered to be one of the architectural wonders of

Detail of the relief sculptures on the towering column in Trajan's Forum. The story unfolds in a 219-feet (67 m) sequence.

the world. To enter the forum you passed through a large, rectangular courtyard flanked by two long porticoes, 367 feet (112 m) in length, and closed off at the northern end by the gigantic two-story **Basilica Ulpia.** The latter, richly decorated in sumptuous colors, marble work, and precious metals, had five aisles separated by columns, with a semicircular apse at each end. Beyond

the basilica was a second, smaller courtyard. Here rises **Colonna Traiana** (Trajan's Column), which tells the story of his military campaigns against the Dacians in magnificent relief work involving 2,600 carved figures that spirals up for about 100 feet (30 m). Made of 29 cylindrical blocks, it has a staircase inside lit by 40 small windows. A giant statue of the emperor was replaced in the 16th century with one of St. Peter. After Trajan's unexpected death in A.D. 117, his remains were put in a golden urn that was placed inside the column's hollow base. Flanking the courtyard were two libraries, one Greek and one Latin.

But wait, there's more. To make space for this forum, Trajan and his court architect, Apollodorus of Damascus, effected what was for the time a technological miracle. They hollowed out much of the high ridge (which was about the same height as the column), linking the Capitoline and the Quirinal Hills. Then there are the **Mercati Traianei** (Trajan's Markets). This three- or four-story semicircular structure was also built by Apollodorus, and was essentially a reconstruction of the neighborhood removed by the forum's construction. An ancient Roman street (Via Biberatica) runs through it, and wandering from shop to shop (there are about 150) gives an idea of what life was like in the second century A.D. The alcove-like shops on the ground floor probably sold dry goods (flour and sugar), flowers, and vegetables. Those off the gallery were probably storehouses for wine and oil. There were also special shops for Eastern spices, and there were fishponds. The world's first mall, with its impressive vaulting, is currently under restoration and will host the new Museo dei Fori Imperiali, scheduled to open in spring 2007. ■

The massive Colosseum has always been Rome's best-known landmark. But only a short distance away you will find other marvels. Imperial monuments alternate with early Christian churches and their glorious frescoes and mosaics.

Colosseo to San Clemente

Detail from the 12th-century apse mosaic in San Clemente

Colosseo to San Clemente

SET IN A VALLEY BETWEEN THREE OF THE SEVEN HILLS (THE PALATINE, THE Esquiline, and the Caelian), the Colosseo (Colosseum) is undoubtedly the Roman landmark that has been most closely identified with the city for the longest time. As the Venerable Bede put it in the eighth century: "*Quandiu stat Colisaeus, stat et Roma; quando cadet Colisaeus, cadet et Roma. Quando cadet Roma, cadet et mundus.*" ("As long as the Colosseum stands, Rome stands; when the Colosseum falls, Rome will fall. When Rome falls, so falls the world.") Beyond a doubt the single best-known site of the Eternal City, it has inspired travelers, historians, and men of letters. "You must look to the East, among the ruins of Palmyra, Balbek, and Petra, to find buildings comparable in grandiosity to the Colosseum," wrote Stendhal in his *Roman Promenades* in the early 1800s. For the French writer, who was of the opinion that the best time to visit the monument was after midnight, "in the company of the woman you love, ... these walls, blackened by time, have the same effect on one's soul as the music of Cimarosa, who knew how to render sublime even the words of a vulgar libretto."

Two thousand years after it was built by the Emperor Vespasian, on the site of the artificial lake that Nero had built for his magnificent pleasure house, the Domus Aurea, the Colosseum is still standing. It looms over one of the most extensive archaeological areas in the world, to remind us of both man's achievements and his cruelty. It cannot be forgotten, after all, that while this was a place of celebration it was also a site of unchecked (human and animal) slaughter.

Not far away is the Arch of Constantine, built in A.D. 315 to celebrate the emperor's victory at Ponte Milvio over his brother-in-law and predecessor, Maxentius. But for all its size (it is the largest of the triumphal arches to have survived) and apparent splendor, the arch, decorated mostly with derivative art, is generally considered to be an indication of Rome's incipient decline.

On the other side of the Colosseum are the remains of the first-century Domus Aurea (Golden House) which, with the exception of Diocletian's Palace in Split (Croatia), is the only floor-to-ceiling Roman imperial structure to have survived. Nero's extensive pleasure palace, which reflects the vast wealth and architectural prowess of imperial Rome, was built in the aftermath of the terrible fire of A.D. 64 which totally destroyed 3 of Rome's 14 neighborhoods. Its exact dimensions are as yet unknown. The Domus was recently closed and is not expected to reopen before 2008.

The surrounding area has many important early churches. San Pietro in Vincoli, the location of Michelangelo's imposing "Moses," was originally named the Basilica Eudoxiana after the empress who built it to hold St. Peter's Chains. The multilevel San Clemente, which lies between the Colosseum and San Giovanni in Laterano, was built in the fourth century to commemorate Clement, martyred in the Crimea sometime during the reign of Trajan (A.D. 98–117). In the 11th century invading Norman armies destroyed the original church, but important treasures from the new church survive, such as the wonderful 12th-century apse mosaic. San Clemente is also a prime example of Rome's architectural stratification, concealing the remains of a fourth-century church as well as older, first-century structures.

The quiet Caelian Hill, facing the Palatine on the opposite side of Via di San Gregorio, offers other jewels of both early Christian culture and Renaissance design. St. Gregory (San Gregorio Magno) built his church and monastery here in the sixth century, although both the church and the three frescoed chapels near it were rebuilt in the 17th century. The Basilica of Santi Giovanni e Paolo has medieval buttresses and a Romanesque campanile, but the church, built over the remains of various late imperial structures, dates back to the fourth (or possibly fifth) century. Villa Celimontana, whose grounds today are a lovely park, testifies to the quality of Renaissance

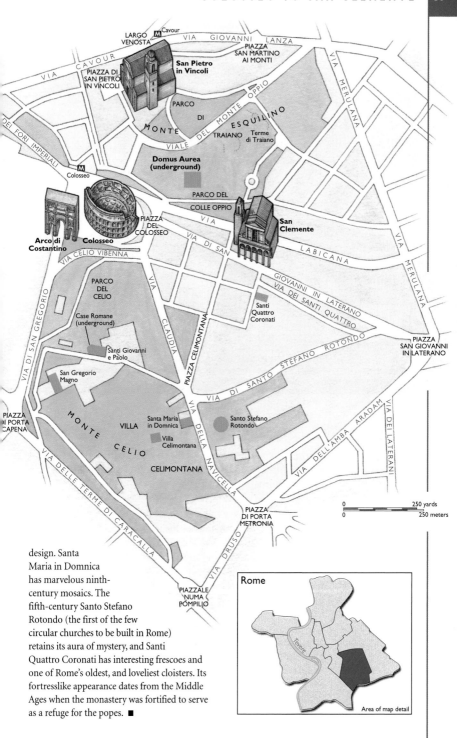

design. Santa
Maria in Domnica
has marvelous ninth-
century mosaics. The
fifth-century Santo Stefano
Rotondo (the first of the few
circular churches to be built in Rome)
retains its aura of mystery, and Santi
Quattro Coronati has interesting frescoes and
one of Rome's oldest, and loveliest cloisters. Its
fortresslike appearance dates from the Middle
Ages when the monastery was fortified to serve
as a refuge for the popes. ■

Colosseo

Colosseo

🅼 Map p. 57

✉ Piazza del Colosseo

☎ 06 3996 7700 or
06 700 5469

💲 $$ (also valid for
Palatino). Audio
guide: $. Tours in
Eng. daily: $

🚌 Bus: C3, 60, 75, 81,
85, 87, 175, 628.
Tram: 3.
Metro: Linea B
(Colosseo)

THE COLOSSEO, OR COLOSSEUM, WAS BUILT BY THE THREE
Flavian emperors, and its proper name is the Flavian Amphitheater. Its
construction was part of the new imperial family's campaign to
promote a good public image. Vespasian (A.D. 69–79), the founder of
the dynasty, was not of noble birth; he became emperor a year after
Nero's suicide, stepping in after the reigns of three short-lived and
unsuccessful emperors. Nero was not missed; his vast land expropria-
tions and other excesses had angered most of the populace. So almost
no one minded when Vespasian decided to drain the artificial lake that
had formed part of Nero's extravagant Domus Aurea complex (see
pp. 64–65) and transform the site into a place for public entertainment.

Probably built with the spoils of the
Temple of Jerusalem at the end of
the so-called Jewish campaign,
waged and won by his son Titus in
A.D. 70, the amphitheater was
inaugurated in A.D. 80—by which
time Titus had ascended to the
throne. Made from travertine
(130,800 cu yards/100,000 cu m,
were hewn from quarries near
Tivoli and hauled to Rome along a
specially built road), the stone oval
(620 feet/189 m long; 512 feet/
156 m wide; and 157 feet/48 m

Most of the holes in the Colosseum, the largest Roman amphitheater anywhere, held the iron grapples that were plundered and reused during the Middle Ages.

high) was the largest amphitheater in the Roman world. Some 300 tons of iron are believed to have been used for the grapples that held the stones together.

It is generally assumed that the name, Colosseum, came into being because of the structure's super size. But many historians believe that the term is derived from the giant, or colossal, bronze statue that stood nearby. Its base, today planted with five trees, is still visible between the arena and the Temple of Venus and Rome. The original statue was of Nero, but political correctness of the time dictated a change and the Flavians very pragmatically added sunbeams around the statue's head, changed the inscription, and came up with an image dedicated to the sun god. The statue remained standing until sometime in the early Middle Ages, when it was removed and probably melted down.

Externally, the Colosseum is composed of a series of three **arcades,** topped by a fourth story, or attic. The columns are disposed on three levels according to classical canons (starting from the ground up, Doric, Ionic, and Corinthian). Running below the fourth-story cornice are 240 small ledges with holes in them used to hold the tall wooden poles that supported the *velarium*, the canvas awning that sailors from the imperial fleet would raise to protect spectators from the summer heat, the rain, or the winter cold, turning it into a first-century Astrodome.

Estimates of crowd capacity in the Colosseum range from 50,000 to almost 90,000. There were three tiers of seats: the *ima* (lowest), the *media,* and the *summa*, plus a standing-room-only balcony at the top for the least important members of society: women, slaves, and the poor. Even on the other levels

seating was arranged according to social status and profession: Members of the imperial family and Vestal Virgins had special boxes. The senators, in their red-bordered white togas, sat on the same level, in the "orchestra" section; then came the knights *(equites)* followed by the *plebs* (ordinary citizens). Special sections were set aside for various professions, such as soldiers, scribes, students with tutors, and foreign dignitaries. Spectators poured into the arena through the 80 arched entrances on the ground floor. They poured in and out through the 160 exits, called *vomitoria*, distributed throughout the tiers on the various levels, allowing for quick exit (some say it could be emptied in 10 minutes) by the often unruly and rambunctious crowds.

The arena had a wood floor that was covered with sand to absorb the blood and stench of the spectacles involving human beings fighting for their lives *(munera)*. The floor has been partially reconstructed. The uncovered portion reveals the **corridors and tunnels** underneath, which celebrities used to avoid the crowds and animals and gladiators used to enter the arena. Vertical shafts held the caged animals (which were brought up to the arena level along ramps or in pulley-system elevators). And not just the lions and tigers dear to Hollywood. The thousands of animals killed in the festivities, which on special occasions could last for three to four months, included hyenas, elephants, hippopotamuses, wild horses, elk, giraffes, and zebras. The program was divided into various parts: Animal hunts *(venationes)* in the morning, public executions at noon, and gladiatorial contests in the afternoon.

There was also a tunnel connecting this understage section with

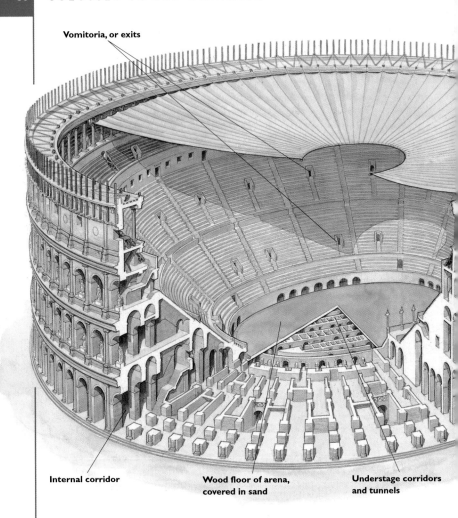

Vomitoria, or exits

Internal corridor

Wood floor of arena, covered in sand

Understage corridors and tunnels

Above: Colosseum reconstruction

the Ludus Magnus, the gladiatorial barracks and training area located between the Colosseum and San Clemente. The gladiators—who were chosen from among condemned criminals, slaves, and prisoners of war—were divided into different categories. There were those who fought heavily armed, with sword and shield; those lightly armed with dagger and arm buckler; and those armed only with nets and tridents as one can see in the Roman floor mosaics in the Galleria Borghese. "*Ave, Imperator,*

muratori te salutant" ("Hail, Emperor, we who are about to die, salute you"), the gladiators scheduled to fight that day would intone during the pre-games parade. Naturally, they all hoped to survive and enjoy the booty they were awarded in the case of victory. But, except for rare cases, survival (or the thumbs up sign from the crowd) generally meant only having to fight again. The lucky few were awarded the laurel crown and allowed to retire. As Christian influence grew in Rome, the Colosseum

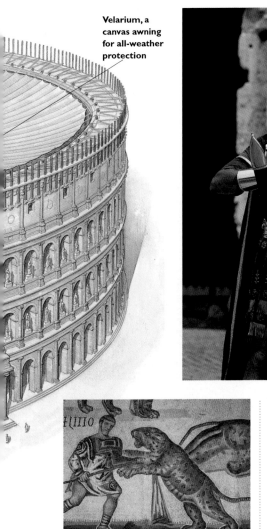

Velarium, a canvas awning for all-weather protection

Above: Ancient mosaic, Galleria Borghese

Top right: The city now regulates latter-day gladiators, once accused of overcharging tourists for photos.

declined in importance. The last recorded gladiatorial games were in the early fifth century, whereas the staged animal hunts lasted another hundred years.

After the decline of Rome, the Colosseum was utilized for a variety of purposes. It was used by the Frangipane family in the Middle Ages, and its southern side collapsed in a major earthquake in 1349. However, time and natural calamity were not the structure's only enemies. Much of the responsibility for its deterioration goes to the Romans themselves. For about 400 years, from the mid-14th to 18th century, it was used as a quarry for marble and travertine building blocks to be used in other city structures, for example the Palazzo Venezia and even the new St. Peter's. This practice ended when Pope Benedict XIV (1740–1758) declared the Colosseum a sacred place because of the Christian martyrs' blood that reportedly had been shed there. In effect, historians are not agreed on this. Since the 19th century, a Way of the Cross ceremony involving the direct participation of the pope has been held here every year on the evening of Good Friday before Easter. ■

Arco di Costantino

CONSTANTINE IS OFTEN REFERRED TO AS THE FIRST
Christian emperor, but you won't find any Christian images on the
arch built in his honor in A.D. 315. His baptism, such that it was, only
took place on his deathbed 22 years later. And, impressive as it seems,
the Arch of Constantine is atypical.

**Constantine built
this arch to mark
his tenth year
in power. He
placed it near
the end of the
Via Triumphalis,
the route taken
by triumphal
processions.**

Arco di Costantino
- Map p. 57
- Between Via di San
  Gregorio & Piazza
  del Colosseo
- Bus: C3, 60, 75, 81,
  85, 87, 175, 628.
  Tram: 3.
  Metro: Linea B
  (Colosseo)

Most of the Arch's decorative work
was, in fact, taken from structures
built by previous emperors,
suggesting that Roman art had
entered a phase of decline. Thus,
the eight **rectangular reliefs** on
both sides of the upper portion
(the attic) originally adorned a
structure dedicated to Marcus
Aurelius (A.D. 161–180) and the
portrait of the emperor was recut
with Constantine's likeness. (The
narrative content of three other
reliefs from the same series, now in
the Capitoline Museums, clearly
shows the Emperor Marcus
Aurelius.) Also plundered from
other monuments were the **round
medallions** over the lateral arches
(four on each side). These hunting
and sacrificial scenes date from the
first half of the second century, a
period coinciding not with the

reign of Constantine but with that
of Hadrian. Eight **statues of barbarians** (the ones wearing
trousers, of course!) on top of the
columns were also derivative.
Naturally, some of the work was
original but, even to the untrained
eye, it appears clearly inferior workmanship. The four **panel friezes**
underneath the above-mentioned
medallions, on both sides, were
sculpted specifically for the arch.
Note the one on the south side
(toward the Circus Maximus), over
the leftmost arch, showing
Constantine and his army besieging
the city of Verona: The figure of the
centurion who is scaling the walls is
dwarfish, and there is a general lack
of perspective. Compare the body
proportions in this relief with the
ones directly above, sculpted about
180 years before. ■

San Pietro in Vincoli

A gash on Moses' knee is said to have been caused when Michelangelo threw a tool at it.

TRY TO SCHEDULE YOUR VISIT TO SAN PIETRO IN VINCOLI (also known as the Basilica Eudoxiana) early in the day, in the hopes that you can beat the crush of tourists coming here to see Michelangelo's "Moses." Situated at the end of the right transept, this is the pièce de résistance of the unfinished tomb of Pope Julius II (1503–1513), the pontiff who built the Sistine Chapel.

Michelangelo's original design for a mammoth, freestanding structure with some 40 statues destined for St. Peter's was never to be. Nevertheless, the **statue of Moses,** shown returning from Mount Sinai with God's Commandments under his arm, is incredibly powerful. Clearly annoyed with his idolatrous brethren for flirting with the Golden Calf, he is scowling (the profile under his lower lip is said to be a Michelangelo self-portrait). The striking statues of Jacob's two wives, Leah and Rachel (symbols of active and contemplative life), were probably finished by one of Michelangelo's pupils, Raffaele da Montelupo.

For Christians, there is a precious relic to see: The chains from St. Peter's two imprisonments (in Jerusalem and Rome) which, when placed side by side, are said to have miraculously fused. The church was built by the Empress Eudoxia to host the chains, displayed under the altar. Also, if you ignore the baroque ceiling, you'll get a good idea of the stark and simple basilica structure that so appealed to the ancient Romans and which was later adopted by many Christian churches. Despite repeated remakes, seen from inside the church the brickwork over the windows of the Renaissance facade still reveals the outline of the five arches of the original fifth-century entrances.

To the left of the main entrance is a lovely 15th-century fresco depicting a 1476 procession against the plague. ■

San Pietro in Vincoli

🅰 Map p. 57
✉ Piazza di San Pietro in Vincoli
☎ 06 488 2865
🕐 Closed 12:30–3:30 p.m.
🚌 Bus: 75, 84. Metro: Linea B (Cavour)

Domus Aurea

INACCESSIBLE SINCE 1983, THIS JEWEL OF WHAT MANY
would call imperial folly has now been reopened to the public,
although excavation and restoration is still going on. On the lower
slopes of the Colle Oppio, the Domus Aurea (Golden House) was
so-called because of the extensive use of gold leaf in the decorations.

**The Octagonal
Room (Room
128) complex is
the focal point of
the Domus's east-
ern pavilion. Light
entered through
an oculus in the
ceiling. The apse
in the rear wall
had a waterfall,
and all the rooms
were paneled in
marble.**

Nero built this structure as a vast
pleasure palace, and it was a complex of reception and banquet halls,
courtyards, porticoes, gardens, and
pools that extended beyond the
artificial lake he created in the valley below to connect up with the
older imperial residences on the
Palatine. Part of this vast estate was
demolished when Vespasian, the
first of the Flavians, came to the
throne in A.D. 69 and built the
Colosseum on the lake-site.

Half a century later, Trajan
completed the job, systematically
removing all precious materials
(including the marble on the
walls), and the statuary, which may

have included famous pieces such
as the "Dying Gaul" (see p. 41) and
the "Laocoön" (see pp. 170, 176).
Trajan built massive supporting
walls and filled the spaces with
rubble to make a foundation for his
imperial baths. Paradoxically, his
attempts to wipe out all traces of
Nero backfired because he unwit-
tingly created the conditions for the
Domus Aurea's preservation
through the centuries.

The existence of the Domus
Aurea, written about by Roman
writers such as Tacitus, Pliny, and
Suetonius, has long been known.
But it was only during the
Renaissance that the collapse of

part of the baths structure above led to its rediscovery. Famous artists including Michelangelo, Raphael, and Pinturicchio visited what seemed caves, or grottoes (sometimes leaving their signatures) to examine the unusual decorations on what we now know were the upper portion of high-ceilinged rooms. This type of decoration is similar to that used on the walls and ceilings of many buildings in Pompeii. The Renaissance artists copied the fantastic motifs—small winged creatures, dragons, floral and leaf patterns—that were probably the work of the famous Roman artist Fabullus, and created a "new" art form. These "grotesques" (from "grotto") were used to decorate many new structures including the Vatican Loggias and the Villa Farnesina. Several 18th-century artists visited the ruins, then erroneously identified as the Baths of Titus, making engravings that today are essential for the understanding of first-century imperial art.

It was only later that archaeologists identified the underground structure as part of Nero's famous domain. So far Italian archaeologists have excavated close to 150 rooms, although only about 30 underground rooms are currently open to the public. In summer, bring a sweater because once inside the temperature plummets.

Naturally, the Domus Aurea today is only a shadow of its former self when it was a riot of colored marbles, stuccos, and gold leaf. Another major change is that Trajan closed in all the terraces that in Roman times exploited the palace's vast southern exposure. But it is still overwhelming, as you will see in the 45-minute tour (choose between guided visits with an Italian archaeologist or "accompanied" visits for which audiocassettes

in English can be rented).

Access to the palace is through one of Trajan's massive galleries, and the tour itself starts in **Room 35** and heads eastward. The highlights include **Rooms 44** and **45,** where you will see a *nymphaeum,* an area decorated to resemble a grotto

with the remains of a fountain and a mosaic decoration depicting Polyphemus (the Cyclops) and Ulysses. There are colorful wall decorations in **Room 70** and **Room 79,** where some of the Renaissance signatures are located. In Nero's day, visitors to **Room 80,** the Room of the Gilded Vault, could look out onto a five-sided courtyard and the valley beyond with its artificial lake, later drained for construction of the Colosseum. You should remember that although these rooms are now underground, in Nero's time they were filled with sunlight and most looked out on magnificent views. **Rooms 123** and **125** contain the first examples of groined vaults in Roman architecture. **Room 128** may have been the famous dining room with the rotating dining platform of which Suetonius wrote. ■

IMPORTANT:
Due to flooding
from heavy rains
in late 2005 and
early 2006, the
Domus Aurea
is closed and is
not expected to
reopen until
at least the
beginning of
2008.

Domus Aurea
⬛ Map p. 57
✉ Via della Domus
Aurea (inside park)
☎ 06 3996 7700
🕐 Closed for
restoration. Expected
to open early 2008.
🚌 Bus: C3, 60, 75, 85,
87, 175. Tram: 3.
Metro: Linea B
(Colosseo)

Above: The
Terpsichore
Room (Room 42)
is dedicated to
the muse of
poetry.

Monks, mosaics, & martyrs walk

Only a short distance from the hue and cry of the Colosseum, the Caelian (Celio) Hill has always been one of the quieter and less populated areas of Rome. Right from the earliest centuries of Christian Rome it was therefore a perfect setting for monastic life and spiritual contemplation.

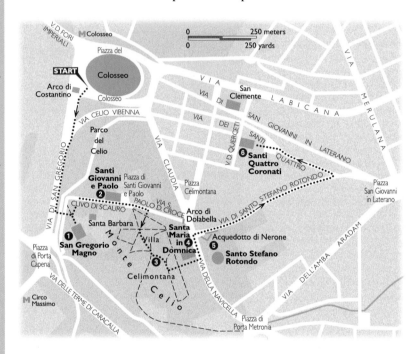

From the Colosseum, follow Via di San Gregorio on the left-hand sidewalk, noting the brick arch across the street, part of an aqueduct built by Nero to supply water to the imperial residences on the Palatine. Just past the arch, steps (on your left) lead up to the imposing facade of **San Gregorio Magno ①**. (Be careful crossing the tram tracks!) The church *(tel 06 700 8227, closed 1–3 p.m.)* was built by Pope Gregory the Great (590–604)—later St. Gregory—on the grounds of his family home. Its baroque facade was added in the 17th century.

The atrium, on the other hand, is typical of the city's early churches, especially those built in sparsely inhabited areas like the Caelian Hill. Note the fresco in the rightmost lunette which shows Gregory in 590, on his way to St. Peter's at the head of a procession (to pray for deliverance from the plague) when he sees the archangel Michael above Hadrian's Mausoleum. The angel is sheathing his sword, a clear sign that the Black Death is over, and the reason why a statue of the archangel stands atop Castel Sant'Angelo. To see the interior, ring the bell on the wall of the atrium's right portico. By the way, it was from here that Pope Gregory, himself a monk, dispatched St. Augustine of Canterbury and 40 Benedictine monks to the British Isles to convert the heathen Angles and Saxons to Christianity and to bring that distant isle back into contact with the classical world. All ties with Rome had been cut in the early fifth century when the last Roman garrisons were withdrawn.

To the left of the church there are three small chapels *(tel 06 7049 4966, open 9:30 a.m.–12:30 p.m. Tues., Thurs., & Sat.–Sun.).* The **chapel of Santa Barbara,** farthest to

Like many Roman parks, Villa Celimontana was the home and gardens of a nobleman.

the left, is frescoed with scenes from the life of St. Gregory, including one showing the pope sending Augustine off on his mission. In it is the stone table at which Gregory usually served meals to 12 paupers. Once, a 13th diner turned out to be an angel. The other two chapels, dedicated to St. Andrew and St. Sylvia (Gregory's mother), contain frescoes by Domenichino and Guido Reni. The adjacent shop *(temporarily closed)* sells honey and other natural products made by the monks.

From San Gregorio, walk up the steep Clivo di Scauro on the left, from where you will have a fine view of the apse of the church of **Santi Giovanni e Paolo ❷.** Walk under its medieval flying buttresses, unusual for this city, to find the Piazza dei Santi Giovanni e Paolo. Underground ruins, accessed from beneath the buttresses, can be visited, and a fine small museum has been opened in the **Case Romane del Celio** (see p. 72). The church was dedicated to John and Paul, two Roman soldiers who suffered martyrdom after refusing to worship pagan idols. Directly ahead, you will see the back entrance to the **Villa Celimontana ❸** (see p. 118), once the gardens to the Renaissance Villa Mattei. After a pleasant stroll past the fountains and ferns, leave the park from its main entrance. You'll find yourself on **Via della Navicella,** named for a Roman votive

boat now placed atop a fountain in the middle of the street to your left on exiting. The fountain stands in front of **Santa Maria in Domnica ❹,** with its superb ninth-century apse mosaic of the "Virgin Enthroned with the Christ Child." Across the street (beyond more remnants from Nero's aqueduct) begins Via di Santo Stefano Rotondo. At No. 7 is the round church of **Santo Stefano Rotondo ❺** (see p. 72). Continue along Via di Santo Stefano Rotondo to a Romanesque portico made with recycled Roman columns. Turn left onto Via dei Santi Quattro, which leads to the medieval fortress that encloses **Santi Quattro Coronati ❻** (Four Crowned Saints church and its monastery, see p. 72). ∎

- Also see area map, p. 57
- ► Colosseo
- 1.5 miles (2.5 km)
- 2.5 hours
- ► Santi Quattro Coronati

NOT TO BE MISSED
- Chapel of Santa Barbara
- Santa Maria in Domnica
- Case Romane del Celio
- Santi Quattro Coronati

San Clemente

THIS MULTILEVEL CHURCH, FOUNDED IN THE FOURTH century to commemorate the martyr Clement, Christianity's fourth pope, is one of the most fascinating in the city. Clement, who had been banished to the Crimea sometime during the reign of Trajan (A.D. 98–117), continued to make converts there until he was weighted down with an anchor (his saint's symbol) and thrown into the sea. Destroyed by the Norman invading armies in 1084, the church was rebuilt (over the rubble of the preexisting church) by Pope Paschal II in the early 12th century.

It has a baroque veneer (primarily the out-of-place gilded ceiling and the pilasters that encase several of the original columns). But these fortunately do not overwhelm the older treasures such as the reconstructed sixth-century *schola cantorum*, the marble barrier defining the monks' choir stall, the colorful pre-cosmatesque (see p. 206) pavement, the porticoed atrium (conceptually part of the main entrance from Piazza San Clemente), and the wonderful 12th-century **apse mosaic.** This has a triumphal cross in the center (with twelve doves symbolizing the Twelve Apostles) between Mary and St. John. From the base of the cross a luxuriant Tree of Life sends out spirals of foliage, each of which encloses images of the learned Doctors of the Church, exotic birds, flowers, and other Christian symbols. The waters of life flow at the base of the mosaic, and if you've brought your binoculars be sure to note the tiny figures performing daily farmyard activities, a return to the classical style that by the fifth century had largely disappeared. Farther below is the Lamb of God, Agnus Dei, in the standard format: the lamb in the center with six sheep on each side. The external arch around the apse is just as interestingly decorated. Jesus is center top, flanked by symbols of the Four Evangelists. Just below, Paul and St. Lawrence are

San Clemente

- Map p. 57
- Via di San Giovanni in Laterano (opposite the pharmacy at No. 108)
- 06 7045 1018
- Underground: $. Audio guide: $.
- Closed 12:30–3 p.m.
- Bus: C3, 60, 75, 81, 85, 87, 673. Tram: 3. Metro: Linea B (Colosseo)

Saints & their symbols

In Roman Catholic iconography, many saints—especially those who were martyred—have a symbol that represents them, often the instrument of their death. Thus St. Bartholomew is represented by a knife because he was skinned alive, St. Cecilia's symbol is a musical instrument because she sang while her persecutors tried to steam her to death, whereas St. Jerome—who was not martyred, but exiled himself in the desert to resist temptation and translate the holy scriptures—is shown as a scantily clad old man with a lion. The church of San Clemente is notable in that you can find the symbols of three saints here. First, of course, is Clement himself, whose symbol, the anchor, is on the canopy over the main altar in both the upper and lower church. The frescoes in the Chapel of St. Catherine show the torture wheel on which she was martyred. And on the arch outside the apse, St. Lawrence is shown with his foot over a flame and grill, his symbol because he was slowly roasted to death. ∎

shown on the left while Peter and Clement are shown in the corresponding spot on the right.

Another must in the main church is the **Chapel of St. Catherine of Alexandria,** immediately to the right of the Via di San Giovanni in Laterano entrance. This chapel contains a series of very celebrated frescoes dating from about 1430 painted by Masolino da Panicale, who was probably helped by his assistant, Masaccio. The far wall is completely covered by a Crucifixion scene, while the ceiling vaults show the Four Evangelists and their symbols as well as the Doctors of the Church. The most interesting frescoes, however, are on the side walls. Those on the right depict scenes from the life of St. Ambrose. Those on the left are scenes from the life of St. Catherine, including, in the middle scene in the lower order, the unsuccessful attempt to murder her on a spiked wheel. Note the 15th-century St. Christopher painted on the outside left wall of the chapel (protected by a glass panel) with some ancient graffiti etched into its lower right-hand section.

But there is more. San Clemente is a microcosmic example of the architectural stratification that is a prime characteristic of Rome. It is an odyssey back through time. You enter, from street level, a 12th-century church, descend to the excavated fourth-century church below, and eventually go down a further level to the remains of several first-century structures. Access (for a small fee) is from the sacristy, and there are generally guides on hand if you want a guided tour.

The subject matter of this 12th-century apse mosaic is unusual. It represents a tree of life, its swirling branches growing out of an acanthus plant at the base of the Crucifix.

Above: Much of the decoration of San Clemente, as well as the facade, is baroque in style, but this hasn't altered its 12th-century essence. Right: The Mithraic altar in San Clemente

How did all the stratification come about? The explanation is simple enough. When Pope Paschal II (1099–1118) decided to build the present church, the rubble from the fourth-century church was simply packed in to form a foundation. The new church was built directly over the old one, which was more or less forgotten. It was rediscovered by accident in 1857. Excavations were begun that led to the discovery of the even earlier Mithraic shrine.

From the sacristy you descend a staircase to find yourself in what was once the entrance portico. In front of you are three doorways, corresponding to the standard three aisles. Note the two frescoes (like the others on this level from the 9th to the 11th century) flanking the middle door. The one on the right narrates one of Clement's miracles. Allegedly, every year the waters of the Black Sea would part to allow the faithful to pray at the spot where Clement drowned. One year an apparently absentminded mother forgot her child and he was submerged. When she returned the next year, she found him safe and

sound (note the fish painted around the border to represent the encroaching sea). Now step inside this door and walk until you are almost parallel with a door leading off to the right aisle. To get an idea of the dimensions of this church, look through the door at a column embedded in a retaining wall. Now look, to your left, at the wall where other columns are embedded. The distance between the columns indicates the width of the central nave of the fourth-century church (which was bigger than the present one), laid out in a typical basilica plan. There are other interesting

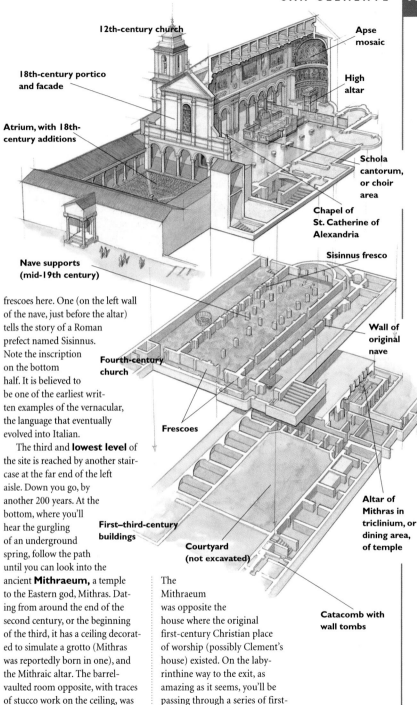

12th-century church

Apse mosaic

18th-century portico and facade

High altar

Atrium, with 18th-century additions

Schola cantorum, or choir area

Chapel of St. Catherine of Alexandria

Sisinnus fresco

Nave supports (mid-19th century)

Wall of original nave

Fourth-century church

Frescoes

First–third-century buildings

Courtyard (not excavated)

Altar of Mithras in triclinium, or dining area, of temple

Catacomb with wall tombs

frescoes here. One (on the left wall of the nave, just before the altar) tells the story of a Roman prefect named Sisinnus. Note the inscription on the bottom half. It is believed to be one of the earliest written examples of the vernacular, the language that eventually evolved into Italian.

The third and **lowest level** of the site is reached by another staircase at the far end of the left aisle. Down you go, by another 200 years. At the bottom, where you'll hear the gurgling of an underground spring, follow the path until you can look into the ancient **Mithraeum,** a temple to the Eastern god, Mithras. Dating from around the end of the second century, or the beginning of the third, it has a ceiling decorated to simulate a grotto (Mithras was reportedly born in one), and the Mithraic altar. The barrel-vaulted room opposite, with traces of stucco work on the ceiling, was probably a vestibule of the temple.

The Mithraeum was opposite the house where the original first-century Christian place of worship (possibly Clement's house) existed. On the labyrinthine way to the exit, as amazing as it seems, you'll be passing through a series of first-century rooms. ■

More places to visit

SANTI QUATTRO CORONATI

The Church of the Four Crowned Saints commemorates nine martyred saints. The four soldiers and five sculptors were killed for refusing either to pray to the Greek god Aesculapius or to sculpt his image. The early 17th-century apse fresco shows the story of their demise. (The soldiers are on the top level, the sculptors below.) Partially damaged during the 1084 Norman invasion, the church was rebuilt and foreshortened by Pope Paschal II (1099–1118); the second of the two outdoor courtyards was once part of the interior. Ring the bell near the door in the left aisle and a nun will admit you to the beautiful, tiny 13th-century cloister, one of the first in Rome. A small offering is expected. To see the frescoes in the **chapel of St. Sylvester** (*closed noon–3:30 p.m. Mon.–Sat., 10:45 a.m.–3:30 p.m. Sun., $*), head for the vestibule marked Suore Agostiniane, ring the bell, and get the key from the nun who answers your ring. The chapel's frescoes seek to explain Constantine's supposed "donation" to Sylvester of the western Roman Empire. ⚠ Map p. 57　✉ Via dei Santi Quattro 20 ☎ 06 7047 5427　🚌 Bus: C3, 60, 75, 81, 85, 87, 175, 673. Tram: 3. Metro: Linea B (Colosseo)

SANTO STEFANO ROTONDO

This is one of the rare circular churches in Rome, and one that is extremely picturesque, not only because you enter the grounds of the church through a portion of the sustaining wall for Nero's aqueduct. The church itself is probably fifth century and is dedicated to St. Stephen, the first Christian martyr. The three arches inside were built in the 12th century for support. To maintain the sense of peace and tranquility the settings afford, don't look too closely at the 34 frescoes that line the walls. Painted by Pomaracio and Antonio Tempesta, and commissioned by Pope Gregory XIII, the frescoes chronologically depict the various methods of torture that were used on early Christian martyrs. ⚠ Map p. 57　✉ Via di Santo Stefano Rotondo 7　☎ 06 7049 3717　🕐 Closed for restoration through 2007.　🚌 Bus: 81, 673.

CASE ROMANE DEL CELIO

A Roman apartment block and villa were joined in the third century A.D. to form a single luxurious dwelling, later the Christian titulus dedicated to the soldier saints Giovanni and Paolo. More than 20 rooms on various levels, some frescoed, are viewable. In the futuristic Antiquarium you can see artifacts from excavations plus a collection of Muslim ceramics. www.caseromane.it　⚠ Map p. 57 ✉ Clivo di Scauro　☎ 06 7045 4544 🕐 Closed 1–3 p.m., Tues.–Wed.　🚌 Bus: 60, 75, 87. Metro: Linea B (Colosseo). ■

Underground Rome

More often than not you can't see it, sometimes you need special permission to get to it, but never forget that it's there. In fact, the two older structures tucked away in the underground recesses of San Clemente are only a tiny part of the ancient hidden city concealed below the surface of Rome. Subterranean structures nestle everywhere, often protected (and obscured) by the tons of dirt and rubble used to construct the foundations of later buildings and by the more or less deliberate landfills that, as you can best see looking down into the Roman Forum, have raised the ground level by several meters. The Domus Aurea was hidden for centuries below the ruins of Trajan's Baths. Under the Colosseum is a network of tunnels. Below many Roman monuments, including Caracalla and the Circus Maximus, are more Mithraea (some bearing traces of animal sacrifices) dedicated to that Eastern god. San Lorenzo in Lucina, a lovely church off Via del Corso, conceals below its marble floor part of the remains of the giant sundial Augustus built in the Campo Marzio. Portions of Pompey's Theater are visible in the cellars of a downtown restaurant, while beneath the Palazzo della Cancelleria water still runs in an ancient canal that once crossed that part of the city. ■

Early Christian churches, Byzantine mosaics, and relics from the Holy Land are some of the gems found in this slice of the city—along with a treasure trove of antiquities in a major museum complex.

Laterano to Terme di Diocleziano

**An angel in Santa
Maria Maggiore**

Laterano to Terme di Diocleziano

AFTER ST. PETER'S, SAN GIOVANNI IN LATERANO IS THE most important Roman Catholic church in the world; along with the Baptistery and Santa Croce, it was one of the few Christian structures built by the Emperor Constantine inside the walls of Rome. And it is, after all, the episcopal seat of the bishop of Rome, that is the pope. "*Omnium urbis et orbis ecclesiarum mater et caput*" ("Mother and head of every church of the city and of the world") is written on the facade and on several of the columns inside.

Before you begin your visit, make sure you realize that the term "in Lateran" means that the Basilica is part of a loosely knit complex of structures that also includes some of Christianity's most important monuments: the Scala Santa, the Sancta Sanctorum, the Baptistery, and the Lateran Palace. The area takes its name from the Roman family, the Laterani, whose *pater familias,* Plautius, participated in a plot against Nero thus losing both his life and the family estate. The land was confiscated by the emperor and later Constantine chose it for San Giovanni since the location was less likely to prove offensive to the city's pagan majority. For centuries, the original Lateran Palace would be the official residence of the popes, who moved to St. Peter's only after their return from a self-imposed exile in Avignon in 1377. In the postwar period, the area has also had a more modern political resonance: It is traditionally the site of the annual May Day rally organized by Italy's unions, and of demonstrations by left-wing political parties.

The area that lies between the Lateran and the Esquiline and Viminale Hills contains other important Christian churches, most notably Santa Pudenziana and Santa Prassede, both known for their mosaics. Here, too, is the imposing Basilica of Santa Maria Maggiore, one of Rome's seven pilgrim churches, dedicated to the Virgin Mary and filled with mosaics celebrating her life. Several popes are buried in this church, which, unusually, has two imposing domes. Also buried here, with surprisingly little ostentation, is the baroque sculptor and architect Gian Lorenzo Bernini. The most famous of Bernini's three "Ecstasies," "St. Teresa in Ecstasy," is nearby in the church of Santa Maria della Vittoria.

In recent years the Museo Nazionale Romano (National Museum of Rome), originally confined within the walls of Diocletian's Baths, has been renovated, refurbished, and decentralized. One of several new branch sites is the Palazzo Massimo alle Terme, across the street from the baths and a stone's throw from the bustling Termini train station, a key junction for Rome's still embryonic but nevertheless useful subway system. Unlike Palazzo Altemps, near Piazza Navona, Palazzo Massimo as a building is of little interest, but it may well be the best organized museum in the city and its exhibition of ancient Roman frescoes and mosaics is unique. The museum's collection of Greek and Roman statues and sculpture is equally magnificent and is effectively organized along thematic, iconographic, and historical lines.

Facing Diocletian's Baths is Piazza della Repubblica, another area that illustrates the architectural stratification of Rome. Built shortly before World War I, the piazza's design follows the outlines of the external perimeter and the *exhedra* (a hemicycle enclosure) of the ancient baths. This busy traffic circle, which the Romans call Piazza Esedra, coincides with what was once the open-air *palestra* or gym of Diocletian's complex. At the break in the exhedra is the onset of Via Nazionale, a major thoroughfare and shopping street which passes by the Palazzo delle Esposizioni, a giant exhibition space, as well as Trajan's Market, to end in Piazza Venezia. The modern fountain in the center of the piazza (Fountain of the Naiads) raised eyebrows when it was unveiled at the beginning of this century because of the generously endowed female statues. ∎

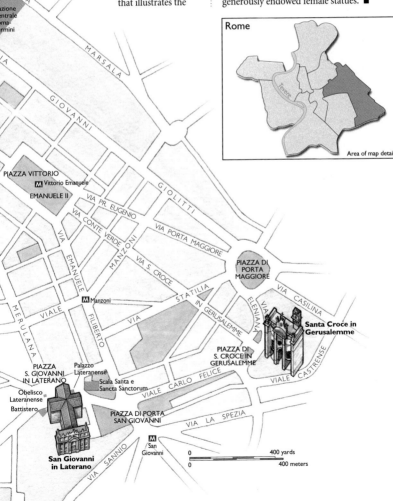

Rome

Area of map detail

San Giovanni in Laterano

FOUNDED BY THE EMPEROR CONSTANTINE IN THE FOURTH century A.D., San Giovanni in Laterano (St. John Lateran), like most Roman churches, has been rebuilt several times over the centuries. In fact, the pope's church—the Cathedral of Rome—only assumed its modern appearance in the 17th century when major overhauls of the interior and the facade took place. The last important architectural change was fairly recent: an enlargement of the presbytery in the 1880s.

The travertine **facade,** divided into a ground-floor portico with a loggia above, was designed by Alessandro Galilei in 1735. It is crowned by 15 giant statues, each about 23 feet (7 m) tall, which can be seen from miles away. The three central statues—Jesus with St. John the Baptist and St. John the Evangelist—are flanked, six on each side, by 12 Doctors of the Church, men or women elevated to this post by the pope for the profundity of their theological thinking. Five doors lead into the barrel-vaulted portico, one for each of the aisles within. The central bronze doors open onto the wide central nave. Originals from the Curia (or Senate) in the Roman Forum, they

were brought here in 1660. The door farthest to the right is the Holy Door which, like that in St. Peter's, is only opened during the Holy Years—generally falling every 25 years.

The interior, in some ways rather cold and unwelcoming (although this is less true of the warmly hued transept), betrays nothing of the church's ancient past. But there is significant grandeur, not surprising since the popes were crowned here until 1870, the year pontifical Rome—until then an independent state—fell to the armies of the Savoy monarchy. But the basilica's monumental magnificence reflects, above all, the creative genius of Francesco Borromini, commissioned by Pope Innocent X in 1646 to do a total renovation for the 1650 Holy Year.

Borromini created the 12 niches flanking the central nave, later transformed into a parade of giant baroque **statues of the Apostles.** If you are not well versed in Apostolic lore, not to worry, the statues are labeled. If you are, you'll be able to identify them by their trademarks: for example, St. Matthew's bag of money (he had been a tax collector), or St. Bartholomew's knife, the symbol of his martyrdom. Artistically, the most interesting are the four sculpted by Camillo Rusconi: Matthew, James the Elder, Andrew, and John. But Borromini's contribution did

**San Giovanni
in Laterano**
- Map pp. 74–75
- Piazza di Porta San Giovanni 4
- 06 7720 7991
- Open daily
- Basilica: Free. Cloister: $. Audio guide: $
- Bus: 16, 81, 85, 87, 218, 360, 665, 714. Tram: 3. Metro: Linea A (San Giovanni)

Left: The Scala Santa is the most impressive of the many relics brought to Rome from the Holy Land by St. Helen, the Emperor Constantine's mother.

Right: The Gothic canopy at the end of the nave in St. John's contains a wooden table that St. Peter may have used to celebrate Mass.

not end here. To preserve something (but not too much) of the church's former style, he selected pieces of medieval monuments or artworks housed in the church, enclosed them in elaborate baroque frames, and created the **funerary monuments** against the pilasters in the outer aisles. The cosmatesque-style pavement (see p. 206) in the central aisle was made during the reign of Pope Martin V (1417–1431), whose bronze floor tomb is in the sunken *confessio*.

The transept of the church was renovated in the late 16th century by Giacomo della Porta and the frescoes (the "Baptism of Constantine," the "Foundation of the Basilica") were painted under the direction of Cavalier d'Arpino, who was responsible for the Ascension over the altar at the end of the left transept. The beautiful frescoed Gothic canopy over the main altar (where only the pope is allowed to say Mass) dates from 1367. Above the frescoes, a grill safeguards two silver bust-shaped reliquaries that contain the **heads of St. Peter and St. Paul,** the two founders of the Church of Rome. Although reconstructed, the **apse mosaic** is striking, and portions of this panoply of figures of varying sizes (depending on their importance) may date from the original fourth-century basilica. The tiny figure kneeling at the feet of the Virgin is Pope Nicholas IV (1288–1292), who commissioned the mosaic's restoration. The even smaller kneeling figures inserted into the row of Apostles on the bottom are the mosaicists, Jacopo Torriti and Jacopo da Camerino.

A door in the left-hand wall, just before the transept, leads to the **cloister** and its accompanying mini-museum. Fashioned between 1215 and 1223 by Cosmati Maestro Pietro Vassalletto and his son, the cloister has a lovely mosaic frieze running around the garden side of the portico and a number of attractive cosmatesque colonettes. The walls are decorated with monuments from the original basilica, including what may be one of the oldest surviving papal thrones.

Leaving the church by the side door (in the right transept), you will be in Piazza San Giovanni in Laterano, with the tallest and oldest obelisk in Rome facing you (see p. 80), the Battistero on your left and, to the right, the Lateran Palace. Note the double brick arch on the other side of the piazza. It was part of the Claudian aqueduct lengthened by Nero to furnish his Domus Aurea with water. If you cross the street, you get an excellent look at the Lateran complex. The basilica's side facade has a portico, surmounted by a loggia designed by Domenico Fontana in 1586. The twin, triangle-topped bell towers of an older 13th-century version of the church are visible above it.

The **Battistero** (Baptistery) also dates back to Constantine and was built into a previous structure that formed part of an imperial residence. In the earliest days of Christianity, only the pope could baptize new converts, usually on Easter, and this was where it was done. With the spread of the new religion, however, this became impractical and parish priests were authorized to perform baptisms. Restored many times, the Baptistery has retained its fourth-century octagonal shape. The circular center space is surrounded by eight porphyry columns surmounted by an architrave with eight smaller white marble columns above. A green basalt urn (for baptisms) stands in the center. The 17th-century frescoes on the outer walls depict scenes from the life of Constantine, and the medallions encompass

Emperor Constantine was baptized on his deathbed in 337. He built this baptistery earlier, and it quickly became a model for future churches.

Battistero
☎ 06 6988 6452
🕐 Closed 12:30–4 p.m.

Scala Santa
☎ 06 772 6641
🕐 Closed winter 12–3 p.m., summer 12–3:30 p.m.

views of Roman churches somehow connected to him. The chapel to St. Venantius, on the left, has magnificent seventh-century Byzantine-style mosaics, although the altar partially obstructs them. Perhaps the most interesting mosaics are in the chapel opposite the door, which until the 12th century was the original narthex (entrance) into the Baptistery. Their classical motifs—acanthus or vine leaves on a blue background—confirm that in the fifth century a real Christian iconography had not yet emerged.

The **Palazzo Lateranense** (Lateran Palace), also built by Fontana, replaced the original papal residence (the Patriarchate), which after a thousand years was reduced to a pitiful state. Fontana salvaged the **Sancta Sanctorum,** the private chapel of the early pontiffs, by moving it to a new though somewhat uninspiring structure across the street. Because of the many relics accumulated there, this chapel was known in the Middle Ages as the holiest site on earth. Renovated in the 13th century, it, too, is a cosmatesque marvel. Above the altar is an *acheiropoieton* image of the Redeemer, meaning it was (supposedly) not painted by human hands.

Also moved there was the **Scala Santa,** the ceremonial staircase, composed of 28 marble steps sheltered by a wooden covering, believed to be the one in Pontius Pilate's Jerusalem palace that Jesus had ascended. The Sancta Sanctorum is at the top of the staircase. Even today the highly religious climb it on their knees. Lateral staircases are available for non-believers and the less energetic. ∎

Obelisks

Hieroglyphics? Obelisks? No, you are not in Egypt. But many of ancient Rome's emperors, or their emissaries, were there, and one of the most popular trophies for a conquering Roman leader was an Egyptian obelisk (*obelisco*). Symbols of divinity and immortality for the pharaohs, they were rated back in Rome as plunder of the highest order and were used as decorative elements for temples, circuses, and mausoleums. After the fall of Rome they lay buried under rubble for centuries. Unearthed during the Renaissance, they were then—paradoxically —given over to the glory of the city's Christian rulers, the popes.

Today, 13 of these stone giants can be found in modern Rome. They embellish some of the city's most beautiful squares and are now as much a part of the Romans' cultural heritage as triumphal columns or arches. Pope Sixtus V (1585–1590), known for his urban planning schemes, obviously had a thing about obelisks: He converted four of them to Christian usage. The Vatican Obelisk in St. Peter's Square was brought to Rome by either Caligula or Nero, and from A.D. 40 on it beautified a nearby circus. It was, amazingly, still standing in 1585, when Sixtus ordered architect Domenico Fortuna to move it to its current location, a feat requiring 900 men, 140 horses, and several dozen giant winches. The pontiff's campaign to Christianize Rome's pagan monuments proceeded with the erection on the Esquiline Hill (behind Santa Maria Maggiore and, incidentally, in front of Sixtus's private villa) of the almost 50-foot (15 m) tall Esquiline Obelisk. Once it had graced the entrance to the Emperor Augustus's Mausoleum but now, says

the inscription, it is "serving the Lord Christ." The Lateran Obelisk (see p. 78) was retrieved from the Circus Maximus along with another erected in Piazza del Popolo, and the Flaminio Obelisk was now "prouder and happier" to be dedicated to Mary.

The obelisks have been so well integrated into Rome's decor that you may almost miss them. Bernini incorporated the Agonale Obelisk into his imposing baroque Fountain of the Four Rivers (see pp. 96, 145) in Piazza Navona, and the Minerva Obelisk, a relative dwarf at only 17 feet (5 m), rides on the back of the whimsical marble elephant in front of Santa Maria sopra Minerva (see pp. 132–33). Renaissance nobleman Ciriaco Mattei placed his in the gardens of Villa Celimontana. The Macuteo Obelisk stands atop Giacomo della Porta's fountain in Piazza della Rotonda.

Sixtus V was not the only obelisk-minded pontiff. Two centuries later, Pope Pius VI (1775–1799) also had a go at relocating them. He put the red granite Quirinal Obelisk in between Castor and Pollux in front of the Quirinal Palace. A similar monument was erected at the top of the Spanish Steps. And in 1792, the obelisk Augustus had used as the needle for his giant Campus Martius sundial was raised in Piazza Montecitorio. Two other obelisks were repositioned in the 19th century: The Antinous Obelisk, originally erected by Emperor Hadrian to honor the memory of his dazzlingly handsome friend and lover, Antinous, was put on the Pincian Hill by Pius VII in 1822. The Termini Obelisk dates from the reign of Rameses II. Excavated in 1883, it has been relegated to a small, somewhat neglected park near the Termini train station. ■

Erected in Piazza del Popolo by Pope Sixtus V in the 1580s, this obelisk dates from the 13th century B.C. and is the second oldest in Rome.

Right: Pope Pius VI placed this obelisk before the Italian parliament. He gave it a pointer like the one it had when it was the needle in Augustus's giant sundial.

Santa Croce in Gerusalemme

SANTA CROCE, A SHORT WALK FROM SAN GIOVANNI DOWN Viale Carlo Felice, was originally part of the palace of St. Helena, Constantine's mother. Its baroque appearance belies its classical origins. Redecorated in the 18th century, the facade's concave and convex movement reveals a strong Borromini influence.

Santa Croce in Gerusalemme

- Map pp. 74–75
- Piazza di Santa Croce in Gerusalemme 12
- 06 7014 779
- Closed 12:30–2 p.m.
- Bus: 649. Tram: 3. Metro: Linea A (San Giovanni)

It is topped by an array of statues, including St. Helen (holding the cross) on the left and her son, Constantine, on the right. The name (Holy Cross in Jerusalem) derives from the church's foundation as a home for the important relics Helen brought back from the Holy Land. Around the back of the church to the right, just through the arches in the Aurelian Wall, and on the left, you can see the outlines of the Castrense amphitheater, used for court performances.

It's hard to discern the original basilica's layout. Only eight of the original granite columns remain: the others are encased in concrete piers. Fortunately, the marvelous cosmatesque pavement (see p. 206) has survived, as has the wonderful fresco in the apse, sometimes attributed to Antoniazzo Romano (ca 1492), showing Jesus and scenes relating to the discovery of the cross. Downstairs are two chapels; the chapel of St. Helen is built over soil that she brought back from the Holy Land. From the left aisle in the church, stairs lead up to the Chapel of the Relics. Here you'll find what are said to be parts of the True Cross, parts of its inscription, two thorns from the Crown of Thorns, a nail from the Cross, and the finger of (the Doubting) St. Thomas. ∎

Like the Lateran, this church was built on the outskirts of the city (on land owned by the imperial family) to avoid offending the pagan majority.

Santa Prassede

The present church was built by Pope Paschal I (817–824) in the early ninth century and was later restored several times, most recently in the 19th century. A typical basilica structure with a restored cosmatesque pavement (see p. 206), it is known for the ninth-century Byzantine mosaics in the apse. The Redeemer is flanked by saints: on the right, St. Peter, Santa Pudenziana (see below), and St. Zeno, with St. Paul, Santa Prassede, and Pope Paschal, holding a model of the church and whose square halo shows he was alive at the time, on the left. These mosaics are Byzantine in character (the two sisters are dressed like Byzantine princesses). A second mosaic masterpiece, one of the most important Byzantine monuments in Rome, is the decoration in the Chapel of St. Zeno. The figures are placed against a gold background, which in Eastern iconography symbolized heaven. ∎

Santa Prassede
- Map pp. 74–75
- Via S. Prassede 9A
- 06 488 2456
- Closed 12–2 p.m.
- Bus: C3, 16, 70 71, 75, 105, 360, 590, 649, 714.
- Metro: Linea B (Cavour)

Santa Pudenziana

It is unclear whether Santa Pudenziana, who was supposed to be Santa Prassede's sister (see above), really existed. The name may stem from a semantic error. Her father was a senator and early Christian named Pudens who had welcomed St. Peter into the family home. Centuries later, the church built on the site was referred to as Ecclesia Pudenziana. In any event, this is believed to be one of the oldest churches in Rome, although frequent restorations have undermined much of its charm. A notable exception is the fourth-century apse mosaic. Classical in style, it shows Jesus seated on a jeweled throne surrounded by ten Apostles (the two others were cut off during a 16th-century restoration). The women standing behind the Apostles, with crowns in their hands, have been variously identified as Prassede and Pudenziana, or as symbols of the early church composed of the ex-circumcized and the ex-Gentiles, as in Santa Sabina (see pp. 208–209). What is significant, is that they are all dressed as Romans and the architectural background, with temples and basilicas, is unmistakably classical. ∎

Santa Pudenziana
- Map pp. 74–75
- Via Urbana 160
- 06 487 2046
- Closed 12–3 p.m.
- Bus: C3, 16, 70 71, 75, 105, 360, 590, 649, 714.
- Metro: Linea B (Cavour)

The Seven Pilgrim Churches

All related to Jesus' Passion, its relics made Santa Croce one of Rome's seven pilgrim churches, Christian places of worship of particular note thanks to their association with important saints or their relics. In medieval and Renaissance times, pilgrims who managed to visit all seven were granted a special indulgence known as a plenary indulgence. A formal itinerary helped them better navigate the distances. The grand tour included the four patriarchal basilicas (St. Peter's, San Giovanni in Laterano, Santa Maria Maggiore, and San Paolo fuori le Mura) plus San Lorenzo fuori le Mura, Santa Croce, and San Sebastiano on the Appian Way. ∎

Santa Maria Maggiore

LEGEND HAS IT THAT IN A.D. 352 POPE LIBERIUS HAD A vision: The Virgin Mary commanded him to build a church dedicated to her on a snow-covered spot. This was quite a presumptuous command because it hardly ever snows in Rome, much less in the summer. Nonetheless, on August 5 it supposedly snowed on the Esquiline Hill, and it was there that Liberius built what was to become one of the four major basilicas of Rome.

Ferdinando Fuga's 17th-century facade belies the early Christian origins of this church, the largest and the oldest of the Roman churches dedicated to the Madonna.

Santa Maria Maggiore

- 🗺 Map pp. 74–75
- ✉ Piazza Santa Maria Maggiore
- ☎ 06 488 1094 (Sacristy), 06 483 195 (Chapel)
- 🕐 Basilica: open all day. Sistine Chapel: Closed Sun. 9:30 a.m.–1:30 p.m.
- 💲 Audio guide: $
- 🚌 Bus: C3, 16, 70, 71, 75, 105, 360, 590, 649, 714. Metro: Linea A or B (Repubblica)

Every August a ceremony is held inside Santa Maria Maggiore to re-enact that miracle, with thousands of white flower petals (the snow) fluttering down from the ceiling. Naturally, the church you see is a later version, built by Pope Sixtus III in the early fifth century, at the tail end of a raging battle among Christian dogmatists over Mary's status: Was she only the mother of Christ the human being (Christokos)? Or was she the mother of Christ in both his human and divine natures (Theotokos)? At the Council of Ephesus in 431 the second view prevailed, giving impetus to the Marian cult. So it shouldn't surprise you that Jacopo Torriti's 13th-century **mosaic** in the apse depicts Mary as a Byzantine princess being crowned by Jesus. By the way, if you have binoculars, you're going to need them here. The 36 fifth-century mosaic panels in the nave, illustrating scenes from the Old and New Testaments, have recently been cleaned, but they are high up and hard to see.

Many additions have been made to this church throughout the centuries, but its basic form—a basilica with three wide aisles divided by 40 massive Ionic columns—faithfully reflects fifth-century canons. The beautiful coffered ceiling was gilded with gold from the New World donated by Ferdinand and Isabella of Spain. The sunken *confessio* holds an 1802 gold and silver relic case said to contain pieces of Jesus' cradle. The giant statue is of Pope Pius IX (1846–1878), who enlarged the confessio.

The two richly decorated, domed chapels on the ends of the transept were added in the 16th and 17th centuries. The one on the left was built by Pope Paul V, who is buried in the Borghese family crypt below. (Another occupant is Paolina Borghese who was sculpted in the nude by Canova, see p. 120.) The other, commissioned by Pope Sixtus V is, like its cousin in St. Peter's, called the **Sistine Chapel.** It is decorated with colored marbles from the Septizodium (a pagan structure which stood below the Palatine Hill) and contains Sixtus's tomb. An underground crypt (open only between Christmas and Epiphany) contains a nearly complete set of magnificent medieval manger figures by Arnolfo di Cambio. (To see them, apply mornings at the church office at Via Liberiana 27.) Near the chapel entrance, in front of the side presbytery banister, a marble slab on the floor marks the **grave of sculptor Gian Lorenzo Bernini** and his ancestors. How peculiar so lavishly baroque an artist should have such a simple, nondescript tomb!

The 18th-century front facade partially covers the early 14th-century mosaics in the loggia. These are worth a visit, anyway, since they tell the story of that miraculous August snowfall. Stop by the piazza at night when, thanks to the Italian genius at artificial lighting, the mosaics glow much as they must have by candlelight. The 14th-century bell tower is the tallest in Rome. The giant marble column in front of the church comes from the Roman forum. ■

The canopy, or *baldacchino*, over the altar covers a sunken *confessio* containing a fragment of the infant Jesus' crib.

Palazzo Massimo alle Terme

IF YOU ONLY HAVE TIME TO VISIT ONE MUSEUM (OTHER than the Vatican), this should be it. Linchpin of the National Museum of Rome's four sites scattered around the city (see p. 31), the Palazzo Massimo alle Terme plays host to some of the museum's finest pieces of Greek and Roman sculpture. Moreso, belying the city's reputation for chaos and confusion, these pieces are displayed in an articulate and happily instructive fashion (in English). Here you'll also find mosaics, frescoes, paintings, and jewelry, as well as the world's premier coin collection. The building, constructed in 1883–1887 to house a Jesuit college, copies the style of early Roman baroque noble residences.

The museum has four display floors, including the **basement** where the massive coin collection dating back to Roman times is enhanced by a charming audio-visual presentation in several languages and a splendid mechanical device: an automated magnifying glass for every one of the vertical display cases that allows you to study in detail any coin you select.

But this is only the beginning. The first thing to do when you get to the museum ticket office is to sign up for the next available accompanied visit to the **top floor** (the second floor, Italian style) which is dedicated to ancient Roman interior decoration, primarily wall frescoes, and wall and floor mosaics. Entire rooms from first-century to late-Roman Empire villas have been reconstructed with their original parietal decoration. While the museum's own guidebook will tell you that the frescoes here do not compare in number with those from Pompeii, "nonetheless, Rome and its suburbs preserved pictorial cycles of exceptional importance and quality." To avoid any security risks, the National Museum of Rome's authorities have decided not to allow visitors to wander freely on this floor, and to make sure everyone gets a chance to visit, they have—unfortunately—set a rather draconian time limit: 45 minutes on weekdays, which should thus take preference over Sundays and holidays when only 30 minutes are allowed. These are not exactly guided visits as we know them and there is no extra charge. But the *accompagnatori*, all of whom speak English, lead you through the area, stopping at the major points of interest to give a brief description of

Decorative mosaic panels from the Basilica of Junius Bassus. The charioteer depicted here is probably Giunio Basso.

Statue of the Emperor Augustus as Pontifex Maximus

what you are to see. They are knowledgeable and courteous and will also answer questions.

Whether or not you've been to Pompeii, however, you probably won't be prepared for the beauty of the summer *triclinium* (dining room) with the garden wall frescoes from the House of Livia. This lady was not just anyone: She was married to Augustus and was the mother of the future emperor, Tiberius. And she had taste. The walls of this room, transported here from a site on the Via Flaminia outside Rome were frescoed to create an imaginary walled garden with trees, plants, flowers, and fruits of all types as well as with exotic birds and animals. Incredibly, experts were able to remove the frescoes from each of the long side walls in a single piece. And take notice of the grotesques—smallish painted decorations on walls and ceilings in which leaves, spirals, and mythological figures generally alternate— and the stucco work on the ceiling.

Another set of staggeringly beautiful **frescoes** come from a first-century villa discovered in 1879 on the grounds of the Villa Farnesina in Trastevere (see pp. 186–87). These frescoes have black backgrounds with friezes and decorative motifs. The mosaics displayed on this floor of the museum are equally enthralling. The four charioteers from a third-century villa belonging to the imperial Severi family show the delicacy of pictorial design. The marble inlay decorations from the Basilica of Junius Bassus are disturbingly modern.

Whether it's before your accompanied tour or after, you won't want

Palazzo Massimo alle Terme

⬛ Map pp. 74–75

✉ Largo di Villa Peretti 1

☎ 06 3996 7700 or 06 4890 3501

🕐 Closed Mon.

💲 $$. Audio guide: $. Guided tours in Italian: Sun.; in English on request $$$$$

🚌 Bus: H, 16, 38, 40, 64, 75, 86, 90, 92, 170, 175, 217, 310, 360, 649, 714. Metro: Linea A or B (Repubblica)

to miss the other two floors (ground floor and first floor) dedicated to the sculpture and statuary that make up the bulk of the Museo Nazionale Romano's ancient art section. The museum has sought, quite successfully, to organize the sculptures thematically and by his-

Apollo" and a magnificent "Crouching Aphrodite." The Lancellotti "Discobolus" (Room VI), the bronze "Dionysus," the amazingly beautiful "Reclining Hermaphrodite," the "Wounded Niobid" (all in Room VII), and the not-to-be-missed Portonaccio

The "Reclining Hermaphrodite," a popular statue found in the ruins of a private garden

torical periods. It would be impossible to mention all the pieces but the ground floor, which deals primarily with the images and accoutrements of power, mainly from the second and first centuries B.C., contains a variety of treasures, some of which are Greek and many of which bear clear Hellenistic influences. Most notable are the multicolored giant cult statue of Minerva (the head is a modern plaster cast of another statue), and the various portraits of Augustus in Room V, which also contains the beautiful Ostia altar, dedicated to Mars. The **frescoes** from the Esquiline colombarium or dovecote tomb and the mosaic floor from a suburban villa (Galleria I) are particularly lovely.

One flight up, on the first floor, there's more. Much more. Here the emphasis is on the iconographic trends in official Roman art, again many with considerable Greek input. The collection is extremely rich. **Room V,** for example, contains marvelous pieces from suburban imperial villas (Anzio, Tivoli, Subiaco), and includes the "Anzio

Sarcophagus **(Room XII),** with its battle scenes between Roman and barbarian soldiers, are all simply thrilling. You'll be amused to note the juxtaposition of the statues in **Room II:** The busts of the Emperor Hadrian, his wife Sabina, and Hadrian's lover, Antinous (the one to whom he dedicated an obelisk), are grouped here together. The busts of the emperors will give you a good idea of what these men really looked like. Another gallery is dedicated to women's head portraits.

Room XIV is also memorable. Grouped under the title "Iconography and celebration from the Severi to the Constantine," the pieces here include several commemorative sarcophagi, the artwork on some of which (for example that of Marcus Claudianus, with its scenes from the Old and New Testaments) indicates that influential Romans were beginning to forsake paganism for Christianity. In general, however, there is only one word for the carved reliefs on these stone coffins: breathtaking. ∎

Terme di Diocleziano

THE BATHS OF DIOCLETIAN (A.D. 284–305), INAUGURATED in A.D. 306, could accommodate about 3,000 bathers. They were built so well that much of the complex's outer structure is still standing. As in Trajan and Caracalla's baths, the *natatio, frigidarium, tepidarium,* and *calidarium* were laid out along a central axis.

In 1561, Michelangelo (age 86) was commissioned by Pope Pius IV (1559–1565) to design a church utilizing part of the structure. The result was **Santa Maria degli Angeli** (*Piazza del Repubblica, tel 06 488 0812, closed noon–4 p.m., Bus: 60, 61, 62, 64, 115, 492, 640, Metro: Linea A/Repubblica*), the imposing entrance to which was built into an apse of the *calidarium* (the hot room), while the vestibule corresponded to the ancient *tepidarium.* In the 18th century, Michelangelo's design was somewhat altered; architect Luigi Vanvitelli changed the axis of the church by creating a new main altar opposite the entranceway and transforming Michelangelo's nave into a somewhat oversized transept. The proportions are awe

inspiring. The eight massive granite columns are 45 feet (14 m) high. The transept is 298 feet (90 m) long, 88 feet (26 m) wide, and over 90 feet (27 m) high—and overwhelming. Don't miss the **Great Cloister,** built in 1565 and attributed to Michelangelo.

In 1889 another portion of the baths was transformed into the **Museo Nazionale Romano** (National Museum of Rome), which has since been decentralized into four different sites (see p. 31). This branch, recently renovated, now holds the **Epigraphic Museum,** where 10,000 inscriptions and funerary monuments, along with mosaics and frescoes, illustrate aspects of ancient Roman daily life— religion, education, professions. ■

The Great Cloister of Santa Maria degli Angeli, part of a Carthusian monastery, was built into a portion of Diocletian's sprawling thermal complex.

Terme di Diocleziano
- Map pp. 74–75
- Viale E. De Nicola 78
- 06 3997 7700
- Closed Mon.
- $$. Audio guide: $. Guided tours in Italian: Sun.; in English on request $$$$$
- Bus: H, 16, 38, 40, 60, 61, 64, 75, 86, 90, 92, 170, 175, 217, 310, 360, 492, 649. Metro: Linea A or B (Repubblica)

More places to visit

AULA OTTAGONA

This octagonal structure between Via Cernaia and Via Parigi was originally the western corner of the central baths complex. Its concrete dome has remained intact, and for this reason in the 1920s it was turned into a planetarium. Since 1986 it has been an annex of the Museo Nazionale Romano (see p. 89) and houses statuary from the Baths of Diocletian, the Baths of Caracalla, and the remains of Constantine's baths on the Quirinal Hill. The marble statue of Aphrodite, a copy of a Greek original dating back to the second or third century, and the fatigued expression on the first-century bronze statue of a boxer are worth seeing.

🄼 Map pp. 74–75 ✉ Via G. Romita 8 ☎ 06 488 0530 🕐 Open 9 a.m.–7:45 p.m., subject to staff availability; closed Mon. 🚌 Bus: H, 40, 60, 61, 62, 64, 70, 84, 170, 175, 492, 590, 910. Metro: Linea A (Repubblica)

played in the giant sunburst over the altar is a copy of one found near the scene of the battle and to which the victory was attributed. The facade was paid for by Cardinal Scipione Borghese (1576–1633) in exchange for a Greek sculpture found on the premises when laying the foundation.

The decoration is the epitome of baroque opulence: Marble, gilded stucco work, sculptures, and paintings abound. This is high baroque at its best, or in any event at its most. Despite the works of artists such as Guercino and Domenichino, the main attraction is Gian Lorenzo Bernini's "The Ecstasy of St. Teresa" in the Cornaro Chapel at the left end of the transept. St. Theresa, enveloped in folds of marble drapery, wounded by an arrow shot by the cherubic angel to her left, lies in the throes of a mystical ecstasy. Members of the Cornaro family are sculpted into what appear to be

The opulent Santa Maria della Vittoria contains carvings by Bernini.

SANTA MARIA DELLA VITTORIA

Built between 1608 and 1620, this church is later than most in Rome. Designed by Carlo Maderno, it was originally dedicated to St. Paul. But in 1622, in commemoration of a victory over Protestant forces in the Battle of the White Mountain near Prague, it was renamed Santa Maria della Vittoria (St. Mary of Victory). The image of the Madonna dis-

theater boxes on the right and left walls of the chapel. This emphasizes the dramatic, theatrical effect so often achieved by Bernini, and is enhanced by the indirect lighting, in this case from above, favored by the artist.

🄼 Map pp. 74–75 ✉ Via XX Settembre 17 ☎ 06 4274 0571 🕐 Closed 12–3:30 p.m. daily & Sun. a.m. 🚌 Bus: H, 16, 60, 61, 62, 84, 90, 175, 492. Metro: Linea A (Repubblica) ■

The Trevi Fountain is one of the biggest crowd-drawers in Rome. But this area also includes other Renaissance and baroque masterpieces, a major museum, and the once glamorous Via Veneto with its luxurious hotels and cafés.

Fontana di Trevi to Via Veneto

Detail from the Fontana del Moro in Piazza Navona

Fontana di Trevi to Via Veneto

TOGETHER WITH THE COLOSSEUM AND THE SPANISH STEPS, THE TREVI Fountain is the other monument that the entire world associates with the Eternal City. It is instantly recognized by travelers from every part of the globe and it, too, has overwhelming, monumental proportions. But the Trevi, hidden away among secondary side streets like St. Peter's was once, gives you a special feeling. Rounding a corner, you almost accidentally discover this travertine giant tucked among narrow city streets. Even in a city like Rome, where fountains abound, you will find it hard not to be overwhelmed, or at least impressed, by Nicola Salvi's dramatic, late baroque masterpiece, cunningly built into the side of a (contemporary) princely palace.

Even though it is right downtown and contains more than one example of Roman majesty, the area around the Trevi has retained much of its traditional character, and you will find simple artisans' shops and boutiques mixed in with baroque masterpieces. The Colonna Palace (with its private art gallery, open only on Saturday mornings) is nearby. Walking uphill along Via della Dataria you will come to the Quirinal Hill and, on top of it, the Quirinal Palace. This was once the summer residence of the popes and is now the home of the president of the Italian Republic, where most afternoons you can see the changing of the guard.

After the late Renaissance popes made this their summer getaway (today's pontiffs head instead to Castelgandolfo on Lake Albano), the surrounding neighborhood became more desirable and several important churches, such as the Jesuit Sant'Andrea al Quirinale and San Carlo alle Quattro Fontane, were built here by major architects such as Bernini and Borromini. These two masters of Italian architecture were thrown together repeatedly; in fact, in the beginning Borromini worked for the older Bernini as a draftsman. They had already collaborated on Palazzo Barberini, the huge baroque palace that Maffeo Barberini, recently elected Urban VIII, had decided to refurbish and expand to make it worthy of the Barberinis' newly exalted status. Decorated by some of the major artists of the 17th century—the ceiling of the great hall of the palace bears the remarkable frescoes of Pietro da Cortona—it is now one of the two sites of the National Gallery (the other is Palazzo Corsini). Its collection includes a series of masterpiece paintings ranging from a Fra Filippo Lippi "Annunciation" to Caravaggio's "Judith Beheading Holofernes."

Near the Palazzo is Piazza Barberini. Today this is both a busy traffic circle and the center of a major shopping area, with the result that despite the repaved traffic island most passersby probably don't even notice Bernini's charming Triton Fountain, one of the first he designed. The Fontana delle Api, which enshrines the Barberini family's bee symbol, is now located across the street. Today, Romans don't pay much attention to it either, but when it was erected in the 17th century things were different. An inscription stated that the fountain had been put up in the 22nd year of the papacy of the Barberini pope, Urban VIII. Unfortunately, it was unveiled a few weeks before the anniversary, making the superstitious Romans nervous. Rightly so, it would seem. Urban died eight days before his 22nd year would have begun.

The Bee Fountain is located at the start of Via Veneto, the long winding avenue that for decades was this city's "great white way" as well as the location of the most elegant hotels and cafés. Once (both in Roman times as well as much later, in the 16th and 17th centuries) a neighborhood of sprawling residential villas, after 1870 this area was wantonly subdivided in a frenzy of real estate speculation. Following World War II, the Via Veneto became known for the dolce vita, an era of glamour and glitter, now vanished, that was depicted in many movies of the time, in particular, Federico Fellini's movie, *La Dolce Vita* (1960). ■

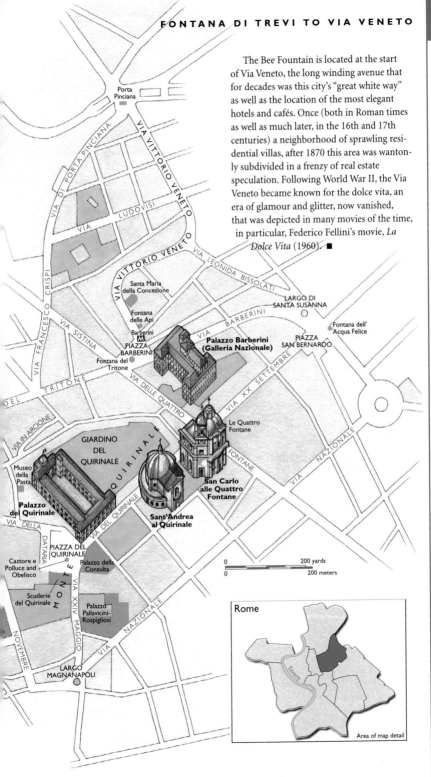

Porta Pinciana

VIA DI PORTA PINCIANA

VIA VITTORIO VENETO

LUDOVISI

VIA

VIA VITTORIO VENETO

VIA LEONIDA BISSOLATI

CRISPI

Santa Maria della Concezione

LARGO DI SANTA SUSANNA

VIA FRANCESCO

VIA SISTINA

Fontana delle Api

BARBERINI

Fontana dell' Acqua Felice

Barberini Ⓜ

PIAZZA BARBERINI

VIA

Palazzo Barberini
(Galleria Nazionale)

PIAZZA SAN BERNARDO

Fontana del Tritone

TRITONE

DEL

VIA DELLE QUATTRO

VIA XX SETTEMBRE

Le Quattro Fontane

VIA IN ARCIONE

GIARDINO DEL QUIRINALE

QUIRINALE

FONTANE

VIA NAZIONALE

Museo della Pasta

San Carlo alle Quattro Fontane

Palazzo del Quirinale

VIA DEL QUIRINALE

Sant'Andrea al Quirinale

VIA DELLA

PIAZZA DEL QUIRINALE

DATARIA

Castore e Polluce and Obelisco

Palazzo della Consulta

0   200 yards

0   200 meters

Scuderie del Quirinale

VIA XXIV MAGGIO

MONTE

Palazzo Pallavicini-Rospigliosi

VIA NAZIONALE

NOVEMBRE

LARGO MAGNANAPOLI

Rome

Tevere

Area of map detail

Fontana di Trevi

BY ROMAN STANDARDS THE FONTANA DI TREVI, OR TREVI Fountain, is almost new; it was, after all, built only some 240 years ago. The water that flows over and through it was brought to Rome by the Aqua Virgo, a largely underground aqueduct originally built by Marcus Vipsanio Agrippa (Augustus's right-hand man) in 19 B.C. to supply water to the baths he constructed in the Campus Martius near the Pantheon. The Aqua Virgo got its name because the spring from which it comes was reputedly revealed to Agrippa's soldiers by a young virgin. You can see her in the relief on the right side of the fountain's upper portion (the *attic*) as she points to the spring. The other relief shows Agrippa approving the plans for the aqueduct's construction. Damaged by the Goths in 537, it was repaired several times and continued to supply the Campus Martius section of town all through the Middle Ages.

Fontana di Trevi

- Map pp. 92–93
- Piazza Fontana di Trevi
- Bus: C3, 52, 61, 62, 63, 71, 80, 81, 85, 95, 116, 119, 175, 492, 590, 628. Metro: Linea A (Barberini)

Opposite: Rome's fussiest English residents used to send their servants here to get water for their afternoon tea. The Acqua Vergine spring (Italian for "Aqua Virgo") is reputed to have the best water in Rome.

A succession of popes thought about building a monumental fountain on this spot, and various projects, including one by Bernini, were presented. It was only in 1732 that Pope Clement XII (whose papal crest is seen at the top of the fountain) approved the design submitted by Nicola Salvi. The project, which took 30 years to complete, emphasizes the central portion of the fountain, dominated by Neptune, while below, among the rocks, two Tritons struggle with two horses (one calm, one bucking to represent the sea in its various moods), while the bubbling and gushing water re-creates the ocean's power and turbulence. These central figures were begun by the little known Giovanbattista Maini but were finished by Pietro Bracci.

The figures in the niches on the right and left represent Abundance (left) and Health (right) and are both by Filippo Valle. The four figures set against the attic, all by different sculptors, represent the beneficial and fertilizing effect of water in the different seasons. As the terminus of the Aqua Virgo aqueduct, the Trevi Fountain is also one of Rome's several *mostre*

d'acqua, a term meant to denote a monumental fountain with enough pressure to push water on to other outlets.

Where and when the custom began of throwing a coin (over your shoulder, if you please!) into the Trevi Fountain in order to guarantee a return trip to Rome is not really known, but to judge from the amount and type of coins pitched in here daily, the practice has become generally accepted by tourists and was, of course, immortalized in the 1954 film, *Three Coins in the Fountain.*

Don't miss the beautiful late 18th-century **aedicola** (niche) on the building at the corner of the piazza with Via del Lavatore. Facing it is the high baroque church of **Santi Vincenzo e Anastasio,** parish church for the popes while they lived on the Quirinal. In the crypt are the hearts and other innards of almost all the popes of the 17th, 18th, and 19th centuries. The practice was discontinued by Pius X (1903–1914). The surrounding streets, Via del Lavatore (where there is a morning food market), Via Panetteria, and Via in Arcione, have grocery and artisans' shops. ■

Fountains & aqueducts

Immortalized in two films, *Three Coins in the Fountain* (1954) and Fellini's *La Dolce Vita* (1960), the Trevi Fountain is certainly the best known in Rome, but it is hardly alone. In effect, fountains (or *fontane*)—small and large, sculpted and plain—are everywhere in the Eternal City. Water spouts from lions' heads, stone tiaras, gargoyles, nymphs, sea gods, masks, barrels, seahorses, a pile of amphorae, and even a heap of stone cannonballs. It trickles, too, from the small neighborhood *fontanelle* from which many Romans once drew their drinking water and today use to wash their cars or quench a summer thirst.

Romans swear by their fontanelle, learning at a tender age that a finger placed over the spigot opening turns a small hole in the top into a drinking spout. It gushes from the *mostre d'acqua* (monumental fonts) that help circulate water throughout the fountain network.

"Nothing can be more agreeable to the eyes of a stranger, especially in the heats of summer, than the great number of public fountains that appear in every part of Rome, embellished with all the ornaments of sculpture, and pouring forth prodigious quantities of cool, delicious water," wrote British writer Tobias Smollett in 1765. In fact, the fountains are omnipresent, testifying both to the grandiosity of the city's ruling class, and to the special relationship that Romans have always had with this life-giving liquid. Historically, Rome had few nearby sources of water, and its

engineers built aqueducts (*aquedotti*) to bring enough of it into the urban area, from as far as 31 miles (50 km) away.

For a fountain lover, Rome is a dream. In the Trident area, on the same aqueduct line as the Trevi, are the Barcaccia, (the "old boat" fountain at the foot of the Spanish Steps), the Pantheon Fountain, and the magnificent 16th-century fountains of Piazza Navona, designed by Gian Lorenzo Bernini. The star attraction in Piazza Navona is Bernini's Fontana dei Quattro Fiumi (Fountain of the Four Rivers), inaugurated in 1651 and financed to the tune of 29,000 scudi by a highly unpopular bread tax. Its four stone giants represent the great rivers of the then known world: the Ganges, the Plate, the Danube, and the Nile, whose veiled countenance stood for the mystery of its (then) uncharted source.

Bernini also designed Il Tritone (the Triton Fountain) and the Fountain of the Bees in downtown Piazza Barberini (see p. 104). These fountains are fed by another mostra d'acqua, the oversize fountain in Piazza San Bernardo near the Grand Hotel. Commonly called the Moses Fountain because of its large central figure, its real name is the Fontana dell'Acqua Felice, after the modern aqueduct built in 1586 by Pope Sixtus V to bring running water to that area. It also sends water to the four charming corner fountains on the intersection of Via delle Quattro Fontane with Via Venti Settembre, and to another beautiful Bernini Triton Fountain in the courtyard at Via della Panetteria 15 (near the Trevi).

A third mostra d'acqua is Fontana dell'Acqua Paola (see p. 189) on the Janiculum Hill, which commemorates the reopening in 1612 of Trajan's aqueduct, built in A.D. 109 to bring water from Lake Bracciano. Probably one of the most beautiful fountains in Rome is the Fontana delle Tartarughe (Tortoises) in tiny Piazza Mattei, a small square tucked away behind the Ghetto (see p. 203). In 1581 Giacomo della Porta's design was executed by Taddeo Landini, who sculpted the four boys and dolphins that make up this lyrical bronze composition. The tortoises, by an unknown artist, were added a century later. ■

Opposite: Detail from Fontana del Moro
Top left: The Barberini family's bees grace a
fountain in their piazza.
Above: This Neptune group was added to a
Piazza Navona fountain in 1878.
Left: A bronze tortoise from the Tortoises
Fountain in Piazza Mattei
Below: Roman aqueduct

Quirinale

THE QUIRINAL HILL (MONTE QUIRINALE), THE HIGHEST OF Rome's famous seven, and just up the street from the Trevi Fountain, is another sight you shouldn't miss, if only because of the magnificent view over the city as far as St. Peter's. Probably named after the ancient Temple of Quirinus which once stood here, it was a site greatly appreciated by Emperor Constantine who chose it for his Imperial Baths. This was probably the source of the enormous statues of the semigods Castor and Pollux and their heavenly steeds that for centuries have graced this piazza (the obelisk and fountain were added later). In the Middle Ages the hill was called Monte Cavallo.

Palazzo del Quirinale

- Map pp. 92–93
- Piazza del Quirinale
- 06 46991
- Open (unless there is an official reception) 8:30 a.m.–noon. Sun. Sept.–June. Changing of the Guard: 3:15 p.m. Mon.–Sat., 4 p.m. Sun., check for summer hours.
- $
- Bus: 40, 60, 64, 70, 170

As far back as the first century B.C., this area had a particular residential cachet. The writer Martial lived here, as did Cicero's good friend, Pomponius Atticus. In the late 1500s Pope Gregory XIII decided to build a summer residence here, where it was somewhat cooler than at the Vatican. Over the decades many important artists—Ponzio, Fontana, Bernini, Maderno, Fuga—worked on the **palazzo,** which has a Renaissance facade facing onto the piazza and a secondary entrance on the wing known as the *manica lunga* (the long sleeve) on the Via del Quirinale.

Also on the piazza are several

other important palazzi. The **Consulta,** on the far side looking toward St. Peter's, was built by Pope Clement XII in the 1730s to house a papal tribunal (today it is the site of Italy's Constitutional Court). Next door is **Palazzo Pallavicini-Rospigliosi,** constructed in 1603 for the Borghese family, while across from the Quirinale are the renovated **Scuderie del Quirinale,** or stables, now used for temporary exhibits. After Italian unification in 1870, Italy's Savoy kings moved into the Quirinale. Since 1947, it has been the residence of the president of Italy. ■

Sant'Andrea al Quirinale

When in 1658 the Jesuits decided to build a new church to serve its novices, they chose the "Strada Pia" (today's XX Settembre), the road designed a century earlier by Michelangelo to connect the Quirinal Palace—which in the time being had become the summer residence of the popes—to the Porta Pia gate. The man in charge was Cardinal Camillo Pamphili and his choice fell on Gian Lorenzo Bernini who had already designed the Piazza Navona fountains for the Pamphili family. Generally consid-

ered Bernini's masterpiece in ecclesiastical architecture, the church is oval in shape. The interior embodies his theory that the visual arts, combined with the effective use of lighting and color, should aim at the creation of an intensely emotional, even theatrical, experience. For Bernini lovers, this is a site not to be missed. Note the colored marbles, the gilded ceiling, and the stucco cherubs on it tumbling down from the small, elliptical dome in a swirl of frenetic activity. ■

Sant'Andrea al Quirinale

- Map pp. 92–93
- Via del Quirinale 29
- 06 4890 3187
- Closed 12:30 p.m.–3:30 p.m.
- Bus: H, 40, 60, 64, 70, 170

Bernini's unusually simple facade gives no clue to the opulence of this church's baroque interior.

San Carlo alle Quattro Fontane

How fitting that the architect of San Carlo alle Quattro Fontane down the street from Bernini's masterpiece should be none other than his archrival, Carlo Borromini, who in his first solo commission seems to have created an antithesis (note the monochromatic off-white interior) to Bernini's opulence. Completed in 1667, the church is so small that it could fit into one of the four supporting pilasters of St. Peter's. Borromini's

genius is exemplified by his sublimely beautiful dome, a beehive of geometric design (crosses, octagons, and hexagons in relief), its windows ingeniously hidden by stucco decorations. Outside, note the four late 16th-century fountains (two river gods and two virtues, Fidelity and Strength) at the intersection with **Via delle Quattro Fontane.** From the intersection's center you can see three of Rome's obelisks—but be careful! ■

San Carlo alle Quattro Fontane

- Map pp. 92–93
- Via del Quirinale 23
- 06 488 3261
- Closed daily 1–3 p.m. & Sat. p.m.
- Bus: C3, H, 40, 52, 60, 61, 62, 63, 64, 70, 71, 80, 95, 116, 170, 175, 492, 590. Metro: Linea A (Barberini)

Palazzo Barberini & Galleria Nazionale d'Arte Antica

AN ARCHITECTURAL MASTERPIECE THAT REFLECTS THE collaboration of celebrated baroque architects Gianlorenzo Bernini and Francesco Borromini, the Palazzo Barberini was the home of Maffeo Barberini, who was elected Pope Urban VIII in 1623. A deep-pocketed art patron, the pope spared no expense, hiring some of the major artists of the 17th century—Pietro da Cortona among them—to decorate the palazzo, which now suitably houses the priceless masterpieces of the National Gallery.

Renovations underway promise to reorganize the collection in a manner worthy of its art. Different sections of the museum will be closed for various periods—and no one knows for how long. Currently, the only working entrance is located in Via delle Quattro Fontane.

The permanent collection is currently displayed on two floors. On the first floor (Italian-style) the first rooms to your left contain some lovely primitives (mostly on wood). Paintings from the 15th and 16th centuries are in the next rooms

and among these, in **Room 3,** are Fra Filippo Lippi's "Annunciation" and a "Madonna and Child," and "Mary Maddalena" by Piero di Cosimo. In **Room 4** you will find several important works by Antioniazzo Romano and Perugino. **Room 6** contains Raphael's famous "La Fornarina" (the "Baker's Daughter," said to have been his mistress), although others attribute it to his pupil, Giulio Romano. Note Raphael's name on her bracelet. Also here are Giovan Antonio (Il Sodoma) Bazzi's "Rape of the

Sabine Women," and Andrea del Sarto's "Sacred Family" and "Madonna and Child." The ceiling vault displays Andrea Camassei's "Creation of the Angels." In contrast, the vast ceiling of **Room 7** is a "Divine Providence" painted by Andrea Sacchi. In **Room 8,** there are several masterpieces: Tintoretto's "St. Jerome," Titian's "Venus and Adonis," Lorenzo Lotto's "Sacred Conversation," and Bronzino's striking "Portrait of Stefano Colonna." **Room 9** features an interesting "Pietà" by a follower of Michelangelo as well as Jacopo Zucchi's "Bath of Bathsheba."

But the pièce de résistance of Palazzo Barberini is without a doubt Pietro da Cortona's magnificent ceiling in the Salone, the "Triumph of Divine Providence over Time," in which you can see a more than queen-size version of the three Barberini bees. The room also includes several of Da Cortona's cartoons. Unfortunately, if a special exhibit is on, you may have to buy a ticket to it in order to see this exceptional masterpiece.

The rest of the collection continues up the staircase designed by Bernini. In the first room you will find several paintings by Guido Reni, including his "Beatrice Cenci," and a "Pietà" by Giovan Battista Gaulli (Il Baccicia). The room down a few steps on the left from this central room has Hans Holbein's "Henry VIII" and leads to yet another chamber where you will find the museum's three Caravaggios ("Judith Beheading Holofernes," "Narcissus," and "St. Francis"). Back in the central room, but on the other side, is a door from which tours of the small but really lovely, 18th-century apartment designed for Princess Cornelia Costanza Barberini start.

What you really want to take note of is the **palazzo** itself, con-

sidered a prime example of baroque Roman patrician architecture. While Bernini and Borromini both contributed greatly to the impressive building, the original design is attributed to Carlo Maderno, Borromini's uncle, who died a year after construction began. Commissioned by the Barberini family in 1625—shortly after Maffeo Barberini became Pope Urban VIII—it epitomizes the level of noble life in 17th-century Rome. Borromini, who began as Bernini's assistant, is believed to have designed the oval staircase in the right wing viewed from Via delle Quattro Fontane. At some point you'll want to walk outside to the garden to get a good look at Bernini's impressive central portico and what was built as the original main facade. ∎

Italian Renaissance painter Andrea Del Sarto's "Sacred Family" (1528–1529) is one of the many prized possessions on display at the Galleria Nazionale d'Arte Antica.

Via Veneto

Via Veneto

IN ANCIENT TIMES, THIS WAS A RESIDENTIAL SUBURB
where the wealthy had their landscaped villas. There are next to no
traces of those first-century buildings or of the extensive gardens
which surrounded most of of them.

The best known were the Horti
Sallustiani, the gardens that surrounded the magnificent home of
Sallust, a Roman general and
scholar who was a contemporary
of Julius Caesar. After the turmoil
of the fifth and sixth centuries A.D.
(barbarian invasions and wars
resulted in an interruption of the
water supply), the area was abandoned in favor of more central
zones. But the suburban tradition
was reborn in the 17th century
when much of this area was occupied by the sprawling Villa

Ludovisi. This was sold in the late
19th century when real estate speculation opened the way for modern
urban development.

By the early 20th century the Via
Veneto (officially the Via Vittorio
Veneto) had become Rome's most
elegant street, the site of the city's
best hotels and restaurants. In the
1950s its upper portion became the
undisputed hub of *la dolce vita* (the
sweet life), a term used during the
economic boom of the 1950s and
'60s to describe the gossip and glitter of Roman night life, the

comings and goings of the Eternal City's international galaxy of stars, and the unrelenting assault of its tabloid photographers on the city's beautiful people.

The era was depicted in many movies of the time, in particular *La Dolce Vita* (1960), one of the finest works of Federico Fellini. The movie includes the unforgettable scene of a voluptuous Anita Ekberg, the prey of the cynical reporter Paolo Rubini (Marcello Mastroianni), immersing herself in the waters of the Trevi Fountain (see pp. 94–95). The most memorable character was Paparazzo, Rubini's photographer sidekick. By then the street's most famous bars and cafés—Doney's, Café de Paris, and Harry's Bar—had become hangouts for actors and directors such as Sophia Loren, Gina Lollobrigida, Vittorio De Sica, Roberto Rossellini, Ingrid Bergman, Liz Taylor, Richard Burton, Burt Lancaster, and many more who went there to see and to be seen.

Today, however, it is simply one of Rome's broader avenues, pleasingly lined with charming (and very expensive) sidewalk cafés, elegant shops, and luxury hotels such as the Excelsior and the Marriott Grand Hotel Flora. At the upper end is **Porta Pinciana,** the fortified gateway built into the Aurelian walls in A.D. 403 by the Emperor Honorius, leading to Villa Borghese and the Galleria Borghese. Its lower end, where you'll find banks, ministries, and other hotels, ends in **Piazza Barberini,** one of downtown's major traffic junctions and the site of two famous Bernini statues (see p. 104). ■

More places to visit

GALLERIA COLONNA

Although only open on Saturday mornings, the art gallery of the magnificent 15th-century Palazzo Colonna is well worth a visit. A masterpiece of baroque architecture with colored marbles, ornate mirrors, and frescoed ceilings (the latter depict the victory of Marcantonio Colonna over the Turks at Lepanto in 1571), the gallery was built between 1650 and 1700 to house the Colonna family's art collection. You'll find works by such masters as Bronzino, Ghirlandaio, Jacopo e Domenico Tintoretto, and Rubens. Walk around the corner to Piazza S.S. Apostoli 66 to look at the facade. Across the street is the **Basilica dei Santi Apostoli** with its 15th-century portico and an 18th-century facade designed by Carlo Fontana.
Map pp. 92–93 Via della Pilotta 17
06 679 4632 Open 9 a.m.–1:00 p.m. Sat.; closed Aug. Bus: H, C3, 40, 46, 60, 62, 63, 64, 70, 81, 84, 85, 87, 95, 119, 170, 175, 628, 715, 716, 780.

GALLERIA DELL'ACCADEMIA DI SAN LUCA

Since the 1930s, when its former neighborhood near the Roman Forum was razed by Mussolini, the Academy of St. Luke has been housed in Palazzo Carpegna, around the corner from the Trevi Fountain. The late 16th-century building, originally designed by Giacomo della Porta, was later modified by Borromini, who built the spiral staircase, ingeniously masked by stucco decoration until you are right upon it. This was one of the little optical diversions that Borromini and his rival Bernini liked to create to trick the eye of the beholder. The staircase is beyond the tiny open garden on the right, which is decorated with 19th- and 20th-century sculptures.

The academy was founded in the late 16th century by a group of artists whose gifts, along with bequests by nonmembers, make up the interesting collection. It was named for St. Luke because the Apostle was supposed to have had artistic inclinations. The collection includes works by Raphael, Titian, Poussin, Bronzino, Rubens, Van Dyck, and Canova, as well as some of the few female artists of the time, including Lavinia Fontana, Angelika Kauffmann, and Elisabeth Vigee-Lebrun.

Nearby, at Via della Stamperia 6, is the **Calcografia Nazionale,** with what may be the largest collection of copperplate engravings in the world. It has more than 20,000 plates including more than 1,400 by G.B. Piranesi and is generally open to the public. Two blocks away in Vicolo di Scanderbeg 117 is the amusing **Museum of Pasta** *(tel 06 699 1120, open 9:30–5:30).*
Map pp. 92–93 Piazza dell'Accademia di San Luca 77 06 679 8850 Closed for restoration Bus: C3, 52, 61, 62, 63, 71, 80, 81, 85, 95, 116, 119, 175, 492, 590, 628. Metro: Linea A (Barberini)

SANTA MARIA DELLA CONCEZIONE (DELL'IMMACOLATA)

From an architectural point of view, the Church of the Cappuccini, as it is generally called after the Franciscan monks that run it, is simple and unprepossessing, an attempt by its founder, Cardinal Antonio Barberini (the younger brother of Pope Urban—he is buried there), to run counter to the then (1626) baroque tide. Inside, however, there is rich decoration. The first chapel on the right has Guido Reni's "St. Michael Trampling on the Devil" and was decorated by Pietro da Cortona; the second has works by Lanfranco; the third by Domenichino; and the fifth by Andrea Sacchi. Most of the church's visitors, however, have something else in mind. In fact, the church conceals several somewhat macabre but nonetheless fascinating underground burial chapels lined with the skeletons (or loose bones) of some 4,000 Capuchins. Take a sweater.
Map pp. 92–93 Via Veneto 27 06 487 1185 Church and Crypt closed noon–3 p.m. Bus: C3, 52, 61, 62, 63, 80, 95, 116, 175, 492, 590. Metro: Linea A (Barberini) ■

With its magnificent Spanish Steps and elegant shops, Piazza di Spagna is the *salotto,* or living room, of Rome. But nearby Piazza del Popolo is also impressive, as is the Villa Borghese park.

Piazza di Spagna to Villa Borghese

Detail of a funerary monument in Santa Maria del Popolo

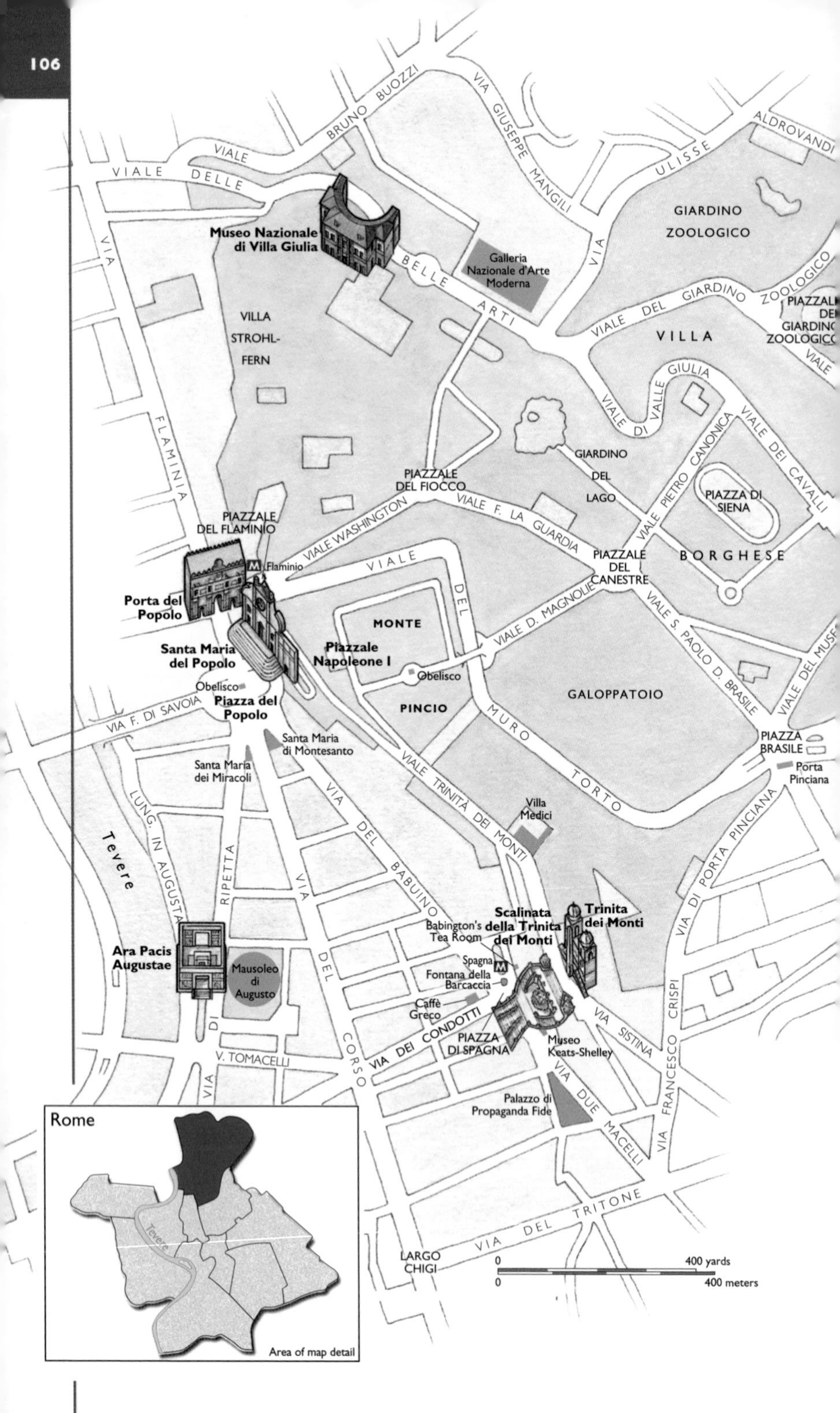

VIALE DELLE

VIALE

VIA BRUNO BUOZZI

VIA GIUSEPPE MANGILI

VIA ULISSE ALDROVANDI

Museo Nazionale di Villa Giulia

GIARDINO ZOOLOGICO

Galleria Nazionale d'Arte Moderna

VIA BELLE ARTI

PIAZZALE DEI GIARDINO ZOOLOGICO

VILLA STROHL-FERN

VIALE DEL GIARDINO ZOOLOGICO

VILLA

VIA

VIALE DI VALLE GIULIA

VIALE DEI CAVALLI

VIALE DEL GIARDINO

FLAMINIA

PIAZZALE DEL FIOCCO

VIALE WASHINGTON

VIALE F. LA GUARDIA

GIARDINO DEL LAGO

VIALE PIETRO CANONICA

PIAZZA DI SIENA

PIAZZALE, DEL FLAMINIO

M Flaminio

VIALE DEL

MONTE

PIAZZALE DEL CANESTRE

B O R G H E S E

Porta del Popolo

Santa Maria del Popolo

Piazzale Napoleone I

VIALE D. MAGNOLIE

VIALE S. PAOLO D. BRASILE

VIALE DEI MUS

Obelisco

Piazza del Popolo

Obelisco

PINCIO

MURO TORTO

GALOPPATOIO

VIA F. DI SAVOIA

Santa Maria di Montesanto

VIALE TRINITA DEI MONTI

PIAZZA BRASILE

Santa Maria dei Miracoli

LUNG. IN AUGUSTA

RIPETTA

VIA DEL BABUINO

Villa Medici

Porta Pinciana

VIA DI PORTA PINCIANA

T e v e r e

Scalinata della Trinità del Monti

Trinita dei Monti

Babington's Tea Room

Ara Pacis Augustae

Mausoleo di Augusto

Spagna M

Fontana della Barcaccia

VIA DEL CORSO

VIA DI

VIA DEI CONDOTTI

Caffè Greco

PIAZZA DI SPAGNA

Museo Keats-Shelley

VIA SISTINA

VIA FRANCESCO CRISPI

V. TOMACELLI

Palazzo di Propaganda Fide

VIA DUE MACELLI

Rome

LARGO CHIGI

VIA DEL TRITONE

Area of map detail

| 0 | | 400 yards |
| 0 | | 400 meters |

Piazza di Spagna to Villa Borghese

WHEN ITALIANS TALK ABOUT A CITY, THEY OFTEN USE the word *salotto*, living room, to describe an area that is both central and welcoming. In that sense the Trident, and in particular Piazza di Spagna, is the salotto of Rome, the neighborhood that best plays host to the city's myriad visitors, those who come to dine and shop and those eager to revisit Rome's architectural, artistic, and archaeological past.

PARCO
DEI
DAINI

Galleria
Borghese

The original design (later dropped) for Piazza del Popolo included a matching tiered garden opposite this one.

The area begins just inside the Porta del Popolo, the gateway in the Aurelian walls (once called Porta Flaminia) that was the terminus of the Via Flaminia, the Roman road built to connect the capital to Rimini on the Adriatic Sea. It includes important archaeological monuments such as Augustus's Mausoleum and the Ara Pacis, Renaissance palaces such as Villa Medici, and innumerable churches, including Trinità dei Monti, with its splendid view of the city. The name, "il Tridente," literally something with three teeth, takes its cue from the street plan developed in the 1500s by the popes of the era, then the city's temporal rulers. In fact, there are three major streets fanning out from Piazza del Popolo: Via Ripetta, which ran to the ancient river port; Via del Babuino, which runs through Piazza di Spagna and on to the Quirinal Hill (then the site of a papal residence); and Via del Corso, which cuts straight through downtown Rome ending at Piazza Venezia and on which important horse races, la Corsa dei Barbari, were held.

For centuries, the area stretching from the Pincio Hill (see p. 112) to the Tiber had been uninhabited: rumored to be haunted by evil spirits, this was a weak point in the city's defenses. With the construction of Santa Maria del Popolo and the other churches of Piazza del Popolo all this was to change, and Via del Babuino's route through Piazza di Spagna would transform the latter into an all-important tourist and shopping center. The Spanish Steps linked the area to the Pincio Hill and, through the latter to the Villa Borghese, a magnificent park that embraces several major museums such as Villa Giulia and, in particular, the magnificently renovated Galleria Borghese. ■

Piazza di Spagna

FOR AT LEAST FOUR CENTURIES, THIS LONG, IRREGULARLY shaped piazza with its un-Italian palm trees has been the heart of nonarchaeological Rome. The elongated square, which boasts one of the city's major monumental attractions, the Scalinata (Spanish Steps), was fashioned into its current form by several important influences: The popes commissioned the best artists to design its major landmarks; the French financed the construction of the three-tiered staircase; and their competitors for the affections of the pope, the Spanish, built their impressive embassy to the Holy See, Palazzo di Spagna (1647), only a stone's throw from Propaganda Fide, the seat of the Vatican's missionary activities. And let's not forget the English, who early on made Rome and this central area of the city an obligatory stop on the Grand Tour for poets and gentlemen alike.

Piazza di Spagna
🅰 Map pp. 106–107
🚌 Bus: 116, 119, 590.
Metro: Linea A
(Spagna)

The **Scalinata della Trinita dei Monti,** or Spanish Steps, is a misnomer. Prior to the inauguration of the Spanish Embassy (across from American Express), the area was

known as Piazza di Francia. Designed by Francesco de Sanctis, the Spanish Steps were built in the 1720s to replace the footpath linking the piazza to the lovely French

church of **Trinita dei Monti** with its double bell towers and the double flight of front stairs. The money to build the 138 travertine steps (24,000 scudi) was bequeathed by a 17th-century French diplomat in his will and then augmented by a contribution of the then king of France, Louis XV.

The steps, a meeting place for young tourists, are particularly lovely in the spring when they are adorned with a magnificent display of flowering azaleas. At Christmastime, a life-size nativity scene is erected there, and every December 8 the pope pays a visit to the narrower, southern end of the piazza where a wreath is placed on the statue of the Virgin Mary atop a Roman column, erected in the nineteenth century to commemorate the 1854 dogma of the Immaculate Conception.

At the foot of the Spanish Steps is the **Fontana** (or fountain) **della Barcaccia** (see p. 96), attributed to Pietro Bernini (Gian Lorenzo's father) and commissioned almost a century before the staircase, in the 1620s, by Pope Urban VIII, a Barberini, as you can tell by the stone bees, the family's

symbol. Because of low pressure, the water does not spout forcefully from the top but rather trickles from nozzles located on the prow, stern, and sides of this marble version of an old, leaky boat. Was this a reference to St. Peter's role as a fisher of men? Or a commemoration of the 1598 flood? It's not clear. The street facing the Steps, **Via dei Condotti,** *the* shopping street of Rome (see p. 110), is named for the underground conduits that Pope Gregory XIII (1572–1585) built to supply the neighborhood with running water.

Beyond the Roman column you'll see, wedged between two streets, the 17th-century **Palazzo di Propaganda Fide,** which houses the Vatican's Congregation for the Propagation of the Faith. Considered an architectural masterpiece, the building combines the work of the two rival geniuses of the era, Gian Lorenzo Bernini and Francesco Borromini. Bernini designed the facade facing the piazza (look, more stone bees here!), while his artistic nemesis, Borromini, was commissioned to create the side facade on Via Propaganda Fide. ∎

In Charles Dickens's day, the Scalinata (Spanish Steps) was a meeting place for artists' models. The Keats-Shelley Memorial House (open to the public) is in the first building on the right. Babington's Tea Rooms is on the left.

The English Quarter

In the 18th century the foreign presence in the Piazza di Spagna area escalated with intellectuals and artists of many nationalities taking up residence in the surrounding streets. But there were so many English visitors that Italians began using the word *"inglesi"* to mean foreigners in general. The major hotels had names like Hotel de Londres and the Hotel des Anglais (even today, a favorite in the area is the Hotel d'Inghilterra). Tennyson and Thackeray had lodgings on Via dei Condotti across the street from

the **Caffè Greco,** a famed meeting place for intellectuals. The young English poet, John Keats, was living at Piazza di Spagna 26 (the rose-colored building to the right of the steps) when he died in 1821, and his apartment now houses the small but interesting **Museo Keats-Shelley** (Keats and Shelley Museum and library). **Babington's Tea Rooms** on the other side of the Steps (great scones!) is an expensive but charming Victorian institution opened to cater to Rome's English-speaking community. ∎

Shopping & fashion

Piazza di Spagna is at the same time the heart of Rome's major shopping district and of the city's fashion world. These days its central position in the universe of Roman *alta moda* is dramatized by the Sotto le Stelle (Under the Stars) fashion show every July when the city's haute couture designers exhibit their fabulous creations on the stone cascade that is the Spanish Steps. The piazza itself and the network of cross-streets that run from here to Via del Corso (the best known are Via dei Condotti, Via Frattina, Via Borgognona, Via delle Carozze e Via della Croce, Via Bocca di Leone, Via Mario dei Fiori, and Via Belsiana) are a fashion victim's delight. Armani, Balestra, Bulgari, Biagiotti, Fendi, Ferragamo, Ferré, Genny, Gucci, MaxMara, Missoni, Prada, Valentino, Versace—all the signature stores are here, as are countless other shops that sell elegant clothing, jewelry, housewares, and objets d'art.

The prices are not low, bargaining is rare, *saldi* (sales) are very often misleading, and tax rebates, while enticing, generally require enormous patience at the airport on your day of departure. (An exception is the Euro Free Tax stores that make a stop at the airport customs office unnecessary.) The clothes are beautiful, eye-catching, and well made and, with some products, particularly leather goods—clothing, shoes, and bags—you may find a real bargain, a trophy to show off at home. Naturally, there are also apparel stores with lower prices. On tiny Via del Gambero you can find bargain blouses and sweaters. On Via del Corso, the long street connecting Piazza del Popolo and Piazza Venezia (adored by writers such as Stendhal for its now vanished 18th-century elegance), there are many shoe stores and casualwear outlets. And the same goes for Via della Croce, which in addition has some nice food stores.

Rinascente at Largo Chigi, one of Rome's oh-so-few department stores, has been totally refurbished in recent years and does a brisk trade in attractive clothing and accessories for both men and women. Like many stores in the center, including those in the newly renovated Alberto Sordi Galleria across the street, it now stays open all day long. Rinascente is open every single day, including Sundays and Monday mornings when clothing stores are generally closed (in summer months they close Saturday afternoons and remain open on Monday mornings).

The streets around the Spanish Steps are not the only important shopping district, however, merely the most elegant, fashionable and…expensive. There are two major alternatives. One is Via Nazionale, the broad cobblestone avenue that runs from Largo Magnanapoli to Piazza della Repubblica (or Esedra), where clothing and leather goods stores abound. Another is Via Cola di Rienzo, across the river in Prati, which is in a similar price range. If you are in this neighborhood, check out Franchi (pronounced FRANCK-ee), known for its expensive-but-worth-it takeout food. If you have a craving for something from home, Castroni, the specialty food shop next door, may well have it. In addition, the area around Campo dei Fiori and Piazza Navona is filled with interesting boutiques and specialty shops.

A few of the many specialty shops that once filled the center still survive and can generally be classified into two groups. They either sell items necessary for a specific clientele or else handmade articles requiring a great deal of time and qualified workmanship. A good example of the first category is the many shops (clustered in the streets behind the Pantheon) that satisfy the haberdashery needs of ecclesiastics. Of the second category, some survivors still sell knotted silk fringes, the tassels for the keys to antique armoires and drapery pull-ropes. One of these *passamanerie* shops is to be found on the Via d'Aracoeli just up the street from Il Gesù, another is near the Parliament.

Despite the overflow of clothing stores, Via del Babuino retains something of its former character as a center for antiques. Shops along here sell everything from silver spoons to antique, marble-topped tables and credenzas. ■

valentino

Many people come to the Italian capital as much for the shopping as for sightseeing. "Made in Italy" has become a well-deserved synonym for excellence.

Pincio

Pincio

◹ Map pp. 106–107

🚌 Bus: C3, 88, 95,
119, 490, 495, 590,
628, 926. Tram: 2.
Metro: Linea A
(Flaminio)

HISTORIANS DISAGREE ABOUT THE ORIGINS OF THE Pincio (pronounced Pin-CHO) Hill, which, by the way, is not one of the famous seven (see p. 191). Was it the location of an imperial residence? The site of the Emperor Nero's tomb? Or simply a suburban residential area inhabited by ancient Rome's patrician families, including the Pinci to whom the hill owes its name? Whatever. At the beginning of the 19th century, the area was transformed into a charming park and promenade that was called the Bois de Boulogne of Rome and figured largely in writings by Stendhal and Henry James.

Domes, bell towers, and terraces form the skyline view from any of Rome's many hills.

The French influence in the layout was inevitable since it was landscaped during a brief period of French administration (1800–

1815). Circular ramps and terraced landings lead from the Piazza del Popolo to a lookout with a magnificent view. Architect Giuseppe Valadier designed circular ramps and terraced landings that lead to the lookout, and the view from here is spectacular (especially at sunset—as guidebooks never fail to point out). The cupolas of Rome, including that of St. Peter's, loom up at you through the gathering dusk, as does the impressive dome of the Pantheon and the all-too-white monument to Victor Emanuel II.

The paths are lined with the busts of Italian patriots added several decades later at the instigation of Giuseppe Mazzini, the 19th-century Italian nationalist. The Egyptian **obelisk** (see p. 80), brought to Rome by the Emperor Hadrian, was placed on the Pincio in 1822 by Pope Pius VII.

Like the **Piazza del Popolo** below, a century ago the Pincio was considered to be the in place for a stroll. Today, however, on weekends there are far more children than lords and ladies, but the view is certainly worth a visit. For those in the mood for a long walk, remember that from the Pincio you can walk to Villa Medici, Trinità dei Monti, and the Spanish Steps or, in the other direction, to the Villa Borghese park (see pp. 118–19). ■

Piazza & Porta del Popolo

Blood once ran in this piazza, where the three streets of the Trident converge. Formerly used for public executions, it was also the starting point for the races held in Via del Corso.

THIS LARGE, OPEN SPACE ECHOES THE MONUMENTAL architectonic style of Paris, and is probably one of the most impressive piazzas in the city, especially now that Rome's municipal government has banned all traffic. Piazza del Popolo takes its name from the church of Santa Maria del Popolo (see pp. 114–115), but it has always been a major landmark. Since Roman times, the Porta has been one of the principal entrances into the city. From an architectural point of view, however, the entire area is primarily a product of the Renaissance, baroque, and neoclassic periods.

In 1589, Pope Sixtus V moved the Egyptian **obelisk** that stood in the Circus Maximus (see p. 207) to the center of the piazza. The foundations for the two churches, whose presence so dramatically enhances the theatrical effect of the square for those entering the city by the Porta del Popolo, were laid in the second half of the 17th century. Although apparently identical, **Santa Maria di Montesanto,** on the left, has an oval dome whereas **Santa Maria dei Miracoli's** dome is round. In 1655, Alexander VII commissioned Bernini to redecorate the inside facade of the Porta to honor the arrival of Queen Christina of Sweden, whose conversion to Catholicism was regarded as a great propaganda coup for the Counter-Reformation. "*Felice faustoque ingressui*" reads the inscription, "For a happy and blessed entrance."

Credit for the piazza's final neoclassic layout, however, goes to Valadier who created the semicircular structures that enclose the piazza, as well as the fountains and the lions. It is a superb mix of French monumentality and Roman warmth. Since the early 19th century, **Piazza del Popolo** has been considered a chic place for a coffee or aperitivo at one of its cafés. ∎

Piazza & Porta del Popolo

Map pp. 106–107

Bus: C3, 81, 88, 95, 119, 490, 495, 590, 628, 926. Tram: 2.
Metro: Linea A (Flaminio)

Santa Maria del Popolo

Santa Maria del Popolo

- Map pp. 106–107
- Piazza del Popolo 12
- 06 361 0836
- Closed Mon.–Sat. 12–4 p.m., Sun. 1:30–4:30 p.m.
- Bus: C3, 81, 88, 95, 119, 490, 495, 590, 628, 926. Tram: 2. Metro: Linea A (Flaminio)

THE REMAINS OF THE EMPEROR NERO WERE SAID TO HAVE been buried on the site of this church, and as part of the medieval penchant for exorcising the remnants of paganism, Pope Paschal II (1099–1118) dug up the supposed gravesite, burning the remains he found there and throwing them into the Tiber. He then built a chapel, dedicating it to the Virgin Mary. Subsequently, Santa Maria del Popolo was redone several times and what we see today—a church with three aisles and many side chapels—is basically the 15th-century Renaissance version. Subsequently, there were some other modifications. Bramante enlarged the apse and Bernini redecorated the interior and added some baroque touches to the facade. In the early 1500s, Martin Luther, the Augustinian monk who only a few years later was to trigger the Protestant Reformation, boarded in the adjoining monastery that today no longer exists.

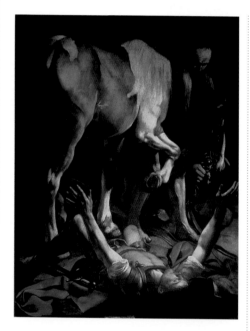

The "Conversion of St. Paul" is one of two dramatic Caravaggio paintings that decorate one of this church's magnificent chapels.

The enormous artistic value of the church lies in its interior decoration, to which some of the most talented artists in the 1500s and 1600s contributed. The Della Rovere Chapel, the first on the right, has frescoes by Pinturicchio, who also painted the "Adoration of the Child" above the altar and the magnificent biblical scenes on the vaulted ceiling of the presbytery. The painting of the "Madonna del Popolo," set into the main altar, which is baroque in style, for centuries was believed to have been painted by St. Luke, until art experts attributed it to the 13th-century Sienese school. The original marble altar designed by Andrea Bregno in 1473 now stands in the sacristy (go through the door at the end of the right transept and down the corridor within). Behind the main altar are the magnificent tombs of Cardinal Ascanio Sforza and Cardinal Girolamo Basso della Rovere, both by Andrea Sansovino.

The star attraction of the church is the **Cerasi Chapel** (to the left of the main altar) with Caravaggio's paintings, the "Conversion of St. Paul" and the "Crucifixion of St. Peter." Also not-to-be-missed is the **Chigi Chapel** by Raphael Sanzio, whose unusual pyramid-shaped marble tombs of the banker, Agostino Chigi, and his brother on the left and right walls of the chapel, may have been inspired by the Roman pyramid of Cestius. The mosaic decoration in the dome of the chapel is based on the designs

(generally known as cartoons) of Raphael. Two of the four corner statues, "Habakkuk" (who in the Old Testament brought food to Daniel in the lion's den) and "Daniel and the Lion," are by Bernini. The "Birth of the Virgin" above the altar is by Sebastiano del Piombo. In the apse (behind the main altar) there are two stained-glass windows. Fairly unusual in Rome to begin with, these are surely among the first in the city. Before you leave, note the somewhat gruesome skeleton sharing a cage with a butterfly (symbolizing rebirth or resurrection) to the right of the rightmost door. ■

Bernini designed the marble floor and hanging bronze lamp—three intertwined cherubs—in the gloriously appointed Chigi Chapel.

Ara Pacis Augustae

Decorated with friezes and acanthus leaves, the Ara Pacis faces the mausoleum of Augustus. It was built after the defeat of Anthony and Cleopatra at Actium (Greece).

ONE OF THE MOST FAMOUS MONUMENTS IN ANCIENT Rome, the Ara Pacis was a ceremonial altar inaugurated in 9 B.C. to commemorate the Pax Romana that followed Augustus's conquest of Spain and Gaul (as France was then known). Dug up (in pieces) back in 1568 near Piazza San Lorenzo in Lucina, it was reassembled (with missing segments reconstructed) in the 1930s. Today it is enclosed in an imposing new construction designed by the well-known American architect Richard Meier.

Made of white Italian (Luna) marble, the altar is set on a rectangular platform and surrounded by four walls with entrances on two sides. The reliefs are a stunning example of the highest quality classical sculpture and are also of great historical interest. The procession represented on the outside of the longer, lateral walls actually took place (on July 4, 13 B.C.). The half-figure on the side facing the nearby mausoleum is Augustus. He is followed by several priests (*flavins*) and family members, including his son-in-law Agrippa, whose place as the second nobleman in the procession indicates he is the heir apparent. An inscription on the outer modern structure reads "*Res gestae Divi Augusti*," the title of the Emperor's own account of his accomplishments.

The Ara Pacis has been the focal point of the grandiose renovation project directed by Meier that, when completed, will also house a conference center, a bookshop, libraries, offices, and new exhibition space.

The overgrown and sorely neglected **Mausoleo di Augusto** next door was once a major monument of ancient Rome, the first of the city's two large circular tombs (the other is Castel Sant'Angelo). The Rome city government is preparing a competition for its long-overdue restoration. ■

Ara Pacis Augustae

- Map pp. 106–107
- Largo Augusto Imperatore
- 06 8205 9127
- Closed for restoration. Expected to open 2006.
- $
- Bus: C3, 81, 119, 224, 590, 628, 926

Villa Giulia

WHAT MORE COULD YOU ASK FOR? NOT ONLY IS VILLA Giulia an absolutely superb example of Renaissance architecture, but since 1889 it has provided the backdrop for one of the most important collections of Etruscan and pre-Roman antiquities in the world. The villa itself was built between 1551 and 1553 by Pope Julius III (1550–55) who commissioned some of the most important architects of the time (Michelangelo, Vasari, Ammanati, and Vignola) to enlarge and ennoble an earlier structure. The resulting building is a consummate expression of the Renaissance architectural concept of exterior–interior "interpenetration" that began with the Villa Farnesina (see pp. 186–87) 40 years earlier.

The mysterious Etruscans dominated central Italy until the sixth century B.C., when power shifted to the Romans who absorbed much of their culture.

Once past the entrance vestibule, you find yourself in a semicircular portico, its ceiling frescoed to create a pergola effect that is in perfect harmony with the courtyard and the gardens with, in the one on the right, a reconstruction of an Etruscan temple. At the other end of the courtyard is a loggia that leads down to a shady, sunken nymphaeum. The two-floor museum **(Museo Nazionale di Villa Giulia)** is housed in the right and left wings of the villa, initial access to which is from the far left-hand side of the portico. The first six rooms display artifacts primarily from the necropolis of Vulci and other digs. There is even a reconstruction of a tomb from Cerveteri, a town in the heart of what was once Etruria.

Not all of this will have general appeal, but who would want to miss **Room 7** with its compelling, life-size terra-cotta polychrome statues of Hercules, Apollo, and a goddess holding a young child, dating from the late sixth century B.C. They were probably done by Vulca, the master sculptor of Veio, who may also have decorated the giant temple to Jupiter that stood on the Capitoline Hill. **Room 9** on the left-hand side of the ground floor is an absolute must. It houses the magnificent world-famous sarcophagus (also sixth century B.C.) of a young husband and wife reclining on a couch. Upstairs are countless objects—domestic implements, bronze utensils, armor, jewelry, and ceramics.

The other wing of the museum exhibits additional material from tombs or temples. The partially reconstructed pediment of the Temple of Apollo allo Scasato is intriguing, and the bust of Apollo is superb. His face, in deep concentration, is turned slightly to the right as if he were listening to a prophetic phrase. ∎

Villa Giulia
- Map pp. 106–107
- Piazzale di Villa Giulia 9
- 06 32 26 571
- Closed Mon.
- $$. Audio guide: $
- Tram: 2, 3, 19

Villas & parks

Rome is one of Europe's greenest cities, and if it has an unusual number of parks it owes this to the city's aristocracy, and—it must be said—to the financial difficulties that forced them, in modern times, to sell their former estates to the State. A major clue to the origins of these vast areas of rolling grassland, normally open from dawn to dusk and ideal for joggers, pensioners, and idlers of all types, is the word *villa,* a sign that the park was once a private house with land surrounding it. Interestingly enough, many of these suburban villas were not built as full-time residences, but for pure leisure, as had often been the case with the estates that ringed the city in ancient Roman times.

The building was called a *casina* or *casino,* literally, a little house, but the word "little" should be used advisedly. Starting in the Renaissance and continuing into the baroque era, as the nobility rushed to build elegant pleasure palaces steeped in verdant and contemplative surroundings, the houses grew ever greater and grander. What were they used for? A day trip for refuge from the summer heat, a picnic, a party, or, as in the case of Villa Borghese, the best known of them all, to house and display a magnificent art collection.

Not all have survived. Villa Ludovisi, which once occupied much of the Via Veneto area, has totally disappeared. The gardens of Villa Giulia, today the Etruscan Museum, have been swallowed up by urban encroachment, as have those of Villa Giustiniani near the Lateran. But fortunately for today's Romans, dozens remain. Villa Ada, Villa Torlonia, and Villa Sciarra are only some of the parks providing a fresh-air outlet for families, lovers, and fitness freaks. Naturally, there are other parks, including those built around ancient monuments, such as the Parco di Traiano (the Colle Oppio) around Trajan's Baths and the Parco degli Scipioni, near the Appian Way, extending around the remains of the tomb of the Cornelii Scipiones, built by that powerful family around the third or second century B.C.

Villa Borghese (pronounced Bor-GAY-zi) is the Roman equivalent of Central Park in New York or St. James's Park in London, and its 198 acres (80 ha) offer the city's residents a downtown escape hatch for strolling, biking, horseback riding, and jogging among extensive greenery, statuary, neoclassic temples, and fountains. There is an artificial lake, a zoo, and a grassy amphitheater (Piazza di Siena) shaded by graceful umbrella pines, where the annual horse show is held every May. The Villa Borghese can be accessed from various points including Porta Pinciana, at the top end of Via Veneto, Piazzale Flaminio, just beyond Piazza del Popolo, and from the Galleria Borghese. Several major museums (Galleria Borghese, see pp. 120–22, the Modern Art Museum— Galleria Nazionale d'Arte Moderna— and Villa Giulia, see p. 117) are in the park.

Heading south from Villa Borghese, between the Pincio (see p. 112) and the Spanish Steps, is Villa Medici. Built for a Tuscan cardinal on the site of the gardens of Lucullus, the famed Roman gourmet and high-liver, this late Renaissance building's gardens were described by Henry James as "a fabled, haunted place." Today it houses the French Academy, which is used for temporary art exhibitions *(tel 06 67611).* In summer, outdoor concerts are held in the spectacular gardens, offering a rare chance to see them.

Among the city's other parks, Villa Doria Pamphili on the Janiculum Hill was laid out in the 17th century for Prince Camillo Pamphili and has a beautiful casino, unfortunately not generally open to the public. With 445 acres (180 ha) and a 5.5-mile (9 km) perimeter, it is the city's largest park, a haven for joggers and fresh-air enthusiasts. Princess Pamphili sold it in the 1960s to settle an enormous tax bill. Villa Celimontana (see p. 67), originally Villa Mattei after the family that built it in the 16th century, is on the Caelian Hill. It is a lovely place for a stroll amid pieces of ancient sculpture, and one of Rome's 13 obelisks (see pp. 80–81); a popular jazz festival is held here in summer. ∎

Right: Ornamental gardens inside the Vatican. Tours of Vatican City can be arranged at the information office in St. Peter's Square.

Above: The Villa Borghese park is a place to relax for Romans and visitors to the city. **Below:** The Janiculum park is one of the few places to see Harlequin and Pulcinella.

Galleria Borghese

CARDINAL SCIPIONE BORGHESE LIVED DOWNTOWN IN HIS princely Roman palace at Piazza Fontanella Borghese, but in the early 1600s he built himself a *casino* (a suburban estate or summerhouse) on his vast estate on what was then the city's outskirts. It was a place to go for picnics, but above all it served to house the family's massive sculpture collection. In 1807 Scipione's descendent, Camillo, who was married to Napoleon's sister Pauline Bonaparte, was forced by his brother-in-law to cede a great chunk of this (374 pieces) to the Louvre. But the collection was later refurbished by new acquisitions and excavations on family-owned land. In 1891 the family painting collection was also moved here and subsequently, in 1902, financial problems forced Prince Paolo to sell the villa and park to the State.

Modified in the 18th century and restored again in recent years, the gleaming white, three-story building today has a facade composed of twin towers flanking a recessed central core or portico. A double ramped staircase (that deliberately imitates Michelangelo's entrance to the Palazzo del Senatore on the Campidoglio) leads up to the main entrance, a mezzanine which is nevertheless considered the ground floor. Stucco work and decorative niches embellish parts of the facade.

The interior decoration of the villa also dates from the 18th century and it must be said that if the outside appears attractive, the inside is simply remarkable. Frescoed ceilings, sumptuous wall coverings, faux marble wall decoration, porphyry mantelpieces, gilded moldings, and marble inlay all vie for our attention with even the most magnificent pieces of art. Remember that every room has a theme, that the ceiling decorations (you mustn't forget to look up) and sculptures are displayed in tandem, and that wherever possible an attempt has been made to extend this thematic link to the paintings on the walls. You'll want to buy a book in the basement bookshop or rent an audio guide.

The sculpture collection, on what passes for the ground floor, or *pianterreno,* contains some of the most famous pieces in the world. Before you lose yourself in those delights, be sure to notice the fourth-century Roman floor mosaics depicting gladiatorial combat scenes in the entrance room. Excavated from a family estate, they are enthralling for their realism. These are portraits (the gladiators' names are written into the mosaic) and those marked with a ø, the first letter in the Greek word *thanatos* (death), got the thumbs down sign and were no more. The frescoed vault depicts a Roman victory over the invading Gauls.

In Room I is Canova's marble **statue of Paolina Borghese,** also known as Pauline Bonaparte, Napoleon's sister. She is reclining, seminude, on a sort of chaise longue, and legend has it that the sculpture was kept under lock and key for years by her husband, Prince Camillo, who was scandalized by her lack of modesty.

Then there are three extraordinary **sculptures by Bernini,** all done while this Roman genius was still in his mid-20s. In Room II you'll find the "David" (ca 1624) in which the young hero is preparing

Galleria Borghese

🅰 Map pp. 106–107

✉ Piazzale Scipione Borghese 5

☎ 06 32810 (for reservations)

🕐 Closed Mon. Advanced booking required.

💲 $$. Audio guide: $. Daily tours in English: $

🚌 Bus: 38, 52, 63, 80, 86, 88, 92, 116, 217, 360, 495, 910

to hurl a stone at his adversary. The face, with its intense and concentrated expression, is a self-portrait of the sculptor. But wait till you get to Room III. **"Apollo and Daphne"** (1622–25), which depicts the young nymph's vain attempts to escape the god (the same scene is painted on the ceiling), has a quasihallucinatory quality. Daphne's hands and feet are in the process of being transformed into a laurel tree. (Remember the laurel wreath? Well, Apollo invented his to keep Daphne ever near him.) The swirling and sensual movement of the two intertwined bodies shows the artist's amazing ability to capture the surface texture of skin and hair, as does his other work (in the next room), the "Rape of Proserpine" (ca 1622). Notice the way Pluto's fingers sink into Proserpine's thigh.

The last room (VIII) on this floor is exceptional more for its paintings than its sculptures. There are six incredible **Caravaggios** here, "St. Jerome" (1605), "David with the Head of Goliath" (1609–1610), and the "Madonna dei Palafrenieri," sometimes called the "Madonna del Serpente," which was removed from an important altar in St. Peter's almost immediately as sacrilegious. The "Bacchino Malato" ("Sick Bacchus") from 1593 is a self-portrait.

Upstairs (a good place to peek out at the gardens in the back) is the painting gallery, or **Pinacoteca,** where one marvelous painting succeeds another and where some of the best known painters in Western history— Bellini, Bronzino, Correggio, Cranach, Domenichino, Fra

Bernini's "Rape of Proserpine" is only one of the magnificent sculptures housed in the refurbished Galleria Borghese, where wall and ceiling decorations vie for your attention.

Bartolomeo, Lanfranco, Lorenzo Lotto, Pinturicchio, Raphael, Reni, Rubens, Titian, and Veronese—are represented.

Room IX is particularly thrilling with Botticelli's richly colored "Madonna con Bambino S. Giovanino e Angeli" (ca 1488) and Raphael's "Ritratto di Giovane Donna con Unicorno" ("Young Woman with a Unicorn"), dated 1506, as well as his very well-known "Deposition" (1507) and many other treasures. In the next room (X) is Bronzino's intriguing "Young San Giovanni Battista" (1525). Note the ceiling. Its theme is Hercules but along with the mythological scenes is a sumptuous prune-colored geometric design. The gilded eagles and dragons are the two symbols of the Borghese family.

Pauline, Napoleon Bonaparte's sister, defied convention and posed as "Venus Victrix" in Canova's magnificent neoclassical sculpture.

You might want to pay special attention to Room XIV, where there are several more works by Bernini, including two self-portraits, the busts of his patron, Scipione Borghese, and the majestic terra-cotta model of a statue of the Sun King, Louis XIV, which was never made. Room XIX contains Domenichino's famous painting of the "Cumana Sibyl," in all her turbaned glory, as well as his "Diana" (1616–17). Federico Barocci's painting of "Aeneas Fleeing the Burning Troy" (1598) inspired Scipione Borghese to commission Bernini to produce the large marble group you saw on the ground floor (Room VI). The gloriously beautiful "Sacred and Profane Love" is among several Titians in Room XX. ■

Galleria Borghese access

Access to Galleria Borghese is more complicated than to other museums. In the first place, you only have two hours to see the museum. Second, if you are carrying anything (including handbags), head straight to the basement check room, otherwise you'll be sent back there from the entrance. Strangely, coats cannot be checked. After seeing the ground floor (sculptures), you may not be able to go directly upstairs without returning first to the basement level. Never mind. What's displayed more than makes up for any organizational defects. ■

This is the heart of modern Rome; a neighborhood where the massive monuments of yesterday—temples in the round, sculpted columns and Corinthian capitals, Renaissance fountains—alternate with major modern political institutions.

Pantheon to Piazza Venezia

Detail from the marble elephant in front of the Minerva church

Pantheon to Piazza Venezia

ARTISANS AND JESUITS, BANKERS AND POLITICIANS, ROMANS AND OUT-OF-towners—the downtown area stretching from the Pantheon to Piazza Venezia is an unusual setting, a melange of ancient, medieval, and Renaissance history. Along the Via del Corso and on Piazza Venezia major Italian banks and insurance companies are ensconced in magnificent stone palaces once owned by Roman princes and noblemen.

Because of its dome, the Pantheon is often called "La Rotonda." Hence the name of the square, Piazza della Rotonda.

In Piazza Colonna the Italian prime minister's office (the 16th-century Palazzo Chigi) looks out on the Marcus Aurelius column, which dates back to A.D. 193. The quality of its workmanship is inferior to that of Trajan's Column, which is 80 years older, but it is interesting for its anthropological detail. The view from the Chamber of Deputies, located in nearby Palazzo del Montecitorio (the facade is by Bernini), includes one of the city's 13 Egyptian obelisks (see p. 80); and in this neighborhood, it is an everyday occurrence to sip a cappuccino against the thrilling backdrop of the Pantheon, a pagan temple built 1900 years ago that subsequently became a church and is today a national monument where kings, a queen, and several painters are buried.

The rulers of Rome have always found it difficult to keep order in Piazza della Rotonda. Recently repaved and today lined with cafés, it is now closed to traffic. But keeping out the mopeds (not an easy task) is somewhat similar to the problems of the 19th century when authorities tried desperately to close down the fish market and other food stands that continued to spring up there. Ironically, at least in the view of many Romans, the plaque erected by Pope Pius VII who tried to rid the area of what he called "disgraceful shops" and "things of unbelievable ugliness" is on the wall of a building that houses one of the newest arrivals to the square, a McDonald's.

Only a short distance away is Santa Maria sopra Minerva, a church steeped in history that belongs to the prestigious Dominican religious order, a major protagonist of both the Inquisition and the Counter-Reformation. The charming small stone elephant in the piazza, designed (but not sculpted) by Gian Lorenzo Bernini, was intended to be a symbol of intelligence. Perhaps more telling, given the political reality of the 16th century, is the overhead bridge spanning Via di Sant'Ignazio (behind the Minerva church); the walkway gave Dominican prelates access to their Jesuit counterparts and to the Jesuit church of Sant'Ignazio.

Across the street from the Collegio Romano—today a high school but once a Jesuit college—is Palazzo Doria Pamphili. That noble Roman family, which boasts both popes and princes among its ancestors, has now turned its imposing block-wide palace with its magnificent private art collection into a very modern museum. A short distance away is the Jesuit mother church, Il Gesù, where baroque opulence has been unstintingly employed to the glory of God.

The Via del Corso terminates at Piazza Venezia which, since several major streets converge there, today seems less a city square than a traffic hub. The helmeted *vigile* (traffic policeman) on his podium in the center of the intersection, is a fixture of the piazza and has appeared in countless films and advertisements. From an architectural point of view Palazzo Venezia can be seen as the start of a modern city, a cross between the medieval and the Renaissance. But it was the construction of the monument to Victor Emanuel II, at the end of the 19th century, that totally changed the look of the square. Then, in order to create a clear view of the monument from Via del Corso, the Palazzetto di Venezia, with its lovely courtyard and

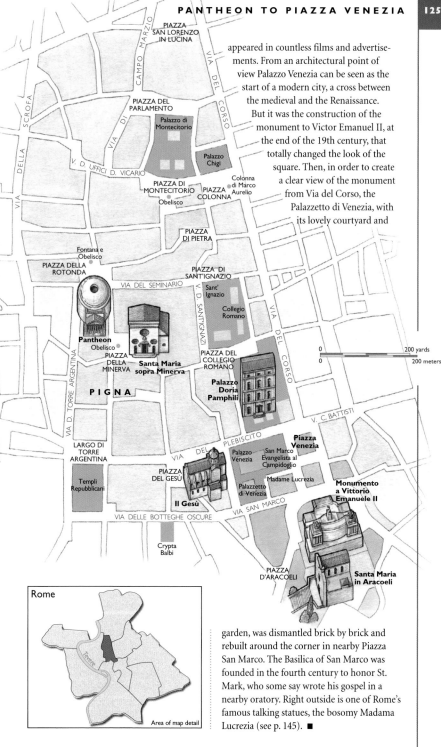

garden, was dismantled brick by brick and rebuilt around the corner in nearby Piazza San Marco. The Basilica of San Marco was founded in the fourth century to honor St. Mark, who some say wrote his gospel in a nearby oratory. Right outside is one of Rome's famous talking statues, the bosomy Madama Lucrezia (see p. 145). ∎

Pantheon

FIRST A PAGAN TEMPLE DEDICATED TO THE GODS (BUT NO one is sure exactly which) and later a Christian church, the Pantheon is generally considered a perfect example of classical architectural harmony. This is largely because of its proportions (its height and diameter are equal) and because the structure, a circular building or rotunda fronted by a rectangular porch that the ancients called a *pronaos* (the latter topped by a triangular pediment), gracefully combines a variety of shapes and forms. Above all, the massive dome of the Pantheon represents an architectural and engineering feat so important that it became a prototype in much of the world.

Pantheon

⬛ Map p. 125

✉ Piazza della Rotonda 12

☎ 06 6830 0230

🕐 Open daily

🚌 Bus: C3, 40, 46, 62, 63, 64, 70, 81, 87, 116, 119, 492, 628.
Tram: 8

With a diameter of 142 feet (43 m) the **cupola,** which was cast by pouring concrete over a temporary wooden frame, is wider than that of St. Peter's. At the base, the dome measures almost 20 feet (6 m), but the thickness gradually diminishes with height, as do the widths of the five rows of coffers lining it. The architectonic function of these was to reduce the weight of the vault, but they also create an optical effect that draws attention towards the center. The opening or "eye" in the ceiling is 30 feet (9 m) in diameter. Apart from any allusion to an eye

looking at the cosmos, the *oculus*, as it is called in Latin, is the only source of light and air in the building, the walls of which are too thick at around 20 feet (6 m) to have made windows an option.

Built by the philosopher-emperor Hadrian between A.D. 118 and 125 to replace an earlier edifice, the Pantheon—it is important to remember—was also built as an astronomical instrument. In ancient times great significance was given to the two equinoxes (March 21 and September 22), the dates when day and night are of equal

From Paganism to Christianity

The Pantheon was the first pagan temple in Rome to be converted into a church, a development of major significance. True, as early as the sixth century other pagan structures had been turned into Christian places of worship (examples are Santi Cosma and Damiano in the Roman Forum, and Santa Maria in Cosmedin near the Forum Boarium, see pp. 200–201), but the buildings involved had been constructed for secular, not religious, purposes.

Furthermore, many of the early Christian churches, such as San Giovanni in Laterano, Santa Croce,

and indeed St. Peter's, were built on what were then the outskirts of the city. If this was partly to make things easy for incoming pilgrims, it was also to avoid offending or incurring the ire of Rome's pagan classes. After all, the spread of Christianity did not take place overnight nor without considerable conflict and resistance. The conversion of a major pagan temple located in the very center of the city was, therefore, of great consequence. It denotes the fact that Christianity had by then become the most important religion in Rome. ∎

Opposite: The Pantheon's large oculus lets in rain as well as light. There are drainage holes below in the center of the pavement.

length, and to the summer and winter solstices (June 21 and December 21 or 22), all of which had a particular significance for agriculture and for checking the accuracy of the calendar. It also had ceremonial possibilities. If every June 21 at noon the beam of light streaming through the oculus hit the floor right in front of the main door, it'd be a good time, wouldn't you think, for an appearance-conscious emperor in full regalia to make a sun-kissed entrance?

The outside **portico,** once preceded by a short staircase, consists of 16 columns of red or gray granite, each 41 feet (12 m) tall and 15 feet (4 m) in circumference and only three of which (on the left

The Pantheon's remarkable state of preservation testifies to the advanced technical expertise of the later Empire's architects and engineers.

side) are replacements. The inscription running below the pediment, *"M. Agrippa F.L.Cos. Tertium Fecit"* ("Marcus Agrippa, son of Lucius, in his third consulate, built this") refers to the earlier structure erected in 27 B.C. by Agrippa to honor his friend and father-in-law, the Emperor Augustus. The bronze letters are new—19th-century fittings made for the original letter holes.

However, there have been changes throughout the centuries. The Byzantine emperor, Constans II, plundered the gilded bronze sheeting that originally covered the dome during his visit to Rome in 663. It was replaced with lead in the 8th century. In the Middle Ages a central bell tower was briefly added,

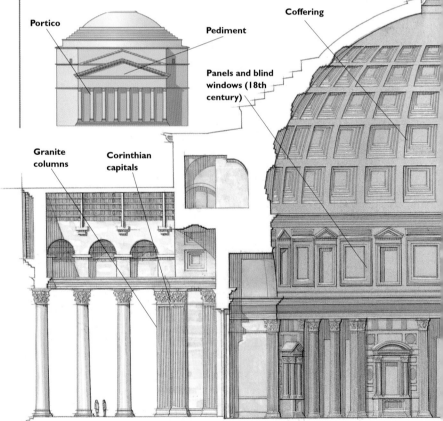

Portico

Coffering

Pediment

Panels and blind windows (18th century)

Granite columns

Corinthian capitals

Interior

only to be replaced in the 17th century by twin turrets designed by Bernini but so hated that they were nicknamed "the donkey's ears" until their removal in 1883. The enormous **bronze doors** are ancient but may have been taken from another structure and placed here. In the mid-1600s, the bronze covering of the portico beams was stripped away to make the cannon for Castel Sant'Angelo and the beautiful spiraled columns for Bernini's *baldacchino*, or canopy, over the main altar in St. Peter's. Pope Urban VIII of the Barberini family ordered this done and his act of sacrilege led the Romans to come up with the famous Latin quip, "*quod non fecerunt barberi, fecerunt Barberini*" ("what the barbarians did not do, the Barberini did").

The Pantheon is the best-preserved ancient monument in Rome, largely thanks to its transformation into a Christian church after the Byzantine emperor Phocas gave the building to Pope Boniface IV in 608 or 609. The interior is awe inspiring. The cavernous **central body** or *cella* (unlike other pagan temples in the Pantheon this cella was accessible to ordinary worshippers and was not, as was usually the case, reserved for priests or notables alone) is divided into three distinct segments. The lower part has six niches (not including the apse), which originally contained statues of the principal gods. In between, there are eight *aediculae* (shrines) flanked by marble columns. The floor, restored in 1872, repeats the colored, geometric patterns of antiquity. Except for a small area, the original marble decoration of the *attic,* the segment that runs around the base of the dome, no longer exists.

The current decor, begun in the 15th century but added to over the following 400 years, contains few major artworks. One exception is Lorenzetto's "Madonna del Sasso" ("Madonna of the Stone"), which stands on the altar in the third aedicula to the left above the **tomb of the painter, Raphael,** who died in 1520. Two Italian kings and a queen are buried here as well as several other painters. This is not surprising since for centuries the Pantheon has been associated with the arts, and one of the most famous artists' groups in Rome, the Accademia dei Virtuosi, had its headquarters in here.

The **fountain** outside, built in 1578, was designed by Giacomo della Porta. The Egyptian **obelisk** was placed on the fountain trough in 1711 by Pope Clement XI. ∎

Oculus

Relieving arches

Walls up to 20 feet thick

Exterior

Coffee & cafés

Whatever you do, don't ask for a "*latte*" (unless, of course, you want a glass of milk). What Americans have taken to calling "latte," here in its country of origin is properly known as a *caffèlatte*, the term Italians mostly use for a breakfast drink of warm milk with a small amount of coffee added. It is normally imbibed at home, especially by children, but can be drunk at the corner bar, where the custom is to take one's pleasure at the counter (although in most places at least some tables are generally available).

The most popular form of coffee outside the home is espresso. But wait! That would be too simple. Everyone crowding the counter seems to have his or her own special request. *Un caffè macchiato* is an espresso with a few drops of warm milk (for cold milk you say "*un caffè macchiato freddo*"). Some prefer a somewhat weaker, more abundant *caffè lungo*. A really strong espresso is, instead, *un caffè ristretto*. And then there are those who don't like cups and want their coffee in a small glass *(un caffè al vetro)*. A decaffeinated espresso is *un caffè Hag* or *un decaffeinato*, while the worker in overalls who's been toiling since 7 a.m. wants *un caffè corretto*, an espresso spiked with something alcoholic—grappa, brandy, or anisette. Then, of course, there is the legion of cappuccino drinkers. Cappuccino, made with less milk than a caffèlatte, is also generally a morning drink (and something an Italian would never even remotely consider drinking after a meal!). But here, too, there are variations. It can be ordered *senza schiuma* (without foam), *chiaro* (light), or *scuro* (dark). A *caffè americano* comes in a larger cup and is probably Nescafé, whereas a *caffè d'orzo* is made from barley.

Coffee has been known to Italy since the 16th century, when a Venetian botanist brought some back from Egypt, and today it comes close to being a national obsession. It can also be a short cut to social interaction. "*Prendiamo un caffè*" can be a successful opening gambit. The Tazza d'Oro on the corner of the Piazza della Rotonda sells excellent fresh-ground for home use in a mocha or neapolitan coffeepot, and Bar S. Eustacchio a couple of blocks away in the piazza of the same name is said to have a secret procedure to make its particularly strong and ristretto brew. But ambience counts, too. And Rome boasts a selection of cafés where the city's denizens go for chat and people-watching, another national sport. Along with the cafés at Pantheon square, there are two in this area that, unusually, offer ample indoor seating: Giolitti, on Via degli Uffici del Vicario 40, also known for its ice cream, and La Caffetteria at Piazza di Pietra.

For decades, the best-known café in Rome was the Caffè del Greco on the fashionable Via dei Condotti, almost facing the Spanish Steps. This was the place where writers and artists gathered to discuss cultural trends and to gossip, and it is still a charming place (indoors only, however) for a rendezvous. But many prefer Rosati and Canova with their outdoor tables on opposite sides of the now car-free Piazza del Popolo. Piazza Navona is lined with cafés, but the Antico Caffè della Pace on Via della Pace a block away has much more atmosphere. Ciampini on the repaved piazza in Lucina (off the Corso) is an in place. And if you happen to be on Trinità dei Monti, above the Spanish Steps, try Ciampini's outdoor café, immersed in greenery and overlooking the rooftops of Piazza di Spagna. The weather-proofed sidewalk cafés that line the Via Veneto are very pricey but can make a nice change. If you're over on the Trastevere side of the river, De Marzio on Piazza Santa Maria di Trastevere, the bar facing the facade of the basilica, isn't fancy but it's where most residents of Rome's "Greenwich Village" gather on weekend mornings. Other popular cafés in the area are Ombre Rosse at Piazza S. Egidio and Friends at Piazza Trilussa. ■

The cafés in Rome allow you to enjoy espresso, sandwiches, and ice cream while feasting your eyes on some of the city's major monuments. Here, convivial conversation takes places in the shadow of the Pantheon, the first version of which was built by Agrippa, Augustus's son-in-law.

Santa Maria sopra Minerva

THIS LOVELY CHURCH, WITH ITS THREE AISLES AND vaulted ceilings, is said to be the one true Gothic church in Rome, although the facade is early Renaissance and the interior, complete with rose windows, has been changed all too often. As an overall structure, the church dates back to the 13th century when its construction as the religious center of the Dominican order was begun by two monks, Brother Sisto and Brother Ristoro, who had already overseen the building of Santa Maria Novella in Florence.

Santa Maria sopra Minerva

Map p. 125

Piazza della Minerva 42

06 679 3926

Open daily

Bus: (3, 40, 46, 62, 63, 64, 70, 81, 87, 116, 119, 492, 628. Tram: 8

This being Rome, however, the monks did not have to break new ground. An earlier church had already been erected in the eighth century amid the remains of a pagan temple probably dedicated to the Roman goddess of war, Minerva. Note the wall plaques on the right side of the facade, which show the waterline from the frequent floods that inundated the area until the 19th-century Tiber embankments were built.

Because of the power and influence of the Dominicans, the order that would later spearhead the Inquisition and (together with the Jesuits) act as standard-bearers to the popes during the Counter-Reformation, this became a very

prestigious church. Four popes are buried here, as are the Tuscan painter Fra Angelico, and St. Catherine of Siena, one of Italy's two patron saints (the other is St. Francis). Many noble Roman families had chapels here, hiring the most famous artists and architects to decorate them. For example, the Carafa family chapel at the end of the right transept boasts a cycle of glorious **frescoes** by Filippino Lippi illustrating the life of the Dominican saint, Thomas Aquinas, as well as a splendid "Assumption" and an "Annunciation." In the "Triumph of St. Thomas" on the right wall, the two small boys are said to be the future Medici popes, Clemente VII and Leo X, who are buried in the church. On the left wall is the tomb of Pope Paul IV, himself a Carafa and the man who bears the blame for shutting Rome's Jews into their 16th-century ghetto.

To the left of the chapel, note the cosmatesque funeral monument (see p. 206), a mosaic "Virgin and Child Enthroned," flanked by two saints on a gold background. The statue to the left of the main altar, **"Christ Bearing the Cross,"** was begun by Michelangelo. In the fifth chapel on the right see the interesting detail in Antoniazzo Romano's "Annunciation," with the Madonna handing money bags (for dowries) to three girls. The seventh has the marvelous Renaissance tomb by Andrea Bregno. The sarcophagus under the main altar holds the remains of St. Catherine, who convinced the popes to return from exile in Avignon. Behind the altar are the wall tombs of Clement VII and Leo X, created by Antonio Sangallo the Younger. On the left, in a poorly lit passageway near the rear door, is **Fra Angelico's** strikingly simple floor **tomb.**

Right: Jesus was originally naked in Michelangelo's statue, but later prelates decided greater modesty called for an added bronze "loincloth."

Ask to see the *sacrestia* (sacristy) where two papal conclaves were held in the 15th century, and the room where Catherine died, which is now a chapel. In the 1566 *chiostro* (cloister), the vaulted ceiling of the fourth arch on the right side of the portico bears the headless images of four Inquisitors who were themselves tried and executed. After all, it was in the adjoining monastery that Galileo was forced to repudiate his belief that the earth moved around the sun. Legend has it that as he was getting off his knees, he whispered under his breath "*E pur si muove*" ("But it does move"). In the piazza outside is the delightful **stone elephant** designed by Bernini in 1667. Pope Alexander VII composed the inscription, which speaks of the elephant's wisdom and intelligence. ■

A walk through the heart of Rome

As it has through the centuries, this area includes some of Rome's major political institutions and is really the heart of contemporary Rome. The walk will take you from Piazza di Montecitorio to Piazza San Marco, enabling you to bear witness to the city's intricate mix of old and even older.

Behind Piazza Colonna looms the Palazzo Wedekind.

Start at Piazza di Montecitorio, where one of the Egyptian obelisks (see pp. 80–81) that Augustus brought back to Rome stands in front of the massive Palazzo dei Montecitorio, now the Chamber of Deputies, the lower house of Parliament. From this piazza, where protesters sometimes gather, walk right toward the Piazza Colonna, named as you will immediately appreciate for the **Colonna di Marco Aurelio** ❶ (Marcus Aurelius's triumphal column), erected in A.D. 193 to celebrate that emperor's victory over the Marcomanni, one of the barbarian tribes that were beginning to threaten Rome. The column stands in front of **Palazzo Chigi** (built in the 16th and 17th centuries), today the prime minister's office and the seat of the Italian government. The column may seem out of place, but, as with the Pantheon, it reminds us that this area was also very important in Roman times.

Leaving Piazza Colonna by Via dei Bergamaschi, you'll see 11 massive Corinthian columns in **Piazza di Pietra** ❷, now paved and closed to traffic. Embedded in the wall of the **Borsa**, or Rome Stock Exchange, these columns were part of the temple to honor Hadrian, built in A.D. 145 by his successor, Antoninus Pius. Continue in the same direction along Via del Burro, and you're in for

another treat. **Piazza di Sant'Ignazio** ❸ is a rococo jewel, constructed by an 18th-century architect to resemble a theatrical stage. View it from the central door of **S. Ignazio** (see p. 140), a major Jesuit church. Now walk along the side of the church (on Via di Sant'Ignazio), noting the overhead arch that connected the Jesuits to their Counter-Reformation allies, the Dominicans, masters of the Minerva church (see pp. 132–133) around the corner. Via di Sant'Ignazio ends at **Piazza del Collegio Romano** ❹, where you'll find the entrance to **Palazzo Doria Pamphili** and Galleria Doria Pamphili (see p. 136).

Turn right on Via di Pie'di Marmo, being sure to note the huge marble foot (from which this street gets its name) at the intersection with Via Santo Stefano del Cacco. Like the obelisk on the elephant in front of the Minerva church, it probably came from a nearby Temple of Isis and Serapis. Facing it at No. 21 is a marvelous chocolate shop. The next cross street along, just before you get to the Minerva church, is Via del Gesù. Turn left, making sure you peek into the courtyards, most of which have fountains (observe the beautiful water clock at No. 62). At the intersection with Corso Vittorio Emanuele II, you'll see the Jesuit mother church, **Il Gesù** ❺ (see p. 137).

Now turn right and walk a block to **Largo di Torre Argentina** ❻, more commonly known as Largo Argentina, to see the remains

---

> 🗺 Also see area map, p. 125
> ▶ Piazza di Montecitorio
> ↔ 1.5 miles (2.4 km)
> ⏱ 2 hours
> ▶ Piazza San Marco
>
> **NOT TO BE MISSED**
> - Column of Marcus Aurelius
> - Piazza di Pietra
> - Sant'Ignazio
> - Il Gesù

of four Republican-era Roman temples **(Templi Repubblicani).** On the other side of the Largo, cross Via delle Botteghe Oscure (Street of the Dark Shops) and walk back along it in the direction you came from. At No. 31 you'll spot the entrance to the **Crypta Balbi,** the section of the Museo Nazionale Romano (see p. 31) dedicated to medieval Rome. It's built over the ruins of a Roman imperial-era theater. Farther on, turn right on Via dei

Polacchi and walk to lovely **Piazza Margana** ❼. Turn left here and take Via Margana to Via d'Aracoeli. On the right stand Santa Maria d'Aracoeli and the Campidoglio. Turn left and return to the Botteghe Oscure, which becomes Via di San Marco. Cross and walk right along Via di San Marco to **Piazza di San Marco** ❽, where you'll see the basilica (see p. 140) and the "talking statue," Madama Lucrezia (see p. 145). ■

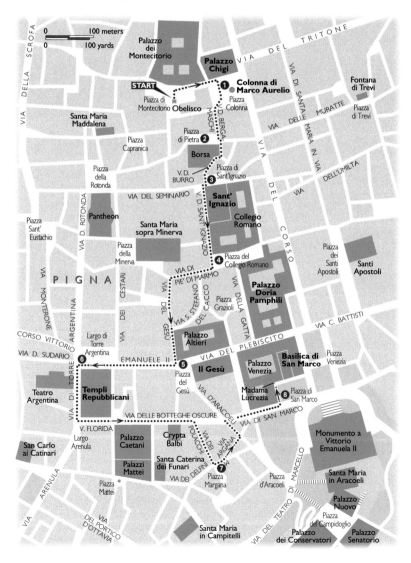

Palazzo Doria Pamphili

You can visit the private apartments of the Doria Pamphili (still inhabited by the family) but only in the mornings.

THIS ENORMOUS BLOCK-LONG BUILDING, WHICH TODAY houses the Doria Pamphili Museum, dates back to 1435 when it belonged to Cardinal Santorio, an obedient prelate who allowed himself to be "convinced" by Pope Julius II to cede the palazzo to the Duke of Urbino, who just happened to be the pontiff's nephew. The rococo facade on Via del Corso, considered notable, was added later.

Palazzo Doria Pamphili

- 🗺 Map p. 125
- ✉ Piazza del Collegio Romano 2
- ☎ 06 679 7323
- 🕐 Closed Thurs.
- 💲 $$. Audio guide: $
- 🚌 Bus: 40, 46, 62, 63, 64, 70, 81, 85, 87, 95, 119, 175, 492, 628

The Pamphilis moved here in the 1700s, bringing with them the collection, begun a century earlier by Donna (or Lady) Olimpia, when the family still lived at Piazza Navona. It is the largest and most important patrician collection still in private Roman hands and the walls are really overcrowded. But as we are talking about works by the likes of Titian, Raphael, Velázquez, and Rubens, it's a minor annoyance. As there are no labels, use the free audio guide included in the entry price, or buy the museum catalog.

The collection is spread through the first floor, the so-called *piano nobile* where the family lived, which runs around a vast courtyard that was once turned into a ballroom to honor a Hapsburg emperor!

The star attraction is probably the corner room (between corridors 1 and 2) in which Velázquez's portrait of Pope Innocent X (1644–1655) is displayed next to Bernini's bust of the same pontiff. Corridor 2 is a triumph of gold, crystal, and mirrors. Two Caravaggios (the "Maddalena" and the "Riposo Durante la Fuga in Egitto") are in Sala del 600, between corridors 2 and 3, and the third (a "San Giovanni Battista") is in corridor 4. There is fine statuary, Roman and otherwise, in the Sala Aldobrandini, where corridors 3 and 4 meet. And don't miss the wonderful bust of Lady Olimpia by Algardi in the corner. The private apartments, with their sumptuous decoration and artwork, are also open to the public. ■

Il Gesù

THE MOTHER CHURCH OF THE JESUIT ORDER, THIS IS A pre-baroque structure that, in ecclesiastical terms, fully embodies the Counter-Reformation spirit. Begun by St. Ignatius Loyola (1491–1556) to complement the new Jesuit headquarters at Collegio Romano, it was consecrated in 1584, although the decoration of the interior continued, to be completed in the 19th century.

This church, like many, is built in the form of a Latin cross, meaning that there is a long central nave, making one of the four arms that radiate out from the center under the dome longer than all the others. The decoration is extremely opulent. These things were done deliberately. To counter the influence of Protestantism (which stressed simplicity and personal responsibility), the Jesuits sought to emphasize the importance of the Church and the clergy. The long nave made processions more dramatic, while darkness encouraged the faithful to focus on the priest who stood on a raised main altar. The ample use of marble, gilded bronze, lapis lazuli, and silver in the decoration of the chapels (especially the two at the opposite ends of the main transept) was another way to stress the magnificence of God.

The chapel on the right by Pietro da Cortona is dedicated to St. Francis Xavier (the relic case is said to contain the saint's arm), that on the left, to St. Ignatius, whose remains are buried here. The silver statue of the saint is attributed to the sculptor Canova. It replaced a more valuable effigy, melted down by Pope Pius VI to pay a tribute to Napoleon. The ceiling fresco and the cupola, decorated with prophets, Evangelists, and Doctors of the Church, are from the end of the 17th century. The ornate bronze banister in front of the chapel is decorated with cherubs and with candelabra set on elaborate marble

bases. Note the cherub at the top holding up a lapis lazuli globe.

Next door at Piazza del Gesù 45 are the **rooms where St. Ignatius lived.** There are paintings in a magnificent trompe l'oeil style by Padre Andrea Pozzo and some memorabilia. ■

Il Gesù

🅰 Map p. 125
✉ Piazza del Gesù 1
☎ 06 697 001
🕐 Closed 12:30–4 p.m.
   St. Ignatius's rooms
   open 4–6 p.m.
   Mon.–Sat., & 10
   a.m.–noon Sun.
🚌 Bus: 46, 62, 63, 64,
   70, 81, 84, 87, 492,
   628, 780

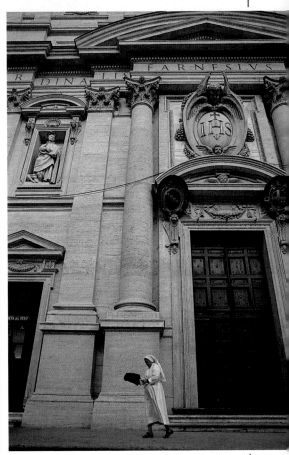

The facade of Il Gesù

Also the site of Italy's Tomb of the Unknown Soldier, the monument to Victor Emanuel II provides spectacular views of the city.

Piazza Venezia

FROM THE POINT OF VIEW OF SIZE AND VISIBILITY, THE Vittoriano, the stark white marble monument to King Victor Emanuel II, the Savoy monarch associated with the Italian Risorgimento and the first king of a united Italy, dominates the piazza. Begun in 1885 and inaugurated in 1911, it commemorates national unification, achieved in 1870. Once considered an eyesore (although attractive at night when lit), under President Carlo Azeglio Ciampi the Vittoriano increasingly has acquired status as a patriotic symbol.

Piazza Venezia
- 🅜 Map p. 125
- 🚍 Bus: H, C3, 40, 46, 60, 62, 63, 64, 70, 81, 84, 85, 87, 95, 119, 170, 175, 628, 715, 716, 780

Vittoriano
- ✉ Piazza Venezia
- ☎ 06 699 1718
- 🕐 Open daily

Museo del Palazzo Venezia
- ✉ Via del Plebescito 118
- ☎ 06 32810
- 🕐 Closed Mon.
- 💲 $

The Vittoriano is also the site of the new Museo Centrale del Risorgimento (see p. 140) as well as a venue, through an entrance on Via dei Fori Imperiali, for important exhibitions.

Built in the late 15th century by Venetian Cardinal Pietro Barbo (the future Pope Paul II), **Palazzo Venezia** was Rome's first important Renaissance palace, although by incorporating a pre-existing medieval tower and some battlements, it can be seen as a transition. The palace was built at a time of significant architectural change in Rome. Until the early 14th century, when the popes fled to Avignon in France, urban development was centered around the

Lateran Palace, then the papal residence. On their return from exile, the Lateran having fallen into disrepair, the popes moved to the Vatican, spurring growth in the area in between.

Over the centuries the palace has served as a papal residence, as the embassy of the Venetian Republic, and, from 1797 to 1916, as the residence of the Austrian ambassador to the Holy See. Under Fascism it was the headquarters of Benito Mussolini, whose major speeches were declaimed from its balcony. The building now houses the **Museo del Palazzo Venezia,** with a vast collection of artworks and objets d'art, which often hosts special exhibitions. ■

Santa Maria d'Aracoeli

PERHAPS NO OTHER CHURCH IN ROME BETTER EMBODIES the stratified nature of Rome's development, and this is not just because its 22 columns were recycled from some important Roman structures. Santa Maria d'Aracoeli (St. Mary of the Altar of Heaven) was built over the ruins of a Roman temple to Juno.

The early Christian church marks the site where, in the first century B.C., Octavius, the future Emperor Augustus, is said to have experienced a vision foretelling the birth of Jesus. He built an altar here and for this reason, in a break with tradition, he is depicted in the fresco on the arch of the apse—quite a place of honor for a ruler of ancient Rome. Rebuilt in the 13th century by the Franciscans, the church has retained the rather austere Romanesque style of that era, intensified by the fact that the facade was never completed. The painfully steep staircase (a reflection of the medieval view that salvation can only be obtained by sacrifice) was built in 1348, probably as a sign of thanksgiving for the end of the Black Death.

Inside, despite the chandeliers and considerable restoration, the church retains its aura of mystery. The cosmatesque pavement (see p. 206) is interspersed with floor tombs (Donatello created that of Archdeacon Crivelli). The ceiling decoration commemorates the European naval victory at Lepanto in 1571. Don't miss the **Bufalini chapel** (the first on the right) with Pinturicchio's magnificently colored rendition of scenes from the "Life of San Bernardino" (1485). Note how the Renaissance realism of this painting contrasts with the stylized Byzantine "Madonna" on the main altar. Other works are by Benozzo Gozzoli, Arnolfo di Cambio, Andrea Sansovino, and Pietro Cavallini. Nearby is the chapel of the

Santissimo Bambino (the Holy Infant). Romans were outraged when, in February 1994, thieves "abducted" its occupant, a gem-studded statue of the Infant Jesus (said to be carved out of olive wood from the garden of Gethsemane) reputed to have miraculous healing powers. It was replaced by a copy. ■

Santa Maria d'Aracoeli

🅰 Map p. 125

✉ Piazza del Campidoglio 4

☎ 06 679 8155

🕐 Closed 12:30–3 p.m. (summer) & 12:30–2:30 p.m. (winter)

🚌 Bus: H, C3, 40, 46, 60, 62, 63, 64, 70, 81, 84, 85, 87, 95, 119, 170, 175, 628, 715, 716, 780

Visitors ascend 124 wide steps to reach the church entrance.

More places to visit

PIAZZA DI SANT'IGNAZIO

This piazza (1727–28) is something really special. Designed by architect Filippo Raguzzini, it resembles a theatrical stage setting, especially when viewed from the central door of the church of **Sant'Ignazio** *(tel 06 679 4560, closed 12:15–3 p.m.).* Historically the official place of worship for the nearby Jesuit Collegio Romano, the church, completed in 1650, was built to celebrate St. Ignatius Loyola, the founder of the Jesuit order. Funds ran out before the cupola could be built. But never mind. Ingenious artists painted a 56-foot (17 m) wide circular trompe l'oeil canvas that magnificently simulates the interior of a dome.

Built in the form of a Latin cross, this church is heavily and ornately decorated with an abundance of stucco, gilt, and colored marbles. The most notable artwork is Padre Andrea Pozzo's ceiling fresco depicting "St. Ignatius' Entrance into Paradise" and, along the sides, his frescoes commemorating the order's worldwide missionary activities. The best view of all is from the yellow marble disk set for this purpose in the floor of the central nave. Note the four large female figures representing the continents on which the Jesuits were active. Guess which one is meant to personify the Americas.
🅼 Map p. 125   🚍 Bus: C3, 62, 63, 81, 85, 95, 116, 119, 175, 492, 628.

SAN MARCO EVANGELISTA AL CAMPIDOGLIO

The basilica of San Marco is one of Rome's 25 titular churches, that is, nonparish churches founded in early Christian times. Established by Pope St. Mark in A.D. 336 and dedicated to his namesake, St. Mark the Evangelist (who some believe may have written his gospel here), it has been rebuilt and restored more than once, leaving it with a decidedly baroque interior. However, the apse mosaic dates from the ninth century. It shows Jesus flanked by saints, his arm lifted in a blessing. Note that the fingers are positioned in the Greek style, with the index and middle fingers raised while

the thumb is crossed over. This is said to mimic the first letter, in Greek, of Jesus' name, while the Western blessing style—the thumb plus the first two fingers—signifies the Trinity. Pope Gregory IV, on the far left, holds a model of the church.

The facade, with a two-story portico, is considered a fine example of Renaissance church architecture and may be the work of Leon Battista Alberti (historians can't decide). Right next door is an entrance to the Palazzo Venezia (see p. 138) from which you can get a good peep at the courtyard with its charming 18th-century fountain and its beautiful, if incomplete, two-story Renaissance loggia.
🅼 Map p. 125   ✉ Piazza San Marco 48
☎ 06 679 5205   🕐 Closed 1–4 p.m.   🚍 Bus: H, C3, 40, 46, 60, 62, 63, 64, 70, 81, 84, 85, 87, 95, 119, 170, 175, 628, 716, 780. ∎

Family & papal heraldic crests

B ears, bulls, castles, bees, fleurs-de-lis, doves, and dragons. These are everywhere in Rome, gracing facades, fountains, occasionally a pavement, and often a ceiling (especially in churches). In case you've wondered about these ubiquitous symbols, they are the heraldic crests of Rome's noble families. These coats of arms may be carved in marble or wood, molded in bronze and in one case (in the Aracoeli Church) represented in stained glass. If the symbol is topped by a papal tiara (a large beehive-shaped crown) and two crisscrossed keys, then there is a pope somewhere on the family tree. (A broad brimmed hat with tassels means a cardinal.) As the city's rulers over centuries, the pontiffs left more traces than most. Some, like Urban VIII Barberini (a baroque period Donald Trump?), went on real building binges; in fact, the Barberini bees are probably more frequent than the Chigi star, the Farnese fleurs-de-lis, the Pamphili dove, or the Borghese dragon and eagle. ∎

This was once a vast and largely uninhabited flood-plain. But the popes' decision in the 14th century to set up house across the river on the Vatican Hill made it a prime residential area for Rome's Renaissance elite.

Campo Marzio

A cupid from the fountain in Piazza Navona

Campo Marzio

THE CAMPO MARZIO OR CAMPUS MARTIUS (FIELD OF MARS) WAS THE NAME given by the ancient Romans to the broad expanse of largely uninhabited land that stretched from the Quirinal Hill to the Tiber River and which, until Trajan's engineering, was separated from the Roman Forum by a land ridge. From about the fourth century B.C. on, this vast floodplain was used, first for military encampment and exercises, and subsequently for games and athletic competitions.

Antique shops abound on some streets of the Campo Marzio area, mainly Via Giulia, Via di Monserrato, and Via dei Coronari.

Numerous porticoes, set among grass and trees, were built for the citizens' enjoyment and relaxation. At first the Campus Martius area included most of what is today downtown Rome, but subsequently it shrank in size and came to be identified primarily with the area tucked into the curve of the Tiber that faces Castel Sant'Angelo and St. Peter's, enclosing more or less everything from Via del Corso to the river. Only in 1377 when the popes returned from Avignon and took up residence across the river in the Vatican did it become a focus for residential construction. In fact, this is one of the oldest parts of modern Rome, and in vast areas much has remained more or less as it was when broad avenues like Corso Vittorio Emanuele II had yet to be even imagined. Then, as now, there was a warren of narrow streets, interrupted only by spacious squares such as Piazza Navona with its magnificent baroque fountains, Campo dei Fiori (a food and flower market), and Piazza Farnese, a study in Renaissance elegance.

Traces of the past are everywhere in this area. The remains of Emperor Domitian's stadium are underneath Piazza Navona, parts of which (several yards below today's ground level) you can see by exiting the square at the north, along Via Agonale, and turning left at the end of it. There are medieval arches and passageways that bring to mind the image of tradesmen in leather jerkins and soldiers in clanking armor. Buildings bear flood marks from the pre-embankment days. It is in this neighborhood that the Renaissance and baroque best meet. Renaissance palaces such as Palazzo Altemps and the Cancelleria alternate with baroque baronies and churches such as Palazzo Pamphili, Sant'Agnese in Agone, or Sant'Andrea della Valle. High-rent elegant streets such as Via Giulia, Via di Monserrato, and Via dei Coronari, with their churches, art galleries, and exquisite antiques shops, give way to humbler crossways. On Via dei Giubbonari (full of cut-rate clothing and shoe shops) and the streets around Teatro di Pompeo or, in the other direction, on Via del Governo Vecchio, you will find countless small *botteghe* (shops of craftsmen and artisans), the direct descendants of the guilds of an earlier era that more often than not gave their names to the streets of today. ■

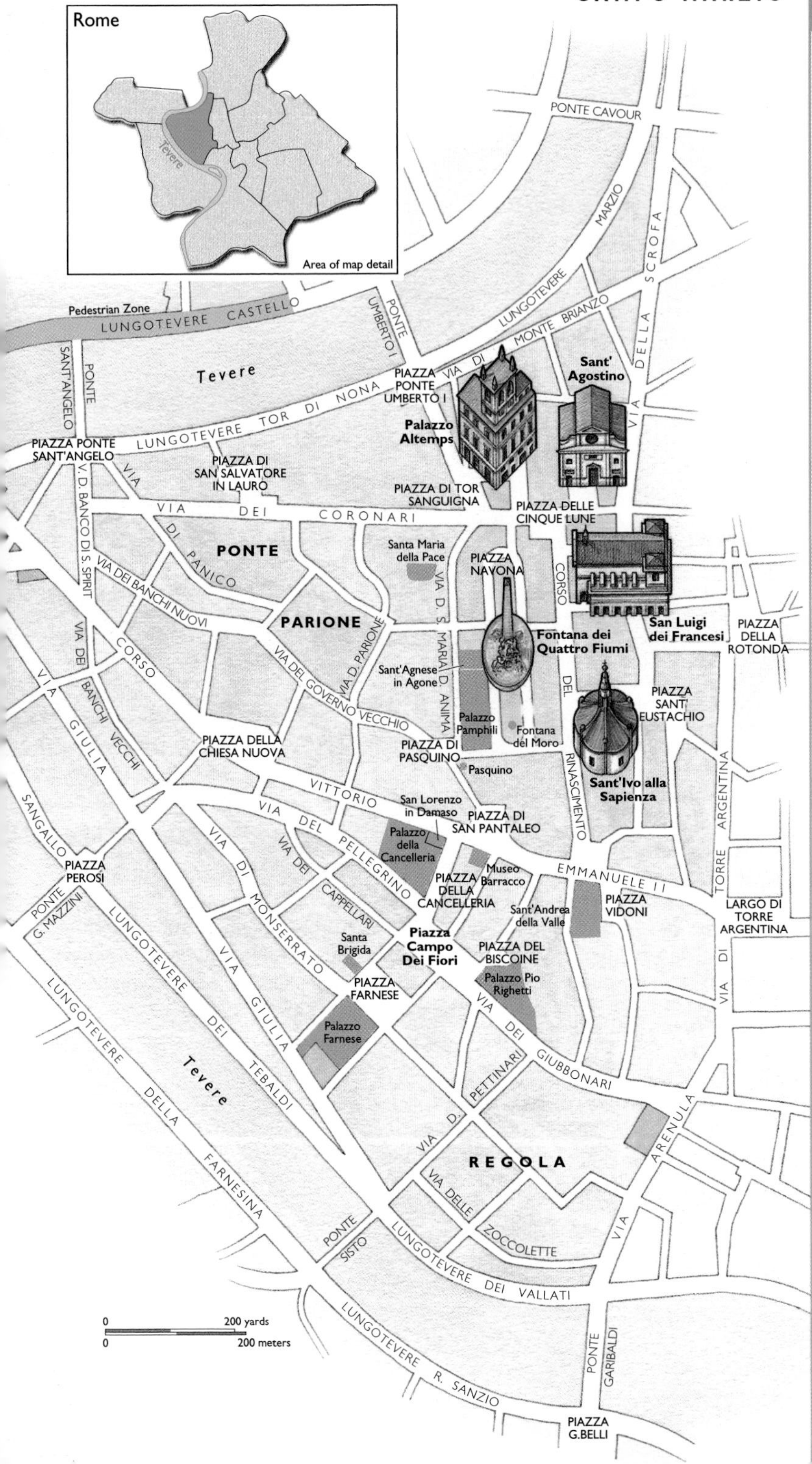

Rome

Area of map detail

Pedestrian Zone

LUNGOTEVERE CASTELLO

Tevere

SANT'ANGELO

PONTE SANT'ANGELO

PIAZZA PONTE SANT'ANGELO

PONTE UMBERTO I

LUNGOTEVERE TOR DI NONA

VIA DI MONTE BRIANZO

LUNGOTEVERE MARZIO

PONTE CAVOUR

VIA DELLA SCROFA

PIAZZA PONTE UMBERTO I

Palazzo Altemps

Sant' Agostino

PIAZZA DI SAN SALVATORE IN LAURO

VIA DEI CORONARI

PIAZZA DI TOR SANGUIGNA

PIAZZA DELLE CINQUE LUNE

PONTE

VIA DI PANICO

Santa Maria della Pace

PIAZZA NAVONA

CORSO DEL RINASCIMENTO

San Luigi dei Francesi

PIAZZA DELLA ROTONDA

V. D. BANCO DI S. SPIRITO

VIA DEI BANCHI NUOVI

PARIONE

VIA DEL GOVERNO VECCHIO

VIA DI S. MARIA D. ANIMA

VIA DEL PARIONE

Sant'Agnese in Agone

Fontana dei Quattro Fiumi

Palazzo Pamphili

Fontana del Moro

PIAZZA SANT' EUSTACHIO

Sant'Ivo alla Sapienza

VIA DEI BANCHI VECCHI

CORSO VITTORIO

PIAZZA DELLA CHIESA NUOVA

PIAZZA DI PASQUINO

Pasquino

San Lorenzo in Damaso

PIAZZA DI SAN PANTALEO

PIAZZA DELLA CANCELLERIA

Palazzo della Cancelleria

Museo Barracco

Sant'Andrea della Valle

EMMANUELE II

PIAZZA VIDONI

VIA TORRE ARGENTINA

LARGO DI TORRE ARGENTINA

VIA GIULIA

PIAZZA PEROSI

PONTE G. MAZZINI

VIA DI MONSERRATO

VIA DEI CAPPELLARI

VIA DEL PELLEGRINO

Santa Brigida

Piazza Campo Dei Fiori

PIAZZA DEL BISCOINE

Palazzo Pio Righetti

VIA DEI GIUBBONARI

PIAZZA FARNESE

Palazzo Farnese

LUNGOTEVERE DEI TEBALDI

LUNGOTEVERE DELLA FARNESINA

Tevere

REGOLA

VIA D. PETTINARI

VIA ARENULA

VIA DELLE ZOCCOLETTE

PONTE SISTO

LUNGOTEVERE DEI VALLATI

PONTE GARIBALDI

LUNGOTEVERE R. SANZIO

PIAZZA G. BELLI

0   200 yards
0   200 meters

Piazza Navona

Giacomo della Porta's Fountain of the Moor was named for the "foreign" features that Bernini gave to its central figure. The small figures are 19th-century copies.

ONE OF THE WORLD'S MOST BEAUTIFUL SQUARES, PIAZZA Navona gives the visitor an opportunity to grasp the complexity of 2,000 years of Roman history. A spectacular baroque composition, the piazza lies within the contours of an ancient Roman stadium. Today it plays host to those who flock here for a moment of relaxation—a chat, an *aperitivo*, a meal—against a backdrop of magnificent man-made beauty.

Piazza Navona
Map pp. 142–143
Bus: C3, 46, 62, 64, 70, 81, 87, 116, 280, 492, 628

Look closely at the buildings that form the perimeter of the piazza. They were built over the tiers of seats of the Circus Agonalis, a stadium constructed by Emperor Domitian in A.D. 86 to host Greek-style games, in which contestants competed nude. Note that as usual one end of the stadium, which could seat 30,000, was rounded.

After the popes returned from Avignon (1377) and chose the Vatican as their new residence, urban development began in earnest in this area. In 1477, for example, Pope Sixtus IV moved the central market here from its historic site at the Capitol (Campidoglio). It remained here for 390 years and survives today in the traditional Christmas stalls

set up every December to sell toys and decorations.

Today's Piazza Navona dates from the 1640s when Pope Innocent X, a Pamphili, chose the square as a site for a new family residence, a plan that included elaborate fountains and a church. Both the resulting Palazzo Pamphili, completed in 1650, and Sant'Agnese in Agone, completed over a decade later, are the work of Girolomo Rainaldi, his son Carlo, and of Francesco Borromini. **Palazzo Pamphili** (now an embassy) has frescoes by Pietro da Cortona depicting the story of Aeneas. **Sant'Agnese in Agone** was built over the spot where 13-year-old Agnes, a fourth-century Christian maiden who rejected the advances of a Roman official's son, was reportedly stripped naked in public. The story goes that, thanks to a miracle, the girl's hair grew so long and so fast as to cover her nudity. Agnes was martyred all the same, beheaded (in A.D. 304) during Emperor Diocletian's anti-Christian persecutions. The church's facade was designed by the temperamental Borromini, who worked on it until falling out with the family in 1657.

The magnificent baroque fountains in the piazza (see pp. 96–97) conceal another tale of the legendary Bernini–Borromini rivalry. Borromini lost his commission for

Right: Originally designed for Greek-style athletic games in which the contestants competed in the nude, today Piazza Navona is a place for repose and relaxation.

the central Fountain of the Four Rivers **(Fontana dei Quattro Fiumi)** because of the savvier, more diplomatic Bernini's successful flattery of Donna Olimpia, the pope's sister-in-law. The story goes that Bernini gave one of the fountain's statues a raised arm to ward off the imminent collapse of

Sant'Agnese, and that Borromini's statue of the saint on the church, her hand on her heart, replies, "I will not fall." But it just ain't so. The fountain was completed in 1651, years before Borromini's facade. The Fountain of the Moor **(Fontana del Moro)** is by Giacomo della Porta but Bernini designed the central figure. ■

Pasquino, the talking statue

Dissidents and anticlerics affixed radical messages to his torso, hoping to incite the populace against the popes. The story of Pasquino, the talking statue (see p. 151), gives us our word "pasquinade" (a brief, anonymous satirical comment, generally on current events). Pasquino, however, was not alone. Named after an out-spoken neighborhood tailor, he had several friends with whom he could converse: Marforio, the river god, now in the Capitoline Museum; the Facchino (the porter) on Via Lata off the Corso; Abbot Luigi on Piazza Vidoni near Corso Vittorio Emanuele; and buxom Madama Lucrezia, who stands outside the Palazzetto di Venezia. ■

Cardinal Marco Sittico Altemps commissioned Martino Longhi the Elder to renovate his palazzo, and the architect created this elegant central courtyard.

Palazzo Altemps

AFTER A LONG PERIOD OF DECLINE AND ABANDON, Palazzo Altemps—once the residence of 16th- and 17th-century noblemen and cardinals—has been superbly restored by the Italian government. Part of the Museo Nazionale Romano complex, it is a site not to be missed. Not only does it contain many priceless pieces of classical statuary but, as you will see, the building's structure and its decor compete for the visitor's attention with the artworks exhibited within. The *altana*, the characteristic Roman belvedere tower over one corner of the building, is believed to be the first of a genre that became a must for any patrician palace. Look up from across the street to see four obelisks, and the family's heraldic symbol, an ibex.

Like many buildings of its era, the palazzo belonged to a succession of noble Italian families. Constructed about 1477 by a Riario, in 1568 it was purchased by Cardinal Marco Sittico Altemps, who amassed a magnificent library and a rich collection of ancient sculpture. Today they are scattered among the world's major museums, although 16 pieces of the original collection have now been returned here. The building remained in the family until it was sold to the Holy See,

Museum is one of a very few that explains this. Panels near the statues use shading to indicate the parts that were added. There are also ample explanations in English.

The Painted Loggia on the first floor (one flight up) is now the setting for the Ludovisi **busts of the Caesars.** In the beautiful, tiny **church of Sant'Aniceto,** richly decorated in high baroque style, you will see some striking examples of marble and mother-of-pearl inlay work. By the way, this church (inaugurated in 1617) may well have been the only private church to house the remains of a saint: Anicetus, an early pope and martyr. The frescoes tell the story of the saint's death by decapitation. In reality, Anicetus's story was altered by the family to fit that of Roberto Altemps, who earlier had been sentenced to death by decapitation (for adultery) by Pope Sixtus V.

Like the Villa Borghese, Palazzo Altemps is as much a protagonist as the objects on display. The original **wall** and **ceiling decorations** have been restored to their former glory, that of a patrician palace whose decor embodies the gradual transition in style from Renaissance to baroque. The **courtyard,** with its statues, four of which are from the original Altemps collections, and its nymphaeum (a curved wall-fountain decorated with mosaic, paste shells, and colored gravel of the type often found in ancient Roman villas), is breathtaking. Don't miss the Fireplace Room, with Cardinal Altemps's monumental fireplace, the room of the Painted Landscapes, and the Cupboard Room. The wall fresco there, in what was the 15th-century reception room, shows wedding gifts and greeting cards received by Girolamo Riario and Caterina Sforza (the palace's first occupants). ■

which turned it into a seminary. In a dismal state, it was purchased by the Italian government in 1982.

The museum's inventory includes artworks from several major Roman art collections, in particular the Boncompagni Ludovisi collection that for years was accessible only to scholars. Now, world-famous pieces such as the magnificent **Ludovisi throne** depicting the birth of Aphrodite, the breathtaking **Grande Ludovisi Sarcophagus** with its violent battles between Roman and barbarian soldiers, the tragically moving "Gaul Committing Suicide," and the inspiring, noble "Ares," the latter restored by Bernini, are all displayed here. In the 16th and 17th centuries, restoration meant reconstructing the missing parts, and the Altemps

Palazzo Altemps

⚠ Map pp. 142–143

✉ Piazza Sant'Apollinare 44

☎ 06 3996 7700

🕐 Closed Mon.

$ $$. Audio guide: $ Tours in Italian on Sun. Tours in English on request: $$$$$

🚌 Bus: C3, 30, 70, 81, 87, 116, 280, 492, 628

Caravaggio's dramatic realism and strong chiaroscuro effects are amply displayed in "The Martyrdom of St. Matthew."

San Luigi dei Francesi

COMPLETED IN 1589, THE CHURCH HAS A RENAISSANCE facade attributed to Giacomo della Porta, but the statues date from the 18th century. Dedicated to Louis IX, the French king who was later made a saint, this is the French national church and you will see that the stone dragons decorating the first story bear the fleur-de-lis.

The interior is somewhat overwhelming, a profusion of marble decoration and monuments. The star attraction, however, is the Contarelli Chapel with its three Caravaggio paintings, all scenes from the life of St. Matthew and masterpieces of dramatic composition, chiaroscuro, and realism. The dramatic content in the "Vocation of St. Matthew," in which Jesus points at Matthew, the indirect lighting from the right, and the incredulous expression on the saint's face are alone enough to rank Caravaggio among the world's great artists. Domenichino's "Scenes from the Life of St. Cecilia" are in the second chapel on the right. ■

San Luigi dei Francesi

🗺 Map pp. 142–143

✉ Piazza San Luigi dei Francesi 5

☎ 06 688271

🕐 Closed 12:30–3:30 p.m. & Thurs. p.m.

🚌 Bus: C3, 30, 46, 62, 64, 70, 81, 87, 116, 280, 492, 628

Caravaggio

His real name was Michelangelo Merisi, and at his birth in September 1573, in the tiny northern town of Caravaggio, no one could have imagined the heights of talent and the depths of torment that his life would encompass. Trained in Milan, far from the centers of classical Renaissance art like Florence, Rome, and Venice, he was to bring to his paintings an extraordinary mix of realism and dramatic lighting. Only 17 when he arrived in Rome, his lifestyle soon took on the characteristics—dissoluteness, drunkenness, and disorderly conduct—that were to bring about his downfall: scrapes with the law, murder (albeit unintentional), impoverishment, illness, and, at only 37, death. The artist was not loved by everyone. For example, the priests of San Luigi rejected his first version of "St. Matthew and the Angel," labelling its extreme realism "disrespectful." For his time, Caravaggio's work was truly revolutionary. He was one of the first to use to its maximum effect the chiaroscuro technique (the use of light and dark). His masterly use of this dramatic method, the wealth of detail, and his ability to depict humanity with all of its defects and frailty (even when painting subjects from scripture) were exceptional. His works can be found in Sant'Agostino and Santa Maria del Popolo as well as in most of the major Rome museums. ■

Sant'Agostino

A wide flight of stairs and an imposing Renaissance facade, possibly one of the earliest in Rome, are your introduction to the church of St. Augustine. Completed in 1483 (but the main altar was refashioned in the 1600s to Bernini's design), this church has several major artworks. Raphael's magnificent fresco of the "Prophet Isaiah" is on the third pilaster on the left, against which stands a lovely sculpture group ("St. Anne, the Virgin and Child," 1512) by Andrea Sansovino. The first chapel on the left houses Caravaggio's remarkable "Madonna dei Pellegrini," highly controversial at the time (1605) because its pilgrims were depicted realistically, that is as old and poor. To the right of the main portal is Jacopo Sansovino's statue, the "Madonna del Parto" (*parto* in Italian means "childbirth") with unusual Junoesque proportions. ■

Sant'Agostino

🅰 Map pp. 142–143
✉ Piazza di Sant'Agostino
☎ 06 6880 1962
🕐 Closed noon–4 p.m.
🚍 Bus: C3, 30, 70, 81, 87, 116, 280, 492, 628

Although it contains several sculptures and paintings that celebrate motherhood, this church was also favored by Renaissance courtesans.

Sant'Ivo alla Sapienza

Named for the patron saint of lawyers, Sant'Ivo is located inside the Palazzo della Sapienza (*sapienza* means "knowledge" in Latin), today the National Archives. Until 1935, this was the site of Rome's La Sapienza University, founded by Boniface VIII in 1303. Many artists were commissioned to work on the structure by a variety of popes, as can be seen from the papal insignias in the courtyard (eagles and dragons for the Borghese family, bees for the Barberini). The 17th-century church was designed by the temperamental Francesco Borromini and is an architectural play of fantasy and mystery with Gothic overtones. The courtyard

and facade, of which the lower portion is concave, were designed by Giacomo della Porta. The convex curves of the cupola culminate in a spiral pinnacle. Inside, the church is all whiteness, again an unusual composition of alternating convex and concave forms.

Outside, around the corner to the right, is a small **fountain:** Books on a shelf with a deer's antlered head and a cross, illustrate the symbol of this neighborhood called Sant'Eustacchio after Eustace, a martyred Roman soldier. He converted to Christianity after suddenly seeing a cross between the horns of a deer he was hunting and was about to kill. ■

Sant'Ivo alla Sapienza

🅰 Map pp. 142–143
✉ Corso Rinascimento 40
☎ 06 686 4987
🕐 Courtyard open daily. Interior open Sun. 9 a.m.–noon.
🚍 Bus: C3, 30, 46, 62, 64, 70, 81, 87, 116, 280, 492, 628

Medieval mystery & Renaissance riches walk

In Roman times, the vast area of the Campo Marzio was given over to army encampments, stadiums, and pleasure porticoes. It's mostly all gone or buried now, but many of the medieval and Renaissance buildings which came later remain, bearing witness to the intrigues and riches of a not-so-distant past.

This walk starts just north of Piazza Navona at **Piazza di Tor Sanguigna,** where you can still see a piece of the past: Below the railing is a chunk of the first-century foundations of **Domitian's Stadium.** Behind you is the medieval tower that gave its name to the piazza. On your left, near the lovely 17th-century wall *aedicola* (shrine) at No. 2, is the start of **Via dei Coronari,** where souvenir vendors once sold *corone* (rosary beads) to Catholic pilgrims. Today it is filled with wonderful (and expensive) antiques stores. The side streets offer intriguing views. Down the Vicolo del Volpe, on your left, is the colorful tiled spire of

A view of what was originally Hadrian's Mausoleum. The angel on the top gave the castle its name, Castel Sant'Angelo.

Santa Maria dell'Anima. On your right, the Vicolo di San Trifone is a really tight fit. Further on is **Piazza di San Salvatore in Lauro ❶,** with the church of the same name. Here you'll want to see the church's beautiful double *chiostro* (cloister).

Now return to Via dei Coronari and walk on (away from Piazza di Tor Sanguigna) until you get to Via di Panico, where you turn right. At No. 40 note the small marble relief on the wall, a stonecutter's shingle. At the end of the street, carefully cross the Lungotevere river road (Lungotevere Tor di Nona) to the onset of **Ponte Sant'Angelo ❷,** from which the view of Castel Sant'Angelo and St. Peter's dome is breathtaking. The bridge is magnificently decorated with monumental Bernini-designed statues, each holding a symbol (a crown of thorns, a whip, a nail) of the Crucifixion.

Crossing back over the Lungotevere Tor di Nona, this time take the Via del Banco di Santo Spirito, the middle street (note the columns of a medieval portico embedded in the corner building) of the three that fan out from what was formerly called Piazza del Ponte, where public executions were once held. Just after the church on your left, there is a dark, medieval passage on the other side of the street, the **Arco dei Banchi,** where an ancient inscription marks the height of the flood waters of 1277. At the Banco di Santo Spirito at No. 3, the road forks. Take the picturesque Via dei Banchi Nuovi on your left to **Piazza dell'Orologio ❸,** named for the large clock on the tower. On the left, take Vicolo degli Orsini, and at the end, sneak a peek at the lush, green inner courtyard of a baronial palace built by the Orsinis. Backtrack to the piazza and continue along the same street (now called Via del Governo Vecchio) to Via della Chiesa Nuova. Turn right here, and right again at the end, and you'll find yourself in front of the late Renaissance church that Romans call the **Chiesa Nuova** ❹ (officially, Santa Maria della Vallicella). Stand near the statue (dedicated to Metastasio) for a better view of the church and the interesting Borromini facade of the **Oratorio dei Filippini** on the left. This has a curious porticoed courtyard and, upstairs on the top floor, a charming if somewhat musty library (the Biblioteca Vallicelliana) designed by Borromini in 1637. The church, which has a ceiling fresco by Pietro da Cortona, has three Rubens paintings over the main altar. Leaving by the side door, return to Via del Governo Vecchio and proceed to **Piazza di Pasquino** ❺, with its "talking" statue (see p. 145). The statue stands against the back wall of Palazzo Braschi, seat of the recently reopened **Museo di Roma.**

Follow the street on the left, Via di Santa Maria dell'Anima, to **Tor Millina,** a medieval

tower. Turn left here and walk a block until you find yourself at the beginning of Via della Pace and, facing you, Pietro da Cortona's spectacularly dramatic facade of the church of **Santa Maria della Pace.** The piazza here has some interesting cafés. ∎

> 🗺 Also see area map, pp. 142–143
> ▶ Piazza di Tor Sanguigna
> ↔ 1 mile (1.5 km)
> 🕐 1.5–2 hours
> ▶ Piazza Santa Maria della Pace

NOT TO BE MISSED
- Domitian's Stadium
- San Salvatore in Lauro
- View from Ponte Sant'Angelo
- Chiesa Nuova
- Oratorio dei Filippini

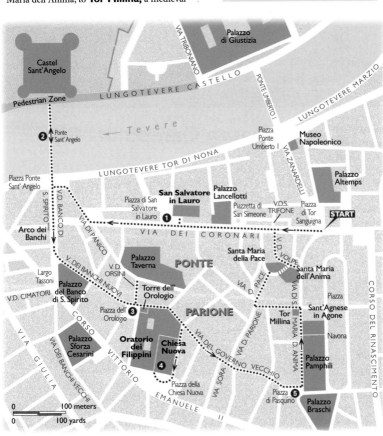

Piazza Campo dei Fiori

ONE OF THE LIVELIEST AND MOST COLORFUL SPOTS IN THE city, Piazza Campo dei Fiori has been an outdoor marketplace since 1869, when the market at the Piazza Navona was closed (its name means "field of flowers"). Morning market stalls Monday through Saturday are stacked high with fresh produce, fish, and flowers, the air filled with vendors' cries. Come evening, young Italians and foreigners alike fill the square's inexpensive trattorias, while bustling wine bars and pubs stay open late into the night.

Piazza Campo dei Fiori

Map pp. 142–143

Bus: C3, 46, 62, 64, 70, 81, 87, 116, 492, 628

Campo dei Fiori is one of the few important squares not linked to a particular patrician family or an important edifice. The only building of note is the **Palazzo Pio Righetti,** at its southeastern end, built over the ruins of Pompey's Theatre. As is true of the rest of the Campo Marzio area, Campo dei Fiori became increasingly central

following the Holy See's decision in the 14th century to set up residence in the Vatican. The square was, after all, directly on the Via Papalis (gone today) and the Via del Pellegrino, the pedestrian routes for pilgrims arriving from the city's south side.

After Pope Sixtus IV built his bridge over the Tiber (Ponte Sisto)

for the 1475 Holy Year, this piazza became a transit point for anyone coming from Trastevere. Not surprisingly, until the 17th century, when most such activity moved to the Spanish Steps area, it was the center of a flourishing tourist trade. Indeed, the Albergo del Sole, just around the corner on Via del Biscione, is reputedly the oldest hotel in Rome. Number 13 on the corner of the Via dei Cappellari and Vicolo del Gallo was an inn, La Vacca, run by Vanozza Cattanei, a grande dame who for a time was the mistress of Rodrigo Borgia (the future Pope Alexander VI), and mother of the lovely, but infamous Lucrezia.

In the past, the piazza's large, open space was well suited to all sorts of games and processions—not to mention, public executions. The heretic Giordano Bruno was burned at the stake by the Inquisition in 1600; his statue stands in the center of the square on the very spot. ∎

Right: Campo dei Fiori straddles two of Rome's *rioni* (neighborhoods), Regola and Parione. See the wall plaques marking their borders at Nos. 14 and 30.

Street names

In medieval and Renaissance times, artisans tended to set up their shops in clusters, a practice often imposed by law as well as by convenience, and many of the streets in this central area of old Rome took (and kept) their names from the tradesmen who worked there. Thus we have Via dei Cappellari, the street of the hatmakers, which starts at the northwest corner of Campo dei Fiori; Via dei Baullari, the street of the trunkmakers, which leads toward Piazza Navona; and Via dei Giubbonari, the street of jacket- or jerkinmakers, which runs toward via Arenula and the Ghetto. Other examples are Via dei Chiavari, the street of the locksmiths; Via dei Sediari, the street of the chairmakers; and Via dei Balestrari, the street of the crossbowmakers. On Via dei Coronari, artisans specialized in the making of rosaries; the Cestari and the Canestrari made baskets; the Funari made ropes; the Staderari weighed things; and, on Vicolo del Bollo, jewelers brought gold or silver to be hallmarked. A small dictionary will help you get a better idea of the historical context. Thus, Piazza del Fico is named after its centuries-old fig tree, Via del Governo Vecchio after the large building that was once the seat of government, while Via dei Soldati, near Piazza Navona, was on a military patrol route. ∎

Piazza Farnese

PALAZZO FARNESE IS WIDELY CONSIDERED TO BE THE most beautiful Renaissance building in Rome, if not in Italy, and the imposing structure cannot be separated from the lovely piazza in which it stands. Begun in 1514 by Alessandro Farnese (the future Pope Paul III), the palazzo's magnificent proportions are the work of some of the major architects of the time, including Antonio Sangallo, Michelangelo, who designed the cornice and the loggia on the facade, and Giacomo della Porta.

The interior was also decorated by the best artists of the era, such as Annibale and Agostino Caracci, Domenichino, and Lanfranco—but most of the artwork is inaccessible since the building houses the French Embassy and is not open to the public. However, the fleurs-de-lis seen everywhere on the exterior and on the fountains have nothing to do with France. These are the Farnese lilies, the symbol of that noble Roman family.

During the Renaissance a piazza was always considered an integral part of any aristocratic residence, and this one was adorned with granite basins from the Baths of Caracalla. It seems to be among the very few in the city not designed by Giacomo della Porta. Della Porta is instead credited with the back facade of the palace, that facing the garden and the river. A project, attributed to Michelangelo, to link the palazzo to property on the Trastevere side of the river with an overhead bridge, was never completed. The only part of the project realized is the lovely arch that romantically spans the Via Giulia. The church of **Santa Brigida** to the left of the palace is the Swedish National Church. The convent next door is where St. Bridget died in 1373. ■

Above: The Caracci Gallery, decorated with mythological love scenes like that of "Jupiter and Juno," was to exert a tremendous influence on 17th-century painting.

Left: Along with the basins, the Farnese pope, Paul III, also removed statues from Caracalla.

Piazza Farnese

⬛ Map pp. 142–143

🚌 Bus: C3, 23, 46, 62, 63, 64, 70, 81, 87, 116, 280, 492, 628

Casa di Santa Brigida

⬛ Map pp. 142–143

✉ Piazza Farnese 96

☎ 06 6889 2596 or 06 689 2497

🕐 Closed 1–4 p.m.; ring bell for access

Right: Bernini's preference for indirect lighting is showcased in the "Blessed Ludovica Albertoni."

"Ecstasies"

The relatively small marble wall relief in the **Casa di Santa Brigida** showing St. Bridget's ecstatic face after a mystical communication with God was probably inspired by Bernini. But it cannot be compared to the Maestro's work. The marble rendering of the ecstasy of the "Blessed Ludovica Albertoni" in **San Francesco a Ripa** (see p. 196) is magnificent. As for the breathtaking and dramatically baroque "The Ecstasy of St. Teresa" in **Santa Maria della Vittoria** (see p. 90), it led one 19th-century traveler to quip, "If that's celestial ecstasy, I've experienced it, too." ■

Among popes & princes walk

This walk will let you feast your eyes on a wealth of Renaissance and baroque detail. Unlike other areas of Rome, the Campo Marzio area is remarkably homogeneous. This is because most construction here took place only after the popes returned from exile in Avignon in 1377 and decided to set up house in the Vatican, setting off a new period of urban development in the area.

An ivy-draped arch over the Via Giulia is the only trace of an unrealized project to link Farnese properties on both sides of the Tiber.

Facing the Palazzo Farnese with its newly restored splendid facade, take Via di Monserrato on the right. Though tiny, the first square you come to, Piazza Santa Caterina della Rota, has three churches. The cream-colored **San Girolamo della Carita** ❶ on your left (1650–1660) is a must. The Spada Chapel, to the left of the entrance, has opulent polychromatic marble decor created by Francesco Borromini. Note the drapery between the two kneeling angels; it looks like cloth but it is marble.

Continue along Via di Monserrato and you'll find yourself at Piazza dei Ricci with its *palazzo istoriato* (painted building)—the L-shaped, 16th-century **Palazzo Ricci** ❷. Continuing on, at the juncture of Monserrato and Via del Pellegrino, where **Via dei**

Banchi Vecchi ❸ begins, don't miss the marble plaque, inscribed in Latin, on No. 145. This marks the perimeter of an ancient Roman neighborhood and dates from the reign of Emperor Claudius (A.D. 41–54). Via dei Banchi Vecchi has charming little shops selling antiques and bric-a-brac. Peek into the old pharmacy at No. 24 (red lanterns hang outside above the door), then cross the street to look at its facade. You'll see why the building is called the **Palazzo dei Pupazzi** (puppets). At No. 118 you'll see the imposing *portone* to the **Palazzo Sforza Cesarini,** originally built by the infamous 15th-century Borgia pope, Alessandro VI.

Continuing on, you will come to Via dei Cimatori, which leads to the most beautiful street in Rome—the Via Giulia—built by Pope Julius II in the early 16th century to provide a better link to the Vatican. To the right is the church of the Florentine residents of Rome, **San Giovanni dei Fiorentini.** Now turn left on **Via Giulia** ❹ where you'll pass some of the most beautiful Renaissance palaces in the city. At No. 85, note the inscription "*Raf Sanzio*" (for Raphael, the painter) above the second-floor balcony. In Renaissance times many famous architects lived right next door to their patrician clients. The travertine "sofas" on the building at No. 62 were part of the grandiose courthouse (Palazzo dei Tribunali) begun by Bramante for Julius II but never completed. Just past the ivy-clad overhead arch is the rear facade of **Palazzo Farnese.** After the arch, you can't miss the striking Mascherone fountain, incorporating a giant marble mask of ancient Roman origin.

Before getting to Ponte Sisto, turn left on to the Vicolo del Polverone. Number 15B is the entrance to the **Galleria Spada** ❺ (*tel 06 687 4896, closed Mon.*), which contains paintings by Rubens, Titian, Guido Reni, Andrea del Sarto, and others, but the palazzo is equally interesting. From the central courtyard you can look at Borromini's famous trompe l'oeil perspective; the optical illusion created by this genius of the baroque makes a tiny statue at the end of a short, 30-foot (9 m) corridor appear to be a colossus at the end of a long and imposing hallway.

After visiting the gallery, continue up the Vicolo del Polverone to the Piazza Capo di Ferro to see the main facade of **Palazzo Spada** with its magnificent stucco decorations, including statues of Caesar, Augustus, and Trajan. From here walk down the Via dei Balestrari, skirt the end of Piazza Campo dei Fiori, and bear right to the Piazza del Biscione. Venture through the iron gate at the far end and down the covered passageway (Passetto del Biscione). You are now on the **Via di Grotta Pinta** ❻. See how the street forms a curve to the right? The buildings are constructed over the bleachers of what was Pompey's Theater

(Teatro di Pompeo), the probable site of Julius Caesar's assassination on March 15, 44 B.C. Now heading left, cross the Largo del Pallaro and follow Via dei Chiavari to Corso Vittorio Emanuele II. The large church on your right is **Sant'Andrea della Valle** (see p. 158), setting of the first act of Puccini's *Tosca*. ■

🗺 Also see area map, pp. 142–143
▶ Piazza Farnese
🔄 1.5 miles (2.5 km)
🕐 2.5–3 hours
▶ Sant'Andrea della Valle

NOT TO BE MISSED
- San Girolamo della Carita
- Via Giulia
- Galleria Spada
- Sant'Andrea della Valle

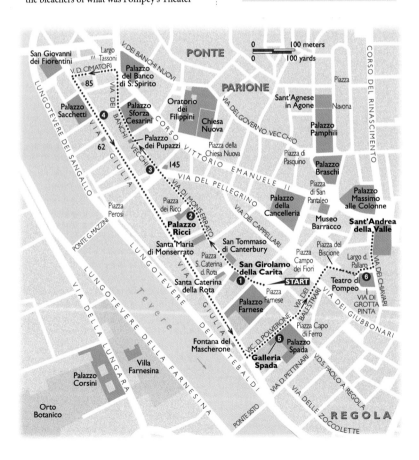

More places to visit

MUSEO BARRACCO

This little-known but delightful museum is commonly called La Piccola Farnesina, despite the lack of connection with Palazzo Farnese. The misunderstanding derives from the fact that its builders, a French noble family named Le Roys, were allowed to use the royal fleur-de-lis in their coat of arms. Built in 1523, probably by Antonio Sangallo the Younger, it has been altered several times. Currently the property of the Rome city government, it now houses the Barracco collection of ancient artwork, primarily sculptures—Egyptian, Greek, Assyrian, Etruscan, and Roman—donated to the city in 1902. It is built over Roman ruins (often accessible to the public) dating from the late empire. ◪ Map pp. 142–143 ✉ Corso Vittorio Emanuele II 168 ☎ 06 6880 6848 or 06 687 5657 ⏱ Closed for restoration; expected to reopen 2006 ⑤ $ 🚌 Bus: C3, 40, 46, 63, 64, 70, 81, 87, 116, 492, 628

PALAZZO DELLA CANCELLERIA

Completed in 1517, this palazzo ranks as one of the finest Renaissance buildings in the city, and its history is intimately linked to that of Roman nobility. It was paid for with the 60,000 scudi that Raffaele Riario, a nephew of Pope Sixtus IV, received from Franceschetto Cibo, the nephew of Pope Innocent VIII as payment for a gambling debt. The stone roses on the facade and in the courtyard (walls and pavement) were the heraldic symbol of the Riario family. Today, it is owned by the Vatican, which at one time used it as a chancellery (hence the name) and enjoys extraterritorial status. Bramante did some work on the palazzo, and you should not miss its marvelous *cortile* (courtyard) with its impressive two-story double loggia.

The **Sala dei 100 Giorni,** the Hundred Days Room upstairs, where concerts are sometimes held, was frescoed by Giorgio Vasari depicting scenes from the life of Pope Paul III, a Farnese. The name comes from Vasari's claim to have painted the room in 100 days and Michelangelo's reported riposte, "*Si vede bene*" ("You can tell"). This is the same Vasari who eventually gained fame with his written biographies (*Lives of the Artists*) of the most important painters of the day. Incorporated into the palazzo on the right is the church of **San Lorenzo in Damaso.** Take note of the columns in the courtyard, some of which were taken from a preexisting fourth-century church. ◪ Map pp. 142–143 **San Lorenzo in Damaso** ✉ Piazza della Cancelleria 1 ☎ 06 6889 1661 ⏱ Closed 12–4:30 p.m. 🚌 Bus: C3, 40, 46, 63, 64, 70, 81, 87, 116, 492, 628

SANT'ANDREA DELLA VALLE

Similar in style to the Jesuit church of Il Gesù (see p. 137), Sant'Andrea della Valle was designed by Giacomo della Porta. But the facade and the dome—the largest in Rome, except of course for St. Peter's—are fundamentally the work of Carlo Maderno, although the travertine facade was added in the 1650s by Carlo Rainaldi. You might want to note the single angel that graces the top of the facade. One story goes that there were supposed to be two of them but the sculptor, irritated by criticisms, told his episcopal patron to "do it himself."

The interior decor is sumptuous. The magnificent dome fresco, the "Glory of Paradise," was done by Lanfranco while his archrival Domenichino only got to paint (brilliantly) the pendentives. Domenchino also did the scenes from the Life of St. Andrew in the upper portion of the apse. Two popes of the Piccolomini family are buried here. The lovely Strozzi chapel is in the Michelangelo style. The Barberini chapel, the first on the left, corresponds to the chapel Puccini chose as the setting for the first act of *Tosca*. It was here that Tosca accused her lover, Cavaradossi, of betrayal when she noticed that the Mary Magdalen he was painting strongly resembled another woman. ◪ Map pp. 142–143 ✉ Piazza Vidoni 6 ☎ 06 686 1339 ⏱ Closed 12–4:30 p.m. 🚌 Bus: C3, 40, 46, 63, 64, 70, 81, 87, 116, 492, 628. ■

The Vatican is the world's smallest independent state, but its importance is immense. The historical seat of Roman Catholicism, it is, with St. Peter's and the Vatican Museums, the repository of some of mankind's major artistic treasures.

Vaticano

Detail from Michelangelo's ceiling fresco of the "Creation" in the Sistine Chapel

Vaticano

ST. PETER'S IS THE CENTER OF ROMAN CATHOLICISM, THE CHURCH BUILT over the tomb of Peter, the Apostle to whom Jesus said, "You are Peter and on this rock I will build my church." This enormous basilica is the largest of Christianity and, with the massive dome created by Michelangelo, is known throughout the world. Built in the 16th century to replace an older church founded by Constantine, St. Peter's contains priceless monuments including Michelangelo's "Pietà" and Bernini's bronze canopy over the altar. However, it represents only the external face of the Vatican, the world's smallest independent city-state. Despite its minuscule geographical dimensions, the Vatican wields immense power and influence, although no longer that of the traditional, temporal sort. "How many battalions does the pope have?" Stalin once asked scornfully.

Behind its walls, built to keep out marauding Saracens, is a miniature urban tapestry. The Vatican has its own post office and stamps, a judicial system, a pharmacy, a gas station, a railway station, a commissary, a television station, and its own special police force, the Swiss Guards corps, which dates back to 1505. It publishes a daily newspaper, the influential *Osservatore Romano*, and beams out daily radio broadcasts in over a dozen languages. The Church once ruled much of Italy; but the Papal States were conquered by Piedmontese troops between 1860 and 1870. As a result the pope did not leave the Vatican for almost 50 years, but in 1929 peace was made with Italy through the signing of the Concordat.

The popes have lived in the Vatican since the end of the 14th

century when they returned from exile in Avignon and found the Lateran Palace (see p. 79) in ruins. Settlement of the Vatican plain (Ager Vaticanus) occurred more slowly than it did on the left bank of the Tiber and was spurred on largely by the presence of St. Peter's shrine. But the papal move to the Vatican accelerated this trend, and the 15th and 16th centuries saw a rash of construction on what was called the Mons Vaticanus. The

Entrance to
Vatican
Museums

VATICANO

VIALE

Museo Gregoriano
Profano

Museo Pio
Cristiano

Pinacotea

Vestibolo dei
Quattro Cancelli

Galleria
degli Arazzi

GIARDINI

Casina
di Pio IV

Biblioteca
Vaticana

Galleria
delle Carte
Geografiche

VATICANI

VIALE VATICANO

VATICANI

Governatorato

Capella
Sistina

Basilica di
San Pietro

German
Cemetery

Aula della
Udienze

Museo Pio-
Clementino

VIA LEONE IV

Museo Egizio,
Museo Etrusco
Galleria dei
Candelabri

Museo
Chiaramonti

PIAZZA DEL
RISORGIMENTO

Cortile
della Pigna

Palazzi
e Musei
Vaticani

Stanze di
Raffaello

VIA DEL MASCHERINO

PIAZZA
CITTÀ
LEONINA

VIA DEL

Obelisco

PIAZZA
SAN
PIETRO

PIAZZA
PIO XII

PIAZZA
DEL
S. UFFIZIO

V.D. PTA. CAVALLEGGERI

GALLERIA PRINCIPE
AMEDEO SAVOIA AOST

0   250 yards
0   250 meters

result was a somewhat labyrinthine complex of interconnected palaces that grew up around St. Peter's in a largely disordered fashion. In the mid-1400s, Nicholas V (1447–1455) enlarged and beautified earlier structures, and his successors were to follow suit. Sixtus IV, for example, built the chapel that bears his name (the Cappella Sistina), Alexander VI (1492–1503) built a tower over that (the Torre del Borgia), and Julius II (1503–1513) arranged for Bramante, Raphael's mentor, to construct the new St. Peter's.

Outside, in the surrounding area, is the Borgo neighborhood, flanked by the remains of the ninth-century Leonine Wall, a portion of which connects the Vatican to Castel Sant' Angelo, first a mausoleum for a Roman emperor, later a fortress and, when necessary, a refuge for the popes. In the 1930s Mussolini gave Pope Pius XI (1922–1939) permission to connect the two by another means, the broad Via della Conciliazione (reconciliation). This made St. Peter's ever more visible but in the process destroyed an ancient neighborhood.

Much of the Vatican today is occupied by the Musei Vaticani or Vatican Museums, which along with the Sistine Chapel and the Rooms of Raphael include the Museo Pio-Clementino, the Pinacoteca, and the Gregorian Profane, the Egyptian, and the Etruscan museums. The

The number of cardinals may vary, but only those under 80 can be members of the conclave that elects a new pope.

entrance is well around the back of Vatican City—beyond Piazza del Risorgimento—on winding Viale Vaticano. To the right of St. Peter's, instead, is the Apostolic Palace with Bernini's Portone di Bronzo, the Papal Apartments (the Pope appears in a window every Sunday when he is in residence to bless the faithful), and the offices of the Secretariat of State (the foreign ministry). It is from here that the pontiff rules his largely (but not entirely) spiritual empire. ■

Basilica di San Pietro

NOBODY KNOWS EXACTLY IN WHAT YEAR PETER CAME TO Rome, other than that it was after A.D. 50. And no one knows the exact year of his martyrdom, only that he was crucified in an Imperial Circus near the Vatican during Nero's persecutions and therefore sometime between A.D. 64 and 67. What we do know is that from early on his gravesite assumed a particular importance for the members of the then recently born Christian sect.

Basilica di San Pietro

- ⚦ Map pp. 160–161
- ✉ Piazza di San Pietro
- ☎ 06 6988 1662
- 🕐 Open daily
- 🚍 Bus: 23, 34, 40, 46, 49, 62, 64, 81, 115, 116, 590, 881, 982, 990

Opposite: The present St. Peter's stands on the site of an earlier fourth-century church, built by the Emperor Constantine over the apostle's grave.

Eager to help (and perhaps to be helped by) the growing religion, in the early fourth century Emperor Constantine laid the foundations for the first St. Peter's. Consecrated by Pope Sylvester I on November 18, A.D. 326, it had a spacious atrium and was elaborately decorated. However, when the popes returned from Avignon, opting for the Vatican over the aging Lateran Palace, they found that the old church had deteriorated and risked collapse. Exactly 1,300 years later to the day (November 18, 1626), a new St. Peter's would open its doors, but its birth was to be slow and painful. Shortly after his reign began, Julius II (1503–1513) commissioned Bramante to build a new church, and in 1506 the foundation stone was laid. But 120 more years were to pass before this massive construction, built over Peter's tomb and known throughout the world, would actually be completed.

Who built St. Peter's? Over the decades, just about everybody. And the fact that so many cooks did not spoil the broth can be considered a minor miracle in itself. The first problem was whether to use a Greek cross (four arms of equal length) or a Latin cross (a long vertical arm and a shorter crossbar towards one end, like the crucifix) as the basic plan. "Greek" said Bramante, who wanted a church similar to Santa Sophia in Constantinople. "Latin" said

Raphael. "Greek" said Baldassare Peruzzi. "Latin" said Antonio Sangallo the Younger. Michelangelo, who joined the fray in 1546 but only (only!) had time to conceive the giant dome that dominates much of the Roman skyline, was also in favor of the Greek cross plan. In the end, decades later, it was Pope Paul V (1605–1621) who finally made the decision, deciding in favor of the Latin cross and, in 1607, awarding the commission to architect Carlo Maderno.

At that time the Catholic Church was fully caught up in the Counter-Reformation, and Paul wanted the church to be at least as big as its predecessor and, for liturgical reasons, to have an even longer nave (615 feet/187 m) to heighten the importance of ritual, making processions and other rites more dramatic. Alas, this meant that Michelangelo's dome was not to be immediately visible to the entering faithful as originally planned. When completed, the dome designed by the 71-year-old maestro was also higher and more elaborately decorated than he had intended. Nevertheless, his mark on the church's structure, including the massive pilasters and the magnificent windows, is indelible.

In contrast, there is no doubt about who created **Piazza di San Pietro** (St. Peter's Square). With its elliptical shape and its two semicircular colonnades, Gian Lorenzo

The newly-restored travertine **facade**—white and ocher, with red and green accents on the Loggia della Benedizione—was also the work of Carlo Maderno and has become an internationally known landmark, although back then not everyone was pleased with the wide (360 foot/110 m), two-story facade: the French painter Henri Matisse once said it looked more like a train station than a church. There are five entrances into the portico (and another five doors into the church). The central loggia is used when the pope delivers his *Urbi et Orbi* ("To the city and to the world") blessing on Christmas and Easter as well as for the "*habemus Papem*" announcement after a successful papal election. Inside the **portico,** where Maderno's stuccoed ceiling has now been gloriously restored, note the two equestrian statues: "Constantine" (by Bernini) at the extreme right and "Charlemagne" (1725) on the extreme left; they represented the temporal power of

Pope Sixtus V moved the ancient Egyptian obelisk to its present place from its original position somewhat to the left of the basilica.

Bernini's design, commissioned by Pope Alexander VII Chigi (1655–1667), has been universally acclaimed as an architectural masterpiece. There are 284 gigantic Doric columns in the colonnade, 88 other pilasters, and 140 statues on top. Statues of Jesus, John the Baptist, and 11 apostles decorate the church facade. Three sets of steps, flanked by statues of St. Peter and St. Paul, lead to the entrance. In the middle of the piazza is an Egyptian obelisk (see pp. 80–81) placed there before the colonnade was created, and two fountains, one by Maderno and a copy done in 1677 by Bernini. Halfway between the obelisk and each fountain is a plain stone disk reading "Centro del Colonnato." Go stand on one and see the four rows of columns in the corresponding hemicycle miraculously line into one.

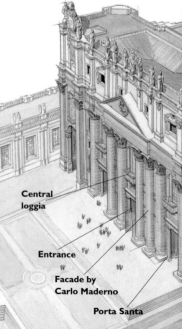

Central loggia

Entrance

Facade by Carlo Maderno

Porta Santa

the Church. Directly over the central doorway, and very difficult to see, is what is left of the famous "Navicella" mosaic ("Jesus Walking on Water") by Giotto, which once graced the atrium of the old St. Peter's built by Constantine. The "Navicella" is best seen if you stand with your back to the central bronze doors to the church itself. Also from Constantine's time, they were decorated in the 15th century by Florentine sculptor, Filarete (Antonio Averulino).

The Holy Door, or Porta Santa, opened only during Holy Years, is that on the far right. The baroque interior of St. Peter's, for which Bernini must get much of the cred-

it, is overwhelming. Stand briefly on the large porphyry circle just inside Filarete's door, where Charlemagne (and others after him) knelt when crowned emperor. Now walk straight up the center nave to the transept. The bronze strips on the floor mark the lengths of other famous, but shorter, cathedrals. Just as Bernini intended, your eyes

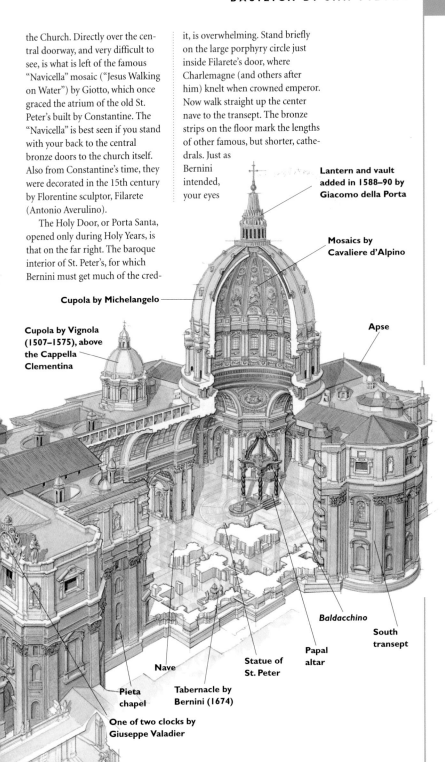

Lantern and vault added in 1588–90 by Giacomo della Porta

Mosaics by Cavaliere d'Alpino

Cupola by Michelangelo

Cupola by Vignola (1507–1575), above the Cappella Clementina

Apse

Baldacchino

South transept

Papal altar

Statue of St. Peter

Nave

Tabernacle by Bernini (1674)

Pieta chapel

One of two clocks by Giuseppe Valadier

go immediately to the enormous bronze canopy **(baldacchino)** over the papal altar, made with bronze stripped from the portico of the Pantheon. Don't miss the "Woman-in-childbirth" sequence on the columns' bases; marble reliefs depict her changing expressions and end with a smiling *bambino* (baby). The sunken *confessio* in front of the canopy, designed by Maderno, is surrounded by a balustrade with 95 perennially lit lamps and marks the tomb of St. Peter which is several levels below. Now head for the *gloria* or sunburst in the apse. This is part of a magnificent baroque monument, the **"Cattedra Petri,"** into which Bernini incorporated an early ninth-century papal throne (once thought to have been Peter's). An alabaster window with a dove (the symbol of the Holy Spirit) is in the center. Flanking this are the tombs of Pope Paul III (left) and Pope Urban VIII (right).

Naturally, you mustn't forget to look up into the **cupola,** Michelangelo's architectural masterpiece, although completed well after his death in 1564. Warmly illuminated by the light from 16 windows and, in the upper portion, divided into 16 wedges by ribs that run up to the lantern at the top where God the Father is depicted, the dome is supported by four enormous pilasters. Note the mosaic decoration in the four pendentives (the triangular spaces where the pilasters reach the dome), each representing one of the four Evangelists. Their proportions are enormous. For example, St. Mark's pen is over 5 feet long (1.5 m). The Latin inscription around the base of the dome repeats an excerpt from St. Matthew (16:18) affirming Peter's importance and that of his successors: "You are Peter and on this rock I will build my church. I will entrust to you the keys to the kingdom of Heaven."

Pope Urban VIII requested that the dome's four enormous **supporting piers** be decorated by Bernini with large *aedicolae* (niches) with oversize statues each more than 16 feet (4.8 m) tall: St. Longinus (done by Bernini, himself), St. Andrew, St. Veronica, and St. Helen. Sometimes precious relics are exhibited on the balconies above them: The lance of St. Longinus (the Roman soldier who prodded the crucified Jesus with his spear), portions of the cross brought back from the Holy Land by St. Helen, and St. Veronica's veil, said to bear the image of Jesus' face. Standing against the Longinus pier is Arnolfo di Cambio's wonderful bronze **statue of St. Peter.** Once thought to be much older, it dates from the late 1200s. Naturally, you won't want to miss Michelangelo's marble **"Pietà"** in the first chapel of the right aisle and, ever since an attack, protected by a transparent bullet-proof panel. This is Michelangelo's only signed sculpture (see his signature on the sash across the Virgin's breast).

At present, 147 popes are buried in St. Peter's and some of the **tombs** are interesting. Check out that of Alexander VII (a Chigi) in a corridor off the left transept. Rich in colored marbles and statuary, this magnificent late Bernini work (1678) shows the pope kneeling in prayer and surrounded by statues representing the virtues. But lo! From underneath the folds of patterned marble, Winged Death—with hourglass in hand—rears his ugly head. The tomb of Innocent VIII stands against a pilaster in the left aisle. It was done by Antonio del Pollaiuolo and is the only papal tomb taken directly from the old St. Peter's, other than those in the Grottoes.

Keep in mind that with only two exceptions (a ceiling fresco over the "Pietà" and a Pietro da Cortona oil in the Cappella del Santi Sacramento) all the "paintings" you see here are mosaic copies of famous paintings in other churches or in the Vatican Museums. Only three monuments in the church are dedicated to women: a queen (Queen Christina of Sweden who abdicated to convert), a countess (Countess Matilda of Tuscany) who sided with the papacy in the 11th-century conflict with the Holy Roman Emperor, and a mother (Maria Clementina Sobieski, mother of the last Stuart pretender to the English throne, the Stuarts).

Other things to see include the **Treasury Museum** (off the left transept) where for a small fee you can see magnificent church vest-ments and crucifixes, a Bernini angel and another Pollaiuolo tomb, and the **Grottoes.** Many popes are buried here, including John Paul II who took John XXIII's slot when the latter's body was put on display upstairs, and it will allow you a glimpse of St. Peter's shrine. Do not miss the **dome** or cupola. An elevator (there is a charge) from the far end of the portico is advisable to get you to the first level. A short climb from there will get you inside the dome where you can really appreciate the church's immense proportions. Another narrow, seemingly endless circular staircase will take you to the balcony atop the cupola from which the view is superb. But be sure you're up to it physically and are not claustrophobic. This closed-in staircase is one way so you can't change your mind halfway up. ■

The inscription around the base of Michelangelo's dome repeats a verse from Matthew's Gospel (16:18), the basis for the Petrine theory, the primacy of the Roman pontiffs.

Musei Vaticani

EVEN IN THE BEST OF CIRCUMSTANCES, NAVIGATION around the Vatican's museum complex is not easy. To make matters worse, the museum authorities open and close entrances throughout the day, to better regulate the heavy flow of visitors. During peak periods, try scheduling your visit later in the morning, around 11:30, if you can. This can help avoid the long lines that form when the museum opens. But be wary: Admittance stops an hour or more before closing time.

The Vatican Museums are immense, and you cannot see everything in one visit. Select the sections that interest you the most and head straight there. Do not try to absorb or read everything along the way. And remember, there is a lot of walking: about 0.3 mile (0.5 km) from the museum entrance to the Sistine Chapel alone!

Once through the brand new entrance on the Viale Vaticano, climb the few steps and take the escalators to the top. The **Pinacoteca** (painting gallery; see p. 176) is to the right. Most first-time visitors will want to head straight for the Rooms of Raphael and the Sistine Chapel. To do this, proceed left to the **Vestibolo dei Quattro Cancelli** (Vestibule of the Four Gates). Note the enormous bronze Roman *pigna,* or pinecone, in the courtyard **Cortile della Pigna,** through the door facing the other side of the *vestibolo.* Now turn left and walk up the stairs to the first landing and the **Greek Cross Room,** part of the Pio Clementine Museum (see p. 175). Don't miss the stupendous fourth-century porphyry sarcophogi; St. Helena, Constantine's mother, was buried in the one on the right, decorated with battle scenes.

Take the stairs to the second floor and walk down the long corridor, which is divided into three sections: the **Galleria dei Candelabri** (candelabras); **Galleria degli Arazzi** (tapestries); and the **Galleria delle Carte Geografiche,** which features interesting map frescoes depicting Italy's and the Church's possessions in the 1580s. From the right-side windows, you are looking at a Renaissance villa, the **Casina di**

Musei Vaticani

- Map pp. 160–161
- Viale Vaticano
- 06 6988 3041
- Open 8:45 a.m.–4:45 p.m. (March–Oct.), 8:45 a.m.–1:45 p.m. (Nov.–Feb. & every Sat.). Ticket office closes 85 minutes earlier. Closed Sun. except last Sun. a.m.
- $$$. Free last Sun. of month. Audio guide: $$. Tours ($$$) every day except Sun. Call 06 6988 4947 for reservations
- Bus: 32, 49, 81, 98, 492, 990

Pio IV, and the **Vatican Gardens.**

The Sala dell'Immacolata, at the end, leads to the Stanze di Rafaello.

STANZE DI RAFFAELLO

Raphael's Rooms (of which there are four) were commissioned by Julius II in 1508, supposedly because the existing papal apartment reminded him too much of his hated predecessor, Alexander VI (a Borgia), and his family, including daughter Lucrezia. The first two, the Stanza della Segnatura and the Stanza di Eliodoro, are considered to be examples of Raphael's greatest work. The Stanza dell'Incendio was based on Raphael's designs but was painted primarily by his assistants. The last room, the **Sala di Costantino,** was finished in 1524 after Raphael's death, and he probably only did some preliminary sketches. The underlying theme of this room, attributed largely to Giulio Romano, Francesco Penni, and Raffaellino del Colle, and told through scenes from the life of Constantine, is the triumph of Christianity over paganism.

The **Stanza della Segnatura** was Julius's library or study. The room is justly famous because among others it contains two of Raphael's best known paintings, the "Disputation of the Sacrament" and the "School of Athens," painted between 1508 and 1511 and meant to glorify respectively faith and philosophy. In the first, Jesus, the Virgin, and St. John the Baptist are flanked by figures from the Old and New Testaments—although only those from the New Testament have halos. Below is an altar with the Host and farther down you see

Above: Papal coats of arms decorate the balustrade of the monumental spiral staircase, designed in the 1930s by Giuseppe Momo.

Above left: The bronze pinecone gave its name not only to this courtyard, but to the neighborhood near the Pantheon where it was found.

Doctors of the Church, saints, and scholars. You can pick out Dante on the right in the lower section. In the "School of Athens," Plato and Aristotle are shown in animated conversation inside a large classical building. Raphael clearly enjoyed painting his contemporaries into historical tableaus, and these abound here. Raphael himself is second to last in the group of hatted gentlemen on the right. Just in front is Bramante, in the guise of Euclid who is bending over, compass in hand, to explain a problem to his students. (Bramante is also in the "Disputation of the Sacrament," leaning over the bannister, on the far

The statue of the Laocoön was found in 1506 minus its right arm, which was discovered 400 years later in a marble-worker's shop and eventually reattached (see p. 176).

left.) The pensive figure seated in the forefront, his head leaning on his left hand and taking notes, is Michelangelo (as Heraclitus, the pessimist).

The **Stanza di Eliodoro** (Heliodorus) is particularly noteworthy for the stunning use of color (note the Swiss Guards in the lower right corner of the "Mass of Bolsena," which depicts a 13th-century miracle) and for the dramatic use of lighting in "The Liberation of St. Peter." This room, originally a bedroom, was decorated between 1512 and 1514. The room also contains the "Expulsion of Heliodorus" (from the temple in Jerusalem), and "Pope Leo Meets Attila the Hun," recounting how St. Leo the Great (Pope Leo I, 440–461) turned Attila and his Huns away during an attack on Rome in the fifth century. Here, Raphael's penchant for painting his contemporaries' faces on historical figures created a problem. After Julius II died, Raphael repainted the face of St. Leo with the features of the new pope, Leo X (1513–1521). However, Leo X's features had already been painted onto one of the accompanying cardinals so he appears twice in the same scene.

The **Stanza dell'Incendio** (fire) was a dining room. Painted between 1514 and 1517 by Raphael's pupils, it depicts events from the lives of two of Leo X's namesakes (Leo III and Leo IV, the pope who built the ninth-century Vatican walls). The most famous painting shows how, in 847, Leo IV quenched a fire in the surrounding Borgo neighborhood by making the sign of the cross. Nearby is the small, private **Cappella di Niccolo V** (Chapel of Pope Nicholas V), which was frescoed by the Florentine artist Fra Angelico. Before reaching the Sistine Chapel, you might want to visit the **Borgia Apartment,** decorated

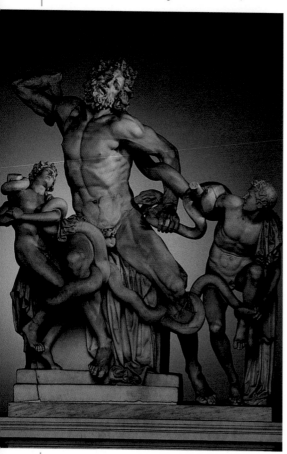

with lovely frescoes by Pinturicchio and his disciples.

CAPPELLA SISTINA

Built by Giovanni di Dolce during the reign of Sixtus IV (1471–1484), this rectangular hall has seen a lot of history. It was the private chapel of the pontiffs, and for centuries it has been the room where the conclaves, or papal elections, are held. The floor is decorated in an exquisite *"opus alexandrinum"* pattern reminiscent of the cosmatesque pavements (see p. 206) from the 13th and 14th centuries, and an elegant sculpted screen—by Mino da Fiesole, Andrea Bregno, and Giovanni Dalmata—divides the chapel into two sections.

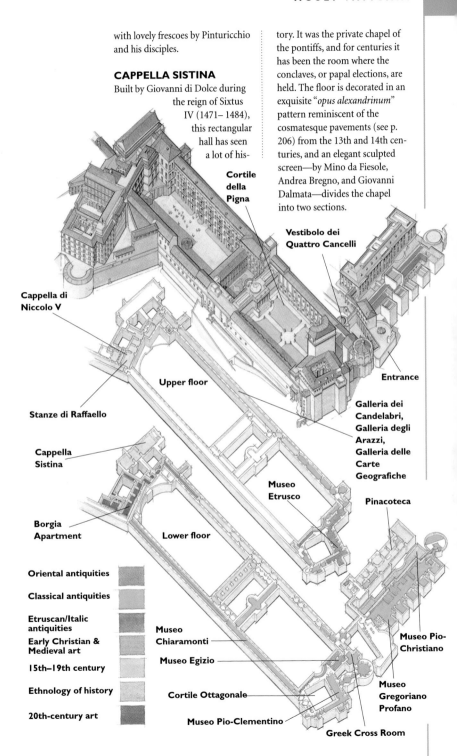

Cortile della Pigna

Vestibolo dei Quattro Cancelli

Cappella di Niccolo V

Upper floor

Entrance

Stanze di Raffaello

Galleria dei Candelabri, Galleria degli Arazzi, Galleria delle Carte Geografiche

Cappella Sistina

Museo Etrusco

Pinacoteca

Borgia Apartment

Lower floor

Oriental antiquities

Classical antiquities

Etruscan/Italic antiquities

Early Christian & Medieval art

15th–19th century

Ethnology of history

20th-century art

Museo Chiaramonti

Museo Egizio

Cortile Ottagonale

Museo Pio-Clementino

Museo Pio-Christiano

Museo Gregoriano Profano

Greek Cross Room

After 20 years of painstaking work, all the frescoes in the Sistine Chapel have been restored to their original glory.

But the room is best known for the recently restored wall and ceiling frescoes, considered by many to be the supreme example of Renaissance, if not universal, art.

The decoration of the Sistine Chapel can be divided into three periods, each coinciding with an important stage in the development of Renaissance art. The frescoes on the long walls were painted between 1481 and 1483; the ceiling was painted by Michelangelo between 1508 and 1512; and his "Last Judgment" was executed some 20 years later between 1534 and 1541.

The **long walls** were decorated by some of the most important 15th-century Renaissance painters (Pinturicchio, Botticelli, Perugino, Ghirlandaio, Rosselli, Signorelli), significantly all of Tuscan or Umbrian origin. It was a time when, under the impetus of a reinvigorated and dynamic papacy, the cultural epicenter of the Renaissance was shifting to Rome from Florence and its environs. On the left, starting from the "Last Judgment," are scenes from the Old Testament including the "Burning Bush" and "Moses Slaying Egyptians" (Botticelli), the

Opposite: The Sistine Chapel is the place where the College of Cardinals elects the successor to St. Peter's Throne after a pope dies.

"Punishment of Korah, Dathan, and Abiram" (Botticelli), and the "Last Days of Moses" by Signorelli. The scenes on the right, from the New Testament, include the "Baptism of Jesus" (Pinturicchio or Perugino), the "Temptation of Christ" (Botticelli), the "Calling of Peter and Andrew" (Domenico Ghirlandaio), and "Jesus Giving the Keys to Peter" (Perugino). On the end wall, opposite the "Last Judgment," are the "Resurrection" by Ghirlandaio and Salviati's "St. Michael," both later repainted.

Michelangelo's decoration of the **ceiling** (originally it was blue with stars on it) coincided with the mood of cultural and political self-confidence that characterized the early Renaissance. Michelangelo was not particularly keen on accepting this commission; he considered himself a sculptor, not a painter, and wanted to keep working on Julius II's tomb, the one which was never finished but did spawn the magnificent "Moses" you saw in San Pietro in Vincoli (see p. 63). When he did accept (possibly to foil his implacable rival, Bramante), he turned a simpler

The Sistine Hall, part of the extensive Vatican Library, was built between 1587 and 1589 across the great Belvedere Courtyard, thus cutting it in two.

project (the "Twelve Apostles") into the more ambitious "Creation." As everyone now knows he spent four years lying on his back on scaffolding to do it.

Michelangelo's choice of subject matter was not accidental. The cosmology of the time divided world history into various epochs: The period before the Law, the period of Law (as given to Moses), and finally the period of Grace which began with the coming of Jesus. The older decoration on the side walls corresponded to the second two eras (Law and Grace), so Michelangelo decided to dedicate the ceiling to the pre-Law era, that is to the Creation, the Garden of Eden, and original sin. The decoration is sublime and has been recognized as such since the start. Hopefully, you've brought your binoculars or

at least a decent-size mirror to view the ceiling comfortably. Remember, start your gazing from the altar end of the room. There are nine central scenes on the ceiling. Alternating in larger and smaller rectangles are: "The Separation of Light and Darkness;" "The Creation of the Sun, the Moon, and Planets;" "The Separation of Land from the Sea" and "The Creation of Plants and Animals;" "The Creation of Adam;" ""The Creation of Eve from Adam's Rib;" "The Expulsion from the Garden of Paradise;" "The Sacrifice of Noah;" "The Flood;" and "Noah Drunk."

Forming a border around them are portraits of prophets (going clockwise Jonah, Jeremiah, Ezekiel, Joel, Zecheriah, Isaiah, Daniel). Alternating with these are the oracles of the ancient world known as

sibyls (clockwise the Persian, Erythrean, Delphic, Cumaean, and Libyan Sibyls). The triangular lunettes between the sibyls and prophets contain images of the forerunners and ancestors of Jesus Christ, while the four larger corner lunettes represent Old Testament scenes. Between the prophets and sibyls and above the triangular lunettes bearing the forerunners of Jesus, we see the figures known as the "Ignudi," athletic male nudes, painted in various poses between low, trompe l'oeil pedestals.

By the time Michelangelo got around to painting **"The Last Judgment,"** commissioned by Pope Paul III (1534–1549), the mood in Rome had changed drastically to one of pessimism. The 1527 Sack of Rome had created insecurity, and the burgeoning Protestant movement was stimulating renewed religious uncertainty and fervor. In the "Last Judgment" (which got far less favorable reviews than the "Creation," with many critics crying obscenity), you can read the drama, terror, and pathos of the era. In the center of the composition is an athletic, beardless, and severe Christ in Judgment, flanked by Mary and a collection of saints. Below, on the left, are the blessed on their way to Heaven (note the two figures suspended by a rosary, a clear anti-Lutheran statement). In contrast, on the right the damned are being pushed down to Hell while Charon, in his boat, watches. Michelangelo gave Minos, the judge of the damned (the figure in the lower right-hand corner with the donkey's ears entwined in a serpent's coils), the face of one of his sharpest critics, Biagio da Cesena, a member of the papal court. And there is a self-portrait: St. Bartholomew (below and right of the Redeemer) is holding his flayed skin (recalling the method of his

Right: Roman pontiffs ruled much of central Italy until the 1860s, using seals like these on important documents.

martyrdom) but has no beard. How so? Because the face is that of the beardless Michelangelo.

MUSEO PIO-CLEMENTINO
Access to the Pio-Clementine Museum is through the ground-floor Cortile della Pigna and up the stairs to the Palazzo del Belvedere, built during the reign of Innocent VIII. This museum has a variety of sections, but the most impressive may well be that of the vast display of classical statuary in the Cortile Ottagonale. You could say that the foundations of the entire Vatican museum complex were laid right here when, in 1503, Pope Julius II placed a statue of Apollo, ever since called the **Belvedere Apollo,** in the Belvedere's courtyard. The papal collection was significantly enlarged by

Clement XIV in 1770, and the museum was opened shortly thereafter.

The list of sculptures is endless, but there are several pieces that are not to be missed, most of which are in the first several rooms. The Cabinet of Apoxyomenos, just beyond the round vestibule, houses the statue of an athlete, called the **"Apoxyomenos Athlete,"** a first-century Roman marble copy of a Lysippus bronze from about 320 B.C. An athlete in the process of scraping oil from his body, it was found in Trastevere in 1849 on the street that is named for it, the Vicolo dell'Atleta. In the Octagonal Court you'll find not only the Belvedere Apollo, but the **"Laocoön,"** possibly the most sublime classical marble group to have survived. Excavated in 1506 on the Esquiline Hill and possibly from the Domus Aurea, it is attributed to three first-century sculptors from Rhodes working from an older bronze original. It tells the story (related by Virgil in the *Aeneid*) of the Trojan priest, Laocoön, and his two sons whose warnings about the wooden horse angered Athena who sent two huge serpents to kill them. Their facial expressions convey human suffering in an unparalleled fashion. The remaining rooms include the Animal Room, the Gallery of Statues, the Gallery of Busts, the Mask Room, and the Hall of the Muses. Near the exit is a domed room with a reconstructed *biga*, or two-horse chariot.

THE PINACOTECA, THE OTHER MUSEUMS, & THE GARDENS

As you can imagine, over the centuries the popes have also built quite a collection of paintings, and these are kept in the **Pinacoteca** (to get here turn right at the top of the escalator instead of left).

Though not enormous, the collection is impressive. This, for example, is where you can see Raphael's "Transfiguration," his "Madonna di Foligno," and his "Coronation of the Virgin," all in the same room. There are also paintings by Giotto, Fra Angelico, Simone Martini, Perugino, Bellini, and Titian, to name only a few.

For more specialized interests there are the **Museo Egizio** (Egyptian Museum), the **Museo Etrusco** (Etruscan Museum), and the **Museo Gregoriano Profano** (Gregorian Profane Museum) which displays several Greek and Roman collections, arranged either by era (Roman sculpture of the first and early second centuries) or thematically (sarcophagi, Greek originals, for example). It is in this museum that you can see the famous mosaics of athletes found in the Baths of Caracalla (see pp. 210–11). The Braccio Nuovo of the **Chiaramonti Museo,** a smaller adjunct to the Pio-Clementino that was organized by the sculptor Canova in the early 19th century, also displays Roman floor mosaics. There you will also find the famous statue of Augustus from the villa of his wife, Livia, at Prima Porta. The **Museo Pio-Christiano** (Pio-Christian Museum) displays early Christian antiquities.

It is also possible to visit the 16th-century **Giardini Vaticani** (Vatican Gardens) on guided tours that last about two hours. You get to see the medieval German cemetery attached to the Teutonic College, several major fountains, and the main buildings (mostly from outside) including the new (1971) Aula delle Udienze (Audience Hall), the Governatorato (Governor's Palace), and Casina di Pio IV, today seat of the Pontifical Science Academy. ∎

Castel Sant'Angelo

THIS BUILDING HAS QUITE A HISTORY. BUILT AS A mausoleum by Emperor Hadrian (but completed after his death by his successor, Antoninus Pius), Castel Sant'Angelo has also been a fortress, a prison, a papal refuge, a barracks, a pleasure palace, and even the setting for the last act of a famous opera, *Tosca*. Like Augustus's mausoleum on the other side of the river, this circular structure with a 210-foot (64 m) diameter was once topped with trees and a large statue of the emperor or, some say, a four-horse chariot.

The mausoleum served its original function for a very short time. In the third century, Aurelian incorporated it into his walls in an attempt to protect the city from barbarian encroachment. Theodoric, the city's fifth-century barbarian ruler (clearly the walls didn't work!), was the first to use it as a prison. The castle got its name only at the end of the sixth century. The city's population was being decimated by the plague when Pope Gregory the Great decided to ask for divine intercession. As he was leading a massive procession to St. Peter's he saw the Archangel Michael above the tomb in the process of sheathing his sword, as if to say that the

scourge was over. Subsequently, a statue of the Archangel was placed atop the tomb, hence the new name, Castel Sant'Angelo. The bronze statue you see dates back to 1753, replacing an earlier stone one by Raffaele da Montelupo that is now in one of the courtyards.

Throughout the Middle Ages, the castle was often the scene of conflict between the papacy and one or other of the noble families vying for control of the city. During the famous Sack of Rome in 1527, Clement VII took refuge here, probably using the secret corridor (*il passetto*) that was built into the Leonine wall in 1277 and which can be seen on a guided tour of the castle.

The ancient Pons Adrianus in front of Castel Sant'Angelo was built in the second century A.D. to afford ready access to the Emperor Hadrian's Mausoleum.

Castel Sant'Angelo

- 🗺 Map pp. 160–161
- ✉ Lungotevere Castello 50
- ☎ 06 3996 7600 or 06 681 9111
- 🕐 Closed Mon.
- 💲 $$. Audio guide: $. Tours in English on request: $$$$$
- 🚌 Bus: 23, 34, 40, 49, 87, 280, 492, 926, 982, 990

For centuries parts of the building were used as a prison. The 16th-century Florentine goldsmith, Benvenuto Cellini, tells in his autobiography of being imprisoned here, and Puccini made it the scene for Tosca's suicide. In the 1930s it was restored and turned into a museum.

Because bits and pieces have been added on over the centuries, you'll need imagination and a discerning eye to separate the original Roman portions from the additions of later eras. In the vestibule downstairs you'll find a very useful model that shows what is left of the original structure. This, like the rooms directly above it, is in the central Roman core of the building. Walk up the long ramp—which dates back to Roman times with portions of the original mosaic flooring—until, turning left, you come to the **Cordonata di Alexander VI,** a very gradual staircase that cuts diagonally across the structure and eventually ends at the **Cortile dell'Angelo.** Along the way you will walk over a drawbridge, which until 1822 could still be pulled up to protect the upper stories of the castle from unwanted intruders. The bridge spans the funeral chamber where Hadrian's remains were originally kept.

At the top is the Cortile delle Palle, named after the cannonballs stored there (the white marble plaques on the walls indicate the diameters of the balls in each pile). This is also known as the Cortile dell'Angelo because da Montelupo's gigantic angel statue was put here after its replacement. The rooms on the left are named after the various popes who inhabited them or the subject matter of their decoration. The **Sala di Apollo** has lovely "grotesque" decoration on the walls. When you come to the **Sala di Giustizia,** once a courtroom, you will be back in the Roman part of the structure. Be sure to note the fresco of the Angel of Justice, over one of the doors, by Perin del Vaga. A corridor from the Apollo Room leads to a courtyard, called either the **Cortile del Teatro,** because theatrical performances were given there during the Renaissance, or the Cortile del Pozzo dell'Olio, because of the wellhead. Just past the entrance, a short flight of stairs (through the door on the right) will take you to **Pope Clement VII's bathroom,** complete with frescoes by Giulio Romano. The other rooms off this circular courtyard were used as **prison cells** for centuries; the ones on this floor were for VIPs, the dingy ones downstairs for ordinary prisoners.

Farther upstairs is the **Loggia of Julius II,** which overlooks the Ponte Sant'Angelo, ancient in origin but lengthened in the 19th century when the walls along the Tiber were built. Up a short flight of stairs from the loggia are the **Papal Apartments** frescoed by Perin del Vaga for Paul III (1534–1549). Note another angel frescoed on the far wall and the amusing portrait of a gentleman peering out of a trompe l'oeil door. A curving corridor, decorated with more grotesques, leads to what was once the library; here, only the upper portion of the walls was frescoed because the lower part was covered by bookcases. Through a door in the center of the wall is the **Camera del Tesoro** or dell'Archivio Segreto. Until 1870 the Vatican kept its secret archives here. This room, too, is in the central core. A narrow winding staircase excavated into the thick walls leads up to the terrace where the bronze statue of the archangel stands and where there is a spectacular view of St. Peter's and the entire city. ■

Trastevere: The other side of the Tiber is a warren of narrow streets and small squares. Under the ancient Romans this was an enclave largely inhabited by foreigners and nonconformists; it still attracts those groups as well as casual visitors.

Trastevere to Gianicolo

Detail of the ceiling of the master bedroom in Villa Farnesina

Trastevere to Gianicolo

TRASTEVERE IS WHAT THE ITALIANS CALL A VERY *POPOLARE* NEIGHBOR-hood, by which they mean one of the few still inhabited by "real" Romans. Until recently this was a working-class area and your typical *Trasteverino* would thus be lower-income, extroverted, sharp-tongued—and possibly a bit arrogant, since the residents of this area consider themselves to be the true descendants of the ancient Romans and are also proud that this was an insurrectionist hotbed during the short-lived 1849 revolt against the papacy.

No one really knows why, but the Trasteverini tend to have loud, rather hoarse voices and to speak with a very heavy Roman intonation, the equivalent—let's say—of a very thick Brooklyn accent. They drink lots of coffee, breakfast on *maritozzi* (a plain, sweet roll filled with fresh whipped cream), and favor heavy dishes such as *spaghetti cacio e pepe* (spaghetti with grated *caciotta* cheese and pepper) or *coda alla vaccinara* (oxtail in tomato sauce). They are a dwindling race, since over the last several decades many have left the area either by choice, preferring the newer, more modern apartments built in the postwar period, or forced out by gentrification and spiraling rents. But enough of them remain to allow the neighborhood to keep much of its traditional color and character.

At the same time this area—the name means trans-Tiber (across the Tiber)—also has a long history as a favorite residential area for foreigners or nonconformists. This was already the case back in ancient Roman times when many outsiders settled here, including tens of thousands of Jews. According to local parish officials, there may once have been as many as ten synagogues in the neighborhood. The first Christians, for the most part converted Jews, settled here as well, explaining the presence of several major early Christian basilicas. And the area's international flavor was certainly heightened following World War II, when many foreigners chose this area because it seemed so Roman and at the time was considerably cheaper than other central neighborhoods.

Artisans abound, as do small local shops, bars, and eateries. In fact, the trattorias of Trastevere have always been a draw for outsiders, especially on weekends or during July's Festa de'Noiantri (Our Own Festival). Nowadays, in the evenings the restaurants have been supplemented by scores of small *locali* (clubs), sometimes only a few tables or a bar counter, which appeal to young people. Many intellectuals—filmmakers, artists, and students—also live here. This, along with an abundance of street peddlers, art galleries, and boutiques, explains why Trastevere is often compared to Soho in London or New York's SoHo or Greenwich Village.

Trastevere is divided into two parts, one stretching upriver from

GALLERIA PRINCIPE AMEDEO SAVOIA AOSTA

PONTE PR. AMEDEO SAVOIA AOSTA

VIA DELLA LUNGARA

LUNGOTEVERE GIANICOLENSE

Tevere

Sant' Onofrio

VIALE

Tasso's Oak

Faro

Passeggiata

MONTE

Monumento ad Anita Garibaldi

Villa Lante

ORTO BOTANICO

delle MURA

Monumento a Giuseppe Garibaldi

PIAZZALE G. GARIBALDI

GIANICOLO

Gianicolo

AURELIE

Porta San Pancrazio

VIA GARIBALDI

PIAZZALE AURELIO

VIALE

DELLE MURA

Viale Trastevere to the Vatican and nestling on the lower slopes of Monte Gianicolo (Janiculum Hill), the other extending beyond the Viale, running by Tiber Island and including lovely Piazza in Piscinula, the church of Santa Cecilia, and, at its outer limit, Porta Portese. The heart of the neighborhood, however, is Piazza Santa Maria in Trastevere, the piazza facing the magnificent basilica of the same name and which, with its cafés and restaurants, newsstand, and pharmacy, is akin to a village square for the area's residents. Many people still shop in the outdoor market at nearby Piazza San Cosimato or buy bread on Sunday mornings at the *forno* in Via del Moro. Passing through Porta Settimiana on Via della Lungara, for centuries the only road linking Trastevere to the Vatican, you come to the Botanical Gardens, once part of the beautiful,

post-baroque Palazzo Corsini, and to Villa Farnesina, on the grounds of which archaeologists found the ruins of a splendid ancient Roman villa (rooms from it have been rebuilt in the Palazzo Massimo Museum). Above looms the Janiculum Hill, where churches such as San Pietro in Montorio and Sant'Onofrio compete for attention with the breathtaking Roman panorama. ■

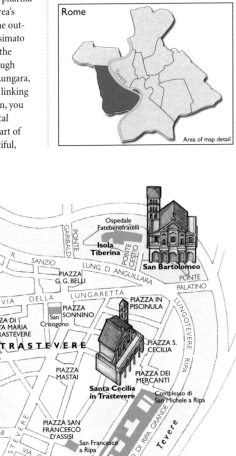

Rome

Area of map detail

Villa
Farnesina

DELLA FARNESINA
PONTE SISTO

Porta
Settimiana
VIA S.
DOROTEA   PIAZZA
TRILUSSA

Palazzo
Corsini

VIA GARIBALDI

VIA DELLA SCALA

VIA DEL MORO

PIAZZA
S. EGIDIO

Santa Maria
in Trastevere

Il Tempietto

Fontana
dell'Acqua   San Pietro in
Paola   Montorio

PIAZZA DI
SANTA MARIA
IN TRASTEVERE

San
Crisogono

PIAZZA
GARIBALDI

PONTE GARIBALDI

Ospedale
Fatebenefratelli

Isola
Tiberina

LUNG.
R.
SANZIO

LUNG. D. ANGUILLARA

PIAZZA
G. G. BELLI

VIA   DELLA   LUNGARETTA

PONTE
CESTIO

San Bartolomeo

PONTE
PALATINO

PIAZZA IN
PISCINULA

PIAZZA
SONNINO

LUNGOTEVERE   RIPA

PIAZZA S.
CECILIA

T R A S T E V E R E

VIA LUCIANO MANARA

PIAZZA DI
SAN COSIMATO

VIA G. MAMELI

VIA E. MOROSINI

VIALE

GLORIOSO

VILLA
SCIARRA

GIANICOLENSI

PIAZZA
MASTAI

Santa Cecilia
in Trastevere

PIAZZA DEI
MERCANTI

Complesso di
San Michele a Ripa

PORTO DI RIPA GRANDE

Tevere

VIA G. INDUNO

VIA G. TRASTEVERE

VIALE   DI

PIAZZA SAN
FRANCESCO
D'ASSISI

San Francesco
a Ripa

PIAZZA DI
PORTA PORTESE

PONTE
SUBLICIO

0   400 yards
0   400 meters

Santa Maria in Trastevere

EVEN MOST TRASTEVERINI DON'T KNOW IT, BUT according to St. Jerome's fourth-century chronicle, at the time of Jesus' birth Trastevere was the scene of a sort of annunciation. In a veterans' hospice, oil gushed from the ground, lasting for an entire day and flowing down to the river; a clear sign, said the saint and scholar, of "the grace of Christ that would come to humanity." Since many early Christians settled in this area, it isn't surprising that in the third century a church was founded (probably by the martyred St. Calixtus) where the miracle supposedly took place. An illegible inscription on the church floor to the right of the altar marks the spot.

Widely believed to be one of the first churches in Rome, Santa Maria in Trastevere was certainly the first to be dedicated to Mary. As we see it today, with its charming *campanile* (bell tower), the basilica—completed in the 1140s—is primarily medieval in style, and somehow the 12th-century aura has lingered, despite later additions such as Domenichino's gilded, coffered ceiling (1617) and Carlo Fontana's portico (1702) with its statues of four saints, including St. Calixtus.

The church is notable for the use of classical Roman architectural forms, which at the time were quite fashionable. The 22 columns in the nave, of various dimensions, types of stone, textures, and colors, were looted from ancient ruins. The straight trabeation (or architrave) over the columns was a throwback to classical Roman construction, a temporary rejection of the arches preferred by earlier and later architects. What truly sets Santa Maria apart are its glowingly beautiful **mosaics,** which mark a return to a tradition that had been largely discontinued. For this we can probably thank Abbot Desiderius of Monte Cassino who, toward the end of the 11th century, brought mosaic workers to Italy from Constantinople and used them, in turn, to train local artisans. In this regard, note the cosmatesque pavement (see p. 206) which, though restored in the 19th century, dates to the 1100s.

The mosaics on the facade date from the 12th or 13th centuries and show a Madonna enthroned, flanked on each side by five women, most probably the Wise and Foolish Virgins from the Gospel, although some historians believe that the work depicts a pro-

Santa Maria in Trastevere

- 🗺 Map pp. 180–181
- ✉ Piazza Santa Maria in Trastevere
- ☎ 06 581 4802 or 06 581 9443
- 🕐 Open daily
- 🚌 Bus: 23, 115, 125, 175, 280. Tram: 3, 8

Left: The 12th-century facade of the church is the major landmark of the Trastevere neighborhood and dominates the piazza of the same name.

cession of eight virgins and two widows. (It's politically incorrect, but the widows, they insist, are the women whose lamps have gone out!) Note the two tiny figures at the Madonna's feet. This was a common way to represent the donors who paid for an artwork.

The mosaics inside the church are even more exceptional. Those in the half-dome of the apse date from the 12th century and show Mary, enthroned, next to Jesus, who has his arm around his mother's shoulder. They are flanked by a collection of saints including, on the left and holding a model of the church, Pope Innocent II, the donor. The prophets Isaiah and Jeremiah are on the two sides of the apse. On the next row down is Pietro Cavallini's 13th-century mosaic of the "Life of the Virgin

Mary" in six masterful scenes. Cavallini also did the mosaic showing the "Madonna and Child between St. Peter and St. Paul" on the apse's central lower segment.

The altar canopy has four porphyry columns. The sumptuous **Altemps Chapel** on the right (designed by Martino Longhi the Elder in the 1580s) has an ornate ceiling and numerous frescoes, including one that depicts the Council of Trent (1545–1563), a major event in Roman Catholicism's response to the Protestant challenge. Also interesting are the marble fragments, embedded in the walls of the facade, bearing Christian symbols—catacomb inscriptions from the third and fourth centuries. Between the gate and the facade are four magnificent medieval floor tombs. ■

In Christian iconography, the 12 Apostles were often shown as sheep in mosaics. In the middle is the Agnus Dei, the Lamb of God or Jesus. On the ends are the holy cities of Bethlehem and Jerusalem.

A taste of Trastevere walk

This walk around Trastevere, divided into two parts, will give you a feeling for a neighborhood that boasts a vast spectrum of sights and sounds. Local artisans, housewives, Italian yuppies, American college students, and transplanted foreigners congregate here to enjoy what many people say is one of the last remaining enclaves of "the real Rome."

Trastevere's old buildings form one of the city's most picturesque old quarters.

Start at Piazza di Santa Maria in Trastevere (see p. 182) where you can enjoy a coffee at the Café De Marzio (the one locals prefer), while taking one more look at the Basilica of Santa Maria's glorious facade. Then, wearing your bags or cameras across your chest (better yet don't carry a bag, a Roman purse-snatcher can spot a tourist a mile off), exit the piazza by the newsstand and take Via della Lungaretta to Viale di Trastevere. On your right you'll see **San Crisogono ❶** (see p. 196), which has an exceptional cosmatesque pavement (see p. 206) that you don't want to miss.

Now cross (carefully) the busy avenue and proceed along the continuation of Via della Lungaretta. This will take you through a deliciously old neighborhood to charming Piazza in Piscinula where the Mattei family once had a palace. Turn right before entering the piazza at the hilly Arco dei Tolomei, which brings you under a fascinating medieval archway. Turn left at the next street (Via dei Salumi) and walk along it. Turn right on Via dei Vascellari, which soon becomes Via di Santa Cecilia and takes you to the piazza and church of the same name, **Santa Cecilia in Trastevere ❷** (see pp. 192–93), another absolute must.

After visiting the church, check out lovely **Piazza dei Mercanti** (between Piazza Santa Cecilia and the river), but avoid the restaurants there, which are for tourists only. Now continue along Via di Santa Cecilia toward Via Madonna dell'Orto. Note the long **Complesso di San Michele a Ripa** building on your left, a 17th-century poorhouse now used for governmental offices (see p. 196). **Santa Maria dell'Orto ❸**, the facade at the end of the Via Madonna dell'Orto curiously decorated with obelisks, was once the headquarters for many guilds of the more humble occupations, such as fruit vendors and chicken keepers. If it's a Tuesday or Thursday afternoon (2–4 p.m), make a brief detour right on Via Anicia and ring the bell at No. 12. The custodian will let you into the magnificent, hidden 15th-century cloister of **San Giovanni dei Genovesi ❹**. Retracing your steps, continue along Via Anicia until you come to Piazza San Francesco d'Assisi and the church of **San**

- Ⓜ Also see area map, pp. 180–181
- ► Santa Maria in Trastevere
- ↔ 1.5 miles (2.5 km)
- ⏱ 2 hours
- ► Villa Farnesina

NOT TO BE MISSED

- Santa Maria in Trastevere
- San Crisogono
- Santa Cecilia in Trastevere
- San Francesco a Ripa
- Villa Farnesina

Francesco a Ripa ⑤ (see p. 196), where one of Bernini's three "Ecstasies" is displayed. Via San Francesco a Ripa, which faces the church, will take you back to Viale di Trastevere. Cross over and at the intersection with Via Luciano Manara, look left up the street at the lovely, moss-covered fountain set against the lower slope of the Janiculum Hill. Continuing along Via San Francesco a Ripa you will come to Piazza di San Callisto and then to **Santa Maria,** where you began.

The second, and shorter, part of this walk starts from the Via della Paglia (the street opposite the newsstand) and takes you to **Piazza Sant'Egidio** ⑥ on the right, where there is a folk art museum (Museo di Roma in Trastevere) and the church's socially activist Comunità di Sant'Egidio. Here you have a choice. If you leave the Piazza by Via della Scala (the street on the left) you will come to

Piazza della Scala, where the Carmelite church **(Santa Maria della Scala)** contains paintings by some of Caravaggio's pupils. The pharmacy outside is also very old. At the end of Via della Scala is the old stone **Porta Settimiana** gateway and Via della Lungara, which takes you to the **Orto Botanico** (Botanical Garden), **Palazzo Corsini,** and **Villa Farnesina** ⑦ (see pp. 186–187). If you take the right-hand exit out of Piazza Sant'Egidio, Vicolo del Cinque, you'll come to **Piazza Trilussa** and the wonderful fountain facing the Ponte Sisto pedestrian bridge spanning the Tevere, or Tiber River. Now take Via Santa Dorotea on the other side of the fountain to Porta Settimiana. The house to the right of the arch, **Casa della Fornarina** (today a restaurant), is said to have been the home of La Fornarina, Raphael's mistress, whose painting hangs in Palazzo Barberini. ∎

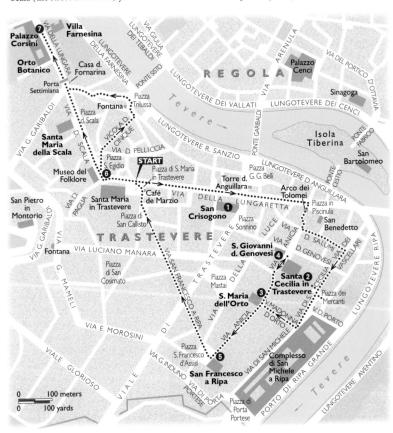

Villa Farnesina

Villa Farnesina

🅰 Map pp. 180–181

✉ Via della Lungara 230

☎ 06 6880 1767

🕐 Open Mon.–Sat. 9 a.m.–1 p.m. Closed Sun.

💲 $

🚌 23, 116, 125, 280

ABOUT A BLOCK FROM PORTA SETTIMIANA, THE crenelated gateway erected by the Borgia Pope Alexander VI in the 1490s, is Villa Farnesina. Built in the early 1500s as a country villa for the Sienese banker and businessman, Agostino Chigi, and later sold to the Farnese family, Villa Farnesina doesn't look like much from the outside, but don't be misled: It is considered a gem of Renaissance architecture. Sienese architect Baldassare Peruzzi believed interiors and exteriors should be integrated, and built what was then an open-air loggia as the main entrance. (Walk around to what is now the back to see the original facade.) In addition, Chigi himself was to spare no expense in furnishing his new residence, decorating it with scenes from Greek and Roman mythology.

In the trompe l'oeil loggias at both ends of the Perspectives Room, the villa's main reception room, Peruzzi tried to eliminate the distinction between interiors and exteriors.

The first room on the ground floor is the **Galatea Room** (also once an open loggia), known primarily for Raphael's "Triumph of Galatea." This wonderful fresco, dated around 1513, shows the sea nymph, wearing a red cloak, riding the ocean waves. Her seashell carriage is pulled by two straining dolphins (one of which is breakfasting on a small squid) and surrounded by cupids. A triton appears to be molesting Galatea's handmaiden. The sumptuous ceiling, done by Peruzzi himself, depicts the planets and constellations at the time of Chigi's birth. Some of the lunettes (by Sebastiano del Piombo) contain scenes from Ovid's *Metamorphoses*. Next is the magnificent Loggia of Cupid and Psyche, which Raphael designed to look like a summertime pergola with fruit and flowers, although most of the artwork was done by his pupils. Craning at the ceiling may give you a stiff neck but never mind because the two large ceiling frescoes—the "Wedding of Cupid and Psyche" and the "Council of the Gods"—are breathtaking. Of the "Three Graces" in the fresco in the corner right of the door, the one with her back to you was probably Chigi's mistress and may have been painted by Raphael himself. The lunettes recount the various stages of Psyche's troubled relationship with the jealous Venus.

The upper floor is equally exciting. In the **Sala delle Prospettive,** the living room, Peruzzi repeated his indoors-outdoors theme, relying amply on trompe l'oeil landscapes and urban scenes with real landmarks such as

Porta Settimiana, an aqueduct, and the campanile of Santa Maria in Trastevere. Note the unfortunate graffiti, left by marauding soldiers during the Sack of Rome in 1527. Next door is the smallish **master bedroom,** a magnificent riot of color, painted mostly by Giovan Antonio Bazzi, generally referred to as Il Sodoma (the Sodomite) because of his homosexuality. The central wall, the "Wedding of Roxanne and Alexander" (the Great), is considered Bazzi's masterpiece. The right-hand wall, "Alexander's Meeting with the Family of Darius of Persia," is less accomplished (the artist reportedly felt he was being underpaid), whereas the central portion of the left-hand wall, the "Taming of Bucephalus" (Alexander's horse), was clearly painted by someone

else: When Chigi's enormous gem-encrusted bed was moved out of the house after his death, it left an empty space that had to be filled.

Chigi was a very wealthy bon vivant with a keen sense of one-upmanship. A lavish reception organized in 1518 in honor of Pope Leo X was staged in the stables (appropriately decorated for the occasion). The idea was to embarrass the Riario family across the street by demonstrating that the Chigi stables were as elegant as the Riario's dining rooms. Later the same year another reception was held at a loggia on the riverbank. Guests were surely impressed (or horrified?) when at the end of each course the servants tossed the silver dishes into the Tiber. But not to worry—Chigi had strung nets below to retrieve them. ∎

Legend has it that Il Sodoma's commission to paint the wedding of Alexander and Roxanne came in the nick of time. He had just been replaced by Raphael in the decoration of the Vatican Stanze 35.

Palazzo Corsini

🅰 Map pp. 180–181

✉ Via della
Lungara 10

☎ 06 6880 2323

🕐 Open Tues.–Sun.
9 a.m.–2 p.m.
Closed Mon.

💲 $

🚌 Bus: 23, 116,
125, 280

Palazzo Corsini

ACROSS THE STREET FROM VILLA FARNESINA IS THE
Palazzo Corsini, an 18th-century remake and amplification of the
Renaissance palace owned by the Riario family in the 15th century,
which in the 17th century became the home of Queen Christina
of Sweden, a convert to Catholicism, who had abdicated and moved
to Rome in 1655. The Corsini, who were Florentines, moved to
Rome after Lorenzo Corsini was elected to the papacy (as Clement
XII) in 1730.

**Fernandino Fuga's
restructuring gave
this Renaissance
palace a decidedly
18th-century
flavor.**

The 18th-century architect
Ferdinando Fuga directed the
restructuring, creating a new light-
filled central body with an impressive and stately ceremonial double
staircase leading up to the gallery
and a monumental three-arched
entry way. He also added another
wing that was used to house the
priceless Corsini library.

In 1883 the building and its art
collection were bought by the
Italian government, and today the
building also houses the Accademia
dei Lincei (1603), an academy of
scholars founded to promote learning, and said to be the oldest of its
kind. The **Galleria Corsini,** a
suite of eight rooms that give off the
atrium (one floor up), contains part
of the collection of the Galleria
Nazionale d'Arte Antica (see pp.
100–101). The paintings, from the
14th to the 18th century, are somewhat haphazardly displayed but
include one Caravaggio ("San
Giovannino, The Young John the
Baptist"), a lovely "Madonna and
Child" by Beato Angelico, and a bust
of Pope Alexander VII, a Chigi, by
Bernini. There are also works by
Rubens, Van Dyck, Murillo, and
Poussin, as well as sculptures,
bronzes, and furniture from
the 1700s.

Despite several remodelings, the
room in which Queen Christina of
Sweden died on April 19, 1689, has
remained as it was. Lavishly decorated, it has two yellow faux marble
columns and elaborate ceilings.
From the back rooms there is a
lovely view of the Botanical Garden
(formerly the gardens of the
Palazzo) and of the lower slopes of
the Janiculum Hill. ■

San Pietro in Montorio & Bramante's Tempietto

From Trastevere a series of steps starting in Via Masi leads up to this landmark church and the adjacent Spanish cultural institute.

THIS MAGNIFICENTLY PLACED FRANCISCAN CHURCH IS generally the first stop for visitors to the Janiculum Hill. The view of the city from the entrance steps is superb and the church itself, with its fine travertine facade, is lovely. Dating from 1481, San Pietro in Montorio once enjoyed special significance in the erroneous belief that the cloister next door was the site of St. Peter's crucifixion.

Inside, there is a beautiful "Flagellation" by Sebastiano del Piombo, and works by Peruzzi, Pomarancio, and Vasari. The second chapel on the left was designed by Bernini. Somewhere underneath is the grave of the young noblewoman Beatrice Cenci, whose 1599 execution at the age of 22 for patricide excited the popular imagination. She was the subject of poems, plays, and paintings, such as Guido Reni's portrait in the Barberini Museum.

In the courtyard of the adjacent monastery is the small, circular **Il Tempietto** ("Little Temple") designed by Bramante and paid for by King Ferdinand and Queen Isabella of Spain to mark the birth of their son. The structure—a colonnade with Doric capitals topped by a balustrade and a cupola—is thought to embody the Renaissance ideal of classical harmony and proportion. Farther up the hill in a commanding position is the **Fontana dell'Acqua Paola** (otherwise known as the Fontanone or Big Fountain). Like the Trevi Fountain, this is the *mostra terminale* of an aqueduct, the point where water first arrives from an extra-urban source. Built of material plundered from the Roman Forum, it is composed of three large central niches flanked by two smaller ones. Water gushes from all five into the pool below (see pp. 96–97). ■

San Pietro in Montorio & Bramante's Tempietto

- ⬛ Map pp. 180–181
- ✉ Piazza di San Pietro in Montorio 2
- ☎ Church: 06 581 3940. Tempietto: 06 581 7377
- 🕐 Church: closed 12–3:30 p.m. Tempietto: closed 12:30–2 p.m. (winter), 12:30–4 p.m. (summer) & Mon.
- 🚌 Bus: 115, 870

Gianicolo

THE GIANICOLO, OR JANICULUM HILL, WHICH RUNS FROM
Trastevere to the Vatican more or less parallel to the Tiber, has little sig-
nificance for ancient Roman history but was intimately associated with
the Italian Risorgimento unification movement of the 19th century.
The Porta San Pancrazio, at the top of the hill, and the surrounding
area saw major battles between the French fighting for the pope, and
Roman and Italian freedom fighters under the command of Giuseppe
Garibaldi. In the 1890s the entire area was turned into a public park.

Gianicolo

Map pp. 180–181

Bus: 115, 870

The Gianicolo Promenade or
Passeggiata del Gianicolo
(the main entrance is on the right
just past the Fontana dell'Acqua
Paola or Fontanone) has a lovely
tree-lined avenue, an equestrian
statue of Garibaldi, another of his
Brazilian wife, Anita, and busts of
the most important Italian patriots.
A favorite place for the *passeggiata*

domenicale (Sunday walk) of many
families, there are souvenir sellers,
pony rides, puppet shows, and, in
the evenings, ample space for cou-
ples to park. The incomparable
view of Rome, however, is the
major attraction. From this vantage
point there is an untrammeled vista
of all of the city's major landmarks
and its magnificent domes. On

clear days, you can see all the way to the Alban Hills. Ever since 1904, a cannon shot has been fired at noon to mark the time. The view is also superb from the *faro* (lighthouse), beyond **Villa Lante,** which was donated to the city by Italians in Argentina in 1911.

Little is left of **Tasso's Oak,** the tree under which the 16th-century poet Tasso liked to sit. Tasso died, in 1595, in the convent of nearby **Sant'Onofrio,** a small single nave church founded in 1419 to honor the Egyptian ascetic, Onophrius. It boasts a lovely two-part "Annunciation" by Antoniazzo Romano and a delightful 15th-century cloister, with frescoes from the life of Sant'Onofrio. ■

The seven hills of Rome

Many people think that the Janiculum was one of the original seven. Wrong. The seven hills of Rome are all on the other side of the Tiber. The Palatine, close to the river, was the site of the earliest settlements and later of the emperors' opulent residences. On the Capitoline were Rome's most important temples, and in between the two hills rose the magnificent Roman Forum. The remaining hills, which to our modern eyes do not seem terribly high, are the Caelian, the Esquiline, the Aventine, the Viminal, and the Quirinal, site of what is now the Italian president's residence (see pp. 92, 98). ■

Santa Cecilia in Trastevere

AN OASIS OF PEACE AND QUIET IN A NOISY NEIGHBOR-
hood, this church was built to honor St. Cecilia, a very important
early Christian saint, martyred by the Romans together with her husband Valerianus. It is said that on her wedding night, the well-born
Cecilia converted her husband and the two then lived together
platonically. The remains of their house, containing some sarcophagi, mosaic floors, and remnants of other classical structures, are
under the church and can be visited during church hours.

**Following a
renovation in 1725,
Cavallini's "Last
Judgment" was
covered up for
nearly 200 years.**

**Santa Cecilia
in Trastevere**

🗺 Map pp. 180–181

✉ Piazza Santa Cecilia
22

☎ 06 589 9289

🕐 Basilica: closed
12:30–4 p.m.
Cavallini fresco: open
Mon.–Fri. 10:15
a.m.–12:15 p.m. &
Sat.–Sun. 11:15
a.m.–12:15 p.m.

🚌 Bus: H, 23, 75, 115,
125, 280, 780.
Tram: 8

Don't expect much enlightenment
unless you can read Italian. The
informational panels describing the
second-century B.C. Roman buildings found here are only in Italy's
native tongue.

Cecilia is the patron saint of
music. Some say she invented the
organ, others that she sang hymns
for three days running while confined to the *calidarium* (steam
bath) of her house in a first,
botched attempt by third-century
Roman authorities to murder her
(she was eventually stabbed in the
neck although decapitation proved,
miraculously, impossible). A basilica was first built on this site by
Pope Paschal I (817–824), who
moved Cecilia's body here after
seeing the location of her grave
in a vision. The church today is a
hodgepodge of styles and colors.

Ferdinando Fuga's monumental
doorway opening onto a garden
with a fountain is early 18th
century, as is the facade. The bell
tower, however, and the portico
with its lovely mosaic decoration,
are 12th century.

Inside, the church has a bland,
18th-century look, probably
because of the rash decision to
encase the Roman columns in
concrete pilasters, but there are
some marvelous remnants of the
more distant past. The ninth-
century **mosaic in the apse**
showing Jesus flanked by St. Paul,
St. Agatha, and St. Valerian on the
right side and by St. Peter and
St. Cecilia on the left is a more
Byzantine version of the one you
saw in Santi Cosma e Damiano (see
p. 46). The figure farthest on the
left, holding a model of the church,

PAVLVS · ET · S · CAECILIAE

is Paschal, who cleverly had himself placed on equal footing with the saints and introduced to Christ by an affectionate St. Cecilia. The cosmatesque pavement (see p. 206) is, of course, medieval. The beautiful Gothic **altar canopy** by Arnolfo di Cambio dates from the late 13th century and is considered that artist's masterpiece. Below is the heart-wrenching statue of the saint sculpted by Stefano Maderno, who was allowed to view the supposedly intact body when the tomb was temporarily opened in 1599. In the chapel at the end of the right aisle there is a damaged, 12th-century fresco depicting the discovery of the saint's body.

Unfortunately, there's a lot in this church that you can't see. Church authorities have closed off the corridor where the calidarium

was located and which also has a Guido Reni canvas. And you can only see into the Ponziani Chapel. But don't despair: Every morning, for a small fee, the Benedictine nuns of the adjacent convent allow you to see the enthrallingly warm colors of **Pietro Cavallini's fresco of the "Last Judgment."** Rediscovered in 1900, but dating from 1293, it is the only major Cavallini to survive. Christ is shown enthroned and surrounded by Apostles, saints, and angels whose multicolored wings run from cream to rose. The nuns of Santa Cecilia have an extra behind-the-scenes job. Every year they are entrusted with two lambs blessed by the pope. They keep them until Easter when their wool—used to make the *pallia* (stoles) given to new patriarchs and archbishops—is shorn. ∎

The sculptor **Stefano Maderno** is said to have carved this statue of the dead **St. Cecilia** after being allowed to view her body when the coffin was temporarily opened in 1599.

Ponte Quattro Capi connects the island to the east side of the Tiber and the Ghetto. The six-story Caetani Tower on the left was recently restored.

Isola Tiberina & San Bartolomeo

A TINY GEMSTONE OF TRAVERTINE AND PLANE TREES, located in the midst of the river, Isola Tiberina (Tiber Island) has long been associated with both medicine and religion. Connected to both shores of the Tevere (Tiber), it is the site of a major hospital, Fatebenefratelli (Do good, brothers) and a small synagogue.

San Bartolomeo

- Map pp. 180–181
- Isola Tiberina 22
- 06 687 7973
- Closed Mon.–Sat. 12:30–3:30 p.m. & Sun. after 1 p.m.
- Bus: H, 23, 63, 125, 280, 780. Tram: 8

Legend has it that in the third century B.C. a delegation of Romans returned from a visit to the sibyl in Epidaurus (Greece) with instructions to build a temple to Aesculapius, the god of healing, if they wanted an outbreak of the plague to be quelled. As they sailed up the Tiber in 219 B.C., they saw a snake like the one wound around Aesculapius's staff (traditionally the doctor's symbol). It supposedly slithered off the ship and swam to the island, indicating its choice of a temple site. Over the centuries, the island became so closely associated with this story that travertine blocks were used to give the island the appearance of a prow and a stern, and vestiges of this construction in the form of a trireme's keel (including a relief depiction of the sacred snake) can still be seen on the side facing the synagogue.

Centuries later the young Holy Roman Emperor Otto III chose the ruins of Aesculapius's temple as a site for a new church dedicated to his friend Adalbert, the first bishop of Prague, who had been martyred a year earlier in A.D. 997. Otto is said to have personally directed the building, using Roman columns and other ancient remnants for the nave and the portico. Somehow, however, poor Adalbert was to get lost in the shuffle. Otto, who would perish shortly thereafter in a skirmish with the rebellious local population, had returned from a trip to Benevento in the Italian south with the remains of the Apostle Bartholomew and deposited them (temporarily, he thought) in his church. But then he died, St. Adalbert was quickly forgotten, and the church was subsequently rededicated to St. Bartholomew.

Rebuilt in 1113 and again in 1624, San Bartolomeo has a 12th-century campanile and a baroque facade. Indoors, a marble wellhead located on the steps leading up to the tribune bears four carved figures: Jesus, St. Bartholomew (holding the knife he was martyred with), St. Adalbert with his bishop's staff (although some believe it to be St. Paulinus of Nola), and Otto III with his crown and scepter. ∎

Il Tevere

It runs right through the city, but nowadays the Tevere, or Tiber, does not play much of a role in the lives of everyday Romans. It's there, it's picturesque, and it is spanned by a variety of bridges, including charming Ponte Sisto from which there is a glorious view that includes St. Peter's. But ever since the end of the 19th century, when high embankments were built to put an end to frequent flooding, the "Biondo Tevere" ("Blonde Tiber," named for its yellowish, muddy bottom) has taken a back seat to other major city rivers. This, however, was not always the case. Romulus and Remus, supposedly the founders of Rome, were discovered on the banks of the Tiber by the she-wolf who adopted them. In ancient times, the Tiber was a major point of access for ships sailing the Tyrrhenian Sea. The Ripa Grande, the large commercial river port in Trastevere, and the smaller Porto di Ripetta (which until the 19th century boasted a monumental, tiered riverside staircase believed to be the inspiration for the Spanish Steps), were of vital importance to the city. ∎

"Tiber in Rome" (1685) by Gaspar van Wittel shows how accessible the Tiber was to Romans before the 19th-century embankments closed it in. Both bridges to the island, still in use today, date back to ancient Roman times.

More places to visit

COMPLESSO DI SAN MICHELE A RIPA

Today the massive 1,099-foot-long (335 m) San Michele complex houses government offices, a branch of the Central Restoration Institute, and is open to the public when temporary exhibits are hosted. Located on the bank of the Tiber once occupied by the ancient river port called Ripa Grande, it was founded in the late 17th century to give refuge, and in some cases to teach a trade to society's rejects: orphans, delinquents, and vagabonds. For this reason its history is linked to that of Roman artisanship. For example, in the 18th century it housed a well-known tapestry workshop. San Michele was also a home for old folks and spinsters—one of the courtyards is named the "Cortile delle Zitelle" (or spinsters). Its upper end faces the Porta Portese gate, one of the entrances to the Sunday flea market.

🗺 Map pp. 180–181 ✉ Via de San Michele 25 ☎ 06 5843 4437 🕐 Varies by exhibit 💲 Varies by exhibit 🚍 Bus: 23, 75, 115, 125, 280. Tram: 3, 8

SAN CRISOGONO

Situated on busy Viale di Trastevere, this large church is often passed over by tourists, but missing it would be an error. Built in the style of a classical Roman basilica, its cosmatesque pavement (see p. 206) may be one of the most beautiful in Rome. Again, the baroque facade and interior decoration give little clue of its medieval beginnings. Only the Romanesque campanile (one of the few in Rome with a triangular top) and the right flank are a giveaway to the church's 12th-century origins. The two porphyry columns supporting the triumphal arch are the largest in Rome. The gilded and blue coffered ceiling is a masterpiece of the genre, but the 17th-century painting on the ceiling (the "Triumph of St. Crisogono" by Guercino) is a copy. The original is in Stafford House in London. The medieval altar has a cosmatesque finish and the framed late 13th-century mosaic in the apse ("The Virgin Between Two Saints") has been attributed to

Pietro Cavallini. The **underground ruins** of the original fifth-century paleo-Christian church are open to the public, although large groups should reserve. During the July Festival of Noiantri the church becomes a Marian sanctuary. "The Virgin of Mount Carmel," an icon, is carried in procession through the streets and put on view in the church for eight days.

🗺 Map pp. 180–181 ✉ Piazza Sonnino 44 (Viale Trastevere) ☎ 06 581 8225 🕐 Upper church: closed 11:30 a.m.–4:15 p.m. Mon.–Sat., 1:15–4:15 p.m. Sun. Underground church: closed 11 a.m.–4:30 p.m. Mon.–Sat., 1–4:30 p.m. Sun. 💲 Underground church: $ 🚍 Bus: H, 23, 125, 280, 780. Tram: 8

SAN FRANCESCO A RIPA

St. Francis took a vow of poverty, but at St. Francis on the Riverbank (named for the ancient riverport that once existed near here) someone may not have been paying attention. When the 13th-century church (erected on the site of a hospice where the saint had once stayed) was rebuilt in the 17th century, it was done in no-holds-barred baroque—the decor is deliciously dramatic with opulent paintings, gold leaf, and stucco everywhere. The **Pallavicini Chapel** at the end of the right aisle nearest the altar is a triumph of multicolored marble; wall tombs sport garishly wicked winged skeletons. The **Altieri Chapel** across the aisle holds one of Bernini's majestic "Ecstasies," the magnificently dramatic statue of the "Blessed Ludovica Albertoni" (1674). Pay no attention to the stucco putto heads gazing down on the blessed Ludovica as she reclines in mystical ecstasy; they were added later. Bernini preferred natural and concealed lighting, but if the light from the side window is not enough for you, ask the sacristan to turn on the electric light for a moment. He'll also take you to visit St. Francis's cell with its stone pillow.

🗺 Map pp. 180–181 ✉ Piazza di San Francesco a Ripa 88 ☎ 06 581 9020 🕐 Church: closed noon–4 p.m., & Sun. 1–4:30 p.m. St. Francis's cell: closed 12–4 p.m., Thurs., & Sun. a.m. 🚍 Bus: H, 23, 115, 125, 280, 780. Tram: 3, 8. ■

Once a busy commercial center for cattle traders and farmers, this area is littered with the remains of ancient temples and monuments. On its borders are Piazza Venezia, the 16th-century Jewish Ghetto, and the quieter Aventine Hill.

Forum Boarium to Aventino

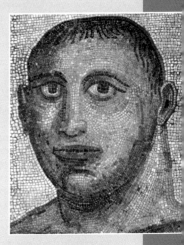

Floor mosaic at Caracalla depicting a gladiator

Forum Boarium to Aventino

MILLING CATTLE, DUSTY HERDSMEN, AND TRADERS SEEKING TO SELL THEIR bovine charges for the best price possible; farmers from outside the city, their carts heaped high with cabbages, asparagus, lettuce, olives, lemons, figs, apples, and even truffles, loudly touting the quality of their produce; barges laden with amphorae filled with olive oil and barrels of grain. Some 2,000 years ago, the area between the Campidoglio and the Tiber was the location for the Forum Boarium and the Forum Holitorium, two bustling outdoor markets for, respectively, cattle and vegetables. Straddling a road that led straight to the city center (the Roman Forum), the Velabrium as it was called, was a marshy expanse, which according to legend was the place where the herdsman, Faustulus, found Romulus and Remus after they had washed up on the shore and been suckled by a friendly she-wolf.

The adjacent area also abounds in vestiges of Roman rule. The remains of the Teatro di Marcellus, designed by Julius Caesar's architects (but completed by Augustus), were incorporated into an elegant 16th-century palazzo. Three columns from the temple of Apollo Sosianus are dramatically outlined against a medieval urban background, and the remnants of the Portico d'Ottavia, which Octavius dedicated to his sister, lie within the area known as the Ghetto, to which the Jews of Rome were confined for centuries.

Today's hustle and bustle, however, differs drastically from that of yore. A large modern thoroughfare, opened in 1933 and now called Via Luigi Petroselli, takes car and bus traffic past the large central Registry Office (the Anagrafe) north to Piazza Venezia. But some remarkable remnants of those earlier times remain, and all you need to enjoy them is a vivid imagination. Picture the cattle traders as they crowded under the Arch of Janus to avoid the winter rain or the scorching summer sun. Imagine how they and their business partners decided to build a second arch (the Arch of the Moneylenders) to honor (let's say, flatter) Emperor Septimius Severus. Surely you can appreciate why an anonymous wealthy cattle-owner would be willing to spend many, many *sesterces* to build a circular temple in honor of Hercules Victor, considered the god of merchants and traders. A second rectangular temple was built to provide offerings to Portunus, the god of ports. The church of San Nicola in Carcere (note the columns embedded in its walls) incorporates the ruins of three other temples. Several of the other churches in the area, in particular San Giorgio in Velabro, San Teodoro, and the hauntingly beautiful Santa Maria in Cosmedin, were once *diaconates*, food distribution centers for the poor run by the early Christian Church. Centuries later, the powerful Crescenzi family built its medieval fortress (again incorporating many classical bits and pieces) to serve as a toll house for the Pons Aemilius (Emilian Bridge). Only a

small section of this remains, and later Romans appropriately named it the Ponte Rotto (Broken Bridge).

To the south, in contrast then as now, lies the Aventine, a tree-lined residential area that is an oasis of tranquility. Despite its proximity to the center, the Aventine has always been somewhat removed from the scramble of everyday life. The municipal rose garden, Il

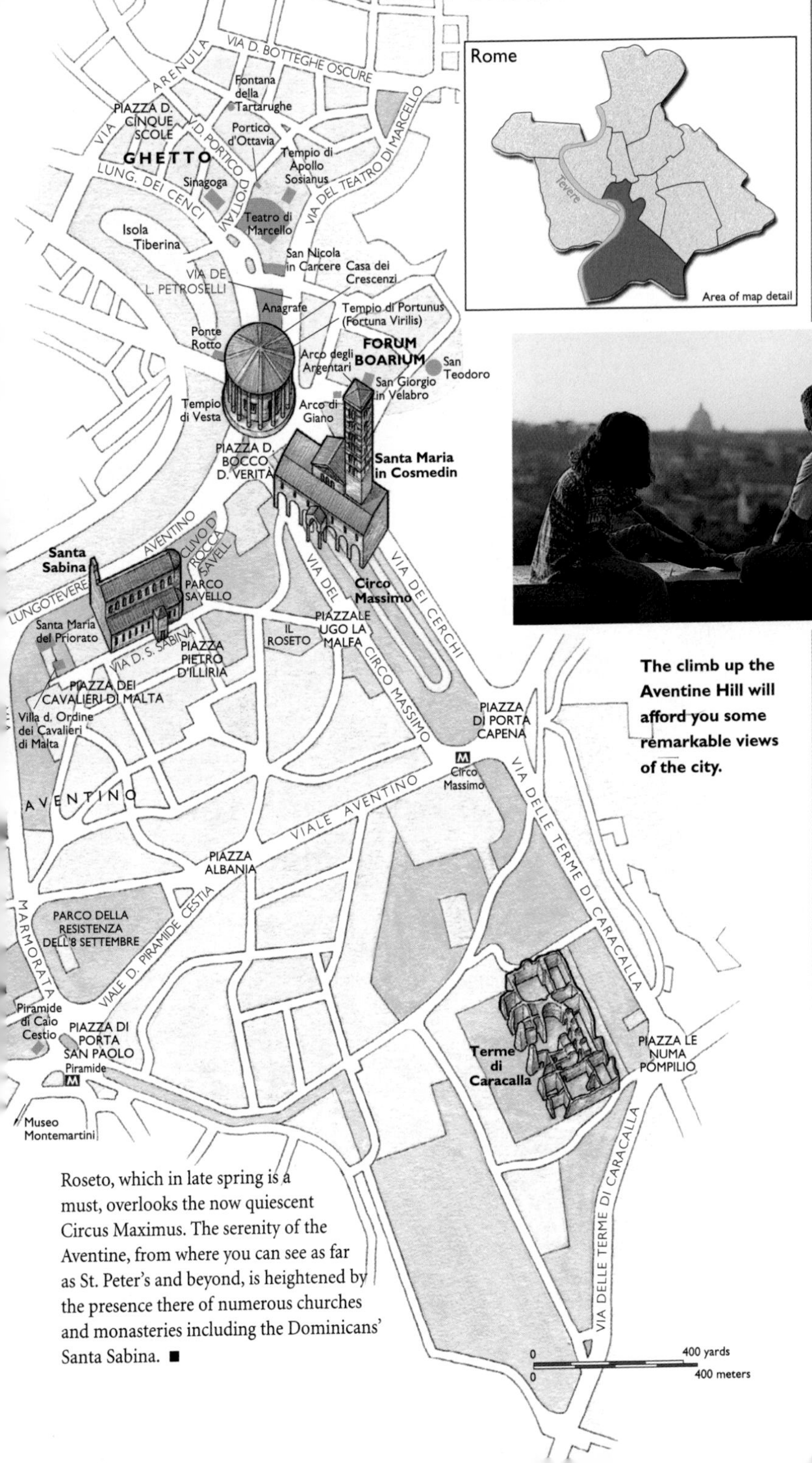

VIA D. BOTTEGHE OSCURE
VIA ARENULA
Fontana della Tartarughe
PIAZZA D. CINQUE SCOLE
V. D. PORTICO D'OTTAVIA
Portico d'Ottavia
GHETTO
Tempio di Apollo Sosianus
VIA DEL TEATRO DI MARCELLO
LUNG. DEI CENCI
Sinagoga
Teatro di Marcello
Isola Tiberina
San Nicola in Carcere
Casa dei Crescenzi
VIA DE L. PETROSELLI
Anagrafe
Tempio di Portunus (Fortuna Virilis)
Ponte Rotto
FORUM BOARIUM
Arco degli Argentari
San Teodoro
San Giorgio in Velabro
Tempio di Vesta
Arco di Giano
PIAZZA D. BOCCO D. VERITÀ
Santa Maria in Cosmedin
AVENTINO
CLIVO D. ROCCA SAVELL
Santa Sabina
LUNGOTEVERE
PARCO SAVELLO
Circo Massimo
VIA DEI CERCHI
VIA DEL CIRCO MASSIMO
PIAZZALE UGO LA MALFA
IL ROSETO
Santa Maria del Priorato
VIA D. S. SABINA
PIAZZA PIETRO D'ILLIRIA
PIAZZA DEI CAVALIERI DI MALTA
Villa d. Ordine dei Cavalieri di Malta
PIAZZA DI PORTA CAPENA
Circo Massimo
VIALE AVENTINO
AVENTINO
VIA DELLE TERME DI CARACALLA
PIAZZA ALBANIA
MARMORATA
PARCO DELLA RESISTENZA DELL'8 SETTEMBRE
VIALE D. PIRAMIDE CESTIA
Piramide di Caio Cestio
PIAZZA DI PORTA SAN PAOLO
Piramide
Terme di Caracalla
PIAZZA LE NUMA POMPILIO
Museo Montemartini
VIA DELLE TERME DI CARACALLA
0 400 yards
0 400 meters
Rome
Tevere
Area of map detail

The climb up the Aventine Hill will afford you some remarkable views of the city.

Roseto, which in late spring is a must, overlooks the now quiescent Circus Maximus. The serenity of the Aventine, from where you can see as far as St. Peter's and beyond, is heightened by the presence there of numerous churches and monasteries including the Dominicans' Santa Sabina. ■

You can't see it, but the fourth-century Arch of Janus stands over the Cloaca Massima, the Roman Forum's main sewage drain which empties into the Tiber.

Forum Boarium's temples, arches, & *diaconates*

THE MASSIVE ARCO DI GIANO, OR ARCH OF JANUS, HASN'T much in common with the triumphal arches built by emperors such as Titus and Septimius Severus, but that's because its purpose was primarily practical. Despite its decorations (the niches on the facades held statues, and various deities are depicted above the archways), this was primarily a covered crossway, erected to protect the cattle traders of the Forum Boarium from the inclement weather.

Forum Boarium

- Map pp. 198–199
- Bus: C3, 23, 81, 95, 170, 280, 715, 716, 780

The same goes for the tiny **Arco degli Argentari** (Arch of the Moneychangers), attached to the church of San Giorgio al Velabro. Erected in A.D. 204 by the cattle merchants and their financial backers, and dedicated to the Severans, it was basically the gateway to the cattle market. If it seems dwarfish, remember that centuries of silt and debris accumulation have raised the ground level, hiding a good part of the bottom section, made of plain travertine to avoid wear and tear from passing bovines. The upper portion, of white marble, is decorated with reliefs showing members of the imperial family performing religious rituals. Septimius Severus and his wife are

on the right and Caracalla (who erased his brother Geta's image after murdering him) is on the left.

Facing the arch, at Via del Velabro 3, is an iron gate and a lovely arched passageway, unfortunately now inaccessible, which leads to an entrance to the Cloaca Massima, the enormous sixth-century B.C. drain system that ran from the Roman Forum to the Tiber.

As for **San Giorgio in Velabro,** this former *diaconate* (food distribution center) is dedicated to St. George (of dragon-slaying fame) who, contrary to popular belief, was not British but rather an early Christian martyr from Palestine. Here you will find a late 13th-century Madonna and Saints fresco attributed to Pietro Cavallini and a lovely 12th-century portico and bell tower. By the way, the saint's relics (including, they say, his head) were brought to this church in the middle of the eighth century when Pope Zaccaria reportedly came across them languishing somewhere in the Lateran Palace.

Across Via Petroselli, only a stone's throw from the river, is the **Tempio di Portunus,** a first-century B.C. temple dedicated to Portunus, the god of harbors, which was long known as Fortuna Virilis (Men's Fortunes). Rectangular, with a colonnaded porch and some remnants of the stucco used to create a white, marblelike effect, it is an excellent example of basic temple architecture, and it is almost intact. Guess why? Starting in the ninth century, this building (like the Pantheon and many others) was turned into a church. The medieval house of the Crescenzi family across the narrow Via del Ponte Rotto has Roman columns embedded in its walls and a classical architrave made from ancient fragments.

Right behind Portunus's temple is the lovely round shrine which for centuries was mistakenly called the **Tempio di Vesta** because of its resemblance to the temple of that name in the Roman Forum. Instead, experts now say, it was almost certainly dedicated to Hercules Victor. This should not surprise us since back then every cattle owner knew that Hercules, who slew the giant Cacus for stealing his cattle, was a god well worth propagating. Indeed, the god's image is on the upper left of the Moneylender's Arch. This temple, too, was turned into a church but the original parts, in white marble, are easy to spot. Many of the 20 Corinthian columns are originals. ■

Right: These three Corinthian columns are all that is left of the temple to Apollo, a Greek god adopted by the Romans. Rebuilt several times, these ruins are from the first century.

Romans, Jews, & Christians walk

This part of Rome encompasses the Jewish Ghetto and the few remains of an area that the ancient Romans dedicated to knowledge and entertainment as well as to commerce. Today it is home to many artisans and merchants, Jewish and not. It is also a desirable address for up-and-coming professionals.

The gateway to the Porticus of Octavia, once about the size of a city block. Greek paintings and statues were displayed here.

Start this walk in front of the Tempio di Portunus and proceed up to the Lungotevere where, traffic permitting, you can cross the street to the other side. If you make it across, you will be rewarded with a magnificent view of **Isola Tiberina** (Tiber Island) with San Bartolomeo and its bell tower. Farther to the right, the restored Torre dei Caetani, or Pierleoni tower (recently renovated), stands like a sentinel over the oldest bridge in the city, the Ponte Fabricio or Ponte Quattrocapi (62 B.C.). At the stoplight by the bridge, cross back (in greater safety) and you will find yourself at the beginning of the **Via del Portico d'Ottavia ❶**, the main street of the Ghetto (see p. 204). The building on your left with the square dome is Rome's modern central *sinagoga,* or synagogue, built a century ago in an odd, but not unpleasing, mock

Assyro-Babylonian style. The synagogue's temple and newly renovated museum *(tel 06 6840 0661, closed Fri. p.m. & Sat.)* are interesting.

The small church on your right is **San Gregorio della Divina Pietà,** one of the churches where the Jews were forced to attend Christian sermons. They could avoid this torment only by paying a bribe or, as many did, using earplugs. Over the door there are inscriptions in both Hebrew and Latin. Now walk down the Via del Portico d'Ottavia to the large marble pediment supported by columns, all that's left of the **Portico d'Ottavia ❷,** the huge colonnade built by Augustus in 23 B.C. for his sister, Octavia. In the Middle Ages, the church of **Sant'Angelo in Pescheria** (*pescheria* means "fish market") was built into its ruins. See the marble plaque on the far right pilaster? It says that any fish head (considered quite a delicacy) longer than the plaque itself was to be handed over to city officials.

Where the street makes a 90-degree turn to the left, note that the buildings on the left are newer than those on the right. Why? Because of poor sanitary conditions in the overcrowded Ghetto, a century ago everything from here to the river was razed and rebuilt. At Nos. 1 and 2 is the **Casa di Lorenzo Manilio ❸,** built in 1497 by uniting several structures. Classical inscription and beautiful Roman reliefs are embedded in the walls. The pastry shop on

---

- ⓜ Also see area map, pp. 198–199
- ▶ Temple of Portunus
- ⟷ 1 mile (1.5 km)
- ⏱ 1.5 hours
- ▶ Santa Maria in Cosmedin

NOT TO BE MISSED

- View of Tiber Island
- Portico d'Ottavia
- Casa di Lorenzo Manilio
- Fontana delle Tartarughe
- Teatro di Marcello

the corner (at No. 1), Boccione, makes delicious Jewish cakes and pastries, but remember that Jewish food in the Mediterranean has little to do with the Eastern European specialties known back home. Backtrack a few paces to the Via della Reginella, which leads to Piazza Mattei with its delightful Tortoise Fountain. The **Fontana delle Tartarughe 4** (see p. 96) was built in the 1580s by Taddeo Landini to a design of Giacomo della Porta. Take Via dei Funari (the Street of the Ropemakers) and peep into the courtyard of Palazzo Caetani at No. 31 to observe the fragments of classical sculpture covering the walls. **Santa Maria in Campitelli 5** (1662–1667), in nearby

Piazza di Campitelli, is architect Carlo Rainaldi's masterpiece.

Exiting the square from its farther end, on your right you'll see the remains of the **Teatro di Marcello** and the three surviving columns of the **Tempio Apollo Sosianus.** The theater was erected between 13 and 11 B.C. and dedicated to Marcellus, Augustus's nephew and, until his premature death in 23 B.C. his probable heir. A short distance on is **San Nicola in Carcere 6,** the medieval church built into the remains of the Forum Holitorium's three temples. Then proceed along Via Petroselli to **Santa Maria in Cosmedin 7** with its seven-story campanile (see pp. 205–206). ■

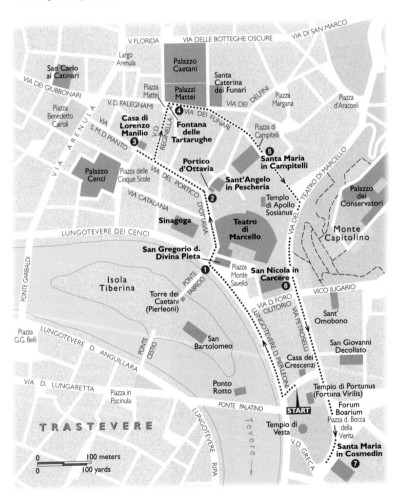

The Ghetto

THE PAPAL BULL ISSUED BY POPE PAUL IV ON JULY 12, 1555, confined the Jews of Rome to a walled-off area of less than 3 acres (1.3 ha) where they were forced to live for more than 300 years. One motive was simple anti-Semitism. But the Counter-Reformation zeal inspired by the Protestant schism probably also played a key role in the creation of the Ghetto, formally abolished only in 1883.

More than half of Italy's 35,000 Jews live in Rome.

Jews have lived in Rome since the second century B.C., settling first in areas favored by foreigners, such as the Aventine and Trastevere. However, by the time the Ghetto was decreed, many Roman Jews, especially merchants, had already moved to this commercially thriving riverport neighborhood. Tiber Island was often referred to as the Pons Judaeorum and the **Piazza delle Cinque Scole** (off today's Via Arenula) had five temples and was called Piazza Giudea by everyone, Jews included.

The papal edict made it illegal for Jews to live elsewhere, barred them from certain professions, and forced them to attend church services. Although enforcement was patchy, severe overcrowding was inevitable. In the 1600s, some 6,000 people crammed into this tiny area when the gates closed at sunset.

Roman Jews are neither Ashkenazi nor Sephardic and pride themselves on being part of a community that preexists the destruction of the Jerusalem synagogue in A.D. 70. This entitles them to enjoy certain privileges such as eating lamb at Passover. But if the kosher restaurants you see start you dreaming of a pastrami sandwich or a bagel, forget it. Jewish people have been in Rome so long that often (pork dishes excluded) the Jewish and Roman cuisines are almost indistinguishable. Some favorites of Jewish origin are *carciofi alla Giudea* (fried, whole artichokes), *filetti di baccalà fritti* (fried codfish fillets), and marinated zucchini. The Jewish bakery on **Via di Portico d'Ottavia** is known for its ricotta cheesecakes (chocolate or berries). The area is dominated by the imposing synagogue. History was made here in 1986 with Pope John Paul II's unprecedented visit. ∎

Santa Maria in Cosmedin

UNFORTUNATELY, THIS CHURCH IS KNOWN PRIMARILY FOR
the Bocca della Verità (Mouth of Truth), a stone disk inside the 12th-
century portico with the carved image of a sea god that inexplicably
tempts hordes of tourists to see whether, as medieval legend had it,
the mouth will bite off a liar's hand. Please don't waste time on an old
cistern cover that has no artistic merit. Set in the heart of an area
rich in ancient monuments and memories, Santa Maria in Cosmedin
has enough real, albeit understated, treasures to further illustrate
this city's perennial transformations.

The two columns flanking the door
inside, the three others embedded
in the left wall, and the freestanding, shorter column in the sacristy
are remnants of an earlier structure. In the fourth century, this was
the seat of the *statio annonae*, the
city office for food distribution and
market inspection. By the sixth
century it had been turned into a
diaconate, a center set up by the
Church to provide food and other
services to the poor. An oratory was
added then, but it was only in the
eighth century that Pope Hadrian
(772–795) turned it into a bona
fide church, donating it to Greek
Christian refugees from the religious turmoil in Byzantium. It thus
became Santa Maria in Cosmedin,
or, as it was sometimes called, Santa
Maria de Schola Graeca.

Whichever name you prefer,
both testify to the Eastern origin of
the new church's parishioners.
Cosmedin is no doubt derived from
Constantinople's famous
Kosmidion Monastery and neighborhood whereas Schola Graeca
(which means "Greek School")
speaks for itself.

Damaged during the Norman
invasion in the late 11th century, it
was restored early in the next
century and the redbrick columned
porch, the portico, and the lovely
seven-story Romanesque bell tower
date from this period. The former
shelters treasures that are far more

interesting than those of the Bocca
della Verita, placed on the left-hand
wall only 370 years ago. The marble
decoration around the portal dates
from the 11th century. The tomb to

The church's
Romanesque
bell tower
stands across
from a baroque
fountain, just one
example of the
city's artistic
stratification.

In medieval times women suspected of infidelity were questioned with their hand inside the sea god's mouth and warned they'd better tell the truth or be bitten.

Santa Maria in Cosmedin

🅰 Map pp. 198–199
✉ Piazza Bocca della Verità 18
☎ 06 678 1419
🕐 Church: closed 1–3 p.m. Bocca della Verita: open daily
🚌 Bus: C3, 23, 81, 95, 170, 280, 715, 716, 780

its right is that of Alfano, the papal chamberlain who supervised the church's 12th-century restoration. The inscriptions on the wall record ninth-century donations. In the hush of the church's penumbra it is easy to feel yourself transported back in time and possibly moved

to spiritual contemplation. This church abounds in Eastern or Byzantine influences, primarily the *schola cantorum,* the walled-off area reserved for worshippers; *matronei,* the balconies reserved for women; and the *iconostasis,* the marble divider delimiting the priests' domain.

The magnificently patterned floor is pre-cosmatesque (12th century), whereas the decorated Gothic canopy over the main altar is dated 1294 and is signed by Deodato, a son of one of the Cosmas (see below). There is cosmatesque decoration on the paschal candlestick (note the stylized lion at its base) just behind the right pulpit. And don't miss the framed eighth-century mosaic in the sacristy with its fine gold background, which comes from the original St. Peter's. The outstretched hand in the bottom left corner (perhaps one of the Magi) has led many experts to conclude that it was a scene from the Adoration of the Three Kings. ∎

The Cosmati marble workers

Cosma must have been a common name in the 12th century; or maybe it was given to the sons of many Roman stonecutters for some other reason. These "Cosmati" can be said to have reinvented mosaic art in Rome. The cosmati technique or cosmatesque are the terms now used to describe their type of inlay decoration which relied on the use of tiny pieces of colored marble—red, green, black, white—to create intricate patterns at times resembling Islamic geometrical motifs. Often, in a break from ancient Roman techniques, the Cosmas combined them with larger stone rounds and strips to make multicolored pavements such as those in Santa Maria in Cosmedin,

San Crisogono, and Santa Maria in Trastevere. Cosmati work was also applied to church accessories such as paschal candlesticks (notable in San Lorenzo), tombs, episcopal chairs and pulpits, and the small columns often used in church cloisters and which glitter like jewels in the sun. The most impressive examples of the latter in Rome are the cloisters of San Giovanni in Laterano and of San Paulo fuori le Mura, both of which are signed by Pietro Vassalletto and his son, masters of this kind of workmanship. The production of cosmati work was interrupted in the 14th century when the popes fled temporarily to Avignon, and never again reached its former levels. ∎

Circo Massimo

IF YOU LOOK DOWN AT THE CIRCO MASSIMO (CIRCUS Maximus) from the imperial residences on the Palatine Hill, you can almost hear the crowds cheering on the city's most popular charioteers as their two-wheeled chariots—probably a *quadriga,* drawn by four horses—rounded the course for the seventh and last time.

Charioteers once raced here, their colors—white, red, green, or blue—signifying membership in one of the *factiones* or parties that paid for the outfitting of the equestrian teams. Today, however, there is little to see here. Archaeologists say that the starting gates and the *spina,* or raised spine that ran down the middle of this race course, still exist. But they have yet to be excavated and here, too, you will have to rely on your imagination to picture what may have been one of the largest stadiums that humankind has known. A long rectangle about the size of a football field, it had a triple tier of stone and wood bleachers that is believed to have held over 250,000 people.

Tucked into the valley between the Palatine and the Aventine (two of Rome's famed seven hills), the Circus Maximus dates back to the fourth century B.C. and is the oldest of the known Roman circuses. During the frequent *ludi* (games), the circus was primarily for horseracing and chariot races, although gladiatorial exhibitions were sometimes held there, as were public executions. Its last use as a Roman circus dates back to A.D. 549, during the reign of the Ostrogoth (barbarian) king, Totila, who had temporarily won control of Rome from the city's then Byzantine rulers. It then gradually fell into disuse (at one point cabbages were grown here). The small medieval tower at the eastern end has absolutely nothing to do with the original circus. It belonged to the Frangipane family, which during the Middle Ages controlled much of this area. ■

More people in ancient Rome watched chariot racing than any other sport, and charioteers vied with gladiators as the era's most popular sports heroes.

Circo Massimo

- Map pp. 198–199
- Bus: C3, 60, 75, 81, 118, 175, 628, 673, 715.
  Tram: 3.
  Metro: Linea B (Circo Massimo)

Aventino

THE MOST PICTURESQUE WAY TO GET UP TO THE AVENTINO (or Aventine Hill) and to Santa Sabina is to walk up the lovely cobblestone street called Clivo di Rocca Savella, which starts about 110 yards (100 m) from Santa Maria in Cosmedin (along Via Santa Maria in Cosmedin, the continuation of Via Petroselli).

Aventino

🗺 Map pp. 198–199

Santa Sabina

🗺 Map pp. 198–99

✉ Piazza Pietro d'Illiria 1

☎ 06 57 941

🕐 Closed 12:30–3:30 p.m.

🚌 Bus: C3, 23, 81, 95, 170, 175, 280, 628, 715, 716

A gate in a medieval wall that was once part of the powerful Savelli family's fortress leads to the **Parco Savello**, also called the Parco degli Aranci because of the orange trees brought from Spain in the 13th century by St. Dominic, founder of the Dominican order. An oasis of peace and quiet, this is one of the loveliest sites in Rome with an unbelievable panoramic view of the city.

The imposing rear view of the Dominican basilica of **Santa Sabina** makes it easy for you to grasp the essentials of fifth-century church architecture. The apse is clearly outlined, and you can see how the center part of the church, over the nave, is higher than the sides, permitting greater illumination through the clerestory windows. When you leave the park (this time through its main entrance), note the wonderful *mascherone* (mask) on the wall to your right, used in the 16th-century fountain by Giacomo della Porta.

By the time this church was built, Christianity had come out of the closet to become a mainstream religion and, as you can see from the 24 fluted Corinthian columns, the remaining mosaic decorations above the entrance door, and the beautiful Roman marble inlay ornamentation above and between the arches, this church was built to be seen. The mosaic over the entrance is particularly interesting: Two female figures, ever so much like two classical Roman matrons, represent the major components of early Christianity, the pagans or gentiles (Ecclesia Ex Gentibus), and the Jews (Ecclesia Ex circumscisione). The gold lettering on a deep blue background is striking. And don't miss the cypress door on the far left of the portico. Its 18 fifth-century paleo-Christian panels depict scenes from the Old and New Testaments, including one of the earliest surviving representations of Jesus' crucifixion.

Some 219 yards (200 m) farther along Via di Santa Sabina you'll come to a quaint piazza with obelisks set atop the surrounding walls, **Piazza dei Cavalieri di Malta,** designed by the 18th-century graphic artist, Giovanni Battista Piranesi. The monumental entrance, also by Piranesi, leads to the residence of the Grand Master of the Knights of Malta, **Villa del' Ordine dei Cavalieri di Malta.** Piranesi (who is buried there) also designed the church inside, **Santa Maria del Priorato.** You can't get in there, but peep through the keyhole to see the justifiably famous picture postcard view of the dome of St. Peter's. ■

About a thousand years ago, the Holy Roman Emperor Otto III is said to have watched from the Aventine Hill as workmen built the church on Tiber Island (see p. 195).

Terme di Caracalla

WHEN SEPTIMIUS SEVERUS TOOK POWER IN A.D. 193, HE WAS concerned—as any new emperor would be—with consolidating the power of his dynasty. Public works were already known to generate popular support so Septimius and his son Caracalla decided to imitate Vespasian (the Colosseum) and Trajan (the Basilica Ulpia) and built the mammoth imperial baths complex which, historians say, covered 119,600 square yards (100,000 sq m) and could accommodate up to 10,000 people. Begun in A.D. 206 and inaugurated in A.D. 217 by Caracalla, the Severans' Baths sought to follow Trajan's lead in going beyond simple hygiene and pleasure to satisfy the needs of a leisured class. You came here not just for a swim and a sauna but, as in any elitist club, to while away a lazy afternoon, to catch up on your reading, or even to do some networking and make a business deal or two.

Terme di Caracalla
- Map pp. 198–199
- Via delle Terme di Caracalla 52 (at the intersection with Via Antonina)
- 06 3996 7700
- $$. Audio guide: $
- Open daily, but closed Mon. after 2 p.m.
- Bus: 60, 75, 118, 628, 673. Tram: 3. Metro: Linea B (Circo Massimo)

The Baths of Caracalla have been "out-of-order" ever since the sixth century when the invading Goths destroyed the aqueducts and cut off their water supply. The majestic ruins which loom in the shadow of the second crest of the Aventine Hill will give you only a partial idea of the Baths' extravagant scale. Along with the bathing rooms, there were libraries (Greek and Latin), art galleries, meeting halls, and a stadium. The buildings were surrounded by a shaded esplanade with fountains, playing fields, and a covered portico. The materials used in the decorations were lavish, as can be seen from the mosaics now in the Vatican Museums, such as the "athletes in training." The sculptures were often monumental; examples are the enormous granite basins incorporated into the fountains of the Piazza Farnese of the so-called Farnese Bull and the Farnese Hercules, both in the Naples archaeological museum.

Plundered repeatedly over the centuries, little is left of the Baths' original grandeur and as in other ancient Roman sites you will have to use your imagination. The main bathing rooms (which could reportedly seat 1,600 people at one time) formed an axis of the central quadrilateral. Secondary rooms were arranged around the *apodyterium* (dressing room), the *palaestrae* (open-air exercise rooms), the *calidarium* (hot room), *tepidarium* (warm room), and the *frigidarium* (cold room). Other structures, like the libraries, were outside the perimeter.

Your visit begins in one of the two workout rooms (palaestrae). This, like its twin on the far side of the complex, contains segments of black-and-white mosaic decoration and patches of multicolor mosaic flooring. A door leading out of the workout room leads to a dressing room with a black-and-white pavement, a vestibule, and then, a few steps down, to the *natatio* (swimming pool). Another brings you to an atrium and then into the frigidarium. If you walk straight through here and the transition room on the other side, you'll come to the other palaestra with its many mosaic panels. Next to nothing remains of the enormous and circular calidarium with its seven plunge baths except two brick pilasters. The dome, now long gone, was said to have been as big as the Pantheon's. ■

Opposite: To build the Baths of Caracalla, an average of 9,000 workers were employed daily for five years.

More places to visit

CIMITERO ACATTOLICO

The cemetery for non-Catholics was founded in 1738 to provide a final resting place for the foreigners who not only visited Rome but died in it as well. These include the famous—such as Keats and Shelley—and the ordinary, such as 16-year-old Rose Bathurst who in 1824 fell off her horse and drowned in the Tiber, and Devereau Plantagenet Cockburn, who died in 1850 (aged 21) after vainly traveling through Europe in search of a suitable climate.

Banked up against a piece of the Aurelian Wall, their final resting place, now almost filled to capacity, is verdantly tranquil, a place of blossom and birdsong and a refuge for some of the city's most beautiful felines. Pull the bell-cord and tell the gatekeeper which tomb you wish to visit. Genuine mourners pay nothing, tourists are asked to make a small donation (a euro or two would be sufficient), and if you're short of time, remember you can see Keats's

In the fifth century, Emperor Honorius doubled the height of Rome's towers, including those of the Ostiense Gate.

grave from outside, through a small window in the cemetery wall at the start of Via Caio Cestio. Interestingly enough, that street is named after the first well-known non-Catholic to be buried in the area: Caius Cestius, a senior Roman magistrate who died in 12 B.C., having built himself a pyramid (on the next corner)

for a tomb **(Piramide di Caio Cestio).** In the third century A.D., like other preexisting monuments, it was incorporated into the walls built to protect the city from the growing threat of barbarian attack. This probably accounts for its survival over the centuries.
🅰 Map pp. 198–199 ✉ Via Caio Cestio 6 ☎ 06 574 1900 🕓 Closed Sun. 🚌 Bus: 3, 23, 30, 60, 75, 95, 175, 280. Tram: 3. Metro: Linea B (Piramide)

MUSEO MONTEMARTINI

This former power station on the Via Ostiense (the road that in ancient times led from Rome to the Basilica of San Paolo and then on to the seaport of Ostia) has transformed into a small branch of the Capitoline Museums. This modern-day industrial structure has proven to be a provocative setting for the classical beauty of these 400-odd Capitoline marbles. The innovative juxtapositioning of ancient statuary with the dark metal machinery of this early 20th-century behemoth is entrancing. Pediment sculptures, friezes from temples and Pompey's Theater, statuary from the *horti* (extensive monumental gardens of ancient aristocratic residences), mosaics, and Republican-era busts are dramatically displayed amid the equipment once in use in the likes of the Machine, Furnace, and Column Rooms. Combining the old with the new is not frequent in rome Here it has been done—and done well.
🅰 Map pp. 198–199 ✉ Via Ostiense 106 ☎ 06 8205 9127 🕓 Closed Mon. 💲 $. Tours in English on request: $$$$$ 🚌 Bus: 23

MUSEO DELLA CIVILTÀ ROMANA

This little-known treasure-trove is in the modern EUR (Esposizione Universale di Roma) quarter. It showcases replicas of artifacts, implements and architectural reconstructions (arches, aqueducts, bridges, baths, etc.) of Roman civilization. Don't miss the set of plaster casts of Trajan's entire column in the basement and a room-size plaster model of the capital as it appeared in Constantine's day (early fourth century).
🅰 Map pp. 198–199 ✉ Piazza G. Agnelli, 10 ☎ 06 5926 135 🕓 Closed Mon. 🚇 Metro: Linea B. ∎

Life didn't stop at the gates of Rome and neither did death. Often built over martyrs' tombs, several early Christian churches lie outside the ancient walls, while Roman tombs dot the lovely Appian Way.

Fuori le Mura (Outside the Walls)

Classical motif detail from Santa Costanza mosaic

Fuori le Mura

FUORI LE MURA, OR OUTSIDE THE WALLS. THESE ARE WORDS THAT HAVE A particular significance for a Roman even if the Aurelian Walls that once totally surrounded the city no longer have the function or the import of the past. Until fairly recently, in fact, almost all of inhabited Rome was inside the 12-mile (19 km) perimeter begun during the reign of Emperor Aurelian (A.D. 270–275), continued by Maxentius, and eventually doubled in height by subsequent emperors, such as Honorius. In a sense Rome (like most ancient settlements) has always been a walled city. A sixth-century B.C. king, Servius Tullius, built fortifications to protect the nascent city, the so-called Servian Walls, of which only a few small sections remain. But the Aurelian Wall was something else. It enclosed all seven hills, the Campus Martius, and Trastevere, which means that almost all of Rome's major monuments are within this area. What remained outside—catacombs, monasteries, vineyards, and farmland—was far more vulnerable. This included San Paolo, San Lorenzo, and Sant'Agnese, all of which have "fuori le mura" attached to their names to distinguish them from other downtown (or later) churches.

As a defensive strategy, the distance between two rampart towers could not exceed the range of arrows.

The mammoth ring of brick wall had an obvious function and a corresponding significance. Aurelian, who had already repelled the Alemanni, built the wall to protect the city in the event of another barbarian onslaught. This was not to happen for another 140 years, until A.D. 410 when the Goths sacked the city, a prelude to the conquest of Spain. The feeling that the walls were necessary was the first step in the decline of an empire which had been deemed invincible. So fuori le mura meant vulnerability, difficulties, and distance.

As built by Aurelian, the wall was interspersed by a series of 18 *porte* (gates), many of which are still in use today, in the sense that city traffic passes through them. The porte often became the gateways or portals for the consular roads (in the Republican era the leaders who took the place of the kings were known as consuls) which, together with the aqueducts, made the Romans famous throughout the world. The first of these, leading out from the massive Porta San Sebastiano, was the Appia Antica, or Appian Way, inaugurated in 312 B.C. and named for the city's then ruler, Appius Claudius Caecus, who also built the first aqueduct (the Appia). The fact is that in the fourth century B.C., Rome was becoming a force to be reckoned with. The Roman Republic, founded in 509 B.C., had quickly conquered the rest of Italy and soon after had begun its expansion into much of the then known world. Military campaigns meant troop movements, and troop movements meant that roads were a major necessity. In its first stage, the Via Appia ran only to Capua in the Italian

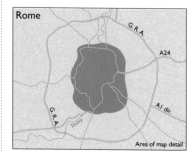

south. Later its importance was assured (the historian, Statius, dubbed it the Regina Viarum, the Queen of Roads) when it was extended to Brindisi and Taranto in Apulia, in the heel of the Italian "boot," effectively becoming a pathway to the Middle East.

The Via Appia, once the site of grandiose funeral processions such as that of Emperor Augustus in A.D. 14 and of triumphal marches into the city by returning army legions, quickly became a cemetery for the rich and powerful as well. The first section of the road was apparently crowded with commemorative tombs, only a small number of which have survived

intact. With its statues, friezes, and once legible Latin inscriptions it was no doubt a sight to behold. Starting in the first century A.D., when Christianity took root and began to spread, and lasting until about the fifth century, catacombs were carved out of the soft tufa rock to build deep, underground cemeteries for the multiple burials of the Christian dead (the Romans considered it unsanitary to bury the dead within the city walls). The damp, underground galleries, which sometimes ran for many miles, have interesting Greek and Latin inscriptions, faded frescoes, imperial seals, and sarcophagi. ∎

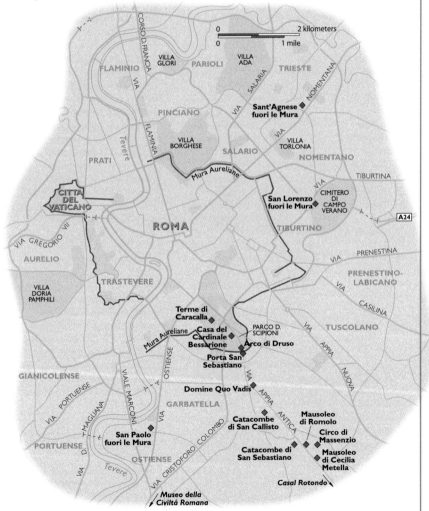

Via Appia Antica

CYPRESSES AND UMBRELLA PINES; THE RUINS OF AN aqueduct silhouetted against the cobalt-blue Roman summer sky, its dried out redbrick arches now only a haven for—who knows?—an owl's nest, some crabgrass, a cluster of wild fennel or caper, a few red poppy blossoms; a long narrow road that stretches unwaveringly ahead, leading southwest, lined with the remnants of marble tombs; and—believe it or not—those large, irregular flagstones that still pave some sections of the road, often rutted by the wheels of carts and chariots that passed here so very long ago, are the originals, hewn by hand from the basaltic lava cliffs of the nearby Alban hills.

Via Appia Antica
- Map p. 215
- Bus: 118, 218, 660, & Archeobus (daily departures from the Termini Station, tel 06 4695 2252, $$)

Museo delle Mura–Porta San Sebastiano
- Via di Porta San Sebastiano 18
- 06 7047 5284
- Open Tues.–Sun. 9 a.m.–2 p.m.; closed Mon.
- $
- Bus: 118, 218, & Archeobus

Opposite: The most graphic evidence of Roman expansion, imperial roads are still visible throughout the Mediterranean, from Morocco to Turkey.

In many ways, given the impact of nature, the scene here has not changed all that much over the centuries. What you are seeing is more or less what St. Peter would have seen when he left Rome, fleeing Nero's persecution, had Jesus not appeared to him at what is now the tiny church of Domine Quo Vadis and convinced him to return to Rome and certain martyrdom. It is also approximately what the Apostle Paul saw when he entered Rome in A.D. 56 as a prisoner.

Today the Via Appia Antica, or Appian Way, is many things to many people: a mecca for pilgrims headed for the Church of San Sebastiano; a destination for the catacombs, where early Christians were buried during the last centuries of the Roman Empire; and a draw for modern-day Romans, eager for a dose of haunting beauty (or a good meal) only a few miles from downtown. The road formally begins at **Porta San Sebastiano,** the gate in the Aurelian Wall (once called Porta Appia) where, by the way, there is a small, interesting **museum** that allows you access to spectacular views from the terrace above and one of the adjacent towers. But on lovely Via di Porta San Sebastiano itself, you will find some interesting sites: the Renaissance house of Cardinal Bessarione; **Casa del**

Cardinale Bessarione (on the right at No. 9; not open to the public); and then, farther up on the left, the verdant **Parco degli Scipioni** with the Scipio family tomb. Out the other side of the park, across Via di Porta Latina, is the picturesque church of **San Giovanni a Porta Latina.** Right before you reach the porta is the **Arco di Druso** (Arch of Drusus), part of the Antoniana Aqueduct which supplied the **Terme** (baths) **of Caracalla.**

About 100 feet (30 m) along the Appian Way is the road's only extant original Roman milestone, and a bit less than half a mile (1 km) farther on, on the left, is the **Domine Quo Vadis** church. Facing it is the entrance to the **Catacombe di San Callisto** (see p. 219). A little farther along is the church of **San Sebastiano fuori le Mura** with its catacombs (also see p. 219). San Sebastiano is one of the seven churches a medieval pilgrim had to visit to earn a plenary indulgence. First built in the early fourth century (the bodies of Peter and Paul were allegedly hidden here during one of the more violent periods of anti-Christian persecution), it was rebuilt in the 17th century.

If you've enjoyed yourself so far, from now on you are really in for a treat. For those with good legs, a car,

The Appia Antica is a popular outings spot for Italians who like to picnic among the ruins.

Circo di Massenzio e Mausoleo di Romulo

- Map p. 215
- Via Appia Antica 153
- 06 780 1324
- Open Tues.–Sun. 9 a.m.–2 p.m.; closed Mon.
- $
- Bus: 118, 660, & Archeobus

Mausoleo di Cecilia Metella

- Map p. 215
- Via Appia Antica 161
- 06 3996 7700
- Closed Mon.
- $
- Bus: 118, 660, & Archeobus

or a bicycle, the next mile or so of the Appian Way becomes increasingly beautiful and evocative. First, on the left, are the fascinating remains of the fortified villa built by Emperor Maxentius (A.D. 306–312), whose siege mentality led him to prefer this location to the Palatine. The site includes the **Mausoleo di Romulo,** the Emperor's young son who died in A.D. 309, and a Roman circus, **Circo di Massenzio,** that, though smaller, is much better preserved than the Circus Maximus and will give you a better idea of what these racecourses were like. The stones on the ground between the remnants of two towers show where the 12 *carceres* (starting gates) were located. You can clearly see the *spina*, once decorated with obelisks and other monuments, which ran down the middle and around which the *bighe e quadrigae* (chariots drawn by two or four horses) would have raced. Built by Maxentius shortly before he was killed by his brother-in-law, Constantine, the circus was never really used. At 1,700 feet (518 m) long it is believed to have had a capacity of about 10,000 people.

Next comes the massive, circular **Mausoleo di Cecilia Metella.** In the 13th century, as you can see from the crenellation around the top, the powerful Caetani family transformed this monument into a sort of medieval fortress for their estate across the road. Originally this was the tomb of the wife and daughter of two of Emperor Augustus's most noble worthies, the consul Quintus Metellus Creticus and M. Licinius Crassus, scion of an extremely wealthy family. The marble frieze has reliefs of flowers, ox skulls, and weapons. Inside there are interesting inscriptions and decorations, probably taken from other tombs. Traveling on you will find yourself increasingly in the open countryside where umbrella pines alternate with funerary remains. Off to the left are the ruins of the impressive Acqua Marcia aqueduct. The last big monument, about 5 miles (8 km) from the Porta, is the **Casal Rotondo,** the largest tomb on the road. A round tomb, this time on a square base (with a house and garden on the top), it is believed to be a memorial to the poet Messala Corvinus erected by his son. ∎

Early Christian symbolism included fish, Greek letters, and animals, but never portraits of Jesus nor scenes of the Crucifixion.

Catacombe di San Sebastiano

Inside the Catacombs of San Sebastiano, four levels have been excavated. The tour of this catacomb, which has second-century **pagan tombs** along with Christian chapels, will take you down a staircase studded with pieces of sarcophagi with imperial seals. Underneath the church, you'll see an area with three decorated pagan tombs with some very attractive frescoes and a floor mosaic. It is believed that both Christian and pagan funerals were held in the elaborate central chapel, the vault of which has acanthus and lotus-leaf stucco decorations. The **Chapel of Symbols** has early Christian symbols carved in it. Up another staircase is a **dining room** for funeral banquets. The graffiti date back to the second century. ■

Catacombe di San Sebastiano
- 🅰 Map p. 215
- ✉ Via Appia Antica 136
- ☎ 06 785 0350
- 🕐 Closed 12–2 p.m. & all day Sun.
- 💲 $
- 🚌 Bus: 118, 660, & Archeobus

Catacombe di San Callisto

The Catacombs of San Callisto are the best known of the Roman catacombs and the first official underground burial site for early Christians, including many second- and third-century martyrs. Excavations have revealed five different levels of *loculi*, niches where the bodies, wrapped in sheets, were placed in tiers. The openings to the loculi were closed with slabs of marble, but these have long since disappeared, as have any artifacts of value. A major attraction of the 40-minute guided tour (available in different languages) is the **papal crypt** with the remains of several martyred early popes. Nearby, with its Byzantine frescoes, is the **Cubiculum of St. Cecilia,** whose body was discovered here by Pope Paschal I and moved to Santa Cecilia in Trastevere (see pp. 192–93). Other cubicles have frescoes and Christian symbols carved on the walls. In the crypt of St. Eusebius is a sarcophagus containing two mummified bodies. ■

Catacombe di San Callisto
- 🅰 Map p. 215
- ✉ Via Appia Antica 126
- ☎ 06 513 01580
- 🕐 Closed 12–2 p.m., all day Wed., & month of Feb.
- 💲 $$
- 🚌 Bus: 118, 218, 660 & Archeobus

San Paolo fuori le Mura

**San Paolo fuori
le Mura**

⬛ Map p. 215

✉ Via Ostiense 186

☎ 06 541 0178

🕐 Open daily

🚌 Bus: C6, 23, 128,
761, 766. Metro:
Linea B (Basilica
San Paolo)

**San Paolo's clois-
ter is considered
by many to be the
most beautiful
in Rome.**

THE CHURCH OF SAN PAOLO FUORI LE MURA (ST. PAUL
Outside the Walls) seems a bit isolated, but remember that until the
eighth century it was physically linked to the city by a long, covered
portico that led to Porta San Paolo, the city's southernmost gate. The
church, originally a simple shrine, was built over the spot where St.
Paul was buried after being beheaded (as a Roman citizen he could not
be crucified) at the nearby Abbey of the Three Fountains (the head
supposedly bounced three times before coming to rest).

A small basilica built here by
Constantine was replaced later in
the same century and enlarged by
subsequent emperors. By the ninth
century (and until the new St.
Peter's was built), it was the largest
church in Rome and reputedly the
most beautiful. Unfortunately, it
was almost totally destroyed by a
fire in 1823. However grandiose its
19th-century replacement may be,
it is lacking in warmth and unlikely
to move you, but a visit will give
you an excellent idea of what a
classical Roman basilica looked like.
San Paolo's construction supposedly mirrors that of Trajan's magnificent Basilica Ulpia (see p. 54), the
grandest of the imperial basilicas.

San Paolo's is immense. The
large central nave is flanked by
two sets of side aisles that are separated by 80 enormous columns.
The **bronze doors,** which survived the fire, were made in
Constantinople in 1070 and decorated with Old and New Testament
scenes. Other pre-fire survivors
include the fifth-century mosaics in
the **Triumphal Arch,** a 13th-
century mosaic in the apse, and, on
the inner side of the arch, more
mosaic decoration, mostly attributed to Pietro Cavallini. The Gothic
canopy over Paul's tomb, dated
1285, is the work of Arnolfo di
Cambio. Don't miss the 18-foot
(5.5 m) 13th-century cosmatesque
paschal candlestick, decorated
with figures of animals, plants,
and scenes from the Passion of
Christ. The Cosmati maestri who
fashioned it also worked on the
cloister which, though small, is
astonishingly lovely with its fluted
and spiraling colonnettes. ■

San Lorenzo fuori le Mura

ANOTHER OF THE SEVEN PILGRIM CHURCHES, SAN LORENZO fuori le Mura (St. Lawrence Outside the Walls) is the only church in Rome to have suffered serious bombing damage during World War II. Mostly, however, it is unusual in that it was formed from the fusion of two early churches, the Minor and Major Basilicas.

The ciborium over the main altar dates from the mid-12th century and stands over St. Lawrence's tomb in a crypt below.

St. Lawrence, one of many early Christian martyrs, died a particularly gruesome death, roasted alive in the year A.D. 258 on a smoldering grid. Like many early Christians, he was buried in a catacomb outside the city on the ancient Via Tiburtina. St. Lawrence's gravesite quickly became a popular destination for pilgrims, and in A.D. 330 Emperor Constantine, by now a true friend of Christianity, built a church in his honor. In the sixth century the Minor Basilica was rebuilt (by Pope Pelagius) right next door to a fifth-century place of worship honoring the Virgin Mary. Centuries later, in 1216, another pontiff (Honorius III) joined the buildings after knocking down their apses. The **chancel** (the area where the priest officiates) and the ten columns with superb Corinthian capitals surrounding it, are from Pelagius's church. In fact, on the inner face of the chancel arch there is a sixth-century mosaic in which Pope Pelagius is seen holding a model of the building.

The **nave** and **aisles,** slightly lower in level, belonged to the second church. Its splendid 12th-century cosmatesque (see p. 206) pavement was reconstructed after the war. Admire the richly decorated cosmatesque paschal candlestick and a magnificent *ambone* (pulpit) in the same style. In the portico, lovely frescoes dramatize the lives of St. Lawrence and of St. Stephen. The remains of both these saints, together with those of St. Justin, are in the crypt. From the sacristy, in the right aisle, you come out into a charming 12th-century cloister. The campanile is from the same period. ∎

San Lorenzo fuori le Mura

🅜 Map p. 215
✉ Piazzale del Verano 3
☎ 06 491 511
🕐 Closed 12:30–3 p.m.
🚌 Bus: C2, C3, 71, 93, 492. Tram: 3, 19

The fourth-century decoration in Santa Costanza was inspired by classical motifs and is a rare example of its kind to survive in situ.

Sant'Agnese fuori le Mura

SANT'AGNESE, WHO WAS ONLY 13 AT THE TIME, WAS martyred in A.D. 304, and her cult became so popular that by the end of the century a basilica had been built over her tomb. Most impressively, the church was founded by a member of Emperor Constantine's family, although experts are still undecided whether it was Constantine's daughter (Costantina or Costantia) or perhaps a granddaughter of the same name.

Sant'Agnese fuori le Mura

- Map p. 215
- Via Nomentana 349
- 06 8620 5456
- Church: closed 12–4 p.m. Catacombs: closed 12–4 p.m. & Mon.
- $
- Bus: 60, 84, 90

Don't let such uncertainty interfere with your appreciation of this site, and of the mausoleum around the back that Costantia/Costantina later constructed for herself, today called Santa Costanza. The mosaics in the two buildings represent different moments in the development of Western art.

Sant'Agnese Outside the Walls was built by Pope Honorius I (625–638) over Agnes's catacomb (open to the public) and into the side of a hill. You enter the complex on ground level from Via Nomentana and then descend a broad staircase (early Christian tombstones and inscriptions are embedded in the walls) to reach the front entrance. The seventh-century **apse mosaic** has a gold background against which Sant'Agnese (clothed like a Byzantine princess and with the sword of martyrdom at her feet) stands between two popes. The figures are totally Byzantine, with no trace of substance or mass beneath their garments.

In contrast, the mosaic decoration in the ambulatory, or arcade, of **Santa Costanza,** the mausoleum originals of which are evident, is an eloquent example of classical mosaic art. Note the absence of any explicit Christian symbolism or iconography, which had probably not yet developed. The ceiling is covered with a variety of motifs—geometric, classical leafy scrolls, amphorae, trees, and animals—all in the best pagan tradition. ∎

Rome lends itself beautifully to the Roman's passion for the *gita fuori porta* (day outing). The city's surroundings include—amid bewitching scenery—seaside resorts, lakes, charming hilltowns, and important historical monuments.

Excursions

Detail of the Fontana della Natura in the Villa d'Este in Tivoli

Excursions

THE REACH OF THE ROMAN EMPIRE WAS EXTENSIVE. AT ITS HEYDAY ITS influence was felt far and wide, as far north as Britain, as far south as North Africa, and by the end of the first century A.D. all of Asia Minor and much of the Middle East had come under its sway. But the first focus of Roman expansion was, as is natural, close to home. Rome was founded in the eighth century B.C., and when the seven early legendary kings started looking around for their first conquests and colonies they looked at their immediate surroundings. The story goes that Ancus Marcius, the fourth king of the nascent city-state, was prescient enough to have founded Ostia, the seaport at the mouth of the Tiber River. However, this is almost certainly just a legend; the earliest remains found at Ostia date from the fourth century B.C., and the colony, in the form of a *castrum* (fortified city), was probably founded at that time.

Legend or not, it was clear from the start that an outlet to the Mediterranean was essential for growth and expansion, and indeed Ostia was to have immense strategic and commercial importance for Rome. It was, for example, the terminus for the massive grain imports from North Africa that allowed Rome to implement its policy of *panem et circensis* (bread and circuses), which proved successful in assuring the affections of the populace. Ostia Antica was the headquarters for the Annona, which was responsible for supplying Rome with grain and distributing it (generally at no cost) to the people. The Annona's presence in Ostia gave impetus to the proliferation of guilds and corporations involved in other kinds of trade. The mosaic remains of their storefronts in the Piazzale delle Corporazioni testify to their importance. So does the advanced level of decorative embellishment in the city in general, the proliferation of baths and temples, and of the *insulae* (multistory apartment houses) that will give you a good idea of what life was like in Rome as well.

Early expansion also looked eastward, and it wasn't long before the Romans set their sights on Tibur in the Sabine Hills. Originally inhabited by tribes such as the Sabines and the Volsci, it was conquered first by Tiburnus or Tiburtus, the son or grandson of a Greek hero named Amphiaraos, and quickly became the object of Roman attentions because of its strategic location on the banks of the Aniene river. Not surprisingly, when conflict between the two finally broke out, Rome emerged as the victor and Tibur's fate was sealed. By the first century B.C. its relatively cool climate and lush vegetation had made it a well-touted holiday resort for well-born, well-off Romans. It was here, in fact, that Augustus came to consult the Albunea Sibyl, who saw in one of the young emperor's dreams the onset of Christianity (thereby winning him an unusual special mention in the iconography of the Aracoeli church on Capitoline Hill in Rome). Brutus and Cassius, Julius Caesar's assassins, had villas here, as did the poets Horace and Catullus. And it was to Tivoli that emperors such as Trajan and his successor, Hadrian, repaired to wait out the hot and sultry summer months far from the heat of Rome. Even Totila, the Ostragoth chieftain who briefly conquered Rome in the sixth century, made Tivoli the capital of his short-lived reign.

It was, however, Hadrian (A.D. 117–138) who really put Tibur on the map. His magnificent imperial villa (Villa Adriana) may well be the major architectural achievement of the philosopher-emperor from Spain to whom one must already feel grateful for the Pantheon and Castel Sant'Angelo. The town's traditional appeal to the Roman elite may have reached its apex during the Renaissance, most notably after 1550 when Cardinal Ippolito II, a scion of the wealthy d'Este family, became governor and settled here. The d'Estes' architects turned an old monastery into a sumptuous palace, embellishing it with magnificently elaborate terraced gardens and a Mannerist complex of secluded grottoes, classical statuary, waterfalls, and cascading fountains. ∎

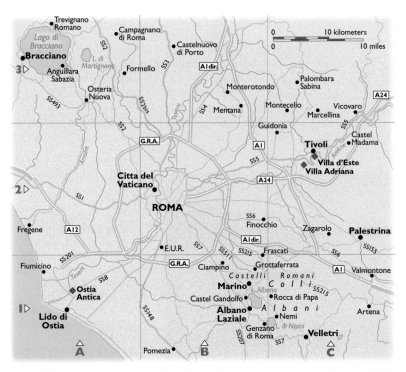

Ancient Tibur was both the home of the Sibyl and the source of travertine—Roman marble.

Ostia Antica

The Baths of Neptune in Ostia got its name from a black-and-white mosaic of the sea god in his chariot.

YOU'VE SEEN THE TIBER AS IT WINDS ITS WAY THROUGH Rome. You know the location of the old river ports where barges and boats laden with everything from fresh produce to squealing livestock ended their upriver course. Now let's follow the river back down to its mouth on the Mediterranean and see what remains of the settlement, Ostia, that grew up there, becoming first a military installation and then a major port. In its heyday, the inhabitants exceeded 100,000 and the city extended over 148 acres (60 ha).

Not far from Rome (14 miles/23 km away), it can be reached easily by car or subway.

Ostia (the name comes from *ostium*, the Latin word for "river mouth") was probably Rome's first colony, and the oldest remains found date from the fourth century B.C. By late Republican times (the second century B.C.), it had become Rome's major port, as well as an important naval outpost. Throughout the first two centuries of the Imperial period, Ostia was to thrive, gradually acquiring the trappings—fora, basilicas, porticoes—

Ostia Antica

- Map p. 225
- Viale dei Romagnoli 717, Ostia
- 06 5635 2830
- Closed Mon. (museum also closed Sun. afternoon)
- $$. Audio guide: $
- Metro Linea B to the Piramide stop then take the train to the Ostia Antica stop.

A visit here will give you an excellent idea of what life was like in a normal city in ancient Rome. Unlike Pompeii, Ostia was not a resort for the rich or a pleasure dome for the powerful. Although its location on the terminus of an international trade route inevitably gave it a cosmopolitan character, it was above all a living, breathing urban complex made up for the most part of ordinary people. Much of its decorative embellishment (for example, its omnipresent mosaics) and its structures—the baths, temples, civic center, and particularly its *insulae* (multistory apartment houses)—can be assumed to be similar to those in Rome and will help you imagine lifestyles in the nearby capital. The site, easily negotiable because of its limited size, is hauntingly lovely.

of an important urban center. It then had to face the competition of Portus, the newer port begun by Emperor Claudius in A.D. 42, completed by Nero, and enlarged by Trajan. It maintained its primacy until Constantine's reign in the early fourth century when a newer port was built nearby. It gradually became more residential, but was to remain an important passenger port for decades to come. For example, when St. Monica died here at the end of the fourth century, she and her son, the future St. Augustine, were awaiting passage to Africa.

In later times Ostia was to be abandoned, ravaged by Saracen invasions and endemic malaria. But at its apex, it had all the amenities, cultural and otherwise: a lovely ancient Roman theater (still used in summer), scores of bathhouses, shops, temples, and taverns, as well as commercial offices, which were concentrated in the Piazzale delle Corporazioni, a sort of ancient mall or port authority.

Who lived (and worked) in the Ostia of yore? Shippers and shipbuilders, merchants and traders, grain weighers, tanners, ropemakers, carters, tavern keepers, prostitutes, and priests. Only about half of the city has been excavated, but digs have brought to light invaluable information about lifestyles and residential patterns. Unlike Pompeii, domestic architecture here mostly eschewed the one-story *domus*, a dwelling built around a central atrium and preferred by the wealthy. The lower- or middle-class dwellings of Ostia were rooms or apartments in buildings that by law were allowed to climb as high as four stories (about 46 feet/14 m high). Windows were probably made of mica or selenite (when not simply covered by fabric). Balconies were frequent and the ground floor was often, though not always, reserved for shops.

To get the best possible sense of this ancient coastal town you'll need several hours. Start at the beginning

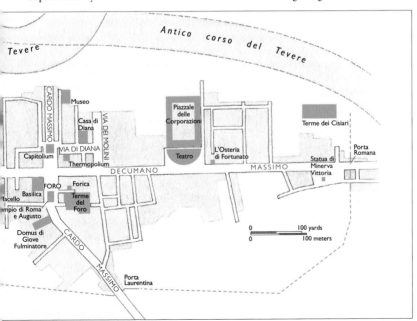

In summer you can still see productions of classical drama in Ostia's theater, built 2,000 years ago by Augustus's son-in-law. Three surviving ancient masks are on the right side of the stage.

of the **Decumano Massimo,** the main drag as it were, lined with shops, baths, theaters, and warehouses. This street was the in-city continuation of the Via Ostiensis (which connected Ostia to Rome), and, as in most Roman colonies, was crossed at midpoint by the Cardo Massimo, which formed the north–south axis. Just inside the Porta Romana, the main gateway to the city, to the left, is a large **Statua di Minerva Vittoria** (Statue of Victory), dating from the first century A.D., which may have once stood atop the gateway. To the right, a path leads to the **Terme dei Cisiari,** Carter Guild's Bathhouse, with a black-and-white mosaic of a cart and driver that you really shouldn't miss. Farther along the Decumanus, at the **Osteria di Fortunato,** or Tavern of

Fortunatus, the mosaic inscription on the floor appears to be a form of early advertising. It reads "Fortunatus says: drink from this bowl to quench your thirst." Continuing on you will come to the **teatro** or theater, built by Agrippa, which held between 2,000 and 3,000 people. Originally, there were three tiers of seats (the top one has not survived) and, like today, there were snack stands in the alcoves between the external arches on the ground floor.

The pulse of second-century Ostia may have beat hardest, however, in the **Piazzale delle Corporazioni,** a huge portico right behind the theater where some 70 local guilds and foreign corporations had their offices and whose trademarks, which have supplied historians with invaluable

depict the day's fare. You can make out eggs, fruits, and vegetables.

If at the next crossroad you turn right, you'll come to the **Museo Ostiense** that displays artworks found during the excavations. A snack bar and bookshop are behind it. Otherwise, continue on to the Cardo Massimo. Turn left and you'll find yourself in the **Foro** or Forum, which is where the Cardo and the Decumano intersect. At one end of the square was the **Capitolium.** Ostia's major temple, dedicated to Jupiter, Juno, and Minerva, still has the broad staircase that leads up to the *cella*, with niches, now empty, for statues of the gods. A second temple, **Tempio di Roma e Augusto,** dedicated to Rome and Augustus, faced it at the opposite end of the forum. The terme, or baths, and the basilica, or law courts, flanked the area on the right and left. And you won't want to miss the *forica* (public latrine) near the baths, with its 20 seats, all in a row.

Farther down the Decumano, you will eventually leave the section corresponding to the *castrum* (the earlier, fortified city) and enter the newer Ostia Antica. Take Via della Foce, to the right, from which a long pathway (to your left) leads to the **Mitreo delle Pareti Dipinte** where the sun god Mithra was worshiped. Continue along the Via delle Foce to the **Insula degli Aurighi,** where frescoed walls depict two charioteers, the sports heroes of yesteryear. Leaving the insula from the other side, find your way back to the Decumano, where there are more baths, a traders' guild (the **Schola di Traiano),** and a market (the Macello). Back behind the Temple of Rome and Augustus, on the Cardo, are a number of elegant one-story houses. The **Domus di Giove Fulminatore** has an interesting welcome mat: a mosaic depicting a phallus. ∎

information, have been immortalized in the arcade's mosaic floors.

Next turn right from the Decumanus onto the Via dei Molini, then take the first street on the left, Via di Diana. The **Casa di Diana,** a large *insula,* or apartment block, gives you a good idea of the architectural layout of the times: shops on the ground floor, apartments with windows on the first floor, and balconies higher up. Next is the **Thermopolium,** a latter-day restaurant or snack bar that is fascinating for the degree to which it shows how little things have changed. The Thermopolium has stone seats near the door (for waiting customers, perhaps?), an L-shaped counter, and near a door leading out to a patio are holes in the wall probably for coat hooks. Above a display shelf, faded frescoes

Tivoli

GREEN HILLS, RIVERS, AND CASCADING WATERFALLS—FOR centuries, ancient Tibur (later Tivoli) was a well-known summer resort. The well-born of Rome were attracted by the gentler summer climate of the Sabine Hills and came here to build their villas or, as in the case of Augustus, to consult the Albunea Sibyl. Poets and princes, emperors and barbarian chieftains frequently chose it as the location of their vacation houses. If contemporary Tivoli has unfortunately lost much of its charm in the onslaught of runaway postwar building construction, the historic center still retains much of the atmosphere of a medieval hill town.

Tivoli
- Map p. 225
- **Visitor information**
- Largo Garibaldi
- 0774 334 522
- Open Mon.–Sat. 9 a.m.–1 p.m. & Tues., Wed., Fri. (& Sat. in summer) 2:30–5:30 p.m.; closed Sun.
- Metro: Linea B to Ponte Mammolo, then CoTral bus to Tivoli. Train: Departures hourly from Stazione Tiburtina in Rome

Villa d'Este
- Map p. 225
- Piazza Trento 1
- 0774 31 20 70 (call ahead to make sure fountains are working)
- Closed Mon.
- $$

Opposite:
Cardinal Ippolito spared no expense in creating his terraced gardens where hundreds of jets of water spring from sculpted fountains.

The **Rocca Pia,** or Fortress, built over the ruins of a Roman amphitheater, dates back to the 15th century. There are some lovely churches. **Santa Maria Maggiore,** a fifth-century church next door to Villa d'Este *(Closed p.m.),* was rebuilt in the 13th century and has a Gothic portal set in a Romanesque facade. The church of **San Silvestro,** charmingly Romanesque except for a hideous, recently built glass front door and a couple of garish shrines, contains some extremely attractive 13th-century frescoes. Next door is an interesting fountainhead and nearby is the attractive Casa Gotica (Gothic House). **San Lorenzo,** the Duomo, unfortunately was rebuilt in the 17th century, but the "Triptych of the Saviour" in wood (12th century) with a gold-and-silver cover (15th century) is definitely worth a look. The same goes for the disturbingly modern 13th-century "Deposition" group.

Walk down Via Valerio and along Via della Sibilla to the Sibilla restaurant to see the remains of both the circular **Tempio di Vesta** and the rectangular **Tempio della Sibilla.** Not far from here on Largo Sant'Angelo is the entrance to the gardens of **Villa Gregoriana,** with its lovely waterfall.

Throughout its history, then, Tivoli has been a favored resort destination, but its fame as a getaway location was heightened by Emperor Hadrian's decision to make it the site of his magnificent imperial villa. The inventiveness of his design enabled him to create a sprawling residence where intellectuals and friends could enjoy the pleasures of a contemplative life. More than a thousand years later a noble (but weren't they all?) Renaissance churchman decided to make life in Tivoli bearable by turning a dilapidated Benedictine monastery into a lovely villa. This was embellished by one of the most fascinating garden and fountain complexes in the world, recently listed by UNESCO as one of Italy's 31 major historical/artistic sites.

VILLA D'ESTE

Cardinal Ippolito II, a son of Lucrezia Borgia, wanted to be pope. But things didn't work out, so in around 1550 this scion of the wealthy d'Este family of Ferrara settled for the governorship of Tivoli and decided to make the best of it. Money was not a problem, and the cardinal wasted no time in engaging the services of major architects to turn an old monastery into a sumptuous palace, the Villa d'Este. After dispossessing many small landowners, they embellished

Organ fountain once played music while the Owl and Bird fountain made hooting and chirping sounds. You can also visit the rooms of the *appartamento nobile,* but make sure you don't miss the Loggia dello Scalone, that is the terrace, from which there is a lovely view.

VILLA ADRIANA

Just a few miles outside of Tivoli are the ruins of Emperor Hadrian's villa, or summer estate, undoubtedly the largest and most elaborate Roman imperial palace ever to have existed. As you can see from the model in the kiosk near the entrance, it extends over a broad area and includes the remains of an enormous villa, with baths, theaters, libraries, and extensive gardens. Choose a nice day and plan on spending several hours here.

Hadrian (see p. 21) ruled between A.D. 117 and 138. He began building this pleasure palace shortly after he ascended the throne and completed it in A.D. 133, although by that time he was ill and grief-stricken by the deaths of his wife and of Antinous, his young lover. Hadrian is known for other architectural achievements such as the Pantheon and Castel Sant'Angelo in Rome, but the villa is his masterpiece. Much traveled and highly educated, when he built the villa (which took about 15 years to complete), Hadrian sought to re-create, or re-evoke, some of the world's architectural wonders. The vast sprawling site (almost 300 acres/121 ha) was designed both as a monument to man's achievements and as a place for study and reflection. Below is a network of tunnels, some large enough for a horse and carriage.

Your best move here is to buy a brochure in the bookstore adjacent to the café, and to follow the suggested itinerary. From the

it with magnificently extensive terraced gardens and an elaborate Mannerist complex of secluded grottoes, classical statuary, and fountains. After the cardinal died, the villa fell into neglect. In the 1920s, it was restored and opened to the public.

Among the most bewitching of the mossy fountains are: the Fontana del Bicchierone (water pours out from a large shell-shaped basin), attributed by many art historians to Bernini; the Rometta fountain is a miniature Rome complete with Tiber, Tiber Island, and a wolf-suckling Romulus and Remus; in the Avenue of the Hundred Fountains, animal heads, lilies, a small boat, basins, and so on all spurt water; the sibyl in the Fontana dell'Ovato watches over naiads and river gods; the Water

Above: The Canopus illustrated how the philosopher-emperor Hadrian sought to create in his villa an atmosphere conducive to study and reflection.

Above left: Fountain depicting the goddess Diana as a fertility symbol, Villa d'Este

Villa Adriana

🅰 Map p. 225

✉ Via di Villa Adriana 204

☎ 06 3996 7900

🕐 Open daily

💲 $$. Audio guide: $. Tours in English on request: $$$$$

🚇 Metro: Linea B to Ponte Mammolo, then CoTral bus (direction Via Prenestina), which stops 300 m from site. Or train from the Stazione Tiburtina to Tivoli, then CAT bus No. 4, which also stops 300 m from site.

parking lot you enter through the high perimeter wall to find yourself at midpoint in the **Pecile**, a large square with an enormous reflecting pool, said to have been modeled on the Stoa Pokile of Athens. It was originally covered over and surrounded by a portico. As you will see, it is also the upper story of a vast construction with hundreds of rooms, probably for slaves and other palace staff. Continuing on you come to the Small Baths and the Large Baths, much of which are still standing. Next is one of the complex's most mystical monuments, the **Canopus.**

This is a reflecting pool, 750 feet (228 m) long, surrounded by columns and statuary (don't miss either the river god or the stone crocodile) and ending in a large nymphaeum (the Serapis) that

once held fountains and statues. It is believed to have been inspired by the canal that linked Alexandria in Egypt to ancient Canopus. Along the west side are six caryatids like those on the Erechtheum on the Acropolis in Athens. Returning via the Stadium, and the Room with Three Exhedrae or apses (probably a large outdoor dining room), are the remains of the **palace proper,** an enormous structure composed of pavilions built around peristyles or courtyards. Don't miss the Fishpool Quadriportico, the Hall of the Doric Columns, the Heliocaminus Baths which may have been heated by solar power, the circular Maritime Theater, and the Republican Villa where you can see the remains of mosaic floors and vault decorations. ■

More excursions from Rome

Italians love Sunday outings and fortunately the regional bus company, CoTral, goes most places *(tel 800 431784 for information)*. If you have a car, so much the better, as all roads leading out of Rome go someplace interesting. Here are some suggestions.

CASTELLI ROMANI

The Castelli Romani (Roman Castles) are small hilltop towns in the Alban Hills southeast of Rome. Situated among the chestnut trees, olive groves, and vineyards that cover the slopes of these extinct volcanoes, they are best known for their white wine, *porchetta* (roast pork), and restaurants.

Frascati, home of the best-known Roman white wine, was founded in the Middle Ages and because of its cooler clime became a resort for the wealthy who built luxurious villas (many of which sadly were damaged by Allied bombing during World War II). The best preserved is Villa Aldobrandini while the park attached to Villa Torlonia has wonderful fountains designed by Carlo Maderno. Nearby is **Tusculum,** an Etruscan settlement said to have been founded by Telegonus, a son of Ulysses, and the siren Circe; the view from the ruins (a forum, a small theater and an amphitheater) is wonderful.

Grottaferrata's beautiful fortified Greek-rite abbey was founded by St. Nilus in the 10th century and later incorporated into a castle. Don't miss the chapel of St. Nilus in the Church of Santa Maria, with Domenichino's wonderful frescoes. **Marino,** on Lake Castelgandolfo (or Albano), is known for its October wine festival, when the town fountains spew forth wine rather than water. There's a Guido Reni painting in the Trinità church and a Mithraeum with interesting frescos. Medieval **Rocca di Papa** is the highest of the Castelli, whereas the most charming is **Nemi,** a tiny hilltown with a Renaissance castle that overlooks a miniscule lake in a crater. The remains of two of the Emperor Caligula's pleasure boats (unfortunately burned by the Germans in 1944) are housed in a small museum. **Genzano,** across

Lake Nemi, with its lovely lakeside restaurants and a 13th-century castle, is known for the June *"infiorata"* when the streets are "paved" with pictures made out of flower petals. Near Albano, once the Castra Albana, headquarters of Rome's Second Legion, is the Etruscan-style Roman tomb of the Horatii and Curiatii. And **Castel Gandolfo's** castle, the Pope's summer residence, was built by Carlo Maderno over an earlier fortress. The fountain in the piazza is by Bernini.

🗺 Map p. 225 **Visitor information**
✉ Piazza Marconi 1, Frascati ☎ 06 942 0331 (for Frascati and Grottaferrata) 🕐 Open 8 a.m.–2 p.m. & sometimes 3–6 p.m.; closed Sun. 🚇 Metro: Linea A to Anagnina then CoTral bus to all Castelli Romani towns. Train: Termini Station to Frascati.

PALESTRINA

Some say ancient Praeneste was also founded by Telegonus. In any event, this medieval-looking town outside Rome is built over the remains of the Sanctuary of Fortuna Primigenia, a Roman shrine that dates back to the second century B.C. This may have been the largest Hellenistic construction in Italy, a series of climbing terraces culminating in a (now) partially reconstructed temple. Its foundations are incorporated into the Palazzo Colonna-Barberini, currently the site of the Museo Nazionale Archeologico Prenestino which hosts numerous statues, artifacts, and reliefs. But its prize possession is the remarkable Nile Mosaic, discovered in the city's ancient Forum. The Cathedral of St. Agapitus has a 12th-century campanile but was built over the remains of a pagan temple. A grill opens on to a small section of Roman Road. The Renaissance musician Giovanni Pierluigi da Palestrina, the creator of contrapuntal composition, was born here.

🗺 Map p. 225 **Visitor information** ✉ Via Barberini 2 ☎ 06 957 3176 🕐 Closed 1–3 p.m. 🚇 Metro: Linea A to Anagnina then CoTral bus to Palestrina. Train: Termini Station to Zagarolo, then CoTral bus to Palestrina. ∎

Travelwise

Traffic policeman

TRAVELWISE INFORMATION

Rome is a very rewarding city to visit and, on the whole, it's also very welcoming. However, some aspects of life here are difficult to understand for those used to a more streamlined (and less idiosyncratic) way of doing things. Although some people feel tales of Italian inefficiency are exaggerated, there is no doubt that the pace of life (and of change) is slower here, and some of the procedures you're likely to have to undertake may take far longer, or be much more complicated, than you would have expected.

PLANNING YOUR TRIP

WHEN TO GO

The peak tourist seasons in Rome are May–June and September–October, when temperatures are perfect for sightseeing. Easter is also busy, with pilgrims flocking to the city for Holy Week. Christmas, on the other hand, attracts fewer visitors. January and February are definitely the quietest months for tourists.

From May through summer, Rome's social life takes place outdoors. Restaurants and bars move their tables onto streets and piazzas, and there is a plethora of open-air cinemas and arts festivals. Many stores and restaurants shut in August, but fewer do so than in previous years. Romans have learned that the city can be enjoyable in August, when traffic jams end and the thermometer drops a bit compared to July.

In recent years hotel prices have risen significantly, but discounts can sometimes be had in summer as well as in January and February.

CLIMATE

Rome has mild, damp winters; the temperature seldom drops below freezing and it rarely snows. Spring and fall tend to be rainy and warmish. Summer is hot—sometimes oppressively so in July and August—and, apart from the occasional dramatic thunderstorm, dry. The rainiest months are October, November and—to a somewhat lesser degree—December. It may, of course, rain at any time of the year—the average rainfall is 31 inches a year—but to make up for it, you're unlikely to have more than two or three days without seeing the sun, whatever the season.

WHAT TO TAKE

Casual clothes prevail except in banking or political circles, so you can pretty much wear what you like. However, if you are planning to visit any churches, make sure not to wear shorts or a very short skirt, and cover your arms to at least the elbow or there is a chance you will not be allowed in. You'll also probably want to have one fairly elegant outfit for the evening. In spring and fall, it's a good idea to dress in layers because, although daytime temperatures are warm and balmy, temperatures in the evenings can drop sharply. In winter, remember that interiors are heated less than in the United States—definitely bring warm clothes.

Bring comfortable shoes because the cobblestoned streets can be hard on the feet. An umbrella is a good idea at any time of year and essential in the spring and fall wet seasons. Sunglasses are also advisable because even the winter sun can be dazzling. Binoculars will help you make the most of views and lavishly decorated interiors.

Other essentials are your passport, driver's license, credit cards, insurance documentation, and, if you're using them, travelers' checks. In Italy you're meant to carry proof of your identity at all times—although you're unlikely to need to produce it.

INSURANCE

Take out enough travel insurance to cover emergency medical treatment, repatriation, and loss or theft of money and possessions.

HOW TO GET TO ROME

PASSPORTS

U.S. and Canadian citizens do not need a visa for stays in Italy of up to three months. By law, however, all visitors are supposed to announce their presence to the local police. Hotels do this for you—leave your passport at reception when you check in and you'll get it back the following morning. You have to do this every time you check into a hotel, even if it's just for one night. Independent travelers and anybody staying for more than three months should contact the central police station (La Questura), tel 064686, to find out what to do.

AIRPORTS

Rome now has two international airports, Leonardo da Vinci-Fiumicino, southwest of Rome, and the smaller Ciampino, southeast of the city, both run by Aeroporti di Roma (tel 0665951, www.adr.it). The website has transport information as well as real-time arrival and departure flight information. Ciampino currently services low-cost airlines such as Ryanair and easyJet, charters, and regional Italian airlines. The Aeroporti di Roma website has plenty of other useful information.

Getting to Rome center from Fiumicino Airport

The "Leonardo Express" train departs every 30 minutes from about 6:30 a.m. to 11:30 p.m. The nonstop trip costs €9.50, and takes about 30 minutes. The FM1 Metropolitan train to Trastevere, Ostiene, Tiburtina, and on to Orte departs every 15 minutes, starting at 5:57 a.m. and ending at 22:36, and costs €5. For exact individual departures times go to www.trenitalia .com/it/treni_stazioni/trasferime nti/index.html#servmetro. A taxi from Fiumicino to Rome center is about €45.

Getting to Rome center from Ciampino Airport

This hub for the low-cost airlines has upgraded transportation to the city center. Taxis to downtown Rome cost between €40 and €50, depending on your destination. Terravision runs buses to Termini railroad station. Show your boarding pass or airline ticket to purchase tickets on board or at the Terravision desk in the Arrivals area. (In Rome, go to Agenzia 365, Via Marsala 22, across from the Termini station.) Round-trip tickets cost €13.50; one way is €8. Cotral (tel 800 150 008, www.cotralspa.it) runs regular airport buses to and from Anagnina (the last stop on the A line subway), as well as a midnight bus from/to Termini (€5). Schiaffini (tel 800 700 805) runs buses every 20 minutes to Anagnina metro or the Ciampino train station, from which you can get trains to Termini.

GETTING AROUND

BY CAR

Car rentals
In Italy:
Avis, tel 199 100133
www.avisautonoleggio.it
Budget, tel 06 482 0966
Europcar, tel 800 014410,
www.europcar.it

Hertz, tel 199 112211
www.hertz.it
Maggiore, tel 848 867 067
Sixt, tel 199 100 666 or, from abroad or from a cell phone, 0039 06 65211, www.sixt.it

Unless you're planning on making a lot of trips out of the city, a car in central Rome is more of a hindrance than a help. Parking is nearly impossible, and the local driving style is daunting. If you do need to rent a car, check prices before leaving home. Rentals booked in the U.S. often cost less. Car rental in Italy is about the most expensive in Europe as, incidentally, is gas.

Driving regulations & conventions

An international driver's license is not required for short-term visitors. When driving, keep all relevant documents (including at least a photocopy of your passport) in the car. Driving regulations in Italy are not always strictly adhered to (although you should do so). Remember also that, despite appearances to the contrary, pedestrians always have right of way. Zebra-stripe crosswalks indicate where pedestrians have precedence over automobile traffic. In contrast, at an intersection with a functioning traffic light, pedestrians must wait for the green to cross.

Italian law makes the use of seatbelts obligatory and—although you never could tell—also prohibits driving while using a cell phone without a headset. On major roads, headlights should be on even in daytime and most drivers use their parking lights in the city on rainy days. Remember that in Italy a car flashing its headlights at you generally means the driver will be taking the right of way and not giving it to you as in the U.K.

Although speeding is a national pastime, there are official limits in Italy. The speed limit in built-up areas is 30 mph (50 kph);

other normal roads, 70 mph (110 kph); and motorways, 80 mph (130 kph). The legal limit for drinking and driving works out to about two drinks.

If you are parked illegally or if your parked car is blocking somebody else's access, the police may tow it away. If you think this has happened, call the Polizia Municipale (tel 06 676 9838) to find out where it is, when to collect it, and how to pay the fine.

Car breakdown
Rental car companies have an emergency number for break-downs. Otherwise call the emergency number of the Automobile Club d'Italia (tel 803 116 and press "3" at the prompt to get an English-speaking operator). Emergency phones are located along the Autostrade toll roads.

PUBLIC TRANSPORTATION

Buses, trams, the metro, and local rail services in Rome are all integrated into one transport system. Tickets can be bought at most tobacconists (tabacchi), newsstands, stations, and from machines near major bus stops. An ordinary ticket (BIT—biglietto integrato a tempo, €1) entitles you to 75 minutes of unlimited bus and/or tram travel plus one journey by train or metro. A day pass (BIG—biglietto integrato giornaliero, €5) is valid until midnight. A BTI (biglietto turistico integrato, €11) is good until midnight of the third day after purchase. A CIS (carta integrata settimanale, €16) is a weekly pass.

All tickets must be validated at the beginning of your first ride and again if you switch to the metro or vice versa. Machines for doing this are on buses or at the entrance to metro and train stations. Keep the validated ticket until the end of your journey in case you are queried by an inspector.

Metropolitana

The Rome subway, where many stations have been spruced up with original mosaics by top contemporary artists, operates from 5:30 a.m. to 11:30 p.m. (Saturday until 12:30 a.m.). Rome has only two subway lines (A and B) which cross at Termini and do not go to many areas of the city. However, the A line does go to Piazza di Spagna and Piazza Barberini, to near the Vatican Museums (Cipro) and out to Cinecittà. Due to ongoing renovations, the A line closes at 9 p.m., after which you can take the replacement bus lines, the MA1 and the MA2. The B line is useful for trips to the Colosseum, the Circus Maximus, the Pyramid (near Cimitero Acattolico–Protestant Cemetery), and St. Paul's Basilica, which is rather out of the way.

Buses & trams

ATAC has a vast bus and tram system, which can take you almost anywhere in the city (at peak hours travel times can be lengthy). On weekdays most lines run until 12 a.m. or 12:30 a.m; there are several nighttime, or *notturni,* lines as well. A series of small, electric buses navigate the historic center's narrow streets and are good for sightseers. The 119 runs every 10–15 minutes and will take you around the historic center; the 117 runs from S. Giovanni to Piazza del Popolo; the 116 from the Gianicolo and Piazza Farnese to near the Borghese gardens; the 115 will take you from Viale Trastevere to the Janiculum park; and the 125 goes around Trastevere.

For information about bus routes call 800 431 784 (Mon.–Sat., 8 a.m.–8 p.m.) or use the excellent ATAC website (www.atac.roma.it) in Italian or English. The Trovalinea box lets you see any bus line's exact route. Be wary of pickpockets, especially on the 64 and 40 lines which serve the Vatican and other tourist areas.

Buses to many towns in the Lazio Region are operated by Cotral (tel 800 150 008, www.cotralspa.it), departing from eight termini coinciding with railway and metro stations. Its website has no English translation but see "*Trasporto, capolinea*" for a list of destinations and "*Linee e Orari*" for the full schedule. People over 70 years of age travel free.

Taxis

Taxis are available at taxi stands, generally marked with blue-and-white or orange-and-black signs saying "Taxi." They can also be hailed in the street, although by law they are not allowed to pick you up within 100 meters of a stand. Almost all Rome taxis are now white although a few yellow cabs remain. When a cab is free the "taxi" sign on the roof is lit up. Rome taxis run on meters, which start at €2.33 and increase about 20 cents every 20 seconds (more if you're traveling out of town or at speeds above 20 km an hour). After 10 p.m. and on Sundays/holidays the start-up charge is, respectively, €4.91 and €3.36. A nighttime charge is added on between 10:30 p.m. and 7:30 a.m. on Sundays and holidays. For rides to the airport and out of town, a second fare system kicks in once you're a certain distance out of town. Additionally, sometimes drivers charge €1.04 for baggage larger than 35 x 25 x 50 cm. Tipping is optional, but a good idea if you ask for added help with your baggage.

Radio-dispatched taxis

Rome's "Radiotaxi" system is surprisingly efficient and increasingly you will find operators who speak English. However, hotels and restaurants will generally be happy to place the call for you. The two larger companies, Radiotaxi3570 and La Capitale (tel 063570 and 064994), have satellite telephone systems, so if you're speaking from a landline they don't need you to give the number or the

address, but they may ask for your name. An automatic system will tell you if a taxi is available and give you its number and the estimated number of minutes you will have to wait. If you understand and accept, just hang up. Otherwise wait until an operator comes on the line. The meter starts working when the driver accepts the call so the longer the wait time the higher the fare. All radio-dispatched taxis in Rome accept reservations but only for trips to Fiumicino or Ciampino airports or to Termini and Tiburtina train stations. If you reserve, you will receive a phone call 10 to 15 minutes before pick-up telling you the number of your taxi. Other companies are Prontotaxi (tel 066645), Tevere (tel 064157), and Cosmo (tel 068822). Drivers prefer cash but most will take credit cards if necessary (many will not take Diners Club or American Express).

Limousine & shuttle services

Airport Shuttle, tel 06 4201 3469.
Airport Connection, tel 06 338 3221.

Traffic

Newcomers to Rome may find the city's undisciplined drivers and darting mopeds intimidating. Many intersections have no traffic lights: White zebra stripes on the ground are supposed to give the pedestrian precedence, but don't count on it. Be careful, but not overly hesitant either as you may confuse drivers. Don't hesitate to hold up your arm in a "stop" gesture. You may look silly, but it helps. Where there are both traffic lights and stripes, you must observe the former.

Trains

Trains to other cities in Lazio or the rest of Italy leave from either the Termini or Tiburtina stations. You can get a specific Roma–Viterbo line from the Ostiense and Trastevere stations and a special metro line to

Viterbo runs regularly from Piazzale Flaminio (near Piazza del Popolo). Tickets can also be bought from selected travel agencies or online at www.trenitalia.it. Call 892021 (no prefix) for information and for Eurostar or Intercity bookings or purchases. You can choose the ticketless option, in which you pay by credit card and get a reservation number to give to the conductor. You can also pick up tickets from automatic teller machines at the station by inserting the same credit card. Eurostar and Intercity trains tickets can now be bought up to 10 minutes before departure if seats are available. Unless you're traveling by Eurostar, remember that before boarding you must punch your ticket in one of the yellow punch boxes scattered throughout the station.

Internal flights
Alitalia flies to most Italian cities. Air One and Meridiana also fly from Rome to other Italian cities and Ryanair has flights from Ciampino to Alghero in Sardinia, Treviso (Venezia) and Brescia (Verona).

Alitalia, tel 062222
Air One, tel 06 488 800
Meridiana, tel 199 111 333

TOURS & SIGHTSEEING

Independent sightseeing
Unless you're short on time, Rome is easy to visit on your own. The key is flexibility. Sightseeing hours at major attractions are much longer than in the past, but because of staff shortages and strikes, official opening hours are not always reliable. In general, archaeological sites are open the whole day, closing an hour before sunset. Museums sell their last tickets an hour before closing. Churches generally close from noon to 3 p.m. and then for the night at around 7 p.m. Most sites offer discounts to children, students, and seniors over 65.

The Rome Tourist Office's help line (tel 06 8205 9127, open 9 a.m.–7 p.m.) can provide information, in English, about events, hours, and transport (press "2" for an English-speaking operator). There are also a dozen information centers in green pagoda-like kiosks scattered throughout the city. The English-language version of the official tourism website (www.romaturismo.it) has a lot of information (see the "Rome Welcomes You" section for important phone numbers, and "Discovering Rome" for other helpful information).

Reservations for most museums and archaeological sites can be made online at www.pierreci.it or by calling 06 3996 7700 (Mon.–Sat. 9 a.m.–1:30 p.m., 2:30–5 p.m. Small fee charged).

Wanted in Rome magazine lists all museums and other cultural events both in print and at www.wantedinrome.com.

Bus tours
Several companies now run moderate cost Stop and Go tours, which in two hours or so give you a good idea of the city. ATAC-Trambus' red double-decker Open 110 departs Termini every 20 minutes (8:40 a.m.–8:20 p.m., €13) and makes 11 stops (10 on weekdays). You can get on at any of the stops and buy your ticket on board, but the upper deck fills up quickly. In peak season, the company suggests early morning departures from Termini; otherwise, the wait could be very long. ATAC's smaller Archeobus leaves Termini every 40 minutes (9:30 a.m.–4 p.m., €8) and drives out to the Ancient Appian Way. The ticket office (tel 06 4695 2252) is in front of the station at platform C.

Trambus and the Vatican Pilgrim Office also run a tour called Christian Rome (Roma Cristiana). It leaves from Termini every hour (starting at 9 a.m.,

€13, ticket valid for 24 hours) and goes by all of Rome's major basilicas. The City Sightseeing Roma red double-decker buses run by Terravision (tel 06 228 3957) leave hourly from Piazza Santa Maria Maggiore (departing from in front of the basilica's entrance) and make six stops. This 1.5-hour ride costs €12 (tickets, valid for 24 hours, can be bought on board). In summer, the last complete tour starts at 6:30 p.m., in winter earlier. For an extra charge, hotel pick-ups can be arranged.

Boat tours
Rome now has its own *bateaux-mouches* running up and down the Tiber. There are several possibilities: A regularly scheduled navigation line takes you one way (€1) from Duca D'Aosta bridge near the Olympic stadium to Tiber Island, both of which have wheelchair access. It runs every hour on the hour and also stops at Ponte Sisto, Ponte S. Angelo, Ponte Cavour, and Ponte Risorgimento. A second, guided-tour boat runs five times a day starting at 9:30 a.m. from Castel S. Angelo (Hadrian's Tomb). The tour lasts one hour and ten minutes and cost €10. Reservations are suggested (tel 06 678 9631, www.battellidiroma.it/en/home .asp). Catered dinner cruises can also be arranged.

Walking tours in English
Our author Michael Brouse and his colleague Dennis Cigler conduct private walking tours in affiliation with *In Italy's Companions* (tel in U.S. 877-655-9221, www.initaly.com).

Scala Reale (tel 06 482 0911, www.scalareale.org) offers tours of the historic center, Vatican, and archaeological area.

Rome Revealed (tel 06 324 741, www.romerevealed.com) offers walking and private tours of the Vatican, Catacombs, fountains, and more.

Bicycle & scooter rental
Rome has about 160 km worth of dedicated bike paths. One path runs along Viale Tiziano; another, barring floods from a rain-swollen Tiber, runs along the river's embankments for 30 km. Many people brave the city's traffic on motorscooters, the quickest way to get anywhere with almost no parking problems. For maps and bike rentals see www.romainbici.it. For other scooter and bike rentals see www.tassoni.it/guide/moto-bike-rent.htm or call Happy Rent (Via Farini 3, tel 06 481 8185. Metro: Termini) or Bici e Baci (Via del Viminale 5, tel 06 482 8443. Bus: H, 40, 60, 64, 75. Metro: Repubblica).

PRACTICAL ADVICE

COMMUNICATIONS

POST OFFICES
The Italian post office, which has branches in every neighborhood, has been largely reorganized in recent years and is far more functional than in previous years. The main post office, at Piazza San Silvestro 19 (open Mon.–Sat. 8:30 a.m.–6:30 p.m), has been totally revamped and has splendid service and a helpful, multilingual information desk. Most tourists' needs will involve mailings (mailing boxes and padded envelopes can be bought here along with stamps), so go straight to the line for *Prodotti postali* and avoid *Prodotti finanziari*, which is for paying bills, picking up pensions, and the like. Most smaller post offices (Mon.–Fri. 8:30 a.m.–2 p.m., Sat. 8:30 a.m.–1 p.m.) now have a number queuing system—but make sure you take a number for the proper sector. Still, unless you are sending a package, your best bet is to buy stamps from a tobacconist. Letters and postcards can be mailed from one of the red boxes you will find outside the tobacconist's or outside a post office. Get the

posta prioritaria (priority mail) stamps. Outside of Italy they don't guarantee faster delivery but they will get on their way quicker. Most mailboxes have two slots, one for the city (*per la città*) and one for everywhere else (*altre destinazioni*).

You can have mail sent to you at the post office by having it addressed "*Fermo Posta*" followed by your name , the branch name, and its address.

Vatican post
The Vatican has its own postal system with two post offices in Piazza San Pietro (one on either side of the basilica). Stamps (or *francobolli*) cost marginally more than they do for the Italian system. There are mailboxes at the post offices and at the Vatican offices on Piazza San Calisto in Trastevere.

Piazza San Pietro, 00193. Bus: 19, 23, 34, 40, 62, 64, 492, 982. Metro: Ottaviano. Open: Mon.–Fri. 8:30 a.m.–7 p.m., Sat. 8:30 a.m.–6 p.m.

TELEPHONES
To call Italy from the United States, dial 011 39 (international and Italian country code) followed by the local number, which always includes the city area code, e.g. 06 for Rome, 055 for Florence, 02 for Milan, 081 for Naples, and 041 for Venice. This goes for in-city calls as well. Be aware that, not counting the area codes, Italian phone numbers can have from four digits (government offices, some embassies) to eight digits. 800 and 848 numbers are toll free. 199 numbers have a higher rate. To make an international call from Italy, dial the international country code (001 for the U.S. and Canada, 0044 for the U.K.) followed by the phone number. For directory assistance call 1254 or visit www.info412.it. To make a collect call, dial 170.

Most public phones are now operated by phone cards, which

can be bought from tobacconists, bars, and post offices. Most have clearly displayed instructions in English. To make a call, lift the receiver, then insert your card (first break off the perforated corner) in the slot. The amount of money available on your card will be shown on an LCD. Dial the number. You can watch how quickly you're using up the card on the LCD—just before it's about to expire, you'll hear a shrill sound. Insert another card to continue the conversation.

INTERNET CAFÉS

They may not be on every corner, but if you need an Internet point you can find it. **Easy Internet Café** (Via Barberini 2, open 8 a.m.–1 a.m. Metro: Barberini. Buses: 52, 53, 80, 630, 116, 119, 630) is the biggest and most modern with more than 250 stations. There's a bar with drinks and snacks, and facilities for printing and copying to disk. **Il Mastello** (Via San Francesco a Ripa 62, open 7 a.m.–10:30 p.m. Bus: H. Tram: 8 from Argentina) in Trastevere allows you to go online while doing your laundry or make long-distance calls at cheap rates at the phone center. **Pantheon Internet** (Via S. Caterina da Siena 48, tel 06 692 0051, open Mon.–Sat. 10 a.m.–8:30 p.m.) offers Internet access as well as printing, scanning, and downloads from your digital camera to a CD. **Navona Cyber Cafe** (Vicolo del Fico 17) offers Internet access, printing, scanning, and coffee.

CRIME

Rome is much safer than most American cities, but tourists are an enticing prey for thieves and pickpockets—it pays to take a few simple precautions to avoid the risk of falling victim. Carry cameras and bags across your body and keep a hand on them in crowded areas; move away if someone asking questions or jostling you on the bus seems to be just a bit too close; and be especially wary of groups of scruffy children waving cardboard or newspaper in your face while their colleagues delve into your pockets and bags. Don't leave anything on tables, chairs, or anywhere from which it could be grabbed by a passer-by. Leave valuables, money, documents, and credit cards that you don't need immediately in a hotel safe, and try not to bring out tempting wads of cash in public when you're paying for anything.

If you are robbed, go to the nearest police station to file a *denuncia* (complaint). You're unlikely to see your valuables again, but at least you can use the denuncia for insurance claims.

ELECTRICITY

Nearly all Italian circuits use 220 volts; American appliances need adapter plugs and those that operate on 110 volts will also need a transformer. These can be bought at a *ferramenta* (hardware store) or before you leave home.

LOCAL CUSTOMS

Say "*buon giorno*" (*buona sera* after lunch) and "*arrivederci*" when entering and leaving shops, restaurants, and bars. Although nobody expects you to speak Italian, an attempt to utter a few words, no matter how basic, is greatly appreciated. In general Italians use "please" and "thank you" (*per favore* and *grazie*) less than English-speakers do, so don't be offended if people seem brusque. If you are giving flowers, avoid chrysanthemums; here they are only put on graves.

MEDIA

NEWSPAPERS
Most downtown newsstands (*edicole*) have a selection of English-language papers and magazines; the *International Herald Tribune* is widely available.

The major Italian dailies are the Milan-based *Corriere della Sera*, and the Rome-based *La Repubblica*. *Il Sole 24 Ore* is the country's leading business daily.

TELEVISION
The main national stations are the state-owned RAI 1, 2, and 3, Mediaset's Italia Uno, Rete Quattro, and Canale 5. La 7 is a privately owned station. All programs are all in Italian (English-language imports are dubbed). Channels such as CNN, BBC, TV5, and CNBC are available via cable or satellite if your hotel or apartment has them.

RADIO
Vatican Radio (93.3 FM) broadcasts news and other programs in a wide range of languages including English. For 24-hour classical music without breaks, try Auditorium (100.3 FM). Radio Centro Suono (101.3 FM) plays a range of dance, reggae, ragga, Afro-Caribbean, and other music. The state-owned stations (RAI-1 on 89.7 FM, RAI-2 on 91.7 FM, and RAI-3 on 93.7 FM) broadcast a mixture of news and chat shows combined with (usually fairly middle-of-the-road) classical and light music.

BOOKS
If you're interested in ancient Rome, read Suetonius' *The Twelve Caesars*, Livy's *History of Rome*, and Tacitus' *The Histories*. Also try Robert Graves' *I Claudius* and *Claudius the God*, Marguerite Yourcenar's *Memoirs of Hadrian*, or the works of Allan Massie—*Augustus*, *Caesar*, and *Tiberius*—which, although they're fiction, give a good idea of what life was like. Literary works set in more recent times include: *Roman Fever* by Edith Wharton; *A Time in Rome* by Elizabeth Bowen; *History* by Elsa Morante; *The Marble Faun* by Nathaniel Hawthorne; and the works of Roman author Alberto Moravia.

MONEY MATTERS

Banca Intesa, Via del Corso 226, tel 06 67121.
American Express, Piazza di Spagna 38, tel 06 67641.
Thomas Cook, Piazza Barberini 21/A, tel 06 4202 0150.
Banca Nazionale del Lavoro (BNL), Via Bissolati 2 (Piazza Barberini), tel 06 47031.

At midnight on January 1, 2002, the euro became the only legal tender in Italy as well as in eleven other European countries. There are 100 cents to the euro which is available, in bills, in denominations of 1, 2, 5, 10, 20, 100, and 500 as well as in coins worth 1, 2, 5, 10, 20, and 50 cents.

To change money, go to any of the financial offices listed above, a major bank, or a store-front exchange office (look for the "*cambio*" sign). The best bet, however, is to use your debit or credit card at one of the hundreds of ATMs in the city. Called Bancomat machines, they generally give you a choice of operating languages. Travelers checks are accepted by many stores and hotels but seem to be falling out of use. The main post office will also change U.S. dollars, British pounds, Swiss francs, and Japanese Yen into euros.

NATIONAL HOLIDAYS

Jan. 1, Jan. 6, Easter Sun., Easter Mon., April 25, May 1, June 2, June 29 (Rome only), Aug. 15, Nov. 1, Dec. 8, Dec. 25, Dec. 26.

OPENING TIMES

Hours in Rome can be erratic, making sightseeing and shopping difficult. Many shops in downtown Rome now stay open all day, but have no obligation to do so. Those in other areas like Trastevere or Testaccio still tend to close at lunchtime (generally 1 or 1:30 p.m.–3:30 or 4 p.m.) so to be sure phone first. Most Italian banks are open 8:30 or 8:45

a.m.–1:30 p.m. and 2:45–4:15 p.m. Mon.–Fri.; a very few are also open Saturday mornings. Many clothing stores are still closed on Monday mornings, as are hairdressers. Supermarkets are now generally open on Sundays as well and, since it's optional, so are some other stores, although most shopkeepers prefer to take the day off.

Bars open in the early morning; some close at 8 p.m. but many in the center stay open until midnight or 2 a.m. Traditional restaurants generally serve between 12:30–3 p.m. and 8–11 p.m. But today some areas of central Rome, such as Trastevere, have many restaurants catering to tourists which open at noon and stay open the entire day. Many businesses close for summer holidays in August.

TIME DIFFERENCES

Europe changes to daylight savings time on the last Sunday of March, one week before the U.S.; both countries return to standard time the last Sunday in October. Therefore, most days when it's midnight in Rome, it's 6 p.m. in New York and 3 p.m. in Los Angeles.

TIPPING

If service is not included on the bill (it appears as a separate charge under "servizio"), add about ten percent—depending on how satisfied you've been—which should be left in cash if you're paying with a credit card. Even when the tip is included, it's normal to leave some small change if the service has been good.

TOILETS

Rome has few public toilets, but bars and cafés must let you use theirs if you ask. One toilet often serves both men and women, so don't be surprised if a member of the opposite sex is using it when you arrive.

Standards of hygiene vary dramatically but tend toward the lower end of the scale; it's a good idea to carry tissues as toilet paper isn't guaranteed.

TRAVELERS WITH DISABILITIES

Rome is not an easy city for people with disabilities. Most museums now have wheelchair-accessible bathrooms and stair lifts, but the entrances and exits of many museums, shops, restaurants, and hotels have not yet been made accessible. The Vatican Museum, which has ten wheelchairs available at its Guardaroba (cloakroom), is a notable exception. Many sidewalks in Rome lack curb cuts or ramps and those that exist are often steep. Stair lifts in museums and churches (even those that appear fairly new) tend to be narrower, shorter, and have a lower weight capacity than those in the U.S. There are elevators at all the metro stations on the B line except for Circo Massimo, Colosseo, and Cavour. Only Cipro (Vatican) and Valle Aurelia have elevators on the A line. (When necessary, Romans will help carry a disabled person up the stairs.)

A reliable but expensive private van service is Fausta Trasporti (tel 06 503 6040). Free guided tours for disabled persons (English-speaking as well as Italians) are available through CO.IN, a nonprofit organization, but book early (tel 06 570 6036).

EMERGENCIES

EMBASSIES & CONSULATES

British Embassy and Consulate, Via XX Settembre 80/A (Porte Pia), 00187, tel 06 4220 0001. Bus: 16, 36, 60, 61, 62, 84, 90, 492. Canadian Embassy, Via G.B. De Rossi 27, 00161, tel 06 445 981. Bus: 36, 60, 62, 84, 90; Metro:

Linea B (Bologna). Canadian Consulate, Via Zara 30, tel 06 445981.

United States Embassy, Palazzo Margherita, Via V. Veneto 119/A, 00187, tel 06 46 741. Metro: Barberini. Consulate, Via V. Veneto 121, tel 06 46 741.

EMERGENCY PHONE NUMBERS & ADDRESSES

Police, tel 113
Carabinieri, tel 112
Fire, tel 115
Emergency medical assistance, tel 118
Italian Red Cross, tel 065510

Nighttime pharmacies:
Piran, Via Nazionale 228, tel 06 488 0754
Farmacia Internazional, Piazza Barberini 49, tel 487 1195

The Vatican Pharmacy (enter Vatican at the Porta Sant'Anna entrance, tel 06 686 4146, open Mon.–Fri. 8:30 a.m.–6 p.m. & Sat. 7:30 a.m.–1 p.m. Bus: 23, 49, 51) has English-speaking staff and a wide range of non-Italian pharmaceutical products.

LOST PROPERTY

Oggetti Rinvenuti, Via Nicolo Bettoni 1 (Trastevere train station), tel 06 581 6040 or 06 581 0583. Bus: H, 780; Tram: 3, 8. Open 8:30 a.m.–1 p.m. Mon.–Fri., also 3–5 p.m. Tues. & 1–5 p.m. Thurs. Termini station at track 24, tel 06 4782 5543. Open 7 a.m.–midnight.

Lost credit cards
American Express, tel 06 72 900 347
Diners Club, tel 800 864 064
MasterCard, tel 800 870 866
Visa, tel 800 819 014

HOTELS & RESTAURANTS

While Rome is not particularly known for its accommodations, both luxurious and charming places do exist, if you know where to look. The cuisine is a different story. It's very difficult to eat badly in Rome—even the humblest of fare in the smallest trattoria is usually lovingly prepared and tasty.

HOTELS

Accommodation in Rome for the most part is scarce and expensive: You should book as much in advance as possible. You'll probably be asked for a faxed confirmation and a deposit or credit card number. Many Rome hotels and restaurants do not take American Express or Diners Club so check if you are planning to pay your final bill with either of those cards.

Central Rome (especially Trastevere and the areas around Piazza Navona and Campo dei Fiori) is noisy until 2 or 3 a.m. every night. If you're booking in these areas ask for a quiet room—and consider ear plugs. Remember, too, that many of the older, renovated hotels in the city have fairly small rooms.

Few hotels have rooms that are specially adapted for disabled travelers, but many will do all they can to accommodate special needs, especially if you let them know in advance.

Street parking is extremely difficult to find in the historic center, but most hotels will help you and arrange for you to use a garage—for which you will usually have to pay an additional daily charge. It's a good idea to inquire in advance about parking if you know you're going to need it.

Grading system

Italian hotels are rated from one to five stars by the Government's Tourist Office according to such facilities as the number of rooms with private bathrooms, rooms with TV, etc., rather than style or comfort. However, this is not always a reliable measure as for tax reasons many hotels opt to stay in a lower category. Unless otherwise noted, all the hotels listed here have private bathrooms in all rooms (upper categories have bathtub and shower, lower only shower). English is spoken at all the hotels listed; however, the amount spoken varies and may only be sufficient to take a booking and deal with the most basic visitor requests. Value-added tax and service are included in the prices, and so is breakfast, unless otherwise noted. Room price categories are given only for guidance and do not take account of seasonal variations.

Alternative accommodations

Many Roman monasteries and convents have comfortable rooms to rent at reasonable prices, although some have curfews. A list compiled by the Santa Susanna church in March 2005 can be seen at www .santasusanna.org/comingToRome /convents.html#R-vatican. For short-term apartment rentals, check out www.VRBO.com, www.Vacationrentals.com, and www.romaclick.com/Roma.htm.

RESTAURANTS

Italians take eating seriously and tend to eat a lot when they go out. A traditional meal consists of *antipasti* and goes on to the *primo* (usually pasta, soup, or risotto) before hitting the main, or *secondo,* course (meat or fish) accompanied by salad or vegetable *contorni.* Desserts or fruit round off the meal followed by an espresso (only foreigners drink cappuccino after a meal). But most restaurants are now used to people only having one or two courses.

Dining hours

Lunch is eaten between about 12:30 p.m. and 2:30 p.m. Dinner is seldom served before 8 p.m. and continues until about 10:30 p.m. or even later. In traditional restaurants, making reservations is often advisable, sometimes essential. Today, however, in areas like Trastevere and around Campo dei Fiori, there are more and more restaurants geared to tourists, which stay open all day and where you can always get a meal. Menus are often displayed outside and one orders à la carte. At some restaurants a *menu di degustazione* allows you to sample several specialities.

Trattorias

These are relatively simple restaurants that are often family run and were originally geared toward serving local people with good, home-style cooking. Their clientele may have widened over the years (people will travel for miles to eat at a good trattoria), but their value for money has, in most cases, remained.

Smoking

Since January 1, 2005, Italy became one of Europe's growing number of nonsmoking countries. This means that smoking is banned in public offices and shops and permitted only in those very, very few bars and restaurants which have installed the powerful ventilation equipment required by law. However, restaurants or cafés with al fresco seating easily accommodate smokers.

Tipping

Some establishments add a place-setting charge to the bill and others don't. When it hasn't already been calculated, leave about ten percent; whether it's been added or not, a few coins left on the table shows that you've enjoyed your meal and service, and is a gesture that will be much appreciated.

One of the anachronisms of Italian dining is the charge for *pane e coperto* (bread and cover), which appears on nearly all restaurant bills and is usually a euro or two per head. It may

HOTELS & RESTAURANTS

seem odd that you should effectively be charged for using the cutlery and table linen, but it's standard practice and not an optional extra that depends on whether or not you've eaten any bread.

ORGANIZATION & ABBREVIATIONS

All sites are listed first by price, then in alphabetical order.

The abbreviations used are:
L = lunch
D = dinner

AE = American Express
DC = Diners Club
MC = MasterCard
V = Visa

ANCIENT ROME

Until a few years ago, the Monti area (which straddles the lower end of Via Cavour) was busy during the day but relatively quiet in the evening. That has all changed. Monti, now full of bars, pubs, and restaurants, has become a nighttime destination, so the late-night Friday and Saturday traffic on Via Cavour is often at a standstill. 🚌 Bus: 60, 75, 84, 85, 87 Metro: Linea B (Colosseo or Cavour).

HOTELS

🏨 FORUM
$$$$ ✪✪✪✪
VIA TOR DE' CONTI 25, 00184
TEL 06 679 2446
FAX 06 678 6479
WWW.HOTELFORUMROME.COM
Tucked in a comparatively quiet corner behind the Imperial Forums, the atmosphere and decor of this grand hotel are reminiscent of an English gentlemen's club. Rooms vary in size, but all are well furnished, and there's a wonderful roof garden restaurant.
🛏 80 P 🔌 📶 📺 All major cards

🏨 NERVA
$$ ✪✪✪

VIA TOR DE' CONTI 3, 00184
TEL 06 679 3764
FAX 06 6992 2204
This friendly hotel, situated just steps from the Roman Forum, underwent a recent renovation. The public areas are pleasingly decorated and the rooms comfortable and sound-proofed.
🛏 18 P 🔌 📶 📺 V, DC

🏨 RICHMOND
$$ ✪✪✪
LARGO C. RICCI 36, 00184
TEL 06 6994 1256
FAX 06 6994 1454
WWW.HOTELRICHMONDROMA .COM.
A small, family-run hotel strategically placed for sightseeing. The rooms are simple and well equipped. In summer breakfast is served on a splendid terrace with magnificent views over the Imperial Forums.
🛏 13 P 🔌 📶 📺 All major cards

RESTAURANTS

🍴 CAVOUR 313
$$
VIA CAVOUR 313
TEL 06 678 5496
This wood-lined wine bar has more than a thousand different wines from all over the world and serves an interesting range of cheeses, salamis, and freshly prepared salads.
🍴 60 🕐 Closed L Sun. & D Sun. June–Sept. 📺 All major cards

COLOSSEO TO SAN CLEMENTE

The streets around the Colosseum, particularly Via Capo di Africa, have undergone a renaissance. New hotels have opened, restaurants serving innovative food thrive, and bars stay open until the early hours of the morning. 🚌 Bus: C3, 60, 75, 81, 85, 87, 175, 673 Tram: 3. Metro: Linea B (Colosseo)

PRICES

HOTELS
An indication of the cost of a double room is given by $ signs.
$$$$$	Over $450
$$$$	$350–$450
$$$	$250–$350
$$	$120–$250
$	Under $120

RESTAURANTS
An indication of the cost of a three-course dinner without drinks is given by $ signs.
$$$$$	Over $80
$$$$	$55–$80
$$$	$40–$55
$$	$25–$40
$	Under $25

HOTELS

🏨 HOTEL DEI GLADIATORI
$$$$ ✪✪✪
VIA LABICANA 125, 00184
TEL 06 7759 1380
FAX 06 700 5638
WWW.HOTELDEIGLADIATORI.COM
An elegant hotel facing the Colosseum and next door to the ancient gladiators' training ground. The rooms are tastefully decorated. The roof terrace offers spectacular views, particularly at sunset and at night when the monuments are lit.
🛏 17 P (extra) 🔌 📶 All major cards

🏨 CAPO D'AFRICA
$$$ ✪✪✪
VIA CAPO D'AFRICA 54, 00184
TEL 06 772 801
FAX 06 772 80801
WWW.HOTELCAPODAFRICA .COM
Located in the shadow of the Colosseum, this four-star hotel is a fusion of contemporary and classic styles. The rooms have been furnished with great attention to detail. There is a wonderful view of the Colosseum from the terrace.

Breakfast extra.
[i] 64 [P] (extra) 🔲 🅢 🅥
🅢 All major cards

CELIO
$$$ ❍❍❍
VIA DEI SANTI QUATTRO 35/C,
00184
TEL 06 7049 5333
FAX 06 709 6377
WWW.HOTELCELIO.COM
Located on a quiet street near
the Colosseum, this family-run
hotel is one of Rome's most
pleasant, featuring bedrooms
frescoed with reproductions
of Renaissance and baroque
artists.
[i] 19 [P] (extra) 🔲 🅢 🅥
🅢 All major cards

RESTAURANTS

CRAB
$$$$
VIA CAPO D'AFRICA 2
TEL 06 7720 3636
A converted warehouse, this
is the place to come to if you
are craving crustaceans—
though there are also
delicious starters and fresh
fish. Wise to book in advance.
🍽 60 🕐 Closed Sun., L
Mon., & Aug. 🅢 🅢 All
major cards

PAPAGIO'
$$$
VIA CAPO D'AFRICA 26
TEL 06 700 9800
A blend of traditional and
innovative cuisine plus efficient
service makes this restaurant
a popular choice. Fish is their
specialty. Outdoor seating.
🍽 55 🕐 Closed Sun. & 2
weeks in Aug. 🅢 🅢 All
major cards

LATERANO TO
TERME DI
DIOCLEZIANO

Although the area immediately
around Termini, the central train
station, is probably best avoided
at night, the atmosphere changes
quickly as you venture slightly
farther out. Here you will find

hotels and restaurants ranging
from the simple to the most
luxurious. For public transport,
see individual listings.

HOTELS

GRAND ST. REGIS
$$$$$ ❍❍❍❍❍
VIA V.E. ORLANDO 3, 00185
TEL 06 47 091
FAX 06 474 7307
WWW.STREGIS.COM
A traditional luxury hotel with
public rooms that are awe-
inspiringly decorated with
marble columns and richly
patterned Oriental carpets.
The spacious and comfortable
guest rooms are furnished
with valuable antiques, and
bathrooms are well-
equipped. Efficient service
matches the slightly hushed,
aristocratic atmosphere.
Breakfast extra.
[i] 161 [P] Garage 🔲 🅢
🅢 All major cards 🚌 Bus:
60, 61, 62, 84, 175, 492, 590,
910 Metro: Linea A
(Repubblica)

RADISSON SAS
$$$$$ ❍❍❍❍
VIA FILIPPO TURATI 171, 00185
TEL 06 444 841
FAX 06 4434 1396
WWW.RADISSON.COM/ROMEIT
Though not in the nicest part
of town, this minimalist-style
hotel is conveniently located
close to the central train
station. It has individually
designed guest rooms on
seven floors, two restaurants,
and a roof terrace with
swimming pool. Breakfast extra.
[i] 262 [P] (extra) 🔲 🅢
🅥 🏊 🅢 All major cards
🚌 Bus: 70, 71 Metro: Linea A
(Vittorio Emanuele)

RESTAURANTS

AGATA E ROMEO
$$$$$
VIA CARLO ALBERTO 45
TEL 06 446 6115
This family-run restaurant is
one of six Rome restaurants
to have earned a Michelin star.

The menu offers exquisite
versions of traditional dishes
(such as *spaghettini all'
amatriciana*, pasta with
broccoli, and beef filet in
balsamic vinegar) and *menu di
degustazione* with suitable
wines to accompany each
dish. No outdoor dining.
🍽 40 🕐 Closed Sat.–Sun. &
Aug. 🅢 🅢 All major cards
🚌 Bus: 70, 71 Metro: Linea A
(Vittorio Emanuele)

F.I.S.H.
$$$$
VIA DEI SERPENTI 16
TEL 06 4782 4962
The restaurant's name, an
acronym for Fine International
Seafood House, aptly
describes the fare. The very
modern interior is divided into
a sushi bar and a restaurant
with a view of the kitchen. The
menu ranges from Italian
Mediterranean to Pan-Asian.
Try the clam soup with ginger.
🍽 42 🕐 Closed Mon. &
Aug. 🅢 🅢 All major cards
🚌 Bus: H, 40, 60, 64, 70, 75,
84, 170

TRATTORIA MONTI
$$
VIA DI S. VITO 13/A
TEL 06 446 6573
A warm welcome is
guaranteed at this elegant yet
cozy, family-run trattoria
serving traditional seasonal
dishes from the Marche
region—lamb with artichokes,
mushrooms, and truffles or
thick winter soups.
🍽 45 🕐 Closed D Sun.,
Mon. & Aug. 🅢 All major
cards 🚌 Bus: 71, 590, 649
Metro: Linea A (Vittorio
Emanuele)

VALENTINO
$$
VIA DEL BOSCHETTO 37
TEL 06 488 0643
No sign announces this cozy,
family-owned trattoria that
was once a beer house
featuring Peroni brews. The
specialty is *scamorza* (grilled
cheese), but it also serves

excellent grilled meats. Good wine list.

🏠 55 🕐 Closed Sun. & Aug. 🔲 🚫 All major cards 🚌 Bus: H, 40, 60, 64, 70, 170

🍴 EST! EST! EST!
$

VIA GENOVA 32
TEL 06 488 1107

This well-loved pizzeria has been here since 1905, and you may have to wait in line to get in. It serves both thin-crust (Roman) and thick-crust (Neapolitan) pizza and the usual range of fried suppli, cod fillets, and zucchini flowers.

🏠 120 🕐 Closed Mon. & Aug. 🔲 🚫 MC, V 🚌 Bus: H, 40, 60, 64, 70, 170

FONTANA DI TREVI TO VIA VENETO

Many of Rome's luxury hotels can be found on the Via Veneto, made famous by Fellini's film La Dolce Vita. Although the glamour of the 1950s is gone, there are plans to revitalize the area.
🚌 Bus: 52, 60, 61, 62, 63, 80, 95, 116, 175, 492, 590 Metro: Linea A (Barberini)

HOTELS

🏨 ALEPH
$$$$$ ✪✪✪✪✪

VIA SAN BASILIO 15, 00187
TEL 06 422 901
FAX 06 4229 0000
WWW.ALEPH.BOSCOLOHOTELS
.COM

This luxury hotel, of the Boscolo chain, was created by the Israeli architect Adam Tihany. In public spaces the theme is paradise to purgatory, while the guest rooms are decorated in an elegant but contemporary style. The Seventh Heaven roof terrace is ideal for relaxing after a hard day's shopping or sightseeing. The Paradise Spa is also open to the general public. Breakfast extra.

🛈 96 🅿 (extra) 🔷 🔲 🚫 All major cards

🏨 EDEN
$$$$$ ✪✪✪✪✪

VIA LUDOVISI 49, 00187
TEL 06 478 121
FAX 06 482 1584
WWW.HOTEL-EDEN.IT

This luxury hotel is a favorite among international celebrities. Every detail has been thought of, from the antique furnishings to the imaginative welcome baskets when you arrive. Stunning views from the famous roof terrace. Breakfast extra.

🛈 121, including some suites 🅿 Garage 🔷 🔲 🚫 All major cards

🏨 EXCELSIOR
$$$$$ ✪✪✪✪✪

VIA VITTORIO VENETO 125, 00187
TEL 06 47 081
FAX 06 482 6205

A dramatically grand hotel, opulently decorated with swaths of rich fabric and antique and reproduction furniture. All the more-or-less uniformly decorated rooms are luxurious, while the suites look like stage sets. Breakfast extra.

🛈 316, including some suites 🅿 (extra) 🔷 🔲 🚫 All major cards

🏨 FONTANA
$$$ ✪✪✪

PIAZZA DI TREVI 96, 00187
TEL 06 678 6113
FAX 06 679 0024
WWW.HOTELFONTANE-TREVI.COM

The view over the Trevi Fountain from this quirky little hotel is breathtaking (also sleep-depriving—in summer the noise can go on all night). Rooms come in all shapes and sizes in this rambling old building.

🛈 25 🔷 🔲 🚫 AE, MC, V

🏨 LA RESIDENZA
$$ ✪✪✪✪

VIA EMILIA 22–24, 00187
TEL 06 488 0789
FAX 06 485 721
WWW.HOTEL-LA-RESIDENZA
.COM

At this converted town house

conveniently situated near Via Veneto, the service is attentive and the rooms comfortable. But the real charm of this hotel is found in the bar, terrace, and warmly decorated lobbies.

🛈 29, including some junior suites 🅿 Garage 🔷 🔲 🚫 All major cards

RESTAURANTS

🍴 GIRARROSTO FIORENTINO
$$$

VIA SICILIA 46
TEL 06 4288 0660

This classic Roman restaurant has been making clients happy for the last 50 years. Known for its open-fire grilled beef, it also has excellent appetizers that are piled onto your table, a large selection of fish and other meat dishes, and a good wine list.

🏠 75 🕐 Closed Dec. 24–26 🔲 🚫 All major cards

🍴 TRATTORIA TRITONE
$$$

VIA DEI MARONITI 1
TEL 06 679 8181

Here you're guaranteed not just excellent Roman cuisine, but courteous, attentive (English-speaking) service and a warm welcome—non-Italian eating habits are courteously accommodated. Underneath the elegant extension are some carefully preserved ancient remains. Il Tritone's popularity with journalists from the nearby Il Messaggero proves its appeal with discerning locals.

🏠 180 🕐 Closed Dec. 25–26 🔲 🚫 All major cards

🍴 TULLIO
$$$

VIA SAN NICOLA DA TOLENTINO 26
TEL 06 474 5560

A Tuscan restaurant particularly famous for its bistecca fiorentina (T-bone steak) and other grilled meats, Tullio also has an extensive

selection of Tuscan wines.
🍴 80 🕐 Closed Sun. & Aug.
❄ 🃏 All major cards

🍴 PICCOLO ARANCIO
$$
VICOLO SCANDERBEG 112
TEL 06 678 6139
A popular and thus packed little
restaurant that extends over
several rooms on a tiny, steep
alleyway near the Trevi Foun-
tain. The food offers a good,
rather than exceptional, range
of Roman standards slightly
adapted for international tastes.
🍴 50 🕐 Closed Mon. & 3
weeks in Aug. ❄ 🃏 All
major cards

PIAZZA DI SPAGNA TO VILLA BORGHESE

Rome's main shopping district
also boasts a variety of
interesting and original hotels
and restaurants. 🚌 Bus: 81, 117,
119, 628, 590, 926 Metro: Linea
A (Spagna)

HOTELS

🏨 ART BY THE SPANISH STEPS
$$$$$ ✪✪✪✪
VIA MARGUTTA 56, 00187
TEL 06 328 711
FAX 06 3600 3995
WWW.HOTELART.IT
Color is the theme of this
hotel. Previously part of an
exclusive private school, the
new space incorporates
elements of the old with
modern minimalism. The
guest rooms are reasonably
large and highly styled.
ℹ 44 ❄ ❄ 🃏 All major
cards

SOMETHING SPECIAL

🏨 DE RUSSIE
In the heart of the city between
the Spanish Steps and Piazza
del Popolo, this hotel is the
ultimate in luxury. The guest
rooms are spacious and
exquisitely decorated. A

stunning feature of the hotel is
its extensive, terraced gardens,
which provide a tranquil oasis
amidst the bustle of central
Rome. A perfect place to pause
for a drink, or a meal at its first
class restaurant. Breakfast extra.
$$$$$ ✪✪✪✪✪
VIA BABUINO 9, 00187
TEL 06 328 881
FAX 06 3288 8888
WWW.HOTELDERUSSIE.IT
ℹ 94 🅿 (extra) ❄ ❄
🃏 All major cards

SOMETHING SPECIAL

🏨 HASSLER VILLA MEDICI
The hotel's enviable location at
the top of the Spanish Steps is
matched by elaborate interior
design (marble columns and
well-upholstered seating) and
bustlingly attentive service.
The good-sized rooms are
comfortably furnished and have
traces of their more than 100-year
history as a hotel. Breakfast extra.
$$$$$ ✪✪✪✪✪
PIAZZA TRINITÀ DEI MONTI 6,
00187
TEL 06 699 340
FAX 06 678 9991
WWW.HOTELHASSLERROMA.COM
ℹ 100, plus suites 🅿 ❄
❄ 🃏 All major cards

🏨 LORD BYRON
$$$$$ ✪✪✪✪✪
VIA GIUSEPPE DE NOTARIS 5,
00197
TEL 06 322 4541
FAX 06 322 0405
WWW.LORDBYRONHOTEL.COM
On the opposite side of the
Villa Borghese from the Via
Veneto, tranquility is the
overriding feature of this well-
run hotel in a chic residential
area. The prettily decorated
rooms are a good size and
equipped with all you'd
expect from a five-star hotel.
ℹ 36, including 9 suites
🅿 Garage ❄ ❄ 🃏 All
major cards 🚌 Bus: 3, 19, 52,
926

🏨 D'INGHILTERRA
$$$$ ✪✪✪✪
VIA BOCCA DI LEONE 14,
00187
TEL 06 69981
FAX 06 6992 2243
WWW.ROYALDEMEURE.COM
Famous for well over a
century as one of the best in
Rome, this hotel can list
Oscar Wilde among its VIP
guests. Antique furnishings
tend toward the lugubrious
but make for an appropriately
historic atmosphere. It's
also perfectly placed for the
city's most exclusive shopping
streets. Breakfast extra.
ℹ 98 ❄ ❄ 🃏 All major
cards

🏨 INN AT THE SPANISH STEPS
$$$$ ✪✪✪✪✪
VIA DEI CONDOTTI 85
TEL 06 6992 5657
FAX 06 678 6470
WWW.ATSPANISHSTEPS.COM
This new, small, family-run
luxury residence sits on
Rome's famed shopping
street, Via dei Condotti.
Quality and style in a
discreetly refined atmosphere,
with a lovely rooftop terrace
for breakfast and aperitifs.
ℹ 24 ❄ ❄ 🃏 All major
cards

🏨 LOCARNO
$$$ ✪✪✪
VIA DELLA PENNA 22, 00186
TEL 06 361 0841
FAX 06 321 5249
WWW.HOTELLOCARNO.COM
This intriguing art deco hotel
is just off Piazza del Popolo.
Both the lobbies and guest
rooms are tastefully decorated,
and in winter there is an open
fire in the bar area. It also
boasts a lovely roof garden.
ℹ 63 🅿 (extra) ❄ ❄
🃏 All major cards

🏨 FORTE
$$ ✪✪✪
VIA MARGUTTA 61, 00187
TEL 06 320 0408
FAX 06 6799 5433
WWW.HOTELFORTE.COM

HOTELS & RESTAURANTS

Located in one of Rome's most charming streets, this recently renovated hotel offers stylishly decorated rooms.

[i] 19 [elevator] [§] [§] All major cards

🏨 MARGUTTA
$$ ○○

VIA LAURINA 34, 00187
TEL 06 322 3674
FAX 06 320 0395
WWW.HOTELMARGUTTA.IT

Excellent value in an expensive part of town. The rooms are simply and traditionally furnished in wood with iron bedsteads. Bath and shower rooms are small but adequate.

[i] 24 [P] Garage [elevator] [§]
[§] All major cards

🏨 PARLAMENTO
$$ ○○

VIA DELLE CONVERTITE 5, 00187
TEL/FAX 06 6992 1000
WWW.HOTELPARLAMENTO.IT

A simple, well-run, and spotlessly clean *pensione* where not all rooms have air-conditioning. Double-glazing reduces outside noise. Breakfast is served on the little roof garden in summer.

[i] 23 [P] Garage [elevator]
[§] Extra fee [§] All major cards

RESTAURANTS

SOMETHING SPECIAL

🍴 BABY DELL' ALDROVANDI PALACE

The Michelin guide has given a well-deserved star to Baby and its well-known chef, Alfonso Iaccarino. This elegant, contemporary restaurant has views onto both Villa Borghese park and the Aldrovandi Palace Hotel's pool. Outdoor seating.

$$$$$
VIA ULISSE ALDOVANDI 15
TEL 06 322 3993
[places] 60 [closed] D only; closed Mon. [§] [§] All major cards
[transport] Bus: 52, 926

🍴 DAL BOLOGNESE
$$$$

PIAZZA DEL POPOLO 1/2
TEL 06 361 1426

This chic restaurant is where the in-crowd gathers to enjoy the time-honored cuisine of Bologna. Try the *bollito* (steamed meats). Outdoor seating.

[places] 160 [closed] Closed Mon. [§]
[§] All major cards

🍴 CAFFÉ DELLE ARTE
$$$

VIA A. GRAMSCI 73
TEL 06 3265 1236

This restaurant is located on the opposite side of the Villa Borghese from the Via Veneto. Unlike many other beautifully situated restaurants, here you don't have to make any compromises on the food, which is good, especially the fish dishes served with olives, aniseed, and a host of other compatible flavors. Reservations essential.

[places] 130 [P] [closed] Closed D Mon. [§] All major cards
[transport] Bus: 3, 19

🍴 MARGUTTA VEGETARIANO
$$$

VIA MARGUTTA 118
TEL 06 3265 0577

This most elegant of Rome's vegetarian restaurants serves varied and tempting dishes. Contemporary art lines the walls of the large dining area.

[places] 150 [§] [§] All major cards

🍴 NINO
$$$

VIA BORGOGNONA 11
TEL 06 678 6752

A classic restaurant serving excellent Tuscan cuisine. With its cozy, old-fashioned interior, this restaurant is a favorite of politicians, journalists, and film stars.

[places] 95 [closed] Closed Mon. & Aug. [§] [§] All major cards

🍴 ANGELINA
$$

VIA MARGUTTA 1
TEL 06 321 1559

Pizzeria (and restaurant) by night, inexpensive lunch place (fixed price) by day, tea room in the afternoon, this downtown trattoria is a real find. High ceilings, well-distanced tables, friendly service, and large portions make this well worth a stop. One block from Piazza del Popolo, it opens onto the charming Margutta arcade. Outdoor seating in summer.

[places] 100 [§] [§] All major cards

SOMETHING SPECIAL

🍴 INTERNATIONAL WINE ACADEMY TERRACE

For a special treat on a sunny day, sip an *aperitivo* on the rooftop terrace of the International Wine Academy overlooking the Spanish Steps. Spectacular setting, excellent wines.

$
VICOLO DEL BOTTINO 8
TEL 06 699 34 1000
[places] 22 [closed] L only; closed Sun.–Mon.

PANTHEON TO PIAZZA VENEZIA

The true heart of Rome includes the parliament and senate buildings, some of the city's oldest monuments, as well as a labyrinth of narrow streets and alleys. It is also home to some of the city's most established restaurants and hotels. [transport] Bus: 40, 46, 62, 63, 64, 70, 81, 87, 116, 119, 492, 628

HOTELS

🏨 GRAND HOTEL DE LA MINERVE
$$$$$ ○○○○○

PRICES

HOTELS
An indication of the cost of a double room is given by $ signs.

$$$$$	Over $450
$$$$	$350–$450
$$$	$250–$350
$$	$120–$250
$	Under $120

RESTAURANTS
An indication of the cost of a three-course dinner without drinks is given by $ signs.

$$$$$	Over $80
$$$$	$55–$80
$$$	$40–$55
$$	$25–$40
$	Under $25

PIAZZA DELLA MINERVA 69, 00186
TEL 06 695 201
FAX 06 679 4165
WWW.GRANDHOTELDELA
MINERVA.IT
Renovated by postmodernist architect Paolo Portoghesi, this 17th-century building has all the comforts of a luxury hotel, including a beautiful roof garden (closed in winter), where you can enjoy a superb view of the "Eternal City." Guest rooms are elegantly furnished and of varying size. Breakfast extra.
🛈 134 🅿 (extra) 🔲 🄢
🞖 🄢 All major cards

🏨 SANTA CHIARA
$$$ ❍❍❍
VIA DI SANTA CHIARA 21, 00186
TEL 06 687 2979
FAX 06 687 3144
WWW.ALBERGOSANTACHIARA
.COM
Located behind the Pantheon, this hotel is known for its pleasant, calm atmosphere and efficient service. Bright rooms combine function with comfort.
🛈 100 🅿 (extra) 🔲 🄢
🄢 All major cards

RESTAURANTS

🍴 LA ROSETTA
$$$$$
VIA DELLA ROSETTA 8
TEL 06 686 1002
Fresh seafood delivered daily from Sicily and simply prepared makes the Michelin-starred La Rosetta one of the best seafood eateries in Rome. Good selection of wines and efficient service. Small outdoor garden for spring and summer dining.
🍴 50 🕘 Closed Sun. & Aug.
🄢 🄢 All major cards

SOMETHING SPECIAL

🍴 CASA BLEVE
A refined, elegant wine bar with stained-glass and stucco ceilings and marble columns. Offers an exceptional selection of wines, an excellent choice of cold dishes, and knowledgeable and efficient service.
$$$
VIA DEL TEATRO VALLE 48/49
TEL 06 686 5970
🍴 40 🕘 Closed Sun.–Mon., L Wed.–Fri., & Aug. 🄢 🄢 All major cards

🍴 SANT'EUSTACHIO
$$$
PIAZZA DEI CAPRETTARI 63
TEL 06 686 1616
Restrained, polite atmosphere with pleasant outdoor dining in summer. The menu features Roman and more elaborate dishes—*saltimbocca* (veal with ham), fried artichokes, salmon *carpaccio*, and satisfying home-made tarts for dessert.
🍴 100 🕘 Closed Sun. & 2 weeks in Aug. 🄢 All major cards

🍴 TRATTORIA
$$$
VIA DEL POZZO DELLE CORNACHIE 2
TEL 06 6830 1427
Constructed on two levels, with bar below and restaurant above. Views of the kitchen

allow you to see chef Filippo La Mantia at work, preparing traditional Sicilian dishes with his own distinctive twist.
🍴 80 🕘 D only. Closed Aug.
🄢 🄢 All major cards

🍴 OBIKA
$$
VIA DEI PREFETTI 26A
TEL 06 683 2630
If you love mozzarella don't miss this place. A number of varieties of fresh and smoked mozzarella are served with a large range of delicious salads. A good choice for lunch. Outdoor seating available.
🍴 140 🄢 🄢 All major cards

🍴 ENOTECA CORSI
$
VIA DEL GESÙ 87
TEL 06 679 0821
This trattoria has managed to maintain its original wine-and-olive-oil shop feel. Here you can order simple tasty Roman food. Order the house wine, or choose from a large selection of bottled wines.
🍴 100 🕘 L only. Closed Sun. & Aug. 🄢 All major cards

CAMPO MARZIO

This area, central Rome at its most charming and typical, is one of the city's busiest areas both day and night. The range of hotels and restaurants offers something to suit all pockets. For public transport, see individual listings.

HOTELS

🏨 RAPHAEL
$$$$ ❍❍❍❍
LARGO FEBO 2, 00186
TEL 06 682 831
FAX 06 687 8993
WWW.RAPHAELHOTEL.COM
Just a step away from Piazza Navona, this hotel is known for its quiet, luxurious charm and stunning terrace (closed

HOTELS & RESTAURANTS

in winter) with bar and restaurant. Guest rooms, though small, are attractively decorated. Breakfast extra.

(i) 58 P (extra) ⊟ 🛇 🔄 🛇 All major cards 🚌 Bus: 70, 81, 87, 116, 280, 492, 628

🏨 DUE TORRI
$$$ ✿✿✿
VICOLO DEL LEONETTO 23, 00186
TEL 06 687 6983
FAX 06 686 5442
WWW.DUETORRIROMA.COM
Elegant furnishings and a warm welcome combine with a romantic atmosphere to make this one of the most attractive hotels in its price category. The 19th-century building, on a quiet street not far from Piazza Navona, used to be the home of bishops and cardinals.

(i) 26 P ⊟ 🔄 🛇 All major cards 🚌 Bus: 70, 81, 87, 116, 280, 492, 628

🏨 RESIDENZA IN FARNESE
$$ ✿✿✿✿
VIA DEL MASCHERONE 59, 00186
TEL 06 6889 1388
FAX 06 6821 0980
WWW.RESIDENZAFARNESEROME.COM
Housed in a converted 14th-century monastery near Campo dei Fiori, this quiet comfortable hotel has pleasant rooms, some with frescoed ceilings, overlooking either the gardens of Palazzo Farnese or Palazzo Spada.

(i) 31 ⊟ 🔄 🛇 All major cards 🚌 Bus: 23, 116, 280

🏨 TEATRO DI POMPEO
$$ ✿✿✿
LARGO DEL PALLARO 8, 00186
TEL 06 6830 0170
FAX 06 6880 5531
WWW.HOTELTEATRODIPOMPEO.IT
A small hotel built over the ruins of a Roman theater, some of which is still visible. The rooms are not large but are tastefully decorated. Street noise can be a problem.

(i) 13 🔄 🛇 All major cards 🚌 Bus: 116

🏨 TEATROPACE33
$$ ✿✿✿
VIA DEL TEATRO PACE 33, 00186
TEL 06 687 9075
FAX 06 6819 2364
WWW.HOTELTEATROPACE.COM
Opened in 2004, this 17th-century cardinal's former residence offers tastefully appointed bedrooms equipped with modern comforts. Conveniently located only 20 yards from Piazza Navona.

(i) 23 🔄 🛇 All major cards 🚌 Bus: 70, 81, 87, 116, 492, 628

Convents and monasteries can be a good-value alternative to hotels. They offer simple and spotless rooms, most have a curfew, but it is usually late enough not to be inconvenient. Some centrally located ones are **Casa di Santa Francesca Romana** ($, Via dei Vascellari 61 [Trastevere], 00153, tel/fax 06 581 2125. Curfew 2 a.m.); **San Giuseppe** ($, Vicolo Moroni 22 [Trastevere], 00153, tel 06 5833 3490, www.sangiuseppe.it); and **Convent Fraterna Domus** (Via Monte Brianzo 62 [Piazza di Spagna], 00186, tel 06 6880 2727, fax 06 683 2691. Curfew 11 p.m.).

RESTAURANTS

SOMETHING SPECIAL

🍴 L'ALTRO MASTAI
Opened in 2003, this elegant restaurant near Piazza Navona quickly became very fashionable and won itself a Michelin star. The interior combines classical elements with rich colors and abstract art. The dishes are inspired by the Mediterranean tradition, with an extra care for detail. It also offers more than 1,200 wines.

$$$$$
VIA G. GIRAUD 53

TEL 06 6830 1296
🍴 50 🕐 D only. Closed Sun.–Mon. & Aug. 🔄 🛇 All major cards 🚌 Bus: 40, 46, 62, 64

SOMETHING SPECIAL

🍴 IL CONVIVIO TROIANI
Three brothers run one of the best and nicest restaurants in Rome. Service is cordial and informative and the food is ambrosial—basically Italian with some touches of creative genius from the chef (one of the brothers). Every dish is a beautifully presented work of art but the desserts are masterpieces. No outdoor dining.

$$$$$
VICOLO DEI SOLDATI 31
TEL 06 686 9432
🕐 D only. Closed Sun. 🔄 🛇 All major cards 🚌 Bus: 30, 70, 87, 186, 492 (Corso del Rinascimento)

🍴 HOSTERIA DEL PESCE
$$$$$
VIA MONSERRATO 32
TEL 06 686 5617
A beautiful display of fresh fish greets patrons at the front entrance, announcing the restaurant's specialty fare. Indeed, the simply prepared seafood is of the highest quality. The interior is casual and noisy. Reservations recommended.

🍴 60 🕐 D only. Closed Sun. & Aug. 🔄 🛇 All major cards 🚌 Bus: 23, 116, 280

🍴 PIERLUIGI
$$$
PIAZZA DE'RICCI 144
TEL 06 686 8717
Although a mecca for visitors in the know (prices have risen and it's always full), this establishment is still a very agreeable place to sample deliciously fresh dishes—pasta with zucchini flowers, fish cooked in various ways, and tasty desserts. A good first

experience of a real Italian restaurant that's used to coping with non-Italians.
🍴 120 🕐 Closed Mon. 🅾
🅰 All major cards 🚌 Bus: 23, 40, 62, 64, 116, 280

🍴 DITIRAMBO
$$
PIAZZA DELLA CANCELLERIA 74
TEL 06 687 1626
Charming staff and attractive decor make for a pleasantly busy atmosphere that is matched by the standard of the ever changing menu. Innovative versions of Italian regional dishes include a potato and broad-bean soup, eggplant croquettes, and lamb with lentils. Tasty homemade bread and pasta. Good value for money. Reservations are essential.
🍴 55 🕐 Closed L Mon. & Aug. 🅾 🅰 MC, V 🚌 Bus: 40, 46, 62, 64, 116

🍴 LA CAMPANA
$$
VICOLO DELLA CAMPANA 18/20
TEL 06 686 7820
This trattoria is one of the oldest in the city and is well known for its traditional Roman cooking. The menu offers a wide choice, but don't miss the *spaghetti alla carbonara*.
🍴 130 🕐 Closed Mon. & Aug. 🅾 🅰 All major cards 🚌 Bus: 70, 81, 87, 116, 492, 628

🍴 CUL DE SAC
$$
PIAZZA PASQUINO 73
TEL 06 6880 1094
A lively wine bar with a good reputation for food. The Cul de Sac offers a variety of light dishes and has a vast selection of wines. Outside tables.
🍴 60 🅾 🅰 MC, V 🚌 Bus: 46, 62, 64, 70, 81, 87, 116, 492, 628

🍴 L'ORSO 80
$$
VIA DEL ORSO 33
TEL 06 686 4904
The *antipasto misto* is the star

of this restaurant. It consists of an endless array of dishes—mozzarella, zucchini, fennel, meatballs, just to mention a few—from which you help yourself. Excellent value. If you can manage more there is a good selection of fresh fish to follow.
🍴 180 🕐 Closed Mon. & Aug. 🅾 🅰 All major cards 🚌 Bus: 70, 81, 87, 116, 280, 492, 628

🍴 TRATTORIA DA LUIGI
$$
PIAZZA SFORZA CESARINI 24
TEL 06 686 5946
This friendly, large trattoria offers an enormous menu that includes the best of Italian cuisine and then some. The dark, wood-panelled interior is pleasant but the best thing about da Luigi is the outdoor dining in a lovely, tree-shaded square that seems more Parisian than Roman.
🍴 240 🕐 Closed Mon. & Dec. 25–26 🅾 Upstairs only 🅰 All major cards 🚌 Bus: 40, 46, 62, 64, 116

🍴 IL BAFFETTO
$
VIA DEL GOVERNO VECCHIO 114
TEL 06 686 1617
One of Rome's most popular and best pizzerias, lingering is not possible here. Unless you come early or late, you'll have to wait for a table and then possibly share it when you are seated.
🍴 100 🕐 Closed L & Aug. 🅰 Cash only 🚌 Bus: 40, 46, 62, 64, 116

🍴 L'INSALATA RICCA
$ (for a salad & desert)
LARGO DEI CHIAVARI 85/86
TEL 06 6880 3656
One of the chain's 11 branches, this is an excellent lunch and/or dinner place for something light like a salad. L'Insalata Ricca means "rich salad" and there are more than 50 to choose from, always fresh and served in generous portions. Pasta and

meat dishes (Argentinian beef is featured) also served. Outdoor seating available.
🍴 85 inside 🚌 Bus: 40, 46, 62, 64, 116 🅾 🅰 All major cards

VATICANO

Much of the solidly respectable residential area around the Vatican dates from the late 19th and early 20th centuries. There are a few unflashy but high quality hotels. With few exceptions most of the touristy eating places close to the Vatican are best avoided. For public transport, see individual listings.

HOTELS

🏨 COLUMBUS
$$$ ✪✪✪✪
VIA DELLA CONCILIAZIONE 33, 00193
TEL 06 686 5435
FAX 06 686 4874
WWW.HOTELCOLUMBUS.NET
A 15th-century building right in front of St. Peter's is the setting for this aristocratically austere hotel. Guest rooms and bathrooms are functional, but public areas make up with a surfeit of carved stone and frescoed walls.
🛏 92 🅿 🖪 🅾 🅰 All major cards 🚌 Bus: 23, 34, 40, 62, 982

🏨 FARNESE
$$$ ✪✪✪✪
VIA A. FARNESE 30, 00193
TEL 06 321 2553
FAX 06 321 5129
WWW.HOTELFARNESE.COM
A charming choice (and value for money) in the residential Prati area near St. Peter's, connected to the center by metro. Tranquil atmosphere with 17th-century decor and comfortable rooms.
🛏 23 🅿 🖪 🅾 🅰 All major cards 🚌 Bus: 70, 224, 280, 590. Metro: Linea A (Lepanto)

🏨 ST. ANNA
$$$ ✪✪✪
BORGO PIO 133/134, 00193
TEL 06 6880 1602
FAX 06 6830 8717
WWW.HOTELSANTANNA.COM
Located in the shadow of St. Peter's, this small family-run hotel offers tastefully decorated, comfortable rooms and caring service. Breakfast is served in a pleasant, inside garden during the summer months.
🛏 20 🅿 (extra) ⬆ 🔌
🔲 All major cards 🚍 Bus: 23, 34, 40, 62, 280, 982

RESTAURANTS

🍴 DA BENITO E GILBERTO
$$$
VIA DEL FALCO 19
TEL 06 686 7769
This small, crowded trattoria has a well-deserved reputation for its high-quality seafood. Reservations recommended.
🍴 30 🕐 D only. Closed Sun.–Mon. & Aug. 🔲 All major cards 🚍 Bus: 23, 34, 40, 62, 982

🍴 TAVERNA ANGELICA
$$$
PIAZZA A. CAPPONI 6
TEL 06 687 4514
Reservations are essential for this romantic little corner restaurant serving delicate, flavorful, and innovative Italian cuisine, like *tagliatelle* with nettles and curry, duck breast in balsamic vinegar, and chocolate crêpes. All are accompanied by a carefully selected wine list.
🍴 45 🕐 Closed L & 2 weeks in Aug. 🔌 🔲 AE, MC, V 🚍 Bus: 19, 23, 40, 62

🍴 DA ROMOLO ALLA MOLE ADRIANA
$$
VIA FOSSE DI CASTELLO 19
TEL 06 686 1603
A trattoria with friendly service and a menu featuring primarily Roman dishes— from delicious pizza to a wide

---

choice of pasta and meats. Romolo observes the tradition of the daily specialty, such as gnocchi on Thursdays, tripe on Fridays, etc.
🍴 100 inside. Some outdoor tables 🕐 Closed Mon. & most of Aug. 🔲 All major cards 🚍 Bus: 23, 34, 40, 62, 982

🍴 DAL TOSCANO
$$
VIA GERMANICO 58
TEL 06 3972 5717
Located conveniently close to the Vatican museums, this well-established restaurant specializes in traditional Tuscan cuisine. Outdoor seating.
🍴 120 🕐 Closed Mon. & Aug. 🔌 🔲 All major cards 🚍 Bus: 32, 81, 590, 982

🍴 IL MOZZICONE
$$
VIA BORGO PIO 180
TEL 06 686 1500
A simple family-style trattoria said to serve one of the best *spaghetti alla carbonara* in the city. In nice weather, you can eat lunch or dinner outside, resting up from your hours in the Vatican museums and St. Peter's.

🍴 40 🕐 Closed Sun. & Aug. 🔲 Cash only 🚍 Bus: 23, 34, 40, 62, 982

TRASTEVERE TO GIANICOLO

Visitors and Romans alike come nightly in search of a good time in this lively area "across the Tiber." It has always been packed with bars and restaurants, but recently a number of appealing hotels have also opened. 🚍 Bus: H, 23, 75, 115, 125, 280, 780 Tram: 3, 8

HOTELS

🏨 HOTEL SANTA MARIA
$$$ ✪✪✪
VICOLO DEL PIEDE 2, 00153
TEL 06 589 4626
FAX 06 589 4815
WWW.HTLSANTAMARIA.COM
A charming, ground-floor hotel set in the tranquil garden of a 16th-century cloister, only a few minutes from Piazza Santa Maria in Trastevere.
🛏 18 🅿 🔌 🔲 All major cards

🏨 SAN FRANCESCO
$$ ✪✪✪
VIA JACOPA DE SETTESOLI 7, 00153
TEL 06 5830 0051
FAX 06 5833 3413
WWW.HOTELSANFRANCESCO.NET
A recently inaugurated hotel, the San Francesco offers pleasant guest rooms, a breakfast area facing a 15th-century cloister, and a terrace with a 360-degree panoramic view over Rome.
🛏 24 🅿 (extra) ⬆ 🔌 🔲 All major cards

🏨 DOMUS TIBERINA
$$ ✪✪
VIA IN PISCINULA 37, 00153
TEL 06 580 3033
WWW.GGROMEHOTELS.IT
This hotel is located in the heart of Trastevere, not far from both Santa Cecilia and

---

Tiber Island. The rooms are comfortable and attractively decorated.

⬛ 10 🔲 🔲 All major cards

🏨 VILLA DELLA FONTE
$$
VIA DELLA FONTE D'OLIO 8, 00153
TEL 06 580 3797
FAX 06 580 3796
WWW.VILLAFONTE.COM
A tiny, welcoming hotel a few yards from Piazza Santa Maria in Trastevere. Guest rooms are comfortable and well-equipped, and a lovely terrace allows guests to relax after a busy day. Breakfast extra.

⬛ 5 🔲 🔲 All major cards

🏨 ORSA MAGGIORE WOMEN'S HOSTEL
$
VIA DELLA LUNGARA 19, 00153
TEL 06 6840 1724
FAX 06 6840 1725
WWW.CASAINTERNAZIONALE DELLEDONNE.ORG/FORESTERIA. HTM
Housed in a 16th-century former convent in Trastevere, the Orsa Maggiore offers accommodations for women only. Completely refurbished but maintaining the building's antique style, the rooms are simple and look onto a peace-ful courtyard. Both singles and dormitory accommodations are available. Restaurant on the premises.

⬛ 10 🔲 🔲 🔲 All major cards 🚌 Bus: H, 23, 75, 115, 125, 271, 280, 780

RESTAURANTS

🍴 ENOTECA FERRARA
$$$$
VIA DEL MORO 1
TEL 06 5833 3920
Two sisters run this excellent and popular wine bar which has an impressive list of wines and after-dinner drinks to accompany a constantly changing menu. The soups are particularly recommended. The decor is original and

pleasing, with touches such as glass panels in the floor allowing you to look down into the all-important cellars.

⬛ 100 🔲 DC, MC, V

🍴 PARIS
$$$$
PIAZZA SAN CALISTO 7/A
TEL 06 581 5378
Civilized surroundings and friendly service at this Jewish-Roman restaurant, whose dishes include elegant versions of such favorites as skate-wing soup, pasta and chickpeas, oxtail, and roast fish and meats with potatoes.

⬛ 90 🕐 Closed Mon., Aug., & D Sun. 🔲 🔲 All major cards

🍴 SABATINI
$$$$
PIAZZA SANTA MARIA 13
TEL 06 581 2026
Tourists love the the stunning setting and archetypal Italian restaurant ambience (complete with serenaders) of this Trastevere locale. The good (sometimes exceptional) mainly fish-based cuisine also draws locals. Super-fresh ingredients.

⬛ 120 🔲 🔲 All major cards

🍴 GLASS HOSTERIA
$$$
VICOLO DEL CINQUE 58
TEL 06 5833 5903
This restaurant in the center of Trastevere offers innovative, quality food (not always easy to find in an area so frequented by tourists) and a good selection of wines. The decor is modern and the service friendly and efficient.

⬛ 70 🕐 D only. Closed Mon. 🔲 🔲 All major cards

🍴 BOTTICELLA
$$
VICOLO DEL LEOPARDO 39/A
TEL 06 581 4738
Tucked away in a small Trastevere alley, this characteristic trattoria serves typical Roman and Roman-

Jewish dishes, such as *carciofi alla giudea* (fried artichokes) and *coda alla vaccinara* (ox-tail). Outdoor dining.

⬛ 40 🕐 Closed Wed. 🔲 🔲 All major cards

🍴 DA LUCIA
$$
VICOLO DEL MATTONATO 2B
TEL 06 580 3601
The same family has run this no-frills trattoria for more than 60 years. In summer tables fill the alley outside. The interior is lined with wooden slats. The unchanging menu includes some standard *primi* followed by dishes such as rabbit *alla cacciatora* and cuttlefish with peas.

⬛ 40 🕐 Closed Mon., 3 weeks in Aug., & Christmas 🔲 Cash only

🍴 LE MANI IN PASTA
$$
VIA DE'GENOVESI 37
TEL 06 581 6017
This inexpensive trattoria, small with a simple interior and a view of the kitchen, offers a wide selection of delicious pastas, fish, and grilled meats. There is a separate dining room for smokers.

⬛ 70 🕐 Closed Mon. & Aug. 🔲 🔲 All major cards

🍴 RISTORANTE LA SCALA
$$
PIAZZA DELLA SCALA 60
TEL 06 580 3763
A former, low-end *birreria* (beer and food joint), this warmly decorated restaurant offers very friendly service, good and abundant food, and low to moderate prices. It also has uninterrupted service to the wee hours of the morning. For those who just want a drink, an adjacent entrance on the right leads to a cozy, wood-panelled bar. Outdoor seating.

⬛ 120 🔲 All major cards

HOTELS & RESTAURANTS

🍴 DAR POETA
$
VICOLO DI BOLOGNA 45/46
TEL 06 588 0516
A lively Trastevere pizzaria offering a wide selection of pizzas and *bruschette* (toasted breads). Arrive very early to get a seat. A few outdoor tables.
🔲 80 🕐 D only 🅂 🅂 All major cards

🍴 PANATTONI
$
VIALE TRASTEVERE 53/57
TEL 06 580 0919
Also known as the "mortuary" *(obitoio)* because of its marble tabletops, this place is an institution for both its pizza and the typical Trastevere atmosphere. Outdoor seating.
🔲 100 🕐 D only. Closed Wed. 🅂 Cash only

FORUM BOARIUM TO AVENTINO

This green, leafy hill just outside the center has been one of Rome's most sought after residential areas since ancient times; it now contains some excellent, tranquil hotels. Many of the nearest restaurants are in the popular Testaccio area or the Ghetto. For public transport, see individual listings.

HOTELS

🏨 RESIDENCE PALAZZO AL VELABRO
$$$ ◆◆◆◆
VIA DEL VELABRO 16, 00187
TEL 06 679 2758
FAX 06 679 3790
WWW.VELABRO.IT
If you are planing to stay a week or more this could be a good choice. Centrally located near the Palatine Hill, it offers quiet, comfortable studio apartments with kitchenettes for 2 to 4 people, some with wonderful views.
🛈 35 🔁 🅂 🅂 All major

cards 🚌 Bus: C3, 81, 95, 170, 715, 716, 628

🏨 FORTY SEVEN
$$$ ◆◆◆◆
VIA LUIGI PETROSELLI 47, 00187
TEL 06 678 7816
FAX 06 6919 0726
WWW.FORTYSEVENHOTEL.COM
Each floor of this new, centrally located hotel is dedicated to a 20th-century Italian artist: Mastroianni, Greco, Modigliani, Quagliata, or Guccione. The guest rooms are large and luminous, many overlooking the surrounding monuments. Roof terrace with views.
🛈 61 🅿 (extra) 🔁 🅂 🔁 🅂 All major cards 🚌 Bus: C3, 81, 95, 170, 715, 716, 628

🏨 SANT'ANSELMO
$$$ ◆◆◆◆
PIAZZA DI SANT'ANSELMO 2, 00153
TEL 06 570 057
FAX 06 578 3604
WWW.AVENTINOHOTELS.COM
Sant'Anselmo's lush garden shaded with orange trees on the Aventine Hill makes the perfect setting for relaxing after sightseeing. And you can wake to the singing of birds yet be at the Roman Forum in minutes. The lobbies and guest rooms are attractively decorated.
🛈 46 🅿 🔁 🅂 🅂 All major cards 🚌 Bus: 175, 715

RESTAURANTS

🍴 GIGGETTO AL PORTICO D'OTTAVIA
$$$$
VIA DEL PORTICO D'OTTAVIA 21A
TEL 06 686 1105
The main street of the Jewish Ghetto is the perfect setting for sampling traditional Jewish-Roman cuisine—starting with fried cod, anchovies, zucchini flowers, and artichokes and finishing with cheesecake and blueberry sauce.
🔲 200 🕐 Closed Mon. & last 2 weeks in July 🅂

🅂 All major cards 🚌 Bus: 23, 46, 62, 63, 64, 70, 87, 119, 280, 492, 780

🍴 PERILLI A TESTACCIO
$$$
VIA MARMORATA 39
TEL 06 574 2415
A classic neighborhood trattoria in Testaccio. Efficient, friendly service for authentic, well-prepared standard Roman dishes. People come from miles around; reservations recommended.
🔲 90 🕐 Closed Wed. & Aug. 🅂 🅂 All major cards 🚌 Bus: 3, 23, 30, 75, 280

🍴 PIPERNO
$$$
MONTE DEI CENCI 9
TEL 06 6880 6629
In the heart of the Jewish Ghetto, this longtime favorite has changed little over the years. Here *carciofi alla giudea* (fried Jerusalem artichokes) are at their best, or try the *fritto misto vegetariano* (lightly fried artichokes, cheese-and-rice croquettes, mozzarella, and stuffed zucchini blossoms). Outdoor seating available.
🔲 75 🕐 Closed D Sun., Mon., & Aug. 🅂 🅂 All major cards 🚌 Bus: 23, 46, 62, 63, 64, 70, 87, 119, 492, 280, 780

🍴 IL SANPIETRINO
$$$
PIAZZA COSTAGUTI 15
TEL 06 6880 6471
Named after the cobblestones of Rome, this stylish restaurant offers high-quality food and service. Good selection of wines.
🔲 53 🕐 Closed Sun., L Mon.–Tues., & Aug. 🅂 🅂 All major cards 🚌 Bus: 23, 46, 62, 63, 64, 70, 87, 119, 492, 280, 780

🍴 SAN TEODORO
$$$
VIA DEI FIENILI 51
TEL 06 679 0849
Lovely setting and atmosphere, both inside and out, charming

service, good selection of wines, and, last but not least, innovative cuisine that's based on some of the most appealing ingredients and dishes from all over Italy.
🛏 80 🅿 🕓 Closed Sun. & 2 weeks in Aug. 🄰 AE, MC, V 🚌 Bus: 81, 95, 170, 628, 715, 716

🍴 REMO
$
PIAZZA SANTA MARIA LIBERATRICE 44
TEL 06 574 6270
Here you can find the traditional Roman pizza—thin and crusty. Arrive early if you don't want to wait for a table.
🛏 85 🕓 D only. Closed Sun. 🄰 Cash only 🚌 Bus: 23, 75, 95, 170, 280, 716

FUORI LE MURA (OUTSIDE THE WALLS)

Italians love the *gita fuori città*, the trip outside the city, and the Castelli Romani area as well as Tivoli and Palestrina have many unpretentious but enjoyable eating spots. Outside the Roman walls, but still in the vicinity of the city, you can also find a variety of hotels and restaurants. For public transport see individual listings.

HOTELS

🏨 CAVALIERI HILTON
$$$$$ ✪✪✪✪✪
VIA A. CADLOLO 101, 00136
TEL 06 35091
FAX 06 3509 2241
WWW.CAVALIERI-HILTON.IT
A shuttle service transports guests to and from central Rome, leaving you free to enjoy the peace of this country location. The well-equipped rooms have balconies, and tennis courts and a jogging track are among the many features typical of this top-of-the-market chain. Breakfast extra.

🛏 347 and 25 suites 🅿 🛗 🄰 💪 🏋 🄰 All major cards 🚌 Bus: 90

🏨 SHANGRI LA CORSETTI
$$$ ✪✪✪✪
VIALE ALGERIA 141, 00144
TEL 06 591 6441
FAX 06 541 3813
WWW.SHANGRILACORSETTI.IT
A peaceful setting, the hotel is surrounded by greenery in the geometrically planned EUR district, which was based on designs commissioned by Mussolini. Excellent service and facilities.
🛏 52 🅿 🄰 💪 🄰 All major cards 🚌 Bus: 714

🏨 HILTON ROME AIRPORT
$$$ ✪✪✪✪
VIA ARTURO FERRARIN, FIUMICINO, 00050
TEL 06 65258
FAX 06 6525 6525
WWW.HILTON.COM
Finally, Rome has an airport hotel. Just 200 yards from Fiumicino, the Hilton's bedrooms are functional and fully equipped. There is a restaurant and snack bar, plus a complimentary shuttle service into central Rome eight times a day. Breakfast extra.
🛏 517 🅿 🛗 🄰 🏋 💪 🄰 All major cards 🚌 See page 237, Fiumicino-Leonardo da Vinci Airport

🏨 TURNER
$$ ✪✪✪
VIA NOMENTANA 29, 00161
TEL 06 4425 0077
FAX 06 4425 0165
WWW.HOTELTURNER.IT
A superb combination of historic charm (in a late 19th-century palazzo) and modern comfort. Decor is elegant and welcoming and the staff is efficient and friendly.
🛏 47 including 2 suites 🅿 Garage 🛗 🄰 🄰 All major cards 🚌 Bus: 60, 62, 84, 90

RESTAURANTS

SOMETHING SPECIAL

🍴 LA PERGOLA DE L'HOTEL ROME CAVALIERI HILTON
Recognized as Rome's best and innovative restaurant, La Pergola's reputation has rocketed since the arrival of Heinz Beck, as of 2005 the only chef in the city awarded three Michelin stars. His dishes show strong Italian and southern Italian influences. The attentive service is superb, the wine list fantastic, and the view of Rome near unmatched.
$$$$$
VIA A. CADLOLO 101
TEL 06 3509 2211
🛏 75 🕓 Closed Sun., Mon., & L 🅿 🄰 🄰 All major cards 🚌 Bus: 990

🍴 ARCHEOLOGICA
$$$
APPIA ANTICA 139
TEL 06 788 0494
A perfect lunch stop when sightseeing along the Via Appia Antica. In winter, the dining areas have open fires, and in summer there is a lovely outdoor seating area studded with Roman statues.
🛏 300 (inside and out) 🕓 Closed Tues. 🅿 🄰 All major cards 🚌 Bus: 118, 218

🍴 TRAM TRAM
$$
VIA DEI RETI 44
TEL 06 490 416
The frequently changing menu at this popular trattoria is oriented toward Pugliese cuisine but makes the most of what's available—for example, spaghetti with octopus, anchovy and endive tart, and bean and chicory purée. Good service but a bit chaotic when it gets busy. Reservations are essential.
🛏 50 🕓 Closed Mon. & 1 week in Aug. 🅿 🄰 🄰 All major cards 🚌 Bus: 71, 492

SHOPPING IN ROME

Combining shopping and sightseeing is one of the delights of Rome. Each shopping district in Rome has its own particular characteristics. Generally, however, most shops are small and specialized, department stores are few and far between, and large shopping malls are situated outside the city.

MAIN SHOPPING AREAS

PIAZZA DI SPAGNA: In the grid of streets around Piazza di Spagna you will find the top names in Italian fashion and design, as well as, on and around Via del Babuino, quality antiques and prints. Less invitingly, Via del Corso is crowded and frenetic, offering much of the same clothes and prices as Via Cola di Rienzo (see below). Bus: C3, 52, 61, 62, 63, 71, 80, 81, 95, 116, 119, 175, 492, 590, 628. Metro: Linea A (Spagna).

PIAZZA NAVONA/CAMPO DEI FIORI: This area is home to several independent designers, as well as some excellent second-hand clothes and accessory shops. Via Giubbonari offers reasonably priced clothes and accessories, largely for the younger generation. Top-quality antiques or prints can be found on Via dei Coronari and lovely (and pricey) Via Giulia. Bus: C3, 30, 40, 46, 62, 64, 70, 81, 87, 116, 280, 492, 628. Tram: 8.

TRASTEVERE: In this labyrinth of narrow streets you will find any number of small shops and street vendors selling unique pieces. Bus: H, 23, 75, 115, 125, 271, 280, 780. Tram: 8.

VIA COLA DI RIENZO: Close to the Vatican Museums, this street offers shops selling mid-range clothes and accessories similar to those in Via Nazionale (see below), department stores, and gourmet food shops. For religious souvenirs head for the shops around St. Peter's. Bus: 23, 32, 49, 70, 81, 280, 224, 492, 590, 990, 982. Metro: Linea A (Ottaviano or Lepanto).

VIA NAZIONALE: Located between Piazza Venezia and the train station, this street is the place to go for affordable fashion. The Monti district, just off Via Nazionale, is full of fascinating boutiques and gourmet stores. Bus: H, C2, 16, 38, 40, 60, 61, 62, 64, 70, 71.

OPENING HOURS

Opening hours are flexible and vary. However, shops are generally open 9:30/10 a.m.–7:30/8 p.m., Mon.–Sat. Some close 1–4 p.m. for lunch; others, like department stores or downtown outlets, stay open all day and, sometimes, on Sundays. In winter, shops generally are closed on Monday mornings, and in summer on Saturday afternoons. Many shops shut in August, the traditional holiday month for Italians. Food shops keep slightly different hours, usually opening earlier, and the lunch break can last until 5 p.m. A number of small supermarkets in central Rome stay open all day and usually on Sundays, or at least Sunday mornings.

TAX FREE SHOPPING

You are allowed to get back 20 percent sales tax on the items purchased. Before paying ask the shop assistant if there is a minimum amount to be spent, and then request the appropriate tax free forms.

SALES (SALDI)

Winter sales start after the 6th of January and go through the end of the month; summer sales start in early July. This is the best time to pick up a bargain: Prices are discounted up to 50 percent and more. Make sure the original price is on the tag, along with the discounted sale price.

MALLS & DEPARTMENT STORES

Although not nearly of the size and scope of their North American cousins, some malls do exist in central Rome. They are open daily, usually until 10 p.m. The **Galleria Alberto Sordi** at Piazza Colonna, on central Via del Corso, not far from Piazza di Spagna, is a small, recently refurbished art nouveau mall. Its soaring atrium and stained glass ceilings make it a pleasant place to browse and pause for a coffee. With its 50 or more shops, the **Forum Termini** mall located at Termini, the central train station, Piazza dei Cinquecento, is an excellent place for one-stop and last-minute shopping needs.

There are two notable department stores in Rome, both selling clothing, leather goods, accessories, cosmetics, and housewares: **Rinascente** (Via del Corso 189, tel 06 679 7691; Piazza Fiume 1, tel 06 884 1231) and **Coin** (Via Cola di Rienzo 179; Piazzale Appio 7, tel 06 708 0020). The Via Cola di Rienzo branch of Coin also has a supermarket on the lower floor.

CLOTHING

Italy leads the world when it comes to designer fashion. Although most major houses have their headquarters in Milan, all have branches here. The chicest stores are in the Piazza di Spagna quadrant; less exclusive clothes shops are around Via Nazionale, Via Cola di Rienzo, and Via del Corso.

PIAZZA DI SPAGNA AREA

Albertelli, Via dei Prefetti 11, tel 687 3793. Classy menswear including wonderful (and expensive) custom-made men's shirts.

Armani, Via dei Condotti 77, tel 06 699 1460. The king of understated elegance for men and women.

Davide Cenci, Via del Campo Marzio 4-7, tel 06 699 0681. Top quality, elegantly conservative men and women's wear and outerwear.

Dolce e Gabbana, Via dei Condotti 51 tel 06 6992 4999.

D&G Line, Piazza di Spagna 93, tel 06 6938 0870. Very "in" and stylish clothes for women.
Emporio Armani, Via Babuino 140, tel 06 3600 2197. More casual and affordable clothes.
Ermenegildo Zegna, Via Borgognona, 7E, tel 06 678 9143. Three floors of classic men's fashion.
Fendi, (Men) Via Borgognona 36, tel 06 696 661; (Women) Largo Goldoni 419. These impressive stores sell everything from furs to gifts.
Gianni Versace, (Women) Via Bocca di Leone 27, tel 06 678 0521; (Men) Via Borgognona 24, tel 06 679 5037; (Jeans) Via Frattina 116, tel 06 678 7681. Flamboyant color schemes and styles beloved of Hollywood stars and the glamour set.
Max Mara, Via dei Condotti 19, tel 06 6992 2104. Wearable, classic styles for women.
La Perla, Via dei Condotti 78, tel 06 6994 1934. Luxury lingerie for women.
Prada, Via dei Condotti 92, tel 06 679 0897; (Sport) Via del Babuino 91, tel 06 3600 4884. Cutting-edge women's clothes and accessories; also menswear.
Tad Concept Store, Via del Babuino 155/A, tel 06 326 951. State of the art fashion, accessories, and home furnishings. There is also a beauty salon, flower shop, and café.
Trussardi, Via dei Condotti 49, tel 06 678 0280. Beautifully tailored suits, and more, for men and women. For casualwear try the **T'Store,** Via del Corso 478, tel 06 322 6055.
Sagripanti, Via Fontanella Borghese 27, tel 06 687 6413. One of a dwindling number of individually owned stores with custom-made and ready-made classic men's and women's wear. Expensive but worth it.
Valentino, (Women) Via dei Condotti 13, tel 06 6920 0618; (Men) Via Bocca di Leone 15, tel 06 678 7585. Chic elegance from Rome's most famous home-grown fashion house.

PIAZZA NAVONA/ CAMPO DEI FIORI AREA
Arsenale, Via Governo Vecchio 64, tel 06 686 1380. Quirky fashions using swaths of luxurious and unusual fabric.
Best Seller, Via dei Giubbonari 96, tel 06 6813 6040. For the younger generation. Discount section at the back of the store.
Degli Effetti, Piazza Capranica 75, 79, and 93, tel 06 679 1650. Major Italian, Japanese, and French designers can be found here.
Origami, Via di Monserrato 40, tel 06 6830 7599. Original designs in stunning colors. Home furnishings are found downstairs.
Le Tartarughe, Via di Piè di Marmo 17, tel 06 679 2240; (Accessories) Via di Piè di Marmo 33. Individual, elegant, high fashion clothes for women.
SBU, Via di Sanpanteleo 68, tel 06 6880 2547. "Perfect" jeans for men.
L'una & L'altra, Piazza Pasquino 75, tel 06 6880 4995. Clothes for feminine sophisticates. Exclusive franchise for Dries Van Noten.

TRASTEVERE AREA
Scala Quattordieci, Via della Scala 14, tel 06 588 3580. Very original but still wearable custom-made women's clothes.

Tip: Always try on clothing and measure gifts, as sizes in Italy are not always uniform, particularly children's clothing. Remember Italian shops rarely make refunds and the smaller shops are often even reluctant to exchange items.

SHOES & BAGS
The Italian leather industry's worldwide reputation is well deserved. Don't leave Rome without a pair of shoes, a bag, or a sampling of the attractive belts, wallets, and gloves available for all tastes and pockets.

PIAZZA DI SPAGNA AREA
Dal Co', Via Vittorio 64, tel 06 678 6536. Highest quality made-to-measure shoes for women.
Fausto Santini, Via Frattina 120, tel 06 678 4114. Trend-setting styles ranging from everyday to eccentric.
Ferragamo, Piazza di Spagna 63/66, tel 06 678 1130. World-famous designer shoes and apparel.
Furla, Via dei Condotti 55, tel 06 679 1973. Smart bags and accessories at accessible prices.
Gucci, Via dei Condotti 8, tel 06 679 0405. The ultimate in elegance, top quality shoes and accessories. Like Ferragamo, a Japanese favorite.
Magli, Via del Gambero 1, tel 06 679 3802. Finely made, conservative shoes for men and women.
Modi di Campagna, Via dei Prefetti 42, tel 06 679 4027. Stunningly beautiful leather goods and clothes.
Tod's, Via Fontanella di Borghese 56/57, tel 06 6821 0066; Via Borgognona 45/46, tel 06 678 6828. Attractive shoes and bags for men and women.

JEWELRY & OTHER ACCESSORIES
Alessandra, Via Monserrato 122a (Campo dei Fiori), tel 06 686 9405. Jewelry using precious and semi-precious stones.
Anelleria, Via dei Banchi Vecchi 37 (Navona), tel 06 6839 2154. Copies of the most famous rings in the world at very reasonable prices.
Bulgari, Via dei Condotti 10 (Spagna), tel 06 679 3876. The ultimate in jewelry design.
La Coppola Storta, Via del Piè di Marmo 4 (Pantheon), tel 06 679 5801. A vast collection of hats and caps.
Fabio Piccone, Via del Boschetto 140 (Nazionale), tel 06 485 511. A real find for costume or vintage jewelry.
Massimo Maria Melis, Via del Orso 57 (Navona), tel 06 686 9188. Beautifully crafted gold jewelry.
Mondello Ottica, Via del Pellegrino 98 (Campo dei Fiori), tel 06 686 1955. Your best bet if you are looking for a very special pair of glasses.
Sermoneta, Piazza di Spagna 61, tel 06 196 0679. Gloves in all colors and styles.

Troncanelli, Via della Cuccagna 15 (Navona), tel 06 687 9320. High-quality versions of many hat styles.

KIDS CLOTHING

Children's clothes don't come cheap in Italy, but they do have that inimitable touch of style.

La Cicogna, Via Frattina 138 (Spagna), tel 06 679 1912. Maternity, baby, and children's wear. Carries designer labels such as Armani and Trussardi.
Mettimi giù, Via Due Macelli 59e (Spagna), tel 06 678 9761. Stylish clothing, accessories, and shoes for 0-14s.
Al Sogno, Piazza Navona 53, tel 06 686 4198. Gorgeous, cuddly toys, some of them life-size. Collectors models, miniature Ferraris, and dolls.
Città del Sole, Via della Scrofa 65 (Navona), tel 06 6880 3805. Educational and environment-friendly toys, books, games, and puzzles for children and adults.
Baby House, Piazza Cola di Rienzo 110, tel 06 320 172. Outlet for children's clothes (2-14).

SPECIALTY SHOPS

Italy is known for its excellence in craftsmanship and specialized production. The following shops offer some of these lovely items that are hard to find elsewhere.

Casali, Via dei Coronari 115; Piazza della Rotonda 82, tel 06 678 3515. A wide range of beautiful prints of varying value.
Cesari, Via del Babuino 195, tel 06 361 3456. Lovely household fabrics and linens.
Crocianelli, Via dei Prefetti 37/40, tel 06 687 3592. Rome's oldest haberdashery sells an amazing variety of tassels, fringes, edgings, and bows in every imaginable color and then some. Worth a visit just to marvel.
Modi e Materie, Vicolo del Cinque 4 (Trastevere), tel 333 407 0748. A tempting selection of linen towels, tablecloths, and napkins that make excellent and reasonably priced gifts. Open

afternoons (Mon.–Sat.), mornings by appointment only.
Officina Profumo Farmaceutica di Santa Maria Novella, Corso di Rinascimento 47, tel 06 687 9608. Products from the ancient Florentine pharmacy made with natural ingredients and the monks' traditional methods.
Stilo Fatti, Via degli Orfani 82, tel 06 678 9662. A wide range of pens, briefcases, and stationary.

TRASTEVERE AREA
Polvere di Tempo, Via del Moro 59 (Trastevere), tel 06 588 0704. Everything for measuring time and space.

GIFTS & SOUVENIRS

Gift and souvenir shops surround Piazza Navona and Campo dei Fiore. Along Corso di Rinascimento you will find Murano glass, ceramics, Roman reproductions, and stationary. Shops selling religious items, including some charming nativity scenes, cluster in the Via dei Cestari area and around St. Peter's.

Tip: Like the Vatican Museums, most Roman museums, galleries, and archaeological sites have excellent gift shops offering a large range of souvenirs at reasonable prices.

TASTE TREATS
Antica Norceria Viola, Piazza Campo dei Fiori 42, tel 06 6880 6114. An impressive selection of salamis, hams, and other pork products, many vacuum-packed for easy transport.
Ai Monasteri, Piazza delle Cinque Lune (Navona), tel 06 6880 2783. This attractive shop sells gourmet goodies, cosmetics, and health products prepared by the monks and nuns of several monasteries and convents.
Bar Sant'Eustachio, Piazza Sant'Eustachio 82 (Navona), tel 06 686 1309. This café selling what is considered the best coffee in central Rome also sells beans or ready ground in a variety of gift packs.

Castroni, Via Cola di Rienzo 196, tel 06 687 4383. Next door to Franchi and, like it, open all day, Castroni sells imported teas and packaged foodstuffs and spices from the U.S., Europe, and Asia.
Enoteca Il Goccetto, Via dei Banchi Vecchi 14 (Navona), tel 06 686 4268. This cosy wine cellar specializes in wines coming from small Italian vineyards.
Franchi, Via Cola di Rienzo 200 tel 06 686 4576. Love to eat? Head for Franchi, the city's best gourmet take-out. Imported cheeses and wines, too.
Moriondo e Gariglio, Via del Piè di Marmo 21 (Pantheon), tel 06 699 0856. Fantastic, home- and custom-made chocolates.
La Peonia Cose di Sardegna, Via delle Carrozze 85 (Spagna), tel 06 678 8432. A wide range of products from Sardinia.
Quetzalcoatl Chocolat Passion, Via delle Carrozze 26, tel 06 6920 2191. Quality chocolates beautifully presented in this very elegant boutique.
Trimani, Via Goito 20 (Nazionale), tel 06 446 9661. Considered the best-stocked wine cellar in Rome. They ship all over the world.
Volpetti, Via Marmorata 47, tel 06 574 2352. This Testaccio area shop is a must for any foodie. It sells the highest quality produce and specializes in aged cheeses. They will vacuum-pack purchases for safe transport home.
Boccione, Via del Portico d'Ottavia 1 (Ghetto), tel 06 687 8637. Closed on Saturdays, this bakery is known for its traditional Roman-Jewish cakes, particularly the *torta di ricotta* (cheesecake) with berries *(visciole)* or chocolate.

BOOKS & MUSIC
There are some excellent English-language bookshops in Rome, with a wide range of books on Rome and Italy. Several Italian stores also carry selections of English books.
The Almost Corner Bookshop, Via del Moro 45 (Trastevere), tel 06 583 6942. A

welcoming treasure trove of fiction, poetry, history, biography, and a wide range of other categories.
Anglo American Bookshop, Via delle Vite 102 (Spagna), tel 06 679 5222. Open Mon. p.m.–Sat. Particularly good for nonfiction titles, catering to a wide range of special interests. At No. 27, a second branch (tel 06 678 9657) specializes in science and technology.
Borri Libreria, atrium of the central train station, tel 06 481 7940. Open daily until 11 p.m. A good selection of foreign language fiction and some guides.
Feltrinelli, Largo Torre Argentina 11 (Navona), tel 06 6866 3001. Open daily. This branch of a major national bookshop chain features an extensive selection of Italian books, a large music section, and some English-language fiction and guidebooks. There is a café and a ticket office where you can buy tickets for events in Rome.
Feltrinelli International, Via V.E. Orlando 84 (Nazionale), tel 06 482 7878. Wide range of books in English and other languages.
Libreria del Viaggiatore, Via del Pellegrino 78 (Campo dei Fiori), tel 06 6880 1048. Open Mon. p.m.–Sat. English-language travel books, guides, and maps.
The Lion Bookshop & Café, Via dei Greci 33/36, tel 06 3265 0437. Open Mon. p.m.–Sun. A large selection of fiction, texts related to teaching English, and children's books, plus a café with home-baked American cakes.
The Open Door Bookshop, Via Lungaretta 25 (Trastevere), tel 06 589 6478. Open Mon.–Sat. Second-hand English books at bargain prices.
Ricordi Media Stores, Via del Corso 506, tel 06 361 2370. One of several branches in Rome, it has a good selection of CDs of all kinds of music.

MARKETS
FRUITS AND VEGETABLES:
Every district in Rome has a fruit and vegetable market, all of

which are open Mon.–Fri. early morning to 2 p.m. Perhaps the most appealing of them all is in **Campo dei Fiori.** The daily food market in Piazza del Testaccio in the area of the same name is equally colorful and also has a few stands selling designer shoes at a third of the original price.

FLEA MARKETS & ANTIQUES:
Rome's biggest flea market is the **Porta Portese Market** (Via Portuense from Piazza Porto Portese to Piazza Ippolito Nievo [Bus: H, 23, 75, 115, 125, 271, 280, 780; Tram 8]). Open 6 a.m.–2 p.m., it's a place where you can find just about anything if you're willing to brave the crowds. Watch out for pickpockets.

A variety of smaller bric-a-brac and antiquities *mercatini* display their wares on all or alternate Sundays (schedules are printed Thursdays in the *TrovaRoma* insert of the Rome daily, *La Repubblica*). Some you'll just stumble upon. **Borghetto Flaminio** (Piazzale della Marina 32, tel 06 588 0517. Open Sun. 10 a.m.–7 p.m.) charges a small entrance fee for great buys in clothes, jewelry, hats, and lots more.

An antiques fair is held twice a month, on the first and second Sundays, at **Piazza Augusto Imperatore** (info at 06 3600 5345). Other antiques fairs are held in **Piazza Cola di Rienzo** and **Piazzale dei Partigiani** (behind the Ostiense train station, tel 06 309 3164).

MISCELLANEOUS:
There are other kinds of markets as well. The charming **Book and Print Market** (Largo delle Fontanella Borghese [Spagna]), is open Mon.–Sat. until sunset. On the **Via Sannio** (behind the Basilica of San Giovanni [Laterano]) you can buy clothes (used and new) and housewares at rock-bottom prices. It's open until 2 p.m. on

weekdays and 5 p.m. on Saturdays (closed Sunday).

Tip: Many street vendors in Rome sell copies of designer bags and cheap CDs. The prices are low and bargaining is a must. One caveat though: It is illegal to buy these goods and, although it is unlikely you'll be stopped by the police, the fines are high.

DISCOUNT OUTLETS
Discount outlets are few and far between in central Rome and their stock is often limited; however, it is possible to pick up a designer item at a bargain price if you are prepared to look.

And, Via delle Carrozze 67 and 20 (Spagna), tel 06 678 852. Check this place out for cashmere sweaters.
Il Discount dell'Alta Moda, Via Gesù e Maria 16/a, tel 06 322 5006. This small but popular outlet sells many famous designer labels.
Fausto Santini Outlet, Via Cavour 106 (Nazionale), tel 06 488 0934. This outlet sells the designer's previous season's collection at a fraction of the price.
Mercatino Michela, Piazza Pitagora 7, tel 06 8069 0510. This store in residential Parioli has rooms of designer label cast-offs.
Regola 33, Via San Paolo alla Regola 33, tel 06 6813 6245. A small outlet near Piazza Navona that sells designer labels, including Dolce e Gabbana, Versace, and Fendi.
Roma Stock, Via Lucrezio Caro 53, tel 06 3600 3360. This large outlet in the Cola di Rienzo area sells designer clothes for women.
The Tad Outlet, Via San Giacomo 5, tel 06 3600 1679. The outlet store for The Tad Concept Store, a homewares emporium.

ENTERTAINMENT

ENTERTAINMENT

Rome has developed into a lively entertainment center. Nightlife has become increasingly active and varied. The opening of the Parco della Musica has added a valuable performance space, which in turn has attracted many international orchestras and stars. The Casa del Jazz, inaugurated in 2004, immediately became a focal point for jazz enthusiasts. The recently opened Casa del Cinema is a must for film buffs. And exhibition spaces such as the Scuderia of the Quirinale and the Complesso of the Vittorino at Piazza Venezia host temporary art exhibitions of international standards. Macro, a former brewery, is the first museum dedicated to contemporary art in Rome and in 2006 MAXXI, the new art and architecture center designed by Zaha Hadid, is due to open. Other than movie houses, the vast majority of places listed here are closed Monday.

Details of what's on and where for the following week are published in Wednesday's *Roma C'è* (which includes a section in English) and Thursday's *TrovaRoma* (an insert in the daily *La Repubblica*). *Wanted in Rome*, published twice a month, also details a selection of concerts, opera, exhibitions, and other events. (Visit their website www.wantedinrome.com.)

Other useful websites for entertainment listings: www.inromenow.com (updated every Friday); www.romaturismo.it; www.romeguide.it (also offers an online booking service).

Chartanet (tel 199 112 112, www.carta.it) and **Hello Ticket** (tel 06 808 8352 or 800 907 080, www.helloticket.it) offer online booking services as well as call centers. Ticket agencies also exist throughout the city: **Orbis** (Piazza dell'Esquilino 37, tel 06 482 7404), which also sells tickets for sports events; **Messaggerie Musicali** (Via del Corso 473, tel 06 6819 2349); and **Feltrinelli** (Largo di Torre Argentina 5/a, tel 06 6830 8596) are just a few. A commission is charged.

Much of cultural and social Rome packs up for the summer, but to make up for this there are lots of outdoor arts festivals in the city and its surroundings. **Estate Romana** (www.estate romana.comune.roma.it), held June through September at venues throughout Rome, is a mind-boggling array of outdoor cinema, theater, opera, music, and dance performances from some of the world's best artists. **Festival Euromediterraneo** takes place July and August in the stunning Villa Adriana at nearby Tivoli and offers a varied program of concerts, drama, and dance. **Romaeuropa Festival** (www.romaeuropa.net), an international cultural event held in November, features a program of dance, theater, and music, with a focus on classical music.

THEATER & DANCE

Nearly all theater is in Italian unless specifically noted. Check *Wanted in Rome*, entertainment websites, and with the theaters themselves for details of any English-language drama. Most theaters offer online booking.
Argentina–Teatro di Roma, Largo Argentina 52, tel 06 6880 4601, www.teatroroma.net. Bus: C3, H, 40, 46, 62, 63, 64, 70, 81, 87, 119, 492, 628, 780. Tram: 8. The repertoire presented at this beautiful, well-restored 18th-century theater includes Italian classics, international contemporary, dance, and festivals.
Colosseo, Via Capo d'Africa 7, tel 06 700 4932. Bus: C3, 60, 75, 81, 85, 87, 175, 673. Tram: 3. Metro: Linea B (Colosseo). Many big names in Italian theater and cinema cut their teeth at this long-established home of experimental productions. It also stages concerts, short films, and dance.
Eliseo and Piccolo Eliseo, Via Nazionale 183, tel 06 488 2114 (Eliseo)/tel 06 488 5095 (Piccolo), www.teatroeliseo.it Bus: H, 40, 60, 64, 70, 170. The Eliseo puts on well-loved classics from Italy and elsewhere. The Piccolo next door concentrates on more contemporary theater.
Quirino Vittorio Gassman, Via delle Vergini 7, tel 06 679 4585, www.teatroquirino.it. Bus: C3, 52, 61, 62, 63, 71, 80, 81, 85, 95, 116, 119, 175, 492, 590, 628. Tram: 8. Home to the Italian National Theater Company, it stages top-quality productions of classics and the best of contemporary theater.
Sistina, Via Sistina 129, tel 06 420 0711, www.ilsistina.com. Bus: C3, 52, 61, 62, 63, 80, 95, 116, 119, 175, 492, 590. Metro: Linea A (Spagna). This spacious venue specializes in dramatic productions and musicals.
Valle, Via del Teatro Valle 21, tel 06 6880 3794, www.teatrovalle.it. Bus: C3, 40, 46, 62, 64, 70, 81, 87, 116, 492, 628. Tram: 8. One of the oldest theater buildings in Rome (built in 1726), the Valle features Italian and international contemporary drama, as well as the occasional non-Italian play in original language.
Vascello, Via G. Carini 72, tel 06 588 1021, www.teatro vascello.it. Bus: 75, 115, 870. There is a bit of everything in this popular venue, though it tends to focus on contemporary dance.

OPERA, MUSIC, & DANCE

As well as the places listed below, look for posters or check www.inromenow.com for details of free classical concerts held in historic churches. These productions are often of extremely high standards and the settings are superb.
Auditorium Parco della Musica, Viale Pietro De Coubertin 15/30, tel 06 8024 1281, www.auditorium.com. Bus: M, C3, 910. Tram: 2. This Renzo Piano–designed complex includes three concert halls offering a wide-ranging program of classical, jazz, contemporary music, and dance, an outdoor

amphitheater, cafés, a restaurant, art gallery, bookstore, and an archaeological area and museum. Home to the Santa Cecilia orchestra, the Parco della Musica offers a rich program of classical music, including guest appearances by some of the world's greatest conductors, soloists, and orchestras. It has also become a performance "must" for non-classical artists such as Lou Reed and Tracy Chapman.
Auditorium Conciliazione, Via della Conciliazione 4, tel 06 6880 1044, www.auditorium conciliazione.it. Bus: 23, 34, 40, 62, 280, 982. The programs here feature classical and contemporary music as well as some dance and film events.
Oratorio del Gonfalone, Piazza B. Gigli 8, tel 06 687 5952. Bus: 23, 116, 280, 870. This glorious, 16th-century setting is entirely appropriate for programs of chamber and choral music, with emphasis on the baroque.
Teatro Ghione, Via delle Fornaci 37, tel 06 4781 8485, www.ghione.it. Bus: 64. It stages concerts of up-and-coming and big-name soloists as well as theater productions.
Teatro Nazionale, Via del Viminale 51, tel 06 4816 0255. Bus: H, 40, 60, 64, 70, 71, 170. Metro: Linea A (Repubblica). A prime venue for ballet company performances and other productions of the Teatro dell'Opera.
Teatro Olimpico, Piazza Gentile da Fabriano 17, tel 06 326 5991, www.teatroolimpico.it. Bus: C3, 910. Home of the Accademia Filarmonica Romana, the program includes music, theatre and dance, with many visiting international artists and companies.
Teatro dell'Opera, Piazza B. Gigli 8, tel 06 481 601 or 800 016 665, www.opera. roma.it. Bus: H, 40, 60, 64, 70, 71, 170. Metro: Linea A (Repubblica).
The home of Rome's Opera and Ballet Company, this theater is host to classical productions as well as some more contemporary ones. In summer, opera and ballet are performed outdoors in the impressive surroundings of the Terme di Caracalla (Bus: 3, 60, 75, 81, 118, 160, 175, 628. Metro: Linea A [Circo Massimo]).
Il Tempietto, tel 06 8713 1590, www.tempietto.it. This classical-music association performs concerts throughout winter at the Sala Baldini (Piazza di Campitelli 9) and at Villa Torlonia (Via Nomentana 7). In summer, it stages concerts each night in the atmospheric outdoor surroundings of the Teatro di Marcello (Via Luigi Petroselli 2) and at Villa Torlonia. Bus (Sala Baldini and Teatro di Marcello): C3, H, 46, 62, 63, 64, 70, 81, 84, 87, 95, 119, 170, 628, 715, 716, 780; (Villa Torlonia): 60, 62, 84, 90.

CONTEMPORARY LIVE MUSIC
Rome has a dynamic live-music scene, with a number of venues offering jazz, soul, rock, and ethnic music. The soccer stadium, race track, and other unusual locations are often settings for concerts and festivals, particularly in the summer months.
Alexanderplatz, Via Ostia 9, tel 06 3975 1877. Bus: 23, 70, 492, 990, 991. Plastered with photos and signatures of visiting performers, Alexanderplatz is one of Italy's most important and well-known jazz clubs. Reservations advised. In summer, the club moves to the outdoor setting of Villa Celimontana (Bus: 3, 75, 81, 117, 175, 204, 673), where one can also enjoy light meals and/or a drink in the evening breeze.
Big Mama, Vicolo San Francesco a Ripa 18, tel 06 581 2551, www.bigmama.it. Bus: H, 75, 115, 125, 780. Tram: 3, 8. The self-styled "home of the blues in Rome" offers an interesting selection of international and Italian musicians with the great names of the past and present. Reservations advised.
Caffè Latino, Via Monte Testaccio 96, tel 06 5728 8556. Bus: 95, 673, 719. Concerts, most of them by local bands, are played nearly every night, followed by a disco playing mainly funk, acid jazz, and black music. On the same street are similar places: **Caruso** (at No. 36, tel 06 574 5019) concentrates on Latin American music; **Radio Londra Café** (at No. 65b, tel 06 575 0044) is more interested in rock, blues, and dance.
Casa del Jazz, Viale di Porta Ardeatina 55, tel 06 704 731 www.casajazz.it. Bus: 118, 715. This recently opened venue hosts top names in Italian and international jazz. Facilities include a bar, restaurant, library, bookshop, and record store.
Ex-Maggazzini, Via dei Maggazzini Generale, tel 06 575 8040. Bus: 23. Located inside the old wholesale vegetable and fruit market, this venue offers live music and dancing, theater, film, and, on Sundays, an ethnic market.
Fonclea, Via Crescenzio 82a, tel 06 689 6302, www.fonclea.it. Bus: 23, 34, 49, 492, 982, 990. This cozy music venue features live jazz, soul, and rock. Nourishment can be had in a good selection of beers and whiskeys and a range of light supper dishes.
Il Locale, Vicolo del Fico 3, tel 06 687 9075. Bus: C3, 40, 46, 62, 64, 70, 81, 87, 116, 186, 492, 628. A chaotically lively and friendly place to hear rock.
La Palma Club, Via Giuseppe Mirri 35, tel 06 4359 9029, www.lapalmaclub.it. Bus: 409, 545. Slightly off the beaten track, La Palma is best known for jazz, both homegrown and imported. This is also the place for Italian, ethnic, and visiting "world" musicians. Restaurant and winebar from 9 p.m. on.
Villaggio Globale, Lungotevere Testaccio 1, tel 06 575 7233. Bus: 170, 719. An architecturally interesting, 19th-century slaughterhouse makes an exotic venue for open-air world music concerts in summer and a variety of year-round cultural events.

CLUBS

Clubs tend to get going late, and although they may be rather a blander version of their London or New York equivalents, they still offer an enjoyable evening, particularly for the younger crowd.

Akab, Via Monte Testaccio 69, tel 06 5730 5177. Bus: 95, 673, 719. Located on "clubbers' row," Akab is one of the oldest and most popular venues. Large dance floor, music varies each night.

Alien, Via Velletri 13, tel 06 841 2212, www.aliendisco.it. Bus: 38, 63, 80, 86, 88, 92, 217, 360, 490, 495. Large disco with three dance floors, popular with the younger crowd.

Alpheus, Via del Commercio 36, tel 06 574 7826, www.alpheus.it. Bus: 23. Many different rooms for a variety of musical styles including house, black, hip hop, blues, rock, techno, etc. Food served.

Baja, Lungotevere Arnaldo da Brescia (Ponte Margherita). Bus: 81, 224, 590, 628, 926. Tram: 2. Metro: Linea A (Flaminio). Moored near Piazza del Popolo, this two-storied barge is a cocktail bar, restaurant, and disco.

Gilda, Via Mario dei Fiori 97, tel 06 678 4838. www. gildabar.it. Bus: C3, 52, 61, 62, 63, 71, 80, 95, 116, 119, 175, 492, 590. Metro: Linea A (Spagna). This well-established disco used to be the place to ogle at the VIPs of Italian politics, culture, and society. A younger crowd patronizes it during the week.

Goa, Via G. Libetta 3, tel 06 574 8277. Bus: 23, 673. Metro: Linea B (Garbatella). The music at this one-room chic club (with corners for dancing) tends to be avant-garde, with some of the best DJs in town at the console.

Jungle Club, Via Monte Testaccio 95, tel 333 720 8694. Bus: 95, 673, 719. This popular Goth venue has two rooms: one for cocktails, the other for dancing.

Piper, Via Tagliamento 9, tel 06 855 5398. Bus: 63, 86, 92. The electrifying mix of music makes this high-tech disco a popular spot for a night out.

Suite, Via degli Orti di Trastevere 1, tel 06 5861 8888. Bus: 23, 280, 125, 870. Contemporary styled, groovy club with top local and international DJs.

BARS

Bars range from the classic *enoteca,* serving wine by the glass or by the bottle, to cool cocktail venues open until late and often serving light meals. In summer many spill onto the street, particularly in Campo dei Fiori, which is transformed from a fruit-and-vegetable market during the day to a lively bar and meeting spot at night.

Wine Bars

Antico Enoteca di Via della Croce, Via della Croce 76b, tel 06 679 0896. Bus: C3, 81, 119, 224, 590, 628, 926. Metro: Linea A (Spagna). Near Piazza di Spagna, this attractive wine bar offers a vast selection of wines and a buffet lunch.

Buccone, Via di Ripetta, tel 06 361 2154. Bus: C3, 119, 224, 628, 926. Established in 1870, this traditional wine bar showcases an excellent selection of wines. Tables available for lunch every day except Friday.

Costantini, Piazza Cavour 16, tel 06 321 3210. Bus: 34, 49, 70, 81, 87, 224, 280, 492, 926, 990. One of the better-known cellars of Rome, Costantini also has a pleasant bar serving wine by the glass.

Ferrazza, Via dei Volsci 59, tel 06 490 506. Bus: C2, C3, 71, 492. A favorite spot for a drink before dinner, Ferrazza also offers light meals in the small dining area. Excellent wine cellar.

Il Goccetto, Via dei Banchi Vecchi 14, tel 06 686 4268. Bus: 23, 40, 46, 62, 64, 116, 280, 870. This cozy wine cellar specializes in wines from small Italian vineyards. The English-speaking owner can guide you in your choice.

Vineria Reggio, Piazza Campo dei Fiori 15, tel 06 6880 3268. Bus: 40, 46, 60, 62, 64, 116. Expats, tourists, and Romans flock here to quaff reasonably priced wines and other drinks at the bar or outside on the pavement.

Enoteca Ferrara, Piazza Trilussa 41, tel 06 5833 3920. Bus: H, 23, 75, 115, 125, 280. Tram: 3, 8. Wine tasting (more than 600 varieties of wine are available) begins at 6 p.m. every day—snacks are available. The accompanying restaurant is interesting, but somewhat pricey.

Il Cantiniere di Santa Dorotea, Via di S. Dorotea 9 (Trastevere), tel 06 581 9025. Bus: H, 23, 75, 115, 125, 280. Tram: 3, 8. Open 5 p.m.–2 a.m. Closed Tues. This less pretentious but extremely cozy *enoteca* features a good selection of Italian and French wines. Light fare is also offered.

Bars

Alibi, Via Monte Testaccio 40, tel 06 574 3448. Bus: 95, 673, 719. One of Rome's earliest gay bars/discos is also one of its most popular—regardless of sexual preference.

BarBar, Via Ovidio 17, tel 06 6880 5682. Bus: 23, 34, 40, 280, 492. Minimalist decor, cocktails, and low-key music. Cool and trendy.

Bloom, Via Teatro Pace 30, tel 06 6880 2029. Bus: C3, 40, 46, 62, 64, 70, 81, 87, 116, 186, 492, 628. Close by Piazza Navona, this ultra-modern bar and fusion restaurant continues to attract a stylish crowd.

Bush, Via Galvani 46, tel 06 572 8691. Bus: 23, 60, 95, 280, 673, 716, 719. This high-tech bar and disco caters to a slightly older crowd, playing house and techno music.

Crudo, Via degli Specchi 6, tel 06 683 8989. Bus: H, 23, 63, 280. Tram: 8. A spacious location with engaging decor. Choose from a wide range of wines and cocktails, or enjoy a meal of steamed or raw fare such as sushi, sashimi, or carpaccio.

Jonathan's Angels, Via della Fossa 16, tel 06 689 3426. Bus: C3, 40, 46, 62, 64, 70, 81, 87, 116, 186, 492, 628. This chaotic, packed cocktail bar is not the place for shrinking violets: You may be pulled into one of the semi-impromptu evening floor shows that sometimes take place. The decorations—wall paintings, statuettes—must be seen to be believed, especially the gorgeous bathroom.

Riccioli Café, Piazza delle Coppelle 10a, tel 06 6821 0313. Bus: C3, 40, 46, 62, 64, 70, 81, 87, 116, 492, 628. Tram: 8. Open from the morning until late at night, this bar/restaurant serves a discerning clientele.

Salotto 42, Piazza di Pietra 42, tel 06 678 5804. Bus: C3, 62, 63, 81, 85, 95, 116, 119, 175, 492, 628. Trendy bar located in front of the Tempio di Adriano. Open from morning until 2 a.m. A great place to savor a coffee or aperitif.

Tazio, Piazza della Repubblica 47, tel 06 489 381. Bus: 40, 60, 61, 62, 64, 70, 84, 170, 492, 590, 910. Metro: Linea A (Repubblica). Located in the Exedra Boscolo Hotel, this attractive bar provides a much needed spot near the Central Train Station where you can have a drink and light meal.

CINEMA
Most films in Italy are dubbed into Italian. There are, however, several cinemas which screen films in original language (listed as VO), either one day a week (usually Monday) or every day.

Alcazar, Via Cardinale Merry del Val 14, tel 06 588 0099. Bus: H, 23, 75, 115, 125, 280. Tram: 3, 8. Shows the latest releases in their original languages on Mondays.

Augustus, Corso Vittorio Emanuele 203, tel 06 687 5455. It sometimes shows films in VO.

Casa del Cinema, at entrance to the Villa Borghese at the top of Via Veneto, tel 06 423 601. www.casadelcinema.it. Daily screenings (in Italian) as well as debates and exhibitions. Bus: 490, 491, 495, 88, 95, 116. Metro: Linea A (Spagna).

Intrastevere, Vicolo Moroni 3a, tel 06 588 4230. Bus: 23, 280, 125. A three-screen, independent cinema that shows quality films, usually dubbed into Italian, but some in their original language.

Metropolitan, Via del Corso 7, tel 06 320 0933. Bus: 81, 95, 119, 224, 490, 590, 628, 926. Metro: Linea A (Flaminio). Tram: 2. One of the four screens here always shows a recently released film in its original language.

Nuovo Olimpia, Via in Lucina 16, tel 06 686 1068. Bus: 75, 119, 116, 492, 628. A two-screen venue where the latest international releases are shown in their original languages.

Nuovo Sacher, Largo Ascianghi 1, tel 06 581 8116. Bus: H, 75, 115, 125. Tram 3, 8. A mecca for cinema fans, the Nuovo Sacher shows recent releases in their original languages on Mondays.

Warner Village Moderno, Piazza della Repubblica 45, tel 06 477 791. Bus: 40, 60, 61, 62, 64, 70, 84, 170, 492, 590, 910. Metro: Linea A (Repubblica). Large, comfortable, five-screen complex. One screen always shows films in their original languages.

SOCCER
Stadio Olimpico, Viale dello Stadio Olimpico, tel 06 323 7333. Bus: C2, 32, 48, 69, 224, 280, 301, 446, 911. By far the most popular spectator sport, soccer is the great national passion. The Olympic Stadium, built for the 1960 Olympics, hosts matches involving one of Rome's two teams, Roma and Lazio, most Saturdays and Sundays from September to June. Tickets can be bought in advance from the Orbis Agency (see above). Be aware that fans can become violent, particularly if the two home teams are playing one another in *un derby.*

ICE CREAM
In Italy ice cream isn't just for kids. Taste it and you'll soon understand why. It's especially delightful on an after-dinner summer stroll through the historic center.

Alberto Pica, Via della Seggiola 12 (Largo Argentina), tel 06 6880 6153. Bus: H, 23, 63, 280. Tram: 8. The 50 or so different flavors sold here include some imaginative inventions, such as rice with cinnamon, as well as classic favorites.

Al Settimo Gelo, Via Vodice 21a, tel 06 372 5567. Bus: 224, 280, 628. Famous for excellent quality and innovative flavors (the Iranian ice cream is made from rose water, almonds, pistachio, and saffron).

Café du Park, Piazza Porta San Paolo (across the street from Porta San Paolo), tel 06 574 3363. Bus: 23, 60, 75. Metro: Linea B (Pyramide). Open daily. This place specializes in *cremolato*—a creation similar to ice cream, but without milk products. Serving all sorts of fruit flavors (fig, raspberry, blackberry, melon, etc.), Café du Park is one of the best taste treats in town.

Duse, Via Duse 1, tel 06 807 9300. Bus: 217, 360. Family-run, Duse serves some of the best ice cream in town. Try the *zabaione* or the *zuppa inglese.*

Giolitti, Via Ufficio del Vicario 40 (Pantheon), tel 06 699 1243. Bus: C3, 62, 63, 81, 85, 95, 119, 175, 492, 628. One of the oldest and best-known *gelaterie* in Rome, Giolitti boasts a vast assortment of traditional and exotic flavors. It also serves tea and pastries. Table-service prices are higher.

Palazzo del Freddo di Giovanni Fassi, Via Principe Eugenio 6, tel 06 446 4740. Bus: 105. Metro: Linea A (Vittorio Emmanuele). This large, art-deco ice cream parlor has dished gelato since the beginning of the 20th century. Its *ninetto,* a chocolate and cream mixture, and Sicilian *cassata* are famous.

San Crispino, Via della Panetteria 42, tel 06 679 3924. Bus: C3, 52, 61, 62, 63, 71, 80, 81, 85, 95, 116, 119, 175, 492, 590, 628. Metro: Linea A (Barberini). The constantly changing and expanding range of flavors here include true innovations such as meringue and hazelnut or pink grapefruit with whiskey.

LANGUAGE GUIDE

USEFUL WORDS & PHRASES

Yes *Si*
No *No*
Excuse me (in a crowd or asking for permission) *Permesso*
Excuse me (asking for attention) *Mi scusi*
Hello (before lunch) *Buon giorno*, (after lunch) *Buona sera*
Hi or Bye *Ciao*
Please *Per favore*
Thank you *Grazie*
You're welcome *Prego*
Have a good day! *Buona giornata!*
OK *Va bene*
Goodbye *Arrivederci*
Good night *Buona notte*
Sorry *Mi scusi* or *Mi dispiace*
here *qui*
there *lì*
today *oggi*
yesterday *ieri*
tomorrow *domani*
now *adesso/ora*
later *più tardi/dopo*
right away *subito*
this morning *stamattina*
this afternoon *questo pomeriggio*
this evening *stasera*
open *aperto*
closed *chiuso*
Do you have? *Avrebbe?*
Do you speak English? *Parla inglese?*
I'm American (man) *Sono americano*, (woman) *Sono americana*
I don't understand *Non capisco*
Please speak more slowly *Potrebbe parlare più lentamente?*
Where is…? *Dov' è…?*
I don't know *Non so*
No problem *Niente*
That's it *Ecco*
Here/there it is (masculine) *Eccolo*, (feminine) *Eccola*
What is your name? *Come si chiama?*
My name is… *Mi chiamo…*
Let's go *Andiamo*
At what time? *A che ora?*
When? *Quando?*
What time is it? *Che ora è?*
Can you help me? *Mi può aiutare?*
I'd like… *Vorrei…*
How much is it? *Quanto costa?*

MENU READER

breakfast *la (prima) colazione*
lunch *il pranzo*
dinner *la cena*
appetizer *l'antipasto*
first course *il primo*
main course *il secondo*
vegetable, side dish *il contorno*
dessert *il dessert*
wine list *la lista dei vini*
the bill *il conto*
I'd like to order *Vorrei ordinare*
Is service included? *Il servizio è incluso?*

PASTA SAUCES

all'amatriciana tomato sauce with chili and bacon
all'arrabbiata ("angry") tomato and chili sauce
alla carbonara with bacon, eggs, and pecorino cheese
alla gricia carbonara without the eggs
alla scoglia ("seashore") with shrimp, mussels, and clams

MEAT

l'abbacchio lamb
l'anatra duck
la bistecca beefsteak
ben cotta well-done
non troppo cotta medium
appena cotta rare
al sangue very rare
il filetto filet steak
il carpaccio finely sliced raw cured beef
il cinghiale wild boar
il coniglio rabbit
il fegato liver
le lumache snails
il maiale pork
il manzo beef
misto di carne mixed grill
il pollo chicken
le polpette meatballs
la porchetta cold roast pork with herbs
il prosciutto ham, *crudo* raw, *cotto* cooked
i rognoni kidneys
la salsiccia fresh, spicy (usually pork) sausage
saltimbocca allo Romano veal and ham in a wine and sage sauce
straccetti pan-fried strips of beef or veal
lo stufato stew or casserole

il tacchino turkey
la trippa tripe
il vitello veal

FISH

l'alici/acciughe anchovies
l'aragosta/astice lobster
il calamaro squid
le cozze mussels
i gamberi prawns
i gamberetti shrimp
il granchio crab
le ostriche oysters
il polipo octopus
il salmone salmon
le sarde sardines
la sogliola sole
la spigola bass
il tonno tuna
la trota trout

VEGETABLES

l'aglio garlic
gli asparagi asparagus
il carciofo artichoke
la carota carrot
il cavolfiore cauliflower
la cipolla onion
i fagioli dried beans, usually haricot or borlotti
i fagiolini fresh green beans
i funghi (porcini) mushrooms
l'insalata mista/verde mixed/green salad
le melanzane eggplant
le patate potatoes
le patate fritte french fries
le patatine potato chips
il peperone bell pepper
i piselli peas
i pomodori tomatoes
il radicchio bitter reddish lettuce
il riso rice
gli spinaci spinach
il tartufo truffle
le zucchine zucchini

FRUIT

l'albicocca apricot
l'ananas pineapple
l'arancia orange
le cilegie cherries
le fragole strawberries
la mela apple
la pera pear
la pesca peach
la pescanoce nectarine
il pompelmo grapefruit
l'uva grapes

INDEX

Bold page numbers
indicate illustrations

ILLUSTRATIONS CREDITS

Abbreviations for terms appearing below: (t) top; (b) bottom; (l) left; (r) right; (c) center.

Cover (r), AA Photo Library/Dario Mitidieri. (l), Images Colour Library. (c), (spine), Superstock. 1, Massimo Listri/CORBIS. 2/3, Steve McCurry/National Geographic Society. 4, Steve McCurry/National Geographic Society. 9, Robert Harding Picture Library. 11, AA Photo Library/Jim Holmes. 12/13, Steve McCurry/National Geographic Society. 14/15, James Stanfield/National Geographic Society. 16/17, Marka s.r.l. 19, James Stanfield/National Geographic Society. 20/21, Tibor Bognar/CORBIS. 23, The Entry of St. Ignatius into Paradise, ca.1707 (fresco) by Andrea Pozzo (1642–1709), Church of St. Ignatius, Rome, Italy/Bridgeman Art Library. 24, Corbis UK Ltd/Bettmann. 25, Rex USA Ltd. 26/27, Victor Boswell/National Geographic Society. 28/29, James Stanfield/National Geographic Society. 30, AA Photo Library/Jim Holmes. 33, Blue Box Toys/epa/CORBIS. 34, Dorling Kindersley/Getty Images. 35, Robert Harding Picture Library. 38/39, Riccardo Musacchio/Farabolafoto. 40/41, Corbis UK Ltd/Carmen Redondo. 44/45, Steve McCurry/National Geographic Society. 46, Corbis UK Ltd/Carmen Redondo. 47, De Camillis/John Sims. 48, Corbis UK Ltd/Carmen Redondo. 51(t), Augustus and the Tiburtine Sibyl (oil on canvas) by Antoine Caron (1520–99), Louvre, Paris, France/Peter Willi/Bridgeman Art Library. 51(bl), Gold coin of the Roman Emperor Nero (a.d. 54–68), Private Collection/Bridgeman Art Library. 51(br), Robert Harding Picture Library. 52, Corbis UK Ltd/Sandro Vannini. 54, Corbis UK Ltd/Vittoriano Rastelli. 55, Corbis UK Ltd/Archivo Iconografico, S.A. 58/59, Corbis UK Ltd/Carol Havens. 61(t), James L. Stanfield. 61(b), Corbis UK Ltd/Archivo Iconografico, S.A. 62, Gettyone/Stone. 63, Corbis UK Ltd/Michael S. Yamashita. 64, Giuseppe Giglia/epa/CORBIS. 65, Pizzoli Alberto/CORBIS SYGMA. 67, Marka s.r.l. 68/69, AA Photo Library/Jim Holmes. 70(t), Corbis UK Ltd/Ruggero Vanni. 70(b), Corbis UK Ltd/Archivo Iconografico, S.A. 73, AA Photo Library. 76, Mecky Fogeling. 77, Mecky Fogeling. 78/79, Corbis UK Ltd/Vanni Archive. 80, John Ferro Sims. 81, De Camillis/John Sims. 82, Marka s.r.l. 84, Marka

s.r.l. 85, John Heseltine/Italian Archive. 86, Museo Nazionale Romano. 86/87, Museo Nazionale Romano. 88, Museo Nazionale Romano. 89, Corbis UK Ltd/Vanni Archive. 90, Musacchio/Farabolafoto. 91, Vannini/Speranza. 95, Robert Harding Picture Library. 96, Robert Harding Picture Library. 97(tl), Corbis UK Ltd/John Heseltine. 97(tr), Franca Speranza. 97(c), AA Photo Library/Jim Holmes. 97(b), Marka s.r.l. 98, Corbis UK Ltd/Hubert Stadler. 99, Musacchio/Farabolafoto. 100, Scala/Art Resource, NY. 101, Araldo de Luca/CORBIS. 102/103, Travel Library. 105, Corbis UK Ltd/Nicolas Sapieha; Kea Publishing Services Ltd. 107, Marka s.r.l. 108/109, SIME/CORBIS. 111(t), Corbis UK Ltd/Vittoriano Rastelli. 111(bl), Corbis UK Ltd /Vittoriano Rastelli. 111(br), The Travel Library. 112, Corbis UK Ltd/Hubert Stadler. 113, Franca Speranza. 114, The Conversion of St. Paul, 1602 (oil on canvas) by Michelangelo Merisi da Caravaggio (1571–1610), Santa Maria del Popolo, Rome, Italy/Bridgeman Art Library. 115, Scala/Art Resource, NY. 116, Corbis UK Ltd/Vanni Archive. 117, Corbis UK Ltd/Massimo Listri. 119(t), Robert Harding Picture Library. 119(bl), Corbis UK Ltd/John Heseltine. 119(br), John Ferro Sims. 120/121, Corbis UK Ltd/Michael S. Yamashita. 122, Corbis UK Ltd/Massimo Listri. 123, Corbis UK Ltd/Dennis Marsico. 124, Robert Harding Picture Library. 127, Corbis UK Ltd/Vanni Archive. 131(t), PowerStock/Zefa. 131(bl),Mecky Fogeling. 131(br), Robert Harding Picture Library. 132, Axiom. 133, Araldo de Luca/CORBIS. 134, 05585701 John Sims/Anthony Blake Photo Library. 136, Corbis UK Ltd/Francesco Venturi; Kea Publishing Services Ltd. 137, AA Photo Library/Jim Holmes. 138, Nagelestock.com/Alamy. 139, Sasso/Farabolafoto. 141, Corbis UK Ltd/Michael S. Yamashita. 142, Corbis UK Ltd/Franz-Marc Frei. 144/145, Stephen Studd/Stone/Getty Images. 145, Corbis UK Ltd/John Heseltine. 146/147, Lanni/Farabolafoto. 148, The Martyrdom of St. Matthew, 1599–1600 by Michelangelo Merisi da Caravaggio (1571–1610), San Luigi dei Francesi, Rome, Italy/Bridgeman Art Library. 149, AA Photo Library/Dario Mitidieri. 150, Axiom. 152/153, 05587201 John Sims/Anthony Blake Photo Library. 153, Mecky Fogeling. 154, Marka s.r.l. 154/155, The 'Galleria di Carracci' (Carracci Hall) detail of Jupiter and Juno, 1597–1604

(fresco) by Annibale Carracci (1560–1609), Palazzo Farnese, Rome, Italy/Bridgeman Art Library. 155, Corbis UK Ltd/John Heseltine. 156, Mecky Fogeling. 159, Robert Harding Picture Library. 161, James Stanfield/National Geographic Society. 163, Steve McCurry/National Geographic Society. 164, Jim Holmes/Axiom. 166/167, Corbis UK Ltd/Archivo Iconografico, S.A. 168, Robert Harding Picture Library. 168/169, Corbis UK Ltd/Franz-Marc Frei. 170, James Stanfield/National Geographic Society. 172, Corbis UK Ltd/Vittoriano Rastelli. 173, Sistine Chapel Ceiling, 1508–12 (fresco) (post restoration) by Michelangelo Buonarroti (1475–1564), Vatican Museums and Galleries, Vatican City, Italy/Bridgeman Art Library. 174/175, James Stanfield/National Geographic Society. 175, Victor Boswell/National Geographic Society. 177, Corbis UK Ltd/Sandro Vannini. 179, AA Photo Library/Jim Holmes. 182, Scala/Art Resource, NY. 182/183, John Heseltine/Italian Archive. 184, Franca Speranza. 186, AA Photo Library/Dario Mitidieri. 187, Corbis UK Ltd/Massimo Listri. 188, John Heseltine/Italian Archive. 189, John Heseltine/Italian Archive. 190/191, John Ferro Sims. 192, John Heseltine/Italian Archive. 192/193, John Heseltine/Italian Archive. 194/195, Corbis UK Ltd/Franz-Marc Frei. 195, Corbis UK Ltd/Ali Meyer. 197, Corbis UK Ltd/Christel Gerstenberg. 199, Jim Holmes/Axiom. 200, Marka s.r.l. 201, Axiom. 202, Marka s.r.l. 204, Corbis UK Ltd/Hubert Stadler. 205, Robert Harding Picture Library. 206, PowerStock/Zefa. 207, John Heseltine/Italian Archive. 208/9, Jim Holmes/Axiom. 211, Robert Harding Picture Library. 212, Corbis UK Ltd/Carmen Redondo. 213, The Grape Harvest (mosaic), Santa Costanza, Rome, Italy/Bridgeman Art Library. 214, AA Photo Library/Peter Wilson. 217, Hubert Stadler/Corbis UK Ltd. 218, Sandro Vannini/Franca Speranza. 219, Corbis UK Ltd/Araldo de Luca. 220, AA Photo Library/Jim Holmes. 221, Corbis UK Ltd/Ruggero Vanni. 222, Ceiling decoration with flowers and birds (mosaic) Santa Costanza, Rome, Italy/Bridgeman Art Library. 223, Robert Harding Picture Library. 225, Robert Harding Picture Library. 226, AA Photo Library/Clive Sawyer. 228/229, AA Photo Library/Clive Sawyer. 231, Robert Harding Picture Library. 232, Corbis UK Ltd/ Macduff Everton. 232/233, Macduff Everton/CORBIS. 235, AA Photo Library/Clive Sawyer.

Founded in 1888, the National Geographic Society is one of the largest nonprofit scientific and educational organizations in the world. It reaches more than 285 million people worldwide each month through its official journal, NATIONAL GEOGRAPHIC, and its four other magazines; the National Geographic Channel; television documentaries; radio programs; films; books; videos and DVDs; maps; and interactive media. National Geographic has funded more than 8,000 scientific research projects and supports an education program combating geographic illiteracy.

For more information, please call 1-800-NGS LINE (647-5463) or write to the following address:

National Geographic Society
1145 17th Street N.W.
Washington, D.C. 20036-4688
U.S.A.

Log on to
nationalgeographic.com;
AOL Keyword: NatGeo.

For information about special discounts for bulk purchases, please contact National Geographic Books Special Sales: ngspecsales@ngs.org.

Printed in Spain

The information in this book has been carefully checked and to the best of our knowledge is accurate. However, details are subject to change, and the National Geographic Society cannot be responsible for such changes, or for errors or omissions. Assessments of sites, hotels, and restaurants are based on the author's subjective opinions, which do not necessarily reflect the publisher's opinion. The publisher cannot be responsible for any consequences arising from the use of this book.

Published by the National Geographic Society
John M. Fahey, Jr., *President and Chief Executive Officer*
Gilbert M. Grosvenor, *Chairman of the Board*
Nina D. Hoffman, *Executive Vice President and President, Book Publishing Group*
Kevin Mulroy, *Vice President and Editor-in-Chief*
Marianne Koszorus, *Design Director*
Elizabeth L. Newhouse, *Director of Travel Publishing*
Barbara A. Noe, *Series Editor*
Cinda Rose, *Art Director*
Carl Mehler, *Director of Maps*
Nicholas P. Rosenbach, *Map Coordinator*
Richard S. Wain, *Production Project Manager*

Gary Colbert, *Production Director*
Rebecca Hinds, *Managing Editor*

Lawrence M. Porges, *Project Editor, 2006 edition*
Jennifer Davis, Steven D. Gardner, Christine Georgeff, Abby Lepold, Carol Stroud, Jane Sunderland, Ruth Thompson, Mapping Specialists, *Contributors to 2006 edition*

Edited and designed by AA Publishing (a trading name of Automobile Association Developments Limited, whose registered office is Norfolk House, Priestley Road, Basingstoke, Hampshire, England RG24 9NY. Registered number: 1878835).
Betty Sheldrick, *Project Manager*
David Austin, *Senior Art Editor*
Allen Stidwill, *Senior Editor*
Bob Johnson, *Designer*
Inna Nogeste, *Senior Cartographic Editor*
Amber Banks, Peter Smith, *Cartographers*
Richard Firth, *Production Director*
Steve Gilchrist, *Prepress Production Controller*
Picture Research by Zooid Pictures Ltd.
Area maps drawn by Chris Orr Associates, Southampton, England
Cutaway illustrations (pp. 42–43, 48–49, 60–61, 71, 128–129, 164–165, and 171) drawn by Maltings Partnership, Derby, England

National Geographic Traveler: Rome, Second Edition (2006)
ISBN-10: 0-7922-5572-0 / ISBN-13: 978-0-7922-5572-7

The Library of Congress catalogued the first edition as follows:
Gilbert, Sari.
    The National Geographic Traveler : Rome / Sari Gilbert and Michael Brouse.
        p. cm.
    Includes index.
    ISBN 0-7922-7566-7
    1. Rome (Italy)--Guidebooks. I. Brouse, Michael. II. Title.

DG804 .G55 2000
914.5'63204929--dc21
                                                    00-021915
                                                    CIP

Printed and bound by Cayfosa Quebecor, Barcelona, Spain. Color separations by Leo Reprographic Ltd., Hong Kong. Cover separations by L.C. Repro, Aldermaston, U.K.

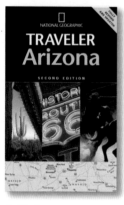

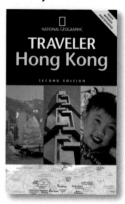